PASSPORT'S GUIDE TO

ETHNIC

NEW YORK

*A Complete Guide
to the Many Faces
& Cultures of
New York*

MARK LEEDS

P9-BYX-706

PASSPORT BOOKS
a division of *NTC Publishing Group*
Lincolnwood, Illinois USA

Cover Photos

American Egg Board (Front, upper left; Back, lower)
Government of India Tourist Office (Front, upper right, lower left; Back, upper left)
Greater Milwaukee Convention and Visitors Bureau, Inc. (Back, upper right)
Korean National Tourism Corporation (Front, lower right)
New York Convention and Visitors Bureau (Front, middle right)
Terry Farmer/Illinois Department of Commerce and Community Affairs (Front, middle left)

Published by Passport Books, a division of NTC Publishing Group,
© 1991 by NTC Publishing Group, 4255 West Touhy Avenue,
Lincolnwood (Chicago), Illinois 60646-1975 U.S.A.
All rights reserved. No part of this book may be reproduced, stored
in a retrieval system, or transmitted in any form or by any means,
electronic, mechanical, photocopying, recording or otherwise, without
the prior permission of NTC Publishing Group.
Manufactured in the United States of America.
Library of Congress Catalog Card Number: 90-61463

0 1 2 3 4 5 6 7 8 9 VP 9 8 7 6 5 4 3 2 1

Contents

Maps

Introduction

New York is an ethnic city with different nations in different territories. The cityscape changes and so do the faces, customs, and languages. It's around the world from barrio to Chinatown to "shtetl." All any explorer needs is a subway token to cross the Alps and the Andes.

Passport's Guide to Ethnic New York is a passport to foreign places right in the city, to Little Odessa and Aleppo in Flatbush. It is an introduction and an appreciation of the nations of New York from Chinese at the tip of Manhattan to Italians in the northern Bronx. It is a cultural itinerary of ethnic restaurants, stores, galleries, museums, and festivals.

The city doesn't stand still: restaurants come and go, ethnics pick up stakes, galleries go broke, and people are always changing the hours. The no-frills store or restaurant of yesteryear is the expensive trend-setting place of tomorrow. In New York, ethnic or not, things are liable to change; the city is always running ahead of itself.

Passport's Guide to Ethnic New York doesn't try to be comprehensive. The foreign nations of New York are endless and the ethnic scene is constantly shifting. The ethnic selections for this book, which spans from Dutch New Amsterdam to the Haitian and Vietnamese boat people, are based on numbers and influence and history and present-day visibility. No doubt, some groups that seem insignificant today will be the power brokers of the future.

New York is a subway city. Parking is a problem and taxis can be prohibitively expensive and buses are too slow, especially during the day. The subway is no beauty to behold; it is New York true grit and part of the texture of the city. It is used by millions of commuters and its dangers during daylight hours can be overstated.

Traveling in the city and trekking to and through ethnic neighborhoods is not shopping-mall antiseptic. New York, high rent or transitional, requires a heads-up attitude and a certain amount of caution. It's best to visit any unfamiliar area during the day. At the same time, minority neighborhoods shouldn't be considered forbidden zones.

New York is a city of regions; in the English tradition, they are called boroughs. The boroughs, five in all, are the principalities of the ethnics. Manhattan has the reputation and the skyscrapers. The other boroughs are sometimes belittled as the outer boroughs of bridge and tunnel people. The image and the reality are different. Brooklyn, the Bronx, Staten Island, and Queens are not burnt-out districts or bland suburbs. Like Manhattan, they have their cultures and other countries; they are places to discover.

Don't try to be inconspicuous when exploring ethnic New York. It is as obvious in most places (as in a foreign country) that you are a stranger. Ask questions and look (don't gawk) and listen. If you are genuinely enthusiastic the local residents will appreciate the interest and open up. Some people inevitably will turn off. Don't be disappointed.

The transportation directions for *Ethnic New York* are the most convenient, direct, and accessible routes. There are no milk-train locals or roundabout buses. The jumping-off points are the midtown stations between 42nd Street and 59th Street. Most of Manhattan is easy to get around with avenues running east and west and streets running north and south, but the older Manhattan neighborhoods, like Chinatown and the Lower East Side, are exceptions.

Ethnic New York doesn't give the admission charges for places of interest or the prices for restaurants for the reason that they often change. It does indicate whether there is an admission fee or contribution and in New York a contribution is anything above a penny. In ethnic areas restaurants tend to be reasonably priced or inexpensive—very inexpensive—and the exceptions are clearly noted.

Passport's Guide to Ethnic New York is not a guide to New York City; it is a guide to New York City's ethnics. The Empire State Building and the Metropolitan Museum of Art are mentioned as footnotes to ethnic experiences. The nuts and bolts of New York touring and sightseeing are left to other books.

This round-the-world of New York covers a lot of territory and I would like to take this opportunity to thank my guides in the neighborhoods and ethnic communities for their extraordinary assistance. Most of all I would like to thank my wife, Dee, without whom this book would never have been written.

The Melting Pot

History

From the days when New York was New Amsterdam the city has been a melting pot. Whether by design or accident, New York has attracted a polyglot pluralistic population. Father Jogues, a French Jesuit missionary to the Mohawk Indians, was the first to comment; he was amazed to find eighteen nationalities in a colony of less than a thousand.

Some Dutch authorities, like the terrible-tempered Peter Stuyvesant, were alarmed by all the foreigners with their ''heretical'' religious practices and questionable morality, but personal preferences took second place to populating the colony. In 1664, New Amsterdam became British property but a policy of open immigration continued. Queen Anne, putting the good of New York above any other considerations, encouraged the emigration of thousands of Palatine Germans to New York, and the city entered the eighteenth century with the British representing less than half of an ethnically and racially mixed population.

While the American Revolution attracted freedom fighters from France to Eastern Europe, it generally slowed the flow of new New Yorkers. The pace of immigration picked up again in 1790 with the announcement of the new republic's two-year (for whites) waiting period for naturalization. America was the hothouse for democracy and all European comers were welcome. Michel de Crèvecoeur, a French ethnic New Yorker, said it all, originating melting-pot imagery: ''There individuals of all nations are melted into a new race of men, whose labors and posterity will one day cause great changes in the world.''

The Louisiana Purchase of 1803 opened up the West to more land-hungry immigrants. The majority first landed in New York and a minority who ran out of money or ran into opportunity stayed. The War of 1812, with its naval blockade, briefly held back the immigration tide, to have it hit its stride again in the port of New York in the 1820s.

The Erie Canal, which began construction in 1817, brought immigrant laborers to New York. While providing pick-and-shovel jobs, once completed it gave the city access to the resources of the northwest frontier and the clear advantage as a port over its Boston and Philadelphia rivals.

The immigrants who rushed to this city of promise were mainly Germans, English, and Protestant Irish. They were motivated by economic hardship, religious persecution, political tyranny, and just a sense of adventure. In the heyday of clipper ships they disembarked at the calm and protected East River ports at the Battery or South Street. The immigrants didn't face Hudson River ice floes, but they had to be on the lookout for con men who steered them to crooked carters and thieving boardinghouses and, when all else failed, picked their pockets.

Between 1840 and 1860 immigration to and through New York took off. The first western European arrivals were artisans and craftsman forced out of work by the Industrial Revolution; they were yeoman farmers who lost their land to large-scale livestock breeding; they were farm tenants who lived off their kitchen gardens, which were suddenly devastated by a common mold.

The potato famine was a disaster of twentieth-century proportions, with slow painful deaths and mass graves. It struck the hardest in Ireland in the 1840s, but it also battered the German farmers of Bavaria and Hanover. The ensuing mass emigration was in an atmosphere of panic, people desperately escaping starvation and disease. Tragically, the emigrants sometimes encountered these twin demons in the steerage of immigrant ships. In the 1850s forty ships never even reached their New York destination.

New Yorkers responded to the problems of the Old World with typical openhearted generosity. There were public subscriptions to aid the victims and immigration assistance for the survivors. Ethnic immigration societies sprang up to finance the unprecedented movement of peoples. The Irish had the greatest need and the largest organization, the Irish Emigrant Society, which worked very closely with the influential German organization, the German Society.

In 1849 the New York government went into action, establishing a commission to deal with the emigration emergency. Its first steps were to provide medical and quarantine facilities on Staten Island and Roosevelt Island. In 1855 the commission, at the urging of emigrant groups, inaugurated the Castle Garden Landing Depot as an official disembarkation point for the mass of emigrants in steerage.

It was a closed-off processing area on an island fort off the Battery. Names were recorded, people examined, money changed, and food purchased. Emigration society representatives offered counsel and advice and even lent money. There were employment agencies and company representatives. The grifters and steerers were kept away from the green immigrants.

The Civil War temporarily interrupted immigration, but the industrial boom of the 1880s coincided with New York's biggest wave of immigration between 1880 and 1914. The Germans, the British, and the Irish predominated in the 1880s and 1890s. They were eventually superseded in numbers by southern and eastern Europeans; southern Italians, Greeks, Czechs, Slavs, Hungarians, Poles, and Jews (of Imperial Russia and Austria-Hungary) were the new immigrants.

Some of these new immigrants had suffered for their religion or a political cause, but in most cases they were peasants living on the edge of subsistence, looking for their place in the sun or at least the money to help their struggling families overseas. Steamships had cut the crossing time from two months to two weeks and the companies had halved the price of steerage. For the first time mass emigration was a reality and even a temporary stay was economically feasible.

The overwhelming majority came just in time to be welcomed by Lady Liberty, her torch held high in New York harbor. Although some New York natives found the new immigrants a bit exotic and even claimed to be shocked by their customs and traditions, the awkward neophytes soon began to build their own bastions in the city.

Castle Garden didn't have the capacity or the facilities to handle the vast number of newcomers. Meanwhile, the Supreme Court conveniently decided that New York didn't have the right to collect fees from the immigrants or shipping companies to defray its Castle Garden costs. Into the breach stepped the federal government to relieve the city's burden with a federally financed and operated immigrant reception center on Ellis Island.

The Ellis Island Immigration Station was all prizewinning architecture and state-of-the-art plumbing, but it was built in 1900 to handle only 1,400 immigrants at a time. It definitely didn't have the capacity to process the 2,000 to 7,000 arrivals who daily passed through its portals before World War I made European immigration dangerous if not impossible.

Even before the "war to end all wars," anti-Catholic and antiforeign groups in New York, like the Know-Nothings and the American Protective Association, were agitating for immigration restrictions, equating Anglo-Saxon blood with American institutions. There were no cries of outrage from New York legislators when Congress passed a law in 1882 excluding Chinese laborers from coming to America. The list of immigration "undesirables" also included idiots, lunatics, and convicts.

Antiforeign feeling was further inflamed by disillusionment with World War I and its diplomatic aftermath. All the lobbying of New York immigrant groups and their government representatives could not buck the trend toward immigration restriction. Congress started the ball rolling in 1917 by forbidding the entry of illiterate foreigners.

In 1921 the Origins Quota Act was passed and grass-roots isolationism became the law of the land. The act was based on the 1911 Dillingham report, which positively proved that recent southern and eastern European emigrants were difficult to assimilate and were bringing down the American standard of living by accepting "slave wages."

The national quotas were based on 3 percent of a nationality in the country at the time of the 1910 census. The Johnson-Reed Act of 1924, which went into effect in 1927, was even more exclusionary, with quotas predicated on 2 percent of the national population in the country in 1890. It was weighted heavily in favor of the British with relatively large quotas for the Germans, the Irish, and the Scandinavians.

Black migration from the South in part replaced foreign-born immigrants, while some of the immigration slack was taken up by nationalities in the Western Hemisphere who were not included in the overall quotas. The first significant numbers of Puerto Ricans emigrated to the city after the Jones Act granted them most of the privileges of citizens. People living in British colonial possessions like Jamaica, Trinidad, and Barbados were able to take advantage of the high British quota. West Indians, who were the largest new immigrant group from the Western Hemisphere, usually set their sights on New York, which had a reputation for racial tolerance.

While the Depression of the 1930s further decreased immigration to New York even from the Western Hemisphere, German Jews and their Christian compatriots fleeing Nazi persecution flocked to the city. Though many were ordinary people, German and Austrian refugees also represented an intellectual elite of writers, artists, and scientists.

During World War II public opinion about restrictive immigration began to slowly shift. In 1943 America recognized the struggle of its Chinese allies by repealing the Chinese Exclusion law. Following the Allies' victory, the Displaced Persons' Act of 1948 opened America's doors to four hundred thousand refugees from Germany and points east outside the official quotas. They were the survivors of the concentration camps and veterans of partisan bands and cold-war casualities of the new map of Europe. Meanwhile, the city was the main destination for the airborne migration of hundreds of thousands of nonquota Puerto Ricans.

Quotas were loosened by the McCarran-Walter Act of 1952 and based on more objective criteria. Immigration eligibility was related to the country's occupational needs and familial and blood ties. But the law still discriminated against the last big wave of immigrants and now restricted immigration from the Western Hemisphere, with West Indian countries like Jamaica limited to a bare hundred immigrants. It had to be amended three times to allow for the entry of European political refugees, Hungarian freedom fighters, and Cuban exiles.

The 1965 Hart-Celler Act attempted to do away with the inequities of the immigration system while retaining immigration ceilings. Emphasis was placed on reuniting families, while there were still large quotas for political refugees and individuals with scarce job skills.

After a brief flurry of applications, the rapid recovery of Europe and Iron Curtain country restrictions interfered with the Act's original intent. Asians, Caribbeans, and Latin Americans provided almost half of the new Americans in the 1960s and 80 percent two decades later. Again the character of the new emigrants to New York changed radically. Besides differences in racial composition and religious background, they were better educated and occupationally prepared than earlier immigrants. Many were trained professionals who didn't have to assimilate culturally to enjoy the city's economic benefits.

New York City was being transformed. The Chinatown of elderly bachelors became a borough-wide community of 90,000 in the space of two decades. The Jamaican population mushroomed from 11,000 to 93,000 from 1960 to 1980. From a small circle of Jewish anti-Soviet activists in 1973, New York's disaffected Soviet Jews were 75,000 strong seven years later. In the 1970s and 1980s the city's political refugees also included thousands of boat people from Haiti, Cuba, and Vietnam.

Since 1976 the Hart-Celler Act has been extended and amended; ceilings and limits have been raised. In 1980 refugees were removed from the overall quotas and they were defined to include people fleeing from noncommunist countries like Haiti or Honduras. In the same year steps were taken to provide benefits for Haitian and Cuban boat people whose status was in doubt.

The 1986 Immigration Reform and Control Act again attempted to revamp the whole system to make it more equitable for immigration groups past and present. Illegal aliens residing in the United States since at least 1982 could now apply for legal residence and there was a special amnesty. At the same time the government provided stricter penalties for employing illegal aliens. It was also now possible for immigrants to enter the country who did not fall within one of the preferential quotas involving work skills or a blood relationship with an American resident.

Today one of every three New Yorkers is foreign born and 90,000 documented immigrants enter the city each year. Whether they come from Odessa, Seoul, Beirut, or Port-au-Prince, they dream the American dream and the sheer vitality of their hopes and ambitions fuels the irrepressible energy of the city. They are the fascinating face of New York: energetic Italians discarding cards in a Bronx social club, Soviet Jews exuberantly toasting the bride and groom in a Brighton Beach nightclub, Indian women scrutinizing fabrics in a Lexington Avenue sari shop, and Senegalese street vendors with studied nonchalance selling watches on the upper East Side. They are Cypriots practicing soccer in Flushing Meadows park next to Jamaicans scoring runs in a leisurely game of cricket.

New York's remarkable new immigrants cluster around occupations and businesses almost to the point of stereotype. Korean greengrocers, Indian newsdealers, Israeli boutique owners, and Hasidic camera and electronics discounters have changed the retail face of the city. New York's famous garment industry now depends on Chinese, Cuban, and Dominican subcontractors with cutters, sewing machine operators, and porters courtesy of the Caribbean, Hong Kong, and Latin America. Gotham's health services are in the capable hands of Korean, Indian, and Middle Eastern physicians with many nurses from the West Indies, Korea, and the Philippines. Korean and Indian pharmacists have filled an important health gap. The legendary New York cabby is likely to be a Soviet refusenik, a Haitian refugee, or a Latino emigrant, while limousine service is provided by Israelis. The cuisines of the Near East and the Far East and the Caribbean have changed the eating habits of the city from fast food to high price trendy. The new ethnics, like the old ones, are reshaping the city in their own image and changing themselves in the process.

Immigration Place Marks

Castle Clinton, *Battery Park (212-344-7220). Free.*

Directions: IRT Lexington 5 to Bowling Green.

Castle Clinton appears properly fortress-like and martial although it never actually engaged in combat from the time it was built in 1807. During the War of 1812 Castle Clinton, then known as the West Battery, guarded the city from a rocky shelf 200 feet off the shore, but it only fired its twenty-eight cannons for target practice.

Directly after the war this dubious fortification was presented to the city and named in honor of Governor DeWitt Clinton. The enterprising city fathers added some flowers and shrubbery, turned the officers' quarters into a bar, and called this exhibition and amusement center Castle Garden. Foreign dignitaries from Lafayette to Edward VII were feted here. It was the scene of the first demonstration of the telegraph and the debut of the Swedish Nightingale, Jenny Lind.

In 1855 it was converted into the country's largest immigration station. Immigrants entered Castle Garden through a great door built through eight-foot-thick walls facing the sea. The reception area was massive but it was difficult to be awed in the crowded atmosphere of money changers and food concessions and ticket sellers. It usually took six hours for the official processing and cursory medical examination; then a long wooden gangplank led directly to the Manhattan shore.

During the Civil War it acted as a recruiting center for immigrants straight off the boat, but later Castle Garden and its emigrant society representatives prepared the immigrants with information about jobs and housing and, if necessary, helped them contact family members or friends in the country. Between 1855 and 1890, 7,690,606 immigrants passed through Castle Garden.

In 1896 Castle Garden went through another major change, becoming the New York Aquarium. By all accounts it was one of the city's most spectacular tourist attractions, with two rings of giant tanks circulating three hundred thousand gallons of water and every variety of aquatic creature. Unfortunately, city politics intervened and the Parks Department closed it down. In 1946 Congress declared it a national monument and it now contains an interesting exhibit dealing with its many transformations.

Off a circular path to the right of Castle Clinton there is a plaque commemorating Emma Lazarus, who wrote the poem that is inscribed on the Statue of Liberty. Emma Lazarus was the daughter of a prominent Jewish family whose ancestors landed in New Amsterdam in 1649. Her most famous poem, "The New Colossus," was her response to seeing the survivors of the first Russian pogrom, who were detained on Wards Island. Two days after she wrote it, the work was auctioned off at a literary gala to raise money for a base for the Statue of Liberty.

Statue of Liberty, *Departure slip, Battery Park (212-269-5755). Daily, April–October, first ferry 9:15 A.M., then every half hour on the hour from 10 A.M., to 5 P.M.; November–March every hour on the hour from 10 A.M., to 5 P.M. Admission charge.*

The ferry for this American symbol, actually titled *Liberty Enlightens the World*, departs from a slip at the foot of the Battery. Though its image is on everything from paperweights to towels, it still has the capacity to thrill.

The Statue of Liberty was the brainchild of Eduard-René Lefebvre de Laboulaye, a staunch French republican, member of the French senate, and author of a history of America. He wanted to seal French-American friendship with a monument to liberty. Frédéric-Auguste Bartholdi was the artist who breathed life into the project, which he conceived on a vast seven-wonders-of-the-ancient-world scale. He adapted the design of an earlier planned work, *Egypt Carrying Light to Asia,* and selected the site of Bedloe's Island.

Alexandre-Gustave Eiffel, who would engineer the Eiffel Tower, devised the revolutionary design of iron pylons that would frame the 151-foot figure. His pioneering work would influence the construction of the first skyscrapers. Although New York's big money scoffed at the idea of Lady Liberty and the respected *New York Times* thought it was a waste of money, Joseph Pulitzer and his crusading *New York World* turned it into a circulation campaign and helped raise the money to put up the magnificent pedestal designed by Richard M. Hunt.

In 1874 the Union Franco-Americaine was formed in Paris to promote the Statue of Liberty. Laboulaye wanted it to be ready by July 4, 1876, in time for America's centennial. He underestimated the enormity of the undertaking. It would take five years just to raise the funds, a million francs, to begin work on the monument, and another five years for Bartholdi to complete his task, using all the best artisans in Paris.

The statue was cast in sections and carried aboard the French ship *Isere* in 214 boxes. On October 28, 1886, President Grover Cleveland dedicated the statue. New York City took the day off to celebrate. Everywhere American flags and tricolors were flying as thousands from France and America marched down Fifth Avenue to the Battery. There was a huge naval procession in the harbor with bands playing and cannon fire in salute. The crowning moment of the day came when Cleveland pulled the cord unveiling the statue.

History repeated itself in 1986, when a completely refurbished *Liberty Enlightens the World* was feted for a second time on her centennial. Lady Liberty was completely cleaned for her party and her interior swabbed out with liquid nitrogen. She was covered with strips of copper and her 98-year-old torch was replaced with a new streamlined one from California.

Her birthday on July 4, 1986, featured a parade of tall clipper ships and the city's biggest display of fireworks ever. When her new torch was hoisted into place, there were in attendance presidents and captains of industry and crowds of the descendants of immigrants she once welcomed.

For those who don't want to make a voyage to the Statue of Liberty, there's and iron replica weighing a modest ton standing on a scaffolding at 219 West Broadway, lighting people's way to the Catalan restaurant, El International, below her.

—American Museum of Immigration—

The American Museum of Immigration is located in the base of the Statue of Liberty, up a single flight of stairs. It recounts the history of immigration from the migrations of the American Indians. Each immigrant group is treated separately with displays of memorabilia and photographs. Dioramas bring to life the immigrant experience. The climb to the pedestal is 161 steps, with another 171 steps to Liberty's crown. The views at each level are spectacular, but the challenge of the spiral staircase is not for everybody. On the grounds of Bedloe's Island, now renamed Liberty Island, there is a group of five lifelike statues by Philip Ratner, which sensitively depict the statue's miwives: Laboulaye, Bartholdi, Eiffel, Pulitzer, and Emma Lazarus.

Ellis Island, *Departure slip, Battery Park (212-269-5755). Daily, first boat 9:15, then every hour until 4 P.M. Admission charge.*

Ellis Island holds the place of honor in America's immigration saga. It is estimated that 85 percent of all Americans are descended from people who came through its reception center.

Before Ellis Island became a landmark it had quite a checkered history. The Indians called it Kioshik Island for its sea gull population, and the British dubbed it ''gibbet island'' for the gallows where a pirate was hung.

Samuel Ellis, for whom the island was named, took title around the time of the revolution, but he preferred to stay on his farm in New Jersey and rented it to a tavern keeper. The government bought it in 1808 to build a fort to protect the harbor. Since the fort was a strategic fiasco it was turned into an ammunition dump. Despite the complaints of residents on the mainland of New Jersey, it fulfilled this function until 1890.

In 1890, when the federal government took control of immigration, Ellis Island became by default the country's main immigration station. Bedloe's Island might have been more appropriate but patriots in France and America thought it would be a desecration. The island was enlarged with a landfill and its pine administration buildings were finished in a hurry in 1892.

Five years later it burned down, along with all the immigration records from 1855 to 1890.

The new station, which opened in 1900, was fireproof. For the first two years immigrants were arbitrarily mistreated and cheated and robbed by greedy concessionaires. Theodore Roosevelt put an end to these abuses but the endemic overcrowding continued.

World War I immigration quotas, with a ceiling of 164,000, and a new policy of processing immigrants in their own countries ended the Ellis Island era. After serving as a detention center for enemy aliens during World War II and a screening center for suspected alien subversives in the early 1950s, it was shut down in 1954. In 1965, at the same time that the Congress was passing a liberalized immigration law, Ellis Island was declared a national monument. A decade later it was open to the public.

New-found feelings of pride in our immigrant heritage have led to recent efforts to restore and preserve the significant Ellis Island chapter in New

York's and the nation's history. The actual buildings of the immigration station are to the right of the ferry slip where visitors disembark. The tall towers of the reception hall dominate the horizon. The reception station itself is not a typical institutional complex. It has high arched windows, brass chandeliers, and a ceiling of Gustavino tile. In the dining hall the WPA created a mural dedicated to immigrant achievements.

Ethnic Extras and Broadcasting

The melting-pot ethos that enables a city to function effectively with a population as varied as the planet does not rule out ethnic individuality and cultural pluralism. Mutual understanding between groups has been enhanced by self-understanding within groups and a stronger sense of identity. Newspapers, radio, and now television are the community resources that have enabled new immigrants from the Irish to the boat people to relate to one another and to their own cultural heritage.

The first immigrant-oriented paper in New York was *The* (Irish) *Shamrock,* which went to press in 1810, while the first foreign-language newpaper goes back to 1827, to the intellectual exiles who started the French-language paper now called *France Amerique.* The German *New Yorker Staats-Zeitung und Herrold* started soon after, in 1834. It would eventually be owned by the Ridders of Knight-Ridder fame, who would build it into a communications empire. The first Italian journal, *L'Eco d'Italia,* was published in 1849 before there was any significant Italian population, and *Il Progresso,* which came out in 1890, was the first successful Italian daily. The Yiddish paper that won the circulation wars in the early years of the twentieth century was the *Jewish Daily Forward.* It empasized social consciousness as much as Judaism.

Before free immigration was blocked in 1924 it seemed as though every foreign-speaking group had its own publication. Between 1898 and 1907 the small Syrian community of New York put out six newspapers to represent all points of view. At that time ethnic papers were similar to the popular press, very partisan and opinionated. Objectivity was secondary to political ideology or religious affiliation and press wars were routine.

The present resurgence in New York's ethnic press mirrors the new waves of immigration. The Hispanic newpaper *El Diario* has the largest circulation—109,000—with its large, predominantly Puerto Rican following. The exploding Chinese community can currently support eight dailies, with *World Journal* readers numbering ninety thousand. The Korean presence in New York, which seems to have grown overnight, already supports six dailies.

New York's ethnic papers, including dailies and weeklies, as of 1986 numbered sixty-eight. They are a new breed of publication—less parochial and more professional. Editor Chin-Fu Woo of *The United Journal,* New York's oldest Chinese daily, is proud to say: "We cover news fairly." Malgorazata Cwiklnska, editor of the Polish language *Nowy Dziennik,* insists on professionalism in serving the non-English-speaking Polish community.

While New York's regular newspapers have decreased in number since World War I, the ethnic press is breaking new records, supplemented by native foreign-language dailies that new immigrants like the Colombians and the Dominicans buy on the newsstands of Jackson Heights and Corona. New York now imports five Colombian papers and seven Dominican ones.

New York's radio has for decades made immigrants feel more at home. Again it has changed with the times and the immigration patterns. WEVD-FM started out in 1927 as the voice of the *Jewish Daily Forward,* but gradually its voice went from Yiddish to Italian to Chinese. While WEVD still has eighty hours a week of Jewish programing in Yiddish, Hebrew, Russian, and English, it also broadcasts Italian, Portuguese, Albanian, Greek, Irish, and Turkish programs.

Most Italian radio, forty-four hours a week, in the metropolitan area is heard on WNWK-FM. There is also a cable radio service offering round-the-clock Italian programing. But the largest non-English-speaking radio audience is Hispanic. There are four full-time Hispanic AM stations—WSKQ, WKDM, WADO, and WJIT. WNWK has plenty of air time for Spanish-speaking Argentines, Dominicans, Peruvians, and Ecuadorians.

Cable television is starting to supersede radio for the larger and more prosperous ethnic groups. WXTV has a twenty-four-hour-a-day Spanish-language programing with Spanish-language films and variety shows from all over Latin America, while WNJJ has a full lineup of Hispanic programs alternating with paid programing. WNYC has programs in Italian, Polish, Japanese, and Chinese, with every type of program from game shows to the news in foreign-language equivalents.

International Place Marks

New York's international character is more than a mingling of immigrants and refugees seeking a better life. New York is a capital of worldwide commerce and a magnet for international deal makers. It is a United Nations of business with branches of the best and the biggest foreign corporations. From the time of the Erie Canal, New York was North America's first port and thoroughly cosmopolitan.

South Street Seaport, *(212-669-9424). The hours for the South Street Seaport exhibits and attractions (though not all the stores and restaurants) are generally from 10 A.M. to 5 P.M. but are subject to seasonal changes.*

Directions: M15 South Ferry bus on Second Avenue to Fulton Street, or the IRT-Lexington Avenue 4 and 5 stopping at Fulton. On the West Side, IND A train to Broadway and Nassau Street. Walk east to the river.

In its prime, the South Street Seaport was the seat of the city's international trade. Clipper ships flying the flags of the sixty nations filled its harbor. It was a cosmopolitan hubbub of longshoremen, seamen, and traders, a Tower of Babel costume ball, people from everywhere speaking every language. As a counterpoint to the relentless activity, there was the on-again, off-again hum of the Fulton Farmer's Market and the Fulton Fish Market.

The opening of the Erie Canal, linking New York to the northwest frontier, only made the port bigger and more frenetic. In one year, over 500 new shipping companies opened offices in the seaport. The firms of South Street built big business New York, opening the lucrative Far Eastern trade and following the Gold Rush out to California. The South Street Seaport glory days were over with the development of the steamship and the Hudson River waterfront.

Nowadays the South Street Seaport still attracts people from around the world, but they are sightseers rather than mariners or merchants. In an eleven-block historic district encompassing piers 15, 16, and 17 along South Street from Peck Slip to Burlingham Slip, the seaport offers a fascinating collection of galleries, historic houses, shops, eating places, and restored clipper ships. The empasis is on historic New York and its connection with the sea.

The seaport is a melting pot of restaurants and cuisines that add flavor to the harborside doings. It's not above fast foods and takeout along with formal dining, but even the informal food has formal prices. This around-the-world-in-restaurants-and-food-shops is located primarily in the main seaport building on Pier 17 opposite Beekman Street, and includes outlets of old New York standbys like Gus's Pickles and Zaro's bread in the restored Fulton Fish Market, as well as originals like Sgarlato's Café and the Pastrami Factory.

Before making the seaport rounds, check in at the Visitors' Center near the Titanic Memorial Tower at 14 Fulton Street and find out about special programs or free concerts. Tickets are available here for all or part of the South Street Seaport scene. Do not miss the multimedia "Seaport Experience" on Pier 17, which depicts its multiethnic past.

International Pavilion of Rockefeller Center, *Fifth Avenue between 49th and 50th Streets.*
Directions: Fifth Avenue buses (M1, M2, M3, M4, M5) stop in front; IND B, D, and F trains to 53rd Street and Fith Avenue.

Rockefeller Center's nineteen buildings cover twenty-two of midtown Manhattan's choicest acres between Fifth and Sixth Avenues and 48th and 51st Streets. Rockefeller Center was the capstone of John D. Rockefeller, Jr.'s career and the first coordinated building development in the city. It includes the RCA building with its bird's-eye observation roof view of Manhattan and the Art Deco glamour of Radio City Music Hall.

Built in the years leading up to World War II, it reflects international interests and concerns. It also reflects a desire to attract foreign tenants. At the focal point of the Center, the British Building is flanked by a building called La Maison Française between 49th and 50th Streets. There is an open European-style promenade separating these buildings with fountains and floral arrangements and decorative pools leading to a lower plaza. The plaza is pure Hollywood, dominated by an eight-ton bronze statue of Prometheus, "the teacher in every art," with a syncopated fountain of fifty jets and colored lights. Above, the flags of most nations hang aloft in a display of unity, while a melting pot of tourists below snaps pictures.

United Nations, *Daily, guided tour every 15 minutes from 9:15 A.M. to 4:45 P.M. Charge.*
Directions: 42nd Street crosstown bus M42 to First Avenue.

Washington is the site of most of the foreign diplomatic offices and all the embassies, but foreign countries in New York have a rich array of official consular, commercial, and tourist offices. The official community has a real presence in the city; they add depth to its cultural life with information offices and institutes. They are a link between the local immigrant populations and their homelands.

In local cab-driver mythology, they are a foreign elite, the bad Old World and the uncivilized New World, ready to take advantage of its diplomatic immunity and imperiously parking their DP-plated cars anywhere. The grumbling can't conceal the pride in being the hub of the world's body politic and the home of the headquarters of the world's governing body, the United Nations.

In 1945 the United Nations Charter was signed and the signers agreed to move the United Nations General Assembly to the United States. John D. Rockefeller, Jr., donated the largest part of the eighteen acres that now contain the UN's buildings, exhibits, and gardens. A committee of architects headed by the American Wallace K. Harrison and representing all the continents except Antarctica created its space-age structures.

Outside the main UN buildings on the west side of the plaza at 43rd Street, a staircase reaches into Ralph J. Bunche Park. It is dedicated to a black peacemaker from the city, who successfully served the UN and gained a Nobel Peace Prize in the process.

The Le Corbusier Secretariat Building dominates the whole complex and has become the symbol for the world organization. This tall slab of glass has a light airy quality as it rises from a contoured base of assemblies, conference rooms, and exhibition areas. The building is entered on the 46th Street side, through doors donated by Canada symbolizing peace, justice, truth, and fraternity. In the lobby there are cultural artifacts of the member nations: a Russian sputnik, a bronze cast of a classical Greek sculpture of Poseidon, and a Mexican mural in the style of Diego Rivera. The international theme continues to the right in the Dag Hammarskjold Memorial Chapel, with stained-glass windows by the renowned Jewish artist Marc Chagall.

Beyond the information desk in the center of the lobby, there is a desk providing tickets for guided tours to the active functioning areas of the UN. The tour includes visits to the Security Council Chamber, the Economic and Social Council Chamber, and the General Assembly Hall.

It is easy to miss the Public Gardens north of the main buildings, but they are definitely worth a stroll just for the change-of-pace trees and greenery. Along the way, there are two heroic statues of the social realism school, provided by Yugoslavia and the Soviet Union.

════════════════ Festivals ════════════════

One World Festival, *Second Avenue at 35th Street.*

Directions: Crosstown bus M34 on 34th Street to Second Avenue.

In the second week of September, 35th Street between First and Second Avenues is closed off to traffic and the city celebrates the One World Festival. The festival is a special gift from New York's Armenian community to all the world's ethnics. The message of this international block party is brotherhood. It's a time to forget the differences and appreciate one another's cultures and talents.

For the weekend a typical New York street becomes an international banquet and bazaar. Thousands eat their way through stands selling Italian sausage, Philippine barbecue, Thai noodles, Armenian *lahmujan,* and Greek *baklava.* They stop to admire Latin American embroidery or African jewelry or thumb through a Middle Eastern cookbook. Meanwhile, in nearby St.

Vartan Park, there is the sweet sound of the Italian Silver Strings or the rumble of the La Roque Bay drummers.

The ethnic entertainment in the park starts at noon or 1 P.M. and lasts the whole afternoon. Ethnic dance companies dominate the program with their nonstop energy and colorful traditional costumes, and the music accompanying the ensembles is much more than background. So pull up a folding chair and watch clog dancers from Ireland, a Hispanic ballet, temple dancers of Bali, or folk dances of the Ukraine. In the magnificent Armenian Cathedral of St. Vartan on Second Avenue between 34th Street and 35th Street, there are classical concerts with an international slant.

Ninth Avenue Fair

Directions: Crosstown bus M42 on 42nd Street or 49th Street M50 to Ninth Avenue.

In the days when the El cast a shadow over Ninth Avenue and Hell's Kitchen's fires were still burning, pushcarts lined Ninth Avenue from 36th Street to 44th Street. New Yorkers called the multiethnic pushcart brigade Paddy's Market. It was the place to go for rare and unusual international food products. Today only a remnant of Paddy's Market remains on Ninth Avenue: Italian salumerias and sausage makers, Greek food and spice shops, and the odd ethnic restaurant, but the spirit of Paddy's Market is renewed in a big way in the annual Ninth Avenue Street Festival.

It happens in mid-May, when the city closes off Ninth Avenue from 37th to 57th Streets for the weekend. Half a million people jam the streets and the sidewalks, sampling food and purchasing crafts and products from around the world. Ninth Avenue ethnic old reliables—with the sons and grandsons and granddaughters of the original owners now in charge—take to the streets. Esposito's Pork Shop's one-of-a-kind hot sausage sizzles while Manganaro's home of the mile-long hero, packs crusty Italian bread with luscious chicken Parmesan. The Greeks at International Foods patiently rotate whole succulent baby lambs on a spit as the ladies in white from the Poseidon hand out Greek *baklava* and spinach pie.

The food is all freshly prepared on open barbecues and grills and even in Chinese woks. There are stir-fried dishes from the Far East and kebabs and *köfte* from the Near East; there are Mexican burritos and Puerto Rican cuchifritos and Jamaican jerk chicken; there are Italian sausage heros and Greek gyros. Occasionally a made-in-New-York hot dog makes an appearance, along with king-size, very salty pretzels. Though American beer is the beverage of choice, there are also Mexican Margaritas and Jamaican ginger beer to wash all the goodness down.

Dancers, bands, and singers from the neighborhoods or aspiring semiprofessionals sponsored by some soft drink or beer company appear on portable stages, while jugglers, mimes in whiteface, and street musicians perform their routines among the crowd. The salsa bands, uptown jazz combos, and Harlem marching bands are usually standouts.

American Ethnic Parade

The American Ethnic Parade is an April-in-New York international entertainment. All the nations of the city dress in native costume and sing and dance their way along the Avenue of the Americas from 56th Street to 37th Street. There are also antique cars, floats with plenty of national character, an angry papier-mâché dragon or two, and the world's largest American flag. In this salute to ethnicity, even the smallest group from Malta or Mali has a chance to strut its stuff and show the colors.

The marchers and performers along the route mostly represent the city's recent immigrants. They still have their roots and the freshness and spontaneity of the first glow of the New York experience. This parade is not an exercise in nostalgia. Peruvian Indians draped with colorful blankets blow on Pan's pipes, and sedate Portuguese serenade on a float resembling the deck of an explorer's ship. People's Republic Chinese in Mao red do a dragon dance, followed by a troop of Taiwanese maidens taking delicate steps in embroidered kimonos. There's an all-Arab float with the children of twenty-two Arab nations, and an all-American Indian float representing ten local tribes. The small community of Kurds has an enthusiastic contingent of three and the populous Dominicans have a long line of marchers, including their own folklorica ballet.

Foreign dignitaries in the reviewing stands solemnly wave to their own national groups. The local elected officials in the same stands keep trying to smile sincerely. Most of the spectators, who represent a fair cross-section of the world, are enthusiastically enjoying the whole show. It is definitely their day.

The International Immigrants Foundation, which is the sponsor of this celebration of cultural diversity, expects to have its own permanent International Culture Center by 1992. Meanwhile, it has offices at 130 West 42nd Street (212-221-7255), where it promotes ethnic culture and provides immigration "consultation, counseling, and documentation processing."

Queens Ethnic Folk Festival, *Czech Hall, 29-19 24th Avenue (718-274-4924).*

Directions: BMT N train to Astoria Blvd/Hoyt Avenue.

About the second week in September, Queens is an all-out ethnic happening. It all takes place in the old-time dance hall of the big brick Bohemian Hall and in its large Old-World backyard. The Czech Hall is located in Astoria, Italian and Greek ethnic territory.

The Queens Ethnic Folk Festival celebrates the music and dance of the people, whether they come from the foothills of Macedonia or the rain forest of Cuba. Every year there are nine or ten ethnic dance troops and music groups performing in the Bohemian Hall from 11 A.M. to 6 P.M. There are no spectators in this special festival; in between acts there are workshops teaching the intricacies of different folk dances.

It's a kaleidoscope of folk culture, from Irish clog dancers and pipers to Pontic Greek dancers and the plaintive note of the clarina and on to a merry concertina and a wild tarantella. After all the dance companies have gone through their energetic paces, it is time for everyone to join in as the festival moves out of doors and under the stars. From 6 P.M. to 12 P.M. there's a lot of strenuous folk dancing along with heavy ethnic eating. Eventually the backyard of Bohemian Hall is transformed into a village and it is difficult to tell the ethnics from the imitation peasants from New Jersey or Manhattan.

chapter two

The Founders

History

The Dutch

The Dutch were the first ethnics to take Manhattan. Henry Hudson, the intrepid English captain of the *Half Moon,* claimed it for the Netherlands in 1609. At the time the friendly locals called it Manna-Hata, the Island of Hills, but Hudson and his crew were more dazzled by the Indian women smoking pipes than by the landscape. Four years later Adriaen Block returned to the island and took a look at some of the outlying boroughs, including Staten Island. After he lost his ship, the *Tiger,* to fire, the Indians helped him build another, the *Onrust* (Restless), and he continued his voyage, collecting valued beaver pelts and their precious oil, which was considered a cure for dizziness, rheumatism, and trembling.

Watching the Spanish and Portuguese get rich on their empires, the Dutch decided to make a profit on their more northerly possessions. The economic future of the island, renamed New Amsterdam, and the whole of New Netherlands became the responsibility of the Dutch West India Company and the "Heeren" XIX, nineteen Lord Directors. Like some future rulers of the Big Apple, greed affected their judgment.

At first New Amsterdam was a stopover on the way to fur trading settlements up the Hudson. In 1625 William Verhulst laid the foundations for a permanent settlement with six farms and a fort. In no time bark houses gave way to stone and the outlines of modern Pearl Street, Beaver Street, and Whitehall Street began to take shape. As an afterthought, Peter Minuit purchased the Big Apple for sixty guilders, or $24, worth of goods. He was more generous in apportioning land to the colony's privileged elite, the patroons, and was eventually recalled for favoritism.

Wouter Van Twiller was the next governor to gain real notoriety. He was a callow and inexperienced twenty-seven, with a weakness for the bottle. When he took office in 1633 New Amsterdam was prospering. Before long he and his corrupt cronies were squandering the company's surplus on private revels and claiming the choice real estate. He was at loggerheads with New Amsterdam's pastor, Everadus Bogardus, and the sheriff, Lubbertus van Dincklage, and his recall was inevitable.

Van Twiller's replacement was a very different personality, incompetent in his own inimitable way. Governor Willem Kieft, who took office in 1638, was a high-handed autocrat with little use for moderation or basic honesty. His attempts to ride roughshod over the Indians, who far outnumbered the Dutch, resulted in bloody Indian wars that depopulated parts of the Dutch possession and turned New Amsterdam into an armed camp. Kieft emptied the treasury fighting senseless wars and crushed the colonists with taxes. Petitions to the company and a remonstrance to the Hague again demanded a governor's recall.

Peter Stuyvesant was the last of this rogues' gallery of Dutch governors. He took charge of the Dutch colony in 1647 and stayed on to the bitter end. Although his personality was no more attractive than that of any of his predecessors, old "Wooden Leg" had a certain stiff-necked honesty, martial skills, and administrative ability. He ruled for seventeen years, longer than anyone in the history of colonial New Amsterdam and New York.

During his term of office he worked hard to overcome the effects of mismanagement and restore order and prosperity. He organized a primitive police force, appointed fire marshals, and established strict laws against fighting and reckless carriage driving. He captured the Swedish colony in present-day Delaware and negotiated a lasting peace with the Indians and a fair treaty with British settlers in New England.

Stuyvesant was quick to anger and had a penchant for feuds. At different times he had disputes with the colony's Jews, Quakers, his own Dutch Reformed Church, the business community, and even the administration of the Dutch West India Company itself. His general intolerance and high-handed approach to government led to company restrictions on his power and the appointment of an advisory council in New Amsterdam.

Finally, in 1664, all his efforts and outbursts came to nothing when Colonel Richard Nicolls handed him an ultimatum from the British Crown. Stuyvesant would have defended New Amsterdam but he had no backing from the Dutch settlers, who welcomed the liberal British peace terms.

The English

Nicolls's lenient peace terms made surrender very easy for the Dutch. In essence, the Dutch were promised the rights of free Englishmen and at least for a time could still ship their tobacco and furs back to Holland. Governor Nicolls was a tolerant man with his own coterie of Dutch advisers, but he had no problem expropriating the Dutch West India Company.

His successor, Colonel Francis Lovelace, was impressed with a city comprised of ethnics that had the "breeding of courts." He saw possibilities everywhere and worked to expand the colony. Lovelace improved transportation and communications, opening a road between New York and Harlem and improving ferry service from Spuyten Duyvil on the Harlem River. This dynamo even attempted to rebuild the colony's defenses but it was too little and too late.

The Netherlands retook New York in 1673 and the local Dutch threw up their hands and declared their neutrality. The new Dutch authorities didn't have time to do more than rename the city New Orange and blow up Fort Amsterdam before their government gave New Orange back to the English in the Treaty of Westminster.

Tensions continued in the city between the Dutch and the British; there were problems in the courts and friction on the city watch. Governor Thomas Dongan, New York's first Catholic governor, took a conciliatory approach, and with the approval of King James II, issued in 1686 the Dongan Charter of Liberties, which guaranteed certain rights and provided for greater self-government. The city was now divided into six wards with a mayor, an alderman, and a city recorder.

Most of the governors who succeeded Dongan thought public office was an easy way to line their own pockets. Governor Montgomery took big bribes from members of the city council to enlarge their powers, and Cosby, who followed him, extorted extra salary from his predecessor and suspended the judiciary. Their actions led to the kind of conflict and protest that triggered the American Revolution.

Even in colonial days New York was a "business first" kind of place. During the French and Indian War, from 1756 to 1763, it became America's second largest city, trading furs and guns with the enemy. Before the Revolution New York's main disagreements with Britain involved commercial interference as well as abstract issues like freedom and the rights of man. It was an import duty on tea that led to New York's own "tea party" on April 22, 1774, in which twenty-two crates of tea were dumped into Manhattan Bay by New Yorkers masquerading as Mohawks.

While Manhattan radicals were holding congresses to form a militia and defend the city against the British in 1775, the British governor, Tryon, was organizing sympathetic loyalists in Queens. When the Revolution stopped talking and started shooting and the statue of George III in Bowling Green was converted into 42,088 bullets, thousands of New Yorkers sought the protection of the British army. New York Tories were everywhere; England was their motherland and New York in most of its essentials was an English city.

The Founders' Legacy

The Dutch Inheritance

The Dutch colony of the seventeenth century set the mold for modern New York. The city is still all about dealing and deal makers, though no longer officially run by a single company and a coterie of merchants. Like seventeenth-century patroons, the city's contemporary power brokers still make fortunes from real estate; the colonial smugglers raking in the guilders on bootlegged pelts also have their twentieth-century equivalents dealing in less benign forms of contraband.

The drinking and roughhousing that characterized New Amsterdam would not disappear despite periodic public crusades in the spirit of Peter Stuyvesant. New York is not effete. It is a convivial town that can sometimes get contentious; the wild good times are in its blood. Cultural pluralism is another part of New York's Dutch inheritance. Even in the days when the population numbered in the hundreds, people were speaking eighteen languages and there were almost as many religious sects. Welcoming foreigners started as a necessity in underpopulated New Amsterdam and quickly became a New York tradition.

The Dutch left a legacy in the New York vocabulary with words like *boss* ("baas"), *scow* ("schouw"), and *snoop* ("snoepen"). Some of New York's favorite treats like the waffle ("wafle") and the cookie ("koekje") are of Dutch origin. Dutch place names can still be found from the Bowery ("bouwerie" means *farm*) to Brooklyn ("Breukelen"). Though the Dutch didn't invent the yule log or the Christmas tree, Santa Claus is derived from the Dutch "Sinter Klass." Even the word *Yankee* comes from the name of a New Netherlands freebooter, Jan Keese. The characteristic New York stoop is a Dutch architectural convention, which in old Amsterdam protected living spaces from floods.

In a footnote to the Dutch founders, there was a small spurt of Dutch immigration to New York in 1953 via a special act of Congress that granted seventeen thousand visas to Dutch emigrants. In 1955, there was a special quota for Dutch citizens leaving their newly liberated colony of Indonesia. Altogether eighty thousand left the Netherlands between 1945 and 1965, with the majority settling in Los Angeles and New York. They eagerly assimilated and were diffused throughout the metropolitan area.

The last Dutch vestiges are preserved in some very special and exclusive organizations:

Holland Society of New York, *122 East 58th Street (212-758-1675).*

All members are direct descendants of the Dutch who settled New York prior to 1675. They meet to discuss their pedigrees and compare genealogies. The society has a 6,000-volume library dealing with Dutch history and culture. The organization's Burgher Guards dress up in seventeenth-century costume and participate in patriotic events and parades.

Netherlands-America Community Association, *One Rockefeller Plaza (212-246-1429).*

The group is a partnership of the Netherlands Benevolent Society (founded in 1905) and the Netherlands-America Foundation (founded in 1921). Its activities are split between community service and promoting Dutch education, literature, and art.

The English Inheritance

The English are New York's nonethnics, the ideal that future ethnics envied and emulated. New York's English imprint has never been lost. It is in the spoken and written language of the city, though slightly obscured by New York's dialects. It is in the courts and the common law and the office of mayor.

New York's buildings imitated English architectural styles from Georgian to Gothic Revival. Chippendale furniture adorned New York drawing rooms, along with made-in-England Mappin and Webb silver and Royal Worcester porcelain. Manhattan enjoyed English drama and English acting companies like the Hallam, and even rioted over a performance by William Macready, the English matinee idol. English higher education set the standard for New York with the establishment of Kings College, which today is Columbia University. New Yorkers kept kennels of hounds and hunted like English squires, or were Sunday sailors like good descendants of a seafaring nation. Some whiled away their leisure hours drinking English gin in English public houses.

Englishmen founded many of the city's most important private institutions from banks to libraries and went on to become the city's unofficial aristocracy in the New York Social Register.

The English tradition continues in a number of organizations with links to the "Mother Country":

St. George's Society of New York, *71 West 23rd Street (212-924-1434).*

This is the granddaddy of all New York "charitable" organizations, having begun life in 1691. It's been a long time since the society helped immigrant Brits find jobs or shelter, although from 1859 to 1909 it did provide cheap passage back to England on the Cunard and White Star lines. It's primarily a social organization for people of British or Commonwealth birth or descent.

English-Speaking Union of the United States, *16 East 69th Street (212-879-6860).*

The organization awards scholarships and travel grants in the process of promoting English-language culture. It has a very British library with the latest English papers and tweedy English types.

Pilgrims of the United States, *74 Trinity Place (212-943-0635).*

Pilgrims is the elite of English overseas organizations. In between toasts for queen and country the old boys promote Anglo-American relations. The British Ambassador comes here to make his inaugural address.

Place Marks

Introduction

Philip Hone, a social commentator of the early nineteenth century, put it very succinctly: "The whole of New York is rebuilt about once every ten years." While New York can be very cavalier with its artifacts and relics, the founders managed to leave behind some curious footprints in the city sands. The landmarks and monuments to New York's Dutch and English colonial founders start at the tip of Manhattan Island, make their way north through Harlem, and are scattered throughout the outer boroughs.

Most of colonial New Amsterdam's or New York's history happened in lower Manhattan. The colonial adventure began at the Battery in 1625 with thirty Dutch families and slowly insinuated itself northward. At the time Peter Stuyvesant paved the streets of New Amsterdam, its northern border was the Wall Street stockade, and even the English waited until 1699 to cross over that line. In 1771, English New York City had expanded to Grand Street and boasted a population of 22,000.

Lower Manhattan

Directions: IRT-7th Avenue 1 train to South Ferry, or the IRT-Lexington Ave 4 or 5 train to Bowling Green. The M1, M6, and M15 buses stop at South Ferry.

Netherlands Memorial Monument

Founders' New York starts at the entrance to Battery Park. The Netherlands Memorial Monument is a flagpole for the ages standing on a granite base that was donated by the Dutch people in 1926. The history lesson on the base shows a map of Dutch Manhattan and Peter Minuit and the Manhattan Indians closing their twenty-four-dollar deal for the island.

The U.S. Customs House

The former U.S. Customs House is beyond the Battery between State and Whitehall Streets on Bowling Green. It's located in the area where the first white settlers built their basic shelters and erected a fort. The British maintained the structure, renaming it Fort George (after the king) in 1664, but victorious New York revolutionaries razed it along with other reminders of this unpopular monarch in 1789.

In 1907 the current U.S. Customs House building, designed by Cass Gilbert, was completed. It's neoclassical facade has an international theme that reinforces the building's original purpose. Four heroic sculptures in front dramatically depict Asia in contemplation, a confident America, a Europe inhibited by history, and Africa asleep between the sphinx and a lion. At the sixth story, above the cornices, twelve statues, representing great commercial civilizations from Greece and Rome to England and France, imperiously survey Broadway. Characterizations of eight so-called races, including Hindu and Eskimo, provide distraction in the window arches.

Bowling Green

The Bowling Green, just north of the Battery dividing Broadway, is a vest-pocket park with plenty of history. The Dutch originally used it as a cattle market, but later it became a place for the game bowls and, under the British, a parade ground. In 1771 officials put a fence around it to protect a statue of a very regal George III dressed up to look like a Roman emperor.

But nothing could stop American patriots in 1776 from tearing it down and melting it into bullets for the Revolution.

Fraunces Tavern, *54 Pearl Street (212-425-1778). Museum open Monday–Friday 10* A.M.*–5* P.M. *Gratis from 10* A.M. *until noon, otherwise there's an admission charge.*

Fraunces Tavern is on the corner of Pearl and Broad Streets between the present financial district and Battery Park. It's a reconstruction and a replica of the old DeLancey mansion, which was built in 1719, and only the west wall contains the original Holland brick. The loyalist DeLanceys made their mansion a Georgian classic, all order and symmetry, with high chimneys and an ornamental balustrade on a hipped roof. In 1763 the DeLancey house became the premises of Samuel Fraunces' Queen's Head Tavern. George Washington made his famous farewell address in the tavern's second-floor dining room in 1783. Nowadays Fraunces Tavern does double duty as a museum of early Americana and as an old-fashioned Yankee restaurant. The exhibitions in the upstairs rooms are all about Washington, the American Revolution, and the restoration and curious history of Fraunces Tavern.

Trinity Church and Churchyard, *74 Trinity Place (212-602-0800).*

The original Trinity Church was constructed in 1697 at Wall Street and Broadway. It was the main house of worship of the established Anglican Church and was built with city taxes. In 1776, while New York was occupied by the British, it was destroyed in a suspicious fire. The current church was erected in 1846 in Gothic Revival style. The spire attempts to soar, but Trinity turns out to be only imitation medieval with decorative buttresses and plaster vaults.

The Trinity Churchyard is two and a quarter tranquil acres in the fast-paced world of Wall Street. There are magnolias in the spring and tombstones from the seventeenth and eighteenth centuries.

St. Paul's Chapel, *Broadway between Vesey and Fulton Streets.*

St. Paul's was built in the New York hinterlands in 1766, and is the oldest building in Manhattan. The church is modeled after London's St. Martin's-in-the-Fields, with a portico more like a Greek temple than an Episcopalian Church porch. The interior of St. Paul's has diamond-faceted Waterford crystal chandeliers, and a magnificent carved pulpit that predates the Revolution. In 1794 a spire and clock tower was added, duplicating the one at St. Martin's.

St. Mark's-in-the-Bouwerie, *131 East 10th Street (212-674-6377)*

St. Mark's started out in 1660 as Peter Stuyvesant's private chapel on his *bouwerie* (Dutch for "farm"), where in his declining years he entertained the British governor. When Stuyvesant died at the age of eighty, he was buried near the chapel door. The church was entirely rebuilt in 1799 in the then-popular Georgian style and a steeple and a portico were added in the nineteenth century. The outlines of the second oldest church in New York are austere without being severe. In 1915 Queen Wilhelmina of the Netherlands presented the church with a statue of Stuyvesant, which now occupies a place near his grave.

The Village of Harlem and Beyond

In simpler colonial times, Harlem was a village governed by loose committees and magistrates selected in an open meeting. The people in Harlem, who all knew one another, represented the best families in the Dutch and later the British communities. Harlem and Harlem Heights were estate areas, a sort of colonial Greenwich or Westport. There were DeLanceys, Beekmans, Rikers, and Coldens. As late as the 1880s, families like the Bensons, Hoppers, and Raubs lived on lands with titles granted in the seventeenth century. It was inevitable that at least part of this legacy would survive. Call ahead before visiting these uptown treasures, and tread lightly in surrounding areas.

Morris-Jumel Mansion, *corner of Edgecombe Avenue and 161st Street (212-923-8008). Tuesday–Sunday 10 A.M.–4 P.M. Admission charge.*

Directions: IND local K train to West 163rd Street. Madison Avenue M2 and M3 buses.

This elegant Georgian mansion (circa 1765) stands serenely in an area between Harlem and Washington Heights. It originally belonged to a Tory named Colonel Roger Morris, who backed the wrong side in the Revolution and left for England on very short notice.

In 1810 the house became the property of a wealthy merchant named Stephen Jumel. It was a present for his ambitious bride and former mistress, Betsy Bowen. She was rumored to have been a lady of easy virtue, and she was eager to gain respectability. While trying to crash polite society, she had the façade of the Morris-Jumel Mansion redone several times, until it resembled a plantation portico. Years after her husband died, leaving her millions, she married the 77-year-old Aaron Burr and attained at least in her own mind the position she craved.

The mansion is open to the public, displaying Madame Jumel's most prized pieces, with English Chippendales in the front parlor and a complete Empire bedroom set on the second floor. There is a study with prerevolutionary American furniture and a room for dipping candles.

Dyckman House, *204th Street and Broadway (212-304-9422). Tuesday–Sunday 11 A.M.–4 P.M. Admission charge.*

Directions: IND-Eighth Avenue A train to 207th Street.

When the Dyckman House was built in 1783, it was a typical Dutch homestead composed of fieldstone, brick, and wood on a very atypical farm covering three hundred acres. The Dyckman farm, which was acquired in stages beginning in 1677, remained the biggest farm in Manhattan for two hundred years.

In 1917, when developers were about to destroy Dyckman House, the Dyckman family restored the old place and rearranged its rooms with Dutch and English period furniture and prerevolutionary toys, clothing, and curios. Behind the building there is a traditional smokehouse and a storage shed. Everyday eighteenth-century life is mirrored in this simple dwelling.

The Bronx

The Bronx was one of the earliest parts of the city to be settled. In 1641 a Scandinavian named Jonas Bronck crossed the Harlem River, bought five hundred acres from the Indians, and started clearing and cultivating the land. The Bronx that was born in that bygone era was a dangerous place, vulnerable to the attacks of Indians and fraught with disputes between the Dutch burghers and English dissenters. The Bronx grew slowly and wasn't really developed until the twentieth century. Some very early Dutch houses were preserved in the Bronx backwater.

Van Cortlandt Mansion, *Van Cortlandt Park near 242nd Street and Broadway (212-546-3323). Tuesday–Saturday 10 A.M.–4:45 P.M. Admission charge.*

Directions: IRT-Broadway-7th Avenue to the 242nd St/Van Cortlandt stop.

The Van Cortlandt Mansion is an evocative return to colonial times, set among broad shade trees and bushes on a bluff in Van Cortlandt Park. The Dutch Van Cortlandt clan owned this section of the Bronx from the late seventeenth to the late nineteenth century. This accomplished family boasted the first native-born mayor of New York (1677) and a general in the Continental Army.

Frederick Van Cortlandt built the mansion in 1748 in a four-square sturdy version of Georgian architecture. This manor house alternates brick and rough fieldstone, the natural materials blending with the natural setting. It has some interesting touches, like the comic masks in the keystones above the double-hung multipaned windows.

The rooms of the house are stuffed with Van Cortlandt family memorabilia and furniture from the Dutch and British colonial eras. The east parlor features a portrait of Augustus Van Cortlandt. There is a Dutch bedroom on the second floor with a Dutch cupboard bed, and the kitchen has an actual Dutch oven. George Washington slept in the Munro room.

Valentine-Varian House, *3266 Bainbridge Avenue (212-881-8900). Saturday and Sunday 10 A.M.–5 P.M. Admission charge.*

Directions: IND-Sixth Avenue D train to 205th St/Bainbridge Avenue, or IRT-Lexington Avenue (4) train to Mosholu Parkway.

The Valentine-Varian House is a simple, unpretentious Dutch farmhouse, compact and rough-hewn, vintage 1758. It is located in the North Bronx in a neighborhood called Norwood near the entrance of Williamsbridge Oval Park.

The Valentine-Varian House was built by Isaac Valentine in 1748 on land he had purchased from the Dutch Reformed Church. He was a farmer and a blacksmith and a man of action who sided with the Sons of Liberty. He and his family were forced to flee their farmstead during the Revolution. It was the scene of violent skirmishes and was even occupied by Hessian troops. The Varians took title to the land along with the house in 1791. There was a Varian mayor and a Varian alderman among generations of prosperous Varian farmers.

Blocking the demolition ball of developers, the Bronx Historical Society preserved the house and filled it with an interesting selection of old pictures, photos, documents, maps, and memorabilia telling the whole story of the Bronx.

Vlissingen: A Stroll Through Historic Flushing

Directions: IRT-Flushing line 7 to Roosevelt Avenue/Main Street.

Vlissingen, now called Flushing, was named for a Dutch town and chartered in 1645. This outlying area of New Netherlands found few Dutch takers and was soon settled by English dissenters. The Quakers who came in the 1640s and 1650s were Vlissingen's leading ''heretics,''

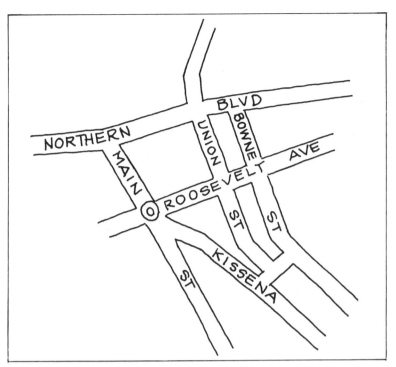

Historic Flushing

and the established Dutch Calvinist Church and its official defenders wanted to close it down.

In 1657 Governor Peter Stuyvesant issued an edict affirming the special status of the Dutch Reformed Church; it was a clear warning to ''abominable sects'' like the Quakers. In the fall Robert Hodgson, a newly arrived English Quaker, was arrested for preaching the Quaker doctrine, whipped by the public executioner, and imprisoned. Despite the threats of Governor Stuyvesant and inquisition-like torture, he refused to submit to forced labor and was banished before the end of the year.

The people of early Flushing took up his cause and made their famous remonstrance to the governor on December 27, 1657. They would not ''persecute'' the Quakers and could not ''in conscience lay violent hands on them.'' Hodgson's stand and the courageous actions of the people of Flushing were a milestone in the fight for religious freedom.

Over the years Quaker farmers were replaced by wealthy Manhattan merchants who used Flushing as a vacation hideaway. Flushing became famous again in 1939, when new highways led to a science-fantasy World's

Fair. The same Robert Moses roads were used by the commuters who flocked to this newly accessible suburb. Still the Quaker tradition of tolerance persists in modern Flushing, a community that accepts people of all races and religious backgrounds.

St. George's Episcopal Church

Just across from the subway stop near the junction of Main Street and Roosevelt Avenue, St. George's was built in 1854. The church is all brownstone respectability with a quaint white wooden steeple. Francis Lewis, a Declaration of Independence signer, was vestryman at the first church on this site in 1761.

Friends' Meeting House, *137-16 Northern Boulevard.*

Walking north toward Northern Boulevard, make a right turn between Main Street and Union, stopping at the site of the historic Friends' (Quakers) Meeting House, which dates from 1694 and was restored between 1716 and 1719. The back of the frame building is on the boulevard; the front faces a tiny cemetery with Quaker headstones without any names. Quakers have been meeting here nonstop since the American Revolution.

Flushing Town Hall, *137-35 Northern Boulevard.*

On the opposite side of the boulevard, the Town Hall dates from 1862. It is all Victorian extravagance with ornamental cornices, decorative turrets, and giant gables. This impressive brick structure keeps changing identity; it has been a courthouse, an opera house, a bank, a library, and a jail. Its halls, which once rang with the voices of Theodore Roosevelt, Ulysses Grant, and P. T. Barnum, are today vacant.

Fox Oaks Rock

A block up is a part of colonial Flushing that really deserves to be called a milestone. This big boulder on 37th Avenue marks the spot where the famous Quaker, George Fox, preached in 1672.

Bowne House, *37-01 Bowne Street (212-359-0528). Friday, Saturday, and Sunday 2:30 P.M.–4:30 P.M. Admission charge.*

At the southeast corner of 37th Avenue is the site of the oldest historic structure in Queens. Today Bowne House is a small museum dedicated to Flushing's colonial past and its part in the struggle for religious liberty. The house is a model of low-key Quaker simplicity. The backyard contains a bronze plaque of the Flushing Remonstrance and an herb garden.

From 1661 to 1945 Bowne House was the residence of the Bowne family. Their ancestor, John Bowne, was another Quaker who dared to stand up to Peter Stuyvesant. Banished to Holland for holding Quaker meetings, he had the last laugh when he convinced the Dutch West India Company to accept the Quakers.

Kingsland Homestead, *143-35 Thirty-Seventh Avenue (718-520-7049). Tuesday, Saturday, Sunday 2:30 P.M.–4:30 P.M. Admission charge.*

This white clapboard farmhouse, which mixes English and Dutch architectural styles, would fit right in an old New England village. Queens preservationists saved this circa 1674 house and opened it as a museum in 1968. It holds a small intimate collection of photos, maps, and other memorabilia of local history.

The house was built by a Quaker named Doughty, who was the first person to free a slave in New York. His son-in-law, Joseph King, who nearly lost his head in the French Revolution, retired here after all the excitement. Kingsland House stayed in the socially prominent Murray family (for whom Murray Hill was named) for more than a century.

The Island with Two Names

The Dutch named it Staten Island and the English named it Richmond. The city fathers officially call it Richmond but mostly everybody else, including mapmakers, calls it Staten Island. For a lot of its history it was so underpopulated no one cared what it was called.

In 1639 the Dutch opened it to colonization but each time they thought they had something going, the Indians chased out the settlers. They had a number of Indian wars with peculiar-sounding names like the Pig War in 1641, the Whiskey War in 1643, and the Peach War in 1655. Every time they made peace with the Indians, the colonists would negotiate another deal to buy the island. They wound up buying it five times.

The original capital of English Richmond was called Cocles Town but when the name became corrupted to Cuckold's Town the people in charge moved that it be changed to Richmond. People were always doing things like that to neglected Staten Island.

For the first two centuries of its life it was a fishing and farming backwater. Later the rich discovered the backwater and made it a luxury resort and literary colony. Inevitably the rich started looking for new places to summer and although Staten Island would have gladly returned to its semirural isolation, industry had different ideas and pollution followed the oil refineries. Finally it took the Verrazano-Narrows Bridge to bring Staten Island into the New York mainstream and make it just another bedroom suburb. Still, the borough's gradual development helped preserve its past, which is alive and well in the Richmond Restoration.

The Richmond Restoration, *intersection of Richmond Road, Clarke Avenue, and Arthur Kill Road, adjoining La Tourette Park (718-351-1617). Wednesday–Friday 10 A.M.–5 P.M.; Saturday– Monday, holidays 1 P.M.–5 P.M. Admission charge.*

Directions: IRT-Lexington Avenue 4 or 5 train to Bowling Green, or IRT-7th Avenue (1) to South Ferry then Staten Island Ferry. S113 bus to Richmond Hill Road near St. Patrick's Place.

Since the Richmond Restoration has more of the Founder's New York than the other four boroughs put together, it is definitely worth the bother of getting there. The first leg of the Staten Island journey is the ferry. It's transporation if you live on Staten Island, but for anyone else it's a bargain— 25 cents for a half hour excursion with spectacular views of the Statue of Liberty, Ellis Island, and the Verrazano-Narrows Bridge. Passengers disembark in St. George, the capital of the borough, in the vicinity of the bus terminal, where the bus leaves regularly for the Restoration. It's just a short walk to the Information Office, a converted courthouse from 1837, for brochures and tickets.

The Richmond Restoration is a thirty-acre village of twenty-five (and soon to be more) representative houses from early America. Ten are at their original Richmond Town sites; the others were retrieved from all over the island through the untiring efforts of the Staten Island Historical Society. Each building reflects a way of life. There's a print shop, a carpenter's shop, a combination bakery-post office, a saddler's and harness maker's shop, and homes of assorted people from a physician to a shipping magnate.

The Restoration is a living museum where guides in period costume explain the intricacies of cooking in a beehive oven or setting type in the nineteenth century. In one house there is a woman in a bonnet turning a potter's wheel; in the next a tall man in overalls is plaiting a straw basket. It contains the oldest elementary school in the United States, dating from 1695, and the Guyon-Lake-Tysen house is the best example of Dutch Colonial architecture in the city. The humble snack bar with homemade brownies (not prepared in the beehive oven) and cider is in the Greek Revival Bennett House, completed in the middle of the last century.

══════ Manhattan Museums ══════

New-York Historical Society, *170 Central Park West at 77th Street, Tuesday–Friday 11 A.M.–5 P.M.; Saturday 1 P.M.–5 P.M. Admission charge.*

Directions: Take the IND-8th Avenue Local BCK to 81st Street, or the IRT-7th Avenue 1 to 79th Street and head east.

The New-York Historical Society is a stickler for tradition, even in the way it spells its name. (There was a hyphen in old New York.) The building looks like a mausoleum from the outside; inside it has the warmth and intimacy of an old country home, very refined.

In its library, the New-York Historical Society has all you want to know about the Founders' New York in books, original manuscripts, periodicals, and prints. There are also exhibits, permanent and otherwise, with paintings by old American masters including Stuart and Copley, prerevolutionary and early American glassware and silver and coaches of every size, age, and purpose in the Fahnestock Collection.

Museum of the City of New York, *Fifth Avenue between 103rd and 104th Streets (212-534-1672). Tuesday–Friday 10:30 A.M.– 4:30 P.M.; Saturday and Sunday 1 P.M.–4 P.M. Free.*

Directions: Madison Avenue M1, M2, M3, and M4 bus, or IRT-Lexington Avenue 6 train to 103rd Street.

The Museum of the City of New York is housed in a handsome rambling neo-Georgian building on Fifth Avenue, and makes the dry essentials of history come to life. The Dutch Gallery on the first floor charts the Dutch colonial adventure from Hendrik Hudson and the *Half Moon* to the Indian War that started over a peach to the Dutch surrender to England. The emphasis is on show rather than capsule-written history, with fascinating dioramas and authentic-looking scale models. The British are given equal time on the same floor in a whole series of maps and pictures detailing their progress after 1664.

The second floor features rooms with Dutch and English period furnishings. There is a portrait gallery that includes famous Dutch and English New Yorkers and a treasure house called the Silver Gallery with the art of Dutch and English silversmiths. The multimedia show tracing the city's story from the Indians to the present is more fun than the usual information-packed seminar and should not be missed.

The English Are Coming

While Anglo-Saxons do not make up a significant portion of the city's new immigrants, New Yorkers are inveterate Anglophiles. Things English are the vogue, from the Princess of Wales to Aquascutum raincoats. It is partly snob appeal. *English* means you've made it and leads a realtor to call his latest luxury highrise Grosvenor House and advertise English services—whatever they are. But mostly in New York, whether its a Royal Shakespeare Company production or a Rolls-Royce, *English* means quality. English retailers have gone trans-Atlantic to meet the New York demand.

English Labels

Alexon, *777 Madison Avenue between 66th and 67th Streets (212-439-9196). Monday–Wednesday, Friday, Saturday 10 A.M.–6 P.M.; Thursday 10 A.M.–7 P.M.*

Sturdy English clothes are brought up to date for the New York professional woman. Alexon won't win medals for imagination and daring, but the clothes are comfortable and work in an office setting.

Aquascutum, *680 Fifth Avenue at 54th Street (212-975-0250). Monday–Wednesday, Friday, Saturday 10 A.M.–6 P.M.; Thursday 10 A.M.–7 P.M.*

It is the old English class act applied to ready-to-wear. There are the internationally known raincoats and much more. The styles are conservative, very careful solids and plaids, simple and functional. The prices are straight-forwardly expensive and the service is respectful.

Berk of Burlington Arcade, *781 Madison Avenue between 66th and 67th Streets (212-570-0285). Monday–Saturday 10 A.M.–6 P.M.*

This shop appeals to the snob in every New Yorker, as if clothes make the class and the title comes with the cashmere. The saleswomen believe in the Berk myth and cater to it.

Burberry's, Ltd., *9 East 57th Street (212-371-5010). Monday–Wednesday, Friday 9:30 A.M.–6 P.M.; Thursday 9:30 A.M.–7 P.M.; Saturday 10 A.M.–6P.M.*

No surprises here—just four floors of Burberry's popular English styles for men and women and all the required plaid linings. The famous raincoat takes center stage with plenty of accessories to go with it—many never seen in London.

Cashmeres of Scotland, *Trump Tower, 725 Fifth Avenue at 56th Street, fifth level (212-758-7621). Monday–Saturday 10 A.M.–6 P.M.*

It's pure Trump Tower luxury, expensive cashmere in an expensive sweater, and nothing else. Scotch sweaters will never be the same—cashmere comes into the fashion present.

Jaeger, *818 Madison Avenue between 67th and 68th Streets (212-628-3350). Monday–Saturday 10 A.M.–6 P.M. 19 East 57th Street (212-753-0370). Monday–Wednesday, Friday, Saturday 10 A.M.–6 P.M.; Thursday 10 A.M.–7 P.M.*

Jaeger is the Regent Street look of conservative style for men and women, though in New York only women's clothes are offered. Since the 1920s it has been the place for camel's hair coats, sweaters, and color-coordinated sportswear. Although spruced up, it is still very set in its ways.

Laura Ashley, *21 East 57th Street (212-752-7300). Monday–Friday 10 A.M.–7 P.M.; Saturday 10 A.M.–6 P.M. 398 Columbus Avenue at 79th Street (212-496-5110). Monday–Wednesday, Friday, Saturday 11 A.M.–7 P.M.; Thursday 11 A.M.–8 P.M.; Sunday noon–6 P.M. 4 Fulton Street (South Sea Seaport) (212-809-3555). Monday–Saturday 10 A.M.–9 P.M.; Sunday noon–8 P.M.*

Laura Ashley is soft and flowered fabrics in gentle English colors. She represents pastoral England with prints and delicate patterns and the return of the romantic.

N. Peal, *118 East 57th Street (212-826-3350). Monday–Friday 10 A.M.–6 P.M.; Saturday 10 A.M.–5:30 P.M.*

The English keep promoting cashmere to compete with the Far East imports. The designs here are so original, who can tell they are sweaters? There's not enough room to explore the merchandise.

The English at Home

Asprey and Company, *Trump Tower, 725 Fifth Avenue at 56th Street (212-688-1811).*

Elegant jewels, fine silver, and splendid accessories are the order of the day. The air is as rarified as the merchandise, but now and again it is possible to find a small enamel box for less than a king's ransom.

Conran's, *160 East 54th Street (212-371-2225). Monday–Friday 10 A.M.–9 P.M.; Saturday 10 A.M.–6 P.M.; Sunday 1 P.M.–6 P.M.*

Conran's-Habitat, *2–8 Astor Place (212-505-1515). Monday–Saturday 10 A.M.–9 P.M.; Sunday noon–7 P.M.*

Good design came to England in the Habitat stores and now it's in New York with well-priced furniture, conservatively modern and country simple, as well as lots of contemporary accessories.

Floris, *703 Madison Avenue (212-935-9100). Monday–Wednesday, Friday 10 A.M.–6 P.M.; Thursday 10 A.M.–7 P.M.; Sunday noon–6 P.M.*

The original is on Jermyn Street at the better end of Piccadilly. There are scented soaps, shaving toiletries, sachets, and natural flower fragrances, all wrapped in the store colors of blue and gold.

Liberty, *630 Fifth Avenue at 51st Street (212-459-0080). Monday–Saturday 9:30 A.M.–6 P.M.*

The twisting turns and dark woods of the Regent Street store can't be found here, but there are plenty of scarves and ties and fabrics and other small items for the home in the famous Liberty prints.

Laura Ashley Home, *714 Madison Avenue (212-735-5000). Monday–Wednesday, Friday, Saturday 10 A.M.–6 P.M.; Thursday 10 A.M.–7 P.M.*

Everything in this store looks as though it came out of English *Country Life* magazine. The same motifs of flower patterns are on the bed linens, towels, fabrics, tea sets, and lampshades. It can get monotonous.

S. J. Shrubsole, *104 East 57th Street (212-753-8920).*

The silver items sold here are practically museum pieces. There are etched tea sets and trays as well as finely crafted Georgian serving pieces.

Pubs and Others

Though *English* and *cuisine* are sometimes seen as a contradiction in terms, the English chophouse is an old New York institution. The combination of prime meat and potatoes in an atmosphere of fireplaces and wainscoting and bronze antiques caught New Yorkers' fancy way before vegetables became a main course. The New York version of the English pub is usually just a gimmick, but there are a couple of authentic ones around with cockles and mussels and steak and kidney pie and real English expats.

Bull and Bear, *301 Park Avenue, in the Waldorf-Astoria (212-872-4900). Monday–Sunday noon–midnight.*

The prime rib and chops *are* prime and the steaks are actually cooked to order. The atmosphere of this last surviving English chophouse is subdued and very clubby and of course it has Waldorf prices.

The Green Man Pub, *133 East 56th Street (212-355-9014). Monday–Friday 10 A.M.–midnight.*

The real McCoy comes complete with English barmaids and Bass ale. English wage slaves from the offices of the local multinationals come in to unwind, trade insults English-style, and play darts.

Lion's Head, *59 Christopher Street, off Seventh Avenue (212-929-0670). Monday–Sunday noon–4 A.M. The kitchen closes at 1 A.M. during the week; 2 A.M. on weekends.*

This bar/restaurant with literary pretensions and book jackets on the walls is certainly no pub. But it brings in the British scriveners and has a running sideshow of regulars that could pass for pub atmosphere.

North Star Pub, *93 South Street (212-509-6757). Monday–Saturday 11:30 A.M. to whenever it cools down (1 or 2 A.M.); Sunday noon–midnight.*

The North Star is a tourist's idea of a pub for the tourists visiting the South Street Seaport. Greasy fried fish and heavy Cornish pasties do not a pub make.

Food Shops

Homesick English expats and fanatical Anglophiles have been known to get yens for such epicurean English fare as Bisto instant gravy and tinned plum pudding. New York's English food shops meet that need.

Myers of Keswick, *634 Hudson Street (212-691-4194). Monday– Friday 10 A.M.–7 P.M.; Saturday 10 A.M.–6P.M.; Sunday noon–5 P.M.*

Peter Myers is an artist if your taste in food includes English savouries, sausage rolls, and pork pies. It's all the best ingredients and family recipes from Keswick in the Lake District.

chapter three

Mittel Europa

Introduction

Mittel Europa is the European heartland, Germanic, Slav, and Magyar. It's Hapsburg and Hohenzollern Europe, a land of empire builders and newly liberated peoples. When the Mittel Europeans came to New York they settled together in the same areas, re-creating their Central Europe. They had their differences, but they had much in common and were comfortable around one another.

Germans

History

Germans are America's largest ethnic group. Before the twentieth century they were consistently New York's second ethnic. Two world wars with Germany destroyed the community's identity, and today the Germans are the city's invisible ethnic.

German refugees from the Thirty Years' War were among the first settlers of New Amsterdam. Hans Kierstede, a native of Saxony, was the first physician, and Ulrich Lupolt was sheriff during the early Indian wars. Even after the British took over in 1664, Jacob Leisler of Frankfort Am Main was

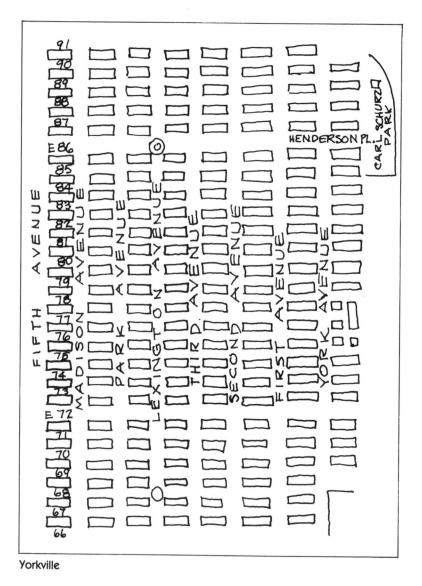

Yorkville

a spokesman for the interests of the Dutch minority and led a New York revolution.

In the eighteenth century, German immigrants from the Palatine entered New York as "redemptionists" and were sold to the highest bidder in a market near City Hall to pay the cost of their passage. They were in great demand for their industry and honesty and skills. Unlike the English, they rarely ran away.

Peter Zenger was one Palatine immigrant who distinguished himself in eighteenth-century New York. Starting as a printer's apprentice, he was soon publishing his own newspaper. In 1734 he had the temerity to attack in print the high-handed and dishonest Governor Cosby. Four members of his paper were consigned to the public hangman and he was sent to jail. His legal vindication set the precedent for press freedom in the city.

The British recruited Germans to put down the American rebellion of 1776. These Hessians, who were dragooned into service, didn't have any real loyalties, and in areas with large German populations some defected to the enemy. Many of the Hessians who occupied New York during the war stayed on to become citizens of the republic.

The dedicated Germans fighting on the revolutionary side included a genuine military genius from Prussia, Baron von Steuben. The Baron's claims to rank and privilege may have been exaggerated, but he knew how to train and organize an army and win wars. Von Steuben continued to take an active part in American public life after the Revolution and was a prominent figure in New York German organizations and society.

In the early years of the Republic, a German named John Jacob Astor from Waldorf became the city's first millionaire. He started out as a butcher's assistant, but quickly learned that there was more money in fur than in meat. His trading posts extended to the Oregon territory. He made his biggest killing investing in New York real estate and the city's first luxury hotels were Astor's.

The defeat of a German revolution in 1848 led to an influx of German political refugees. They were intellectuals and freethinkers who contributed to the overall intellectual life of the city. Franz Lieber taught international law at Columbia University and Carl Schurz championed reform as editor of the very liberal *New York Evening Post*.

German intellectuals were intent on preserving German culture in America's largest city. By the end of the 1850s they had established fifty German schools, ten bookstores, four daily newspapers, and a German theater. They had also formed local "turnverein," gymnastic societies that combined physical education with progressive politics.

But the "Forty-eighters" were more than thinkers: they were also men of action. They took their abolition seriously and six thousand German political exiles were among the first to volunteer for the city's militia. Germans filled the ranks of ten New York regiments. The versatile Carl Schurz led German-American armies along with that other outstanding German, Franz Lieber. Both were generals.

The immigrants of 1848 were followed by emigrants from Germany's own potato famine. There were also immigrants dispossessed from large estates and urban Germans who were casualties of the Industrial Revolution. These Teutonic New Yorkers were more expansive than the political refugees. They enjoyed the camaraderie of the volunteer firehouse and the culture of the beer garden. They preferred marching bands to concert halls.

The established German community organized the German-American Society to aid new arrivals and joined forces with the Irish to create the Board of Commissioners to oversee emigration. Frederich Kapp was the leading German spokesman on the board and helped found the Castle Garden Emigration Station to safeguard emigrants from fraud and exploitation. By 1860 New York's German-born community numbered over a hundred thousand.

In the boom following the Civil War, New York industry beat the bushes for talented German craftsmen and artisans, and set them to work making elegant furniture and cabinets and fine musical instruments. They rolled cigars, baked bread, and brewed beer. When they got tired of working for someone else, they started their own factories and workshops and retail businesses.

There were many German success stories like Heinrich Engelhard Steinweg, who came to New York from Brunswick with his four sons. He was an Old-World master, crafting concert pianos with the quality of Stradivarius violins. In New York, Steinweg became Steinway, and concert pianos became big business. In 1872, William Steinway and his workers left the piano workshop in Manhattan for a four-hundred-acre company town on the East River near Astoria. Steinway had its own park, library, ball field, schools, and row housing.

In the Gilded Age, New York had more German-American breweries than St. Louis and Milwaukee combined. The Rupperts were the leading brewing family and the first to promote sports with their beer. In 1923 Jacob Ruppert built Yankee Stadium in the Bronx with a short right wall so another German by the name of Ruth could hit more home runs. George Steinbrenner is the latest German-American to own the Yankees.

New York's Germans were great music lovers and many joined glee clubs and choirs. They belonged to classical music singing groups like the Liederkranz, which was started in 1847, and the Arion, which was formed after the Liederkranz first admitted women. The Liederkranz chorale was world renowned and even commissioned a work by Richard Wagner for the 1876 presidential inauguration. German singing groups periodically gathered to entertain one another and compete for prizes. One *sangerfeste* in 1900 in Brooklyn involved 6,000 singers and 774 groups. Germans were great joiners. German New Yorkers enjoyed one another's company in every kind of group from shooting clubs to church sodalities to amateur drama societies. Holidays, profane and religious, were a time when the ordinarily restrained Germans could let go. They observed the Sabbath with picnics and outings, shocking some of their prim Protestant neighbors.

German immigrants originally resided in the lower East Side's *Kleine Deutschland,* but there were also pockets of Germans on Dutch Hill at 40th Street and First Avenue and in Hell's Kitchen. German society, families like the Rhinelanders and the Schermerhorns, had staked out Yorkville as early as the 1830s, and by the 1890s wealthy German brewers had mansions there. Brooklyn also had a substantial German community in Williamsburg and Bushwick. They were a typical German mix of tobacconists, tailors, lithographers, and brewers. In 1904 the tragic sinking of the excursion ship *General Slocum* changed the ethnic map of the city as thousands of bereft Germans deserted Kleine Deutschland for Yorkville.

No one doubted the loyalty and patriotism of German New Yorkers in 1901; more than 90 percent had their first citizenship papers. But European power politics and propaganda would change the positive image of German New Yorkers. The industrious Teuton overnight became the bestial Hun as neutral countries were invaded and German U-boats threatened neutral shipping at the start of World War I.

Even before America entered the war, a German newspaper publisher was ordered by the New York mayor to remove the German flag from outside his office. In Brooklyn, government authorities decreed that the name of Hamburg Avenue be changed to Wilson Avenue. There was harassment and vandalism of German schools and cultural organizations. In July of 1916 the whole German community became suspect when a ship carrying British war munitions blew up in New York harbor.

After war was declared, German participation in Liberty Bond drives and service in the foxholes of France didn't change the anti-German attitude on the home front. Germans were forced to deny their heritage. Some anglicized their names and in self-defense started their own Americanization programs.

German-American New Yorkers were the glamour and glitter of the roaring twenties. The great showman Florenz Ziegfield was the toast of Broadway and café society. His *Ziegfield's Follies* was the musical event of the season and his showgirls were the twenties' ideal.

In the years of the Great Depression, New York became a center for Nazi propaganda, and German New Yorkers were a prime target. But most weren't interested in Hitler's hate sheets and some groups, like the German Workers Club, actively distributed anti-Nazi publications.

Fritz Kuhn and his Nazi Bund recruited in the streets of Yorkville. Although the Bund claimed to have a following of 250,000 German-Americans, the FBI estimated it was closer to 6,500. Before Kuhn went to jail for embezzlement in 1939, his group sold out Madison Square Garden twice and had the president of the Olympic Committee as a guest speaker.

While a small minority of German-American extremists were making a lot of noise in Yorkville, a German New Yorker was making history in the U.S. Senate. Born in Germany, Robert Wagner made his way from the State Assembly to become one of the key legislators of Franklin D. Roosevelt's New Deal. The legislative act that bears his name finally gave the working class the right to organize and bargain collectively without fear of retaliation.

German New Yorkers didn't wait to be drafted after the sneak attack on Pearl Harbor. They served in both theaters of the war and a disproportionate number were commissioned officers. German-Americans like Donald Roebling, the great-grandson of the Brooklyn Bridge–builder, John Roebling, used their scientific ability to devise "miracle weapons" such as the amphibious tank.

In the postwar prosperity a second generation Wagner, Robert F. Wagner, Jr., became mayor of New York. Calm and low-key, Wagner went about thoroughly reconstructing the city. He knocked down the Third Avenue El, redeveloped the West Side around Columbus Circle, and built over a hundred thousand units of medium-income housing. New York's master builder also went about dismantling Tammany's political machine.

In the 1950s another kind of German emigrated to New York. Thousands of technicians and scientists came to the city in the first stages of the "brain drain." But as the German economy improved in the 1960s and even began to outperform the U.S. economy in the 1970s, the only Germans who came to New York were employed by German banks and international corporations.

Deutschland on the Lower East Side

Before Germans staked out Yorkville they lived on the Lower East Side. Turn-of-the-century Germans, first and second generation, were concentrated in Kleine Deutschland from 12th Street to Houston and the Bowery east to the river. The neighborhood was completely German-speaking, with big signs in Gothic letters. The population was mainly from the German south—Baden, Bavaria, Wertenberger, and Rhineland—with a reputation for being more "Latin" and lighthearted than northern Germans.

The streets surrounding Tompkins Square Park were filled with German groceries, delicatessens, *konditorei*, and rathskellers. The beer gardens that lined the Bowery were spirited scenes of polkas and accordion playing. The waitresses were beer hall Brunhildes who had no problem hefting the liter steins. Kleine Deutschland was also very keen on sports such as soccer, shooting, and gymnastics.

The intellectual elite of the German neighborhood provided German lending libraries and a *volkstheater* with German productions of Hauptmann and Shakespeare and Ibsen. There were competitions between German singing societies and classical concerts and band concerts in the park. In 1904 a tragic accident ended the era of Kleine Deutschland. It was a fine June morning when 2,000 neighborhood people, mostly women and children, boarded the paddle-steamer *General Slocum* for a picnic on Long Island Sound. The ship was too old and overcrowded; she was a bad-luck ship with a history of other accidents. The immediate cause of the fire was a careless match and a carelessly cleaned boiler. When the *General Slocum* began burning out of control, instead of tacking to shore, the captain panicked and sailed straight into the wind, fanning the flames. Over a thousand people died. Kleine Deutschland would never recover.

Kleine Deutschland

Directions: IRT Lexington Avenue 6 to Astor Place/Fourth Avenue, or M15 Bus to East 7th Street.

Four remnants of Kleine Deutschland are still visible in the East Village of Slavs and the avant-garde.

The headquarters of the Deutsch-Amerikanische Scheuetzen Gesellschaft was located at 12 St. Mark's Place. It is one of the few remaining buildings where German clubs—in this case a shooting club—flourished.

The Freie Bibliothek und Lesehalle lends dignity to an East Village street that has seen better days. Anna and Oswald Ottendorfer, the proprietors of the New York *Staats Zeitung,* donated this attractive red brick building at 135 Second Avenue to the community for a library.

The German Dispensary at 137 Second Avenue was also a gift of the Ottendorfers to Kleine Deutschland. Built to house a medical clinic, it was adorned with terra cotta busts of renowned doctors and scientists from Hippocrates to Humboldt. World War I anti-German hysteria forced the occupants to change the building's name from the German Poliklinik to the Stuyvesant Clinic.

Off Avenue A on the 10th Street side of Tompkins Park, there is a monument to the *General Slocum* disaster. It is a simple statue of a girl and boy gazing at a steamboat, which expresses both loss and hope. The park, which was once a pleasant village green for the Slav and Hispanic ethnics, is currently a crash pad for the homeless and not the kind of place to relax under the shade trees.

Yorkville Era

Directions: IRT Lexington Avenue subway 4, 5, or 6 to 86th Street, or Madison Avenue bus M1, M2, M3, or M4 to 86th Street.

In the eighteenth century, Yorkville was country estates separating commercial New York from the wide-open spaces of Harlem. At first it attracted old German class like the Schermerhorns and the Rhinelanders. When the New York and Harlem Railroad made Yorkville more accessible, the new German money—the brewers and the sausage kings—came in droves. Solid townhouses kept the solid upper classes coming for over a century.

After the *General Slocum* disaster, these buildings were broken up into apartments to handle the influx of German families turning their backs on the Kleine Deutschland past. Yorkville—or at least a substantial part of Yorkville—became in the process the new German colony.

German Yorkville extended north from 84th Street to 89th Street and west from the East River to Central Park. The thriving colony was reinforced by immigration in the 1920s. Germans took advantage of their relatively high quota under the new restrictive immigration law to escape the unstable political and economic conditions of Weimar Germany.

These post–World War I immigrants had a deep nostalgia for a mythic Germany of country maidens and romantic waterfalls. They sang sentimental songs about the "fatherland" in their clubs and societies. Some members of the Yorkville community accused them of being cut off from contemporary American society.

Yorkville's Broadway was 86th Street. It had loud wild Bavarian beer halls with singing waiters and oompah bands. Barkers in lederhosen and alpine hats stood in front of the all-night German clubs, buttonholing the browsers. There were elegant Viennese cafés with candlelight and rich pastry and hunting lodge hofbraus with fireplaces and wild boar.

The Yorkville Casino, at 210 East 86th Street, was one of several theaters showing German movies. There were theaters with German actors and actresses and cabarets with German entertainers. In the neighborhood places, people played cards and talked politics or enjoyed a large selection of German newspapers from a rack.

In the thirties, Yorkville was a hotbed of politics. In and out of the cafés and bars, an army of true believers from anarchists to Nazis were handing out pamphlets and getting into brawls. At 178 East 85th Street, Fritz Kuhn had the offices of the German-American Bund and its mouthpiece, the *Deutscher und Beobachter*. Occasionally he'd parade his bullyboys down 86th Street in regulation-issue Storm Trooper uniforms. Once at the Yorkville Casino some American Legion Germans had enough and there was a bloody free-for-all.

The Nazi episode and World War II changed Yorkville. After the war the German DPs who landed in the German East Side community didn't "identify with the romantic, nostalgic Old World culture." They wanted to start careers as quickly as possible and assimilate into mainstream America. Gradually German Yorkville was moving to the suburbs and the neighborhood was losing its character. First the big beer halls and dance halls closed and the theaters stopped showing German movies. Restaurants that depended on the German family trade folded and traditional German bakeries started baking strawberry shortcake. Finally,landmarks like Jaeger's and the Yorkville Casino were gone. Suddenly there were more fast-food franchises than German delis and cafés on 86th Street, and it was getting hard to find a German-language newspaper.

But a kernel of the old Yorkville remains along with the old German holdouts who haven't been gentrified out of their walkups. They still fondly remember a Yorkville of closeness and caring, when being German was more than wurst and lager and the Von Steuben Day Parade.

Yorkville Place Marks

Carl Schurz Park

Carl Schurz was the most influential German-born American of the nineteenth century. He was an Illinois senator, a New York newspaper editor, and a general in the Union army. He was an intimate of President Lincoln and served in another president's cabinet in 1877. He retired to Yorkville and was active in German community affairs.

The park that bears his illustrious name is a green belt and concrete promenade (Finley Walk) overlooking the East River and running from 84th Street to 90th Street and Gracie Square. It is the place to watch the barges and the joggers pass, and to survey the smokestacks of Queens and the currents of Hell Gate. New Yorkers who can't get to the Hamptons lie on the grass or across a bench and bake in the sun.

Henderson Place

In the early part of the nineteenth century, when Yorkville was estate territory occupied by first German families like the Rhinelanders and the Schermerhorns, John Jacob Astor purchased a country seat that included the present-day Henderson Place. When the estates were broken up and developed, other notable German families like the Ehrets and Rupperts of brewery fame lived here. In 1881, John C. Henderson built a picturesque series of houses on the street that now bears his name. Twenty of the original thirty-two have survived in all their extravagant Queen Anne glory with turrets, gables, and paired entrance ways with sweeping staircases.

Kraut and Konditorei

German cooking has no pretensions to haute cuisine; it doesn't mind being obvious. The tastes are satisfying and full-bodied; the seasoning doesn't strain for effect. It's simple meat-and-dumplings kind of food: roasted meats and brown gravies, with maybe a pickled vegetable, some sauerkraut or red cabbage on the side. Some basics are *wiener schnitzel* (golden-fried veal cutlet); *sauerbraten* (sweet-and-sour pot roast), and *kassler ripchen* (smoked loin of pork swimming in dark gravy)—all stick-to-the-ribs foods to be energetically enjoyed.

For a quick bite, New York's Germans popularized the ubiquitous frankfurter. Their endless varieties of wurst made the delicatessen a New York institution before the Jewish deli came along. German pastry can compete with the French for sheer richness and whipped cream, but it also has a simpler strudel and coffee ring side with the emphasis on a natural fruit taste.

Cafe Geiger, *206 East 86th Street (212-737-7130). Daily 10 A.M.– midnight.*

The windows are pure German kitsch, a miniature Bavarian village with waterfalls and evergreens and a Gothic castle overlooking the Rhine. The dining room itself is all old-fashioned wainscoting and landscape paintings. The entrees are unfortunately no match for the atmosphere, though the Black Forest cake and other desserts are luscious.

Kleine Konditorei, *234 East 86th Street (212-737-7130). Daily 10 A.M.–midnight.*

This *konditorei* looks like the real thing, with pastries in the window and at the front counter. There is an elegantly turned-out dining area full of flowers and polished brass. Evenings it's darkly lit and intimate; couples sip Liebfraumilch and dine on schnitzel. Midmorning, white-haired German regulars sit down for *kaffee mit kuchen* topped up with *schlag* (fresh whipped cream).

Ideal, *238 East 86th Street (212-535-0950). Daily 7 A.M.–10 P.M.*

The Ideal has been on the scene since 1932. It's your basic luncheonette with a long counter and stools that turn and several tables and chairs on a spare mezzanine. The surroundings may be functional, but the food is deliciously authentic at prices unheard of in Manhattan. The *sauerbraten* with red cabbage and a potato dumpling is tartly satisfying and the sizzling potato pancakes are surprisingly light and tasty. The *schweinebraten* (fresh ham) with home-fried potatoes sounds ordinary but is lean, moist, and very special.

Heidelberg Restaurant, *1648 2nd Avenue (212-650-1385). Daily 11 A.M.–11 P.M.*

The restaurant is upbeat with Student Prince conviviality. Diners lift glasses brimming with rare German brews like Spaten or Dinkel Acker. The German basics are best here, a plate of wurst or schnitzel.

Torte and Strudel

Germans and their Austrian country cousins must plead guilty to a sweet tooth; having cookies or cake between meals and cookies and cake between cookies and cake is a Teutonic habit. Bakeries once lined the streets and avenues of Yorkville to cater to this German addiction and some exceptional ones still remain.

Kramer's Pastries, *1643 Second Avenue between 85th and 86th Streets (212-535-5955). Monday–Saturday 7 A.M.–7 P.M.*

German fraus with sturdy linebacker figures still wait on line for the *Sachertorte* (chocolate cake layered with apricot preserves), and the *schwarzwalder kirsch torte* (chocolate Black Forest cake with cherries and whipped cream). Come Christmas, there is a rush on the stollen, crusted with sugar and studded with nuts and raisins.

Glaser's Bakery, *1670 First Avenue between 87th and 88th Streets (212-289-2562). Tuesday–Friday 7 A.M.–7 P.M.; Sunday 7 A.M.–4 P.M.*

Glaser's is well worth a long wait but should be avoided on busy Sundays. The fine assortment of cookies, plain and fancy, and *linzer torte,* with rich raspberry filling, are local favorites.

G&M Pastries, *1006 Madison Avenue between 77th and 78th Streets (212-288-4424). Tuesday–Friday 7:30 A.M.–6:30 P.M.; Sunday 8 A.M.–5 P.M.*

G&M Pastries is slightly off the German Yorkville beaten track in location, but its *linzer torte* and apple strudel are worth the extra steps. Frank Gattnig, who started G&M in 1958, is a no-nonsense Austrian who refuses to stint on quality. His marzipan, whether it looks like a berry or a banana, is the essence of almond.

There is more to German sweets than strudel and Black Forest cake. Germans are great candy lovers and makers.

Elk Candy Company, *240 East 86th Street (212-650-1177). Monday–Saturday 9 A.M.–6:45 P.M.; Sunday 9 A.M.–6 P.M.*

Marzipan is the main treat. The almond paste acorns and berries are a feast for the eyes as well as the sweet tooth. The Elk also has its own hand-dipped chocolates, Florentine butter cream, fruit and nuts, and chocolate-dipped marzipan.

The German Deli

Ever since the first Astor set up shop as a butcher, German New Yorkers have been renowned for their meats. Their smoked meat and sausages, especially the frankfurter, struck the fancy of the city and their delicatessens became an institution.

Schaller & Weber, *1654 Second Avenue between 85th and 86th Streets (212-879-3047). Monday–Saturday 9 A.M.–6 P.M.*

Schaller & Weber is a Yorkville institution dating from 1937, offering German delicatessen in all its varieties, with wurst ranging from *brat* to *bauern* to *knock*. The *nuss Schinken* (Westphalian ham) is the filet mignon of ham and their Oldenburger onion liverwurst makes liverwurst into a pâté. It has all the right cuts for German cooking, like *kassler ripchen* (smoked pork loin), and old German hands behind the counter to advise the uninitiated.

Ridgewood

Directions: IRT-Lexington Avenue 6 to Canal Street. Change to the Nassau Street local M train for Seneca Avenue stop.

Ridgewood was one of the many areas that Peter Stuyvesant opened up for settlement toward the end of the Dutch era of New Amsterdam. In the seventeenth century, this adjunct of the village of Bushwick was all field-stone Dutch farmsteads. Later, English landholders referred to the region, which is now on the Brooklyn–Queens border, as the Ridge because of its most obvious physical feature. The terrain, which was supposed to resemble rural Germany, appealed to the Hessian troops who were billeted here during

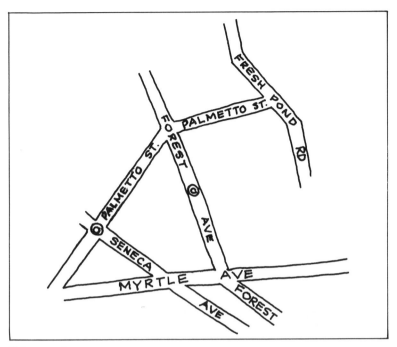

Ridgewood

the Revolution, and they were the first German ethnics to start living here after the war.

The largest wave of German immigrants settled in Ridgewood before the turn of the century. They found work in the nearby breweries and knitting mills and started their own retail businesses to cater to special German tastes. Many of the new arrivals belonged to the Gottscheers, a pietist religious sect that could trace its roots back to the fifteenth century.

The neighborhood was scrupulously neat and respectable with hausfraus regularly scrubbing down their front stairs. German Ridgewood was a quiet family kind of place, different from the more "strident" immigrant areas that surrounded it.

Times changed in the 1960s and 1970s as German families completely deserted adjacent Bushwick and started leaving Ridgewood for the picket-fence suburbs of Queens and Long Island. But neighborhood people, third- and fourth-generation German-Americans, attempted to reclaim Ridgewood. Paul Kerzner, president of the Ridgewood Restoration Corporation, and other concerned citizens secured a landmark designation and the Myrtle Avenue Local Development Corporation was awarded a two-and-a-half-million-dollar federal grant to revive Myrtle Avenue. Ridgewood activists lifted local morale in one easy step when they won the right to become part of Queens, but that didn't stop the German exodus.

While the neighborhood is predominantly German, in recent years they have been joined by other ethnics including Yugoslavs, Rumanians, Chinese, Italians, and Arabs, but Ridgewood has retained the German ethnic authenticity that left Yorkville years ago. There are flyers in store windows for bierfests and local groups with names like the Edelweiss Club. The mass at St. Mathias is said in German and there are more than a hundred small German knitting companies in the neighborhood.

Rudy's Bakery, *905 Seneca Avenue (718-821-5890). Monday– Thursday 6 A.M.–7 P.M.; Friday 6 A.M.–7:30 P.M.; Saturday 6 A.M.–6 P.M.*

Rudy's is a real German bakery, down to the accents of its saleswomen. It makes stollen (Christmas fruit cake) all year round and features *Schillerlocken,* a creamy pastry named for the poet's long locks, and *swartzwalder* and *bienenstich.*

Jobst & Ebbinghaus, *676 Seneca Avenue at Gates Avenue (718-821-5747). Monday–Friday 8 A.M.–6 P.M.; Saturday 7 A.M.–5 P.M.*

A German butcher that covers all bases: wild game, wurst, and prime cuts of beef, lamb, and pork. Where else are moose and bear for sale? This unusual shop has a Museum of Natural History deer in the window with lifelike game birds. Every variety of wurst dangles from the ceiling over the counter, along with smoked pork ribs. There are herrings, pickled vegetables, and breads imported from Germany.

Murken's Confectionery, *59-05 Myrtle Avenue (718-821-9482). Daily 7 A.M.–6:30 P.M.*

Murken's is a flashback to a yesteryear ice cream parlor. White-haired German ladies sit in the booths over strawberry ice cream sundaes topped with whipped cream the counterman has whipped in front of them. Tutti-frutti and pistachio are the best of the homemade flavors. The waitresses come with warm natural smiles.

Karl Ehmer, *63-35 Fresh Pond Road (718-456-8100). Monday– Friday 9 A.M.–6:45 P.M.; Saturday 9 A.M.–6 P.M.*

Karl Ehmer is the flagship of the fifty-four-store butcher and delicatessen chain. It sells a hundred varieties of wurst and the freshest cuts of pork, veal, lamb, and beef. Ehmer also carries German smoked fish and herring, and German breads from *bauernbrot* to pumpernickel.

Building Bridges

Directions: IRT-Lexington Avenue 4, 5, or 6. Change at Brooklyn Bridge for IND Eighth Avenue A and CC to Cadman Plaza West.

The Brooklyn Bridge, which spans the East River from the vicinity of City Hall Park to downtown, is one of the city's genuine masterpieces with its massive pylons linking fine lines of woven cable. The first steel suspension bridge in the world was the brainchild of John A. Roebling, an emigrant from Prussia. It took him years to convince New York politicians of its value. He died in a freak accident the year that construction started. His son, Washington A. Roebling, followed his father's dream, directly supervising the construction until he was crippled by the bends. Roebling watched the progress of the bridge through a telescope, periodically dispatching his wife with instructions for the builders. The bridge was completed on May 24, 1883, winning the approval of ordinary people as well as artists and writers. A later critic exclaimed that "all modern New York . . . started with the Brooklyn Bridge."

In 1973 the city showed its appreciation on the bridge's ninetieth birthday by giving it a fresh coat of paint in the silver and two shades of buff chosen by Roebling. For the bridge's centennial, the city held a huge party, and the national media ran cover stories raving about this architectural wonder. Despite all the hoopla, the city forgot to maintain the bridge and rust did the rest. The walkway of the bridge is now closed till further notice.

German Classics

German political exiles were a catalyst for concert music in the city. Twenty-three revolutionary refugees started the Germania Orchestra in 1848. The group performed 829 concerts in six years. It introduced German classics like Beethoven's Ninth Symphony to New York and the American classical repertoire. After the orchestra disbanded, individual members helped form classical ensembles throughout the nation.

Carl Bergmann became the director of the New York Philharmonic, and later, Theodore Thomas of Essen became the orchestra's conductor. Leopold Damrosch made the big transition from leading the German Liederkranz Society Orchestra to founding the New York Symphony and directing the Metropolitan Opera. His son, Walter, followed in his footsteps, promoting German composers like Richard Strauss and refining the symphony to meet exacting European standards. The German connection with the symphony continued with immigrant conductors like Otto Klemperer and Bruno Walter, who were refugees from Nazi Germany.

Avery Fisher Hall, *Lincoln Center, Broadway at 65th Street (212-874-2424).*

German classical music excellence is alive and well at Avery Fisher Hall, which is named for the building's donor, a hi-fi component manufacturer of German descent. The hall's acoustics have been a source of problems in the past but the symphony has maintained Damrosch standards. Behind the Lincoln Center glitz is Damrosch Park, offering free concerts that the father and son would have enjoyed.

Manhattan Culture from Goethe to Abstract Art: Institutes and Museums

Goethe House, *1014 Fifth Avenue, temporarily at 666 Third Avenue, at 42nd Street (212-972-3960). Tuesday and Thursday 11 A.M.–7 P.M.; Wednesday, Friday, Saturday noon–5 P.M.*

The cultural outlet of the Federal Republic of Germany has a sixteen-thousand-volume, mostly German, library and the latest German newspapers. There are exhibits, lectures, and films of German or German-American cultural interest. The mansion is being sandblasted and refurbished; Goethe House is temporarily headquartered in a small space on 666 Third Avenue.

Deutsches Haus, *42 Washington Mews (212-998-8660).*

Deutsches Haus is an outlet of Goethe House at New York University. It's hidden away in a brick mews conversion from Henry James's era Washington Square. German-language classes are offered throughout the year. Deutsches Haus has sponsored cultural events such as a series of German auteur films.

Austrian Institute, *11 East 52nd Street (212-759-5165). Monday–Friday 10 A.M.–5 P.M.*

The Austrian Institute is an unheralded outpost of modern Germanic culture. Upstairs in this stylish midtown townhouse there is a small library filled with German and Austrian books and publications and recent Austrian newspapers. There's an art gallery on the main floor with professionally mounted exhibits of the best of the Austrian avant-garde, from junk sculpture to minimalist abstractions.

Germans are the masters of fine porcelains and ceramics. While contemporary Meissen and Rosenthal are on display in the city's upmarket stores, the choice pieces are on exhibit in the Metropolitan Museum of Art.

Metropolitan Museum, *Fifth Avenue and 82nd Street (212-535-7710). Tuesday–Thursday, Sunday 9:30 A.M.–5:15 P.M.; Friday, Saturday 9:30 A.M.–8:45 P.M.. Contribution.*

Gallery 29, off the large Medieval Sculpture Hall, has fine eighteenth-century Meissen on display. The high-born ladies, perching birds, and Aesopian animals are delicate and exquisitely detailed. The royal hunting cup created by J. J. Kandler is remarkable.

Downstairs, below the Medieval Tapestries Hall, there are more German and Austrian ceramics in galleries 52 and 53. The eighteenth-century Meissen porcelain goats and the Swan table service have a touch of the Oriental.

Festivals

Von Steuben Day Parade

In the third week in September, usually on a Saturday or Sunday, the German community of the metropolitan area unites to honor the Revolutionary War hero Von Steuben with a parade along upper Fifth Avenue. It's a wholehearted German spectacle that rivals the grand Munich parade for Octoberfest.

The German drum and bugle corps are something special: medieval banners held aloft, brass regally blaring, and drummers stepping lively and raising their arms high in time to the big bass beat. A Steuben society comes dressed for the Revolutionary War in knee britches and ruffled shirts and three-cornered hats, marching to the strains of "Yankee Doodle Dandy." German folk dancers, men and women in embroidered Bavarian village costumes, dance along the line of march. The men whirl the women around and perform a humorous slap dance in time with the music. There is a bucolic float with a waterfall and a fetching German beauty queen followed by a float resembling the bow of a clipper ship from a German shipping line.

Following the Octoberfest tradition, there are old-fashioned brewery wagons carrying attractive blonds, with the barrels pulled by heavy draft horses. The German marchers are joined by local high school bands, many representing communities in New York, New Jersey, and Pennsylvania that were founded by Germans. The crowd is lively, often calling out from the sidelines in German to particular marchers. For a change the refreshment stands along the route are serving real wurst rather than anemic hot dogs, and the big salty German pretzels aren't stale.

Hungarians

History

The Magyar man on horseback, Colonel Michael Kovat, trained the cavalry force that finally defeated the English. This hero of the American Revolution died while leading a cavalry charge at Charleston. Though he wasn't a New Yorker, the Hungarians of the city have honored him with a statue.

There's also a statue in the city dedicated to Louis Kossuth, the leader of the 1848 Magyar revolution, who spent his exile in New York. He was the first Hungarian to attract New York's attention. In 1851 and 1852 the Hungarian hero was acclaimed and admired and generally treated like a matinee idol. Meanwhile, Kossuth spread the message of a free and democratic Hungary, trying to drum up donations to continue his fight.

He was feted by the city's commercial establishment and intellectual elite, but later fickle New York attacked him for his liberal views and his refusal to take positions regarding American politics. He left New York confused by the city's "celebrity treatment" and disappointed by its lack of support for his campaign against the Hapsburg Empire.

Many fellow Hungarians, veterans of the 1848 battles, stayed behind in the city, forming New York's first Hungarian community. These men were writers and thinkers. In 1853 Karoly Kornis started *Magyar Szamuzottek* (Hungarian Exile's News), the first Hungarian-American newspaper. The New York Hungarian Society, which was founded in 1865 after some false starts, was more than a mutual benefit society; it offered a platform for the free exchange of ideas.

Hungarian New Yorkers put their revolutionary fervor to work for the Union cause. These fighters of 1848 fought for the Union in 1861. They filled half the places in New York's famed "Garibaldi Guard" and were an important element in the city's "Black Rifles." Hungarians made up a disproportionate share of the Union officer corps, with two major generals and five brigadier generals. Joseph Pulitzer, the future publisher of the *New York Sun,* was also an officer for the northern side.

While the first wave of Hungarian immigrants, from 1850 to 1870, were political exiles and adventurers, the next wave, from 1880 to 1914, were economic emigrants. They were mostly single men: landless peasants, unskilled industrial workers, and day laborers. They were poor men with simple needs who wanted money to feed their families and to later buy land and homes in their native country.

The Hungarian peasant was not afraid to make sacrifices to save for the future. Hungarians lived collectively, at times twenty to forty-five men in a New York boardinghouse, four to ten to a room. The boarding-house collective appointed a married man to be their *burdos gazda* and oversee their living arrangements. He had the easy job, purchasing provisions, paying the rent, and handling the accounts, while his wife slaved at the cooking, cleaning, and washing.

New York's Hungarians averaged $8.70 a week for the most hazardous employment. They were frequently underpaid even by the standards of the time, but they were in the habit of taking orders from authority, and in their closed world the New York pittance was a Hungarian fortune. Even the worst New York workplaces had a freedom and informality that the Hungarian newcomers welcomed.

Despite the difficulties of work and boardinghouse living, Hungarians enjoyed an active community life. In New York City alone there were seventy-eight associations. The Hungarian Sick Benefit Society was started in 1884 to help workers in medical emergencies. The First Hungarian Self-Culture Society of New York, started in 1888, offered the workingman a program for self-improvement, including lectures, literary readings, and plays. Politically active Hungarian New Yorkers joined the American Hungarian Federation to promote Hungarian freedom.

Culture flourished in choirs, traveling theaters, and literary societies. While New York and Brooklyn had lodges and associations for Hungarians from different geographical areas, local branches of national groups like the Verhovay and Rakoczi Aid Societies united Hungarians from all around America. Newspapers like New York's *Amerikai Magyar Nepszava* (American Hungarian People's Voice), first published in 1899, also created a sense of group solidarity.

The destiny of New York's Hungarians was also shaped by events across the sea. Patriotic Hungarians supported Hungary in the propaganda battle prior to World War I and backed up their words by enlisting in the Hungarian army in 1914. But America entered the war on the other side, allied with France and England. New York Hungarians did not know how to deal with their divided loyalties.

Surrounded by a city caught in a patriotic all-American war fever, the New York Hungarian community in its Yorkville enclave felt cut off and resentful. It was difficult to rally to the cause and sell war bonds and be part of an industrial effort that shed Hungarian blood. In the peace that was supposed to end all wars, their nation lost more than 70 percent of its territory and more than 60 percent of its population.

When the war was over, Hungarian community leaders were preaching the gospel of Americanization. The future was in the United States. Hungarians' lives became more settled; they opened shops and sent for their wives. The boardinghouse was a thing of the past, and New York's Hungarian neighborhood in Yorkville began to thrive.

But Hungarian New Yorkers had not lost their ethnic pride. In 1928 the community erected a statue of Louis Kossuth to the applause of 500 Hungarian dignitaries and officials. In 1931 two brave Hungarian-American aviators displayed the Hungarian colors in a Lindbergh-like flight from New York to Budapest in a one-engine plane named *Justice for Hungary*.

Hungarian political refugees who came to New York between the wars were a genuine source of pride. The urbane playwright Ferenc Molnár took literary New York by storm, and the innovative composer Béla Bartók was hailed by the city's music critics. Hungarian physicists Leo Szilard, Eugene Wigner, and Edward Teller were among the great scientific minds of the age; their work on the Manhattan Project produced the atom bomb.

Hungarian New Yorkers had less ambivalent feelings when World War II again put them on the opposite side of America and her allies. They saw Hungary as an unwilling hostage to Hitler, and their loyalty to America was absolute. After the war was won, Hungarian New Yorkers set about helping Hungarian victims of the war and aiding refugees in resettlement.

The first group to enter New York were called the Forty-fivers. They were displaced persons, Hungarian Royal Soldiers, and politicians fleeing the relentless Soviet army. These men of the old order often had a hard time adjusting to a new land.

The Forty-fivers were soon joined by the Forty-seveners. They were liberals of a western stripe who were forced out of the Hungarian government by the Stalinist dictator, Mátyás Rákosi. They became a significant part of New York's Hungarian community.

In 1956, Hungarians rebelled against authoritarian Stalinist rule and Russian tanks rumbled through the streets of Budapest. Outgunned Hungarians fought valiantly, but the freedom fighters, like earlier Hungarian revolutionaries, were forced into New York exile. The Fifty-sixers joined forces with earlier refugee groups to form a new political organization to represent the Hungarian community, but the real voice of these politically committed exiles was the Hungarian Freedom Fighters Federation, organized by General Bela K. Kiraly, a former leader of the Hungarian National Guard.

New York's Hungarians have hopes for a new Hungary in an era of Magyar glasnost and perestroika. They have been heartened by Hungary's more open society and the public memorial for the fallen leader of the 1956 revolution, Imre Nagy. Many members of New York's small but culturally active emigré community are thinking of returning home.

Hungarian Yorkville

Introduction

New York's first Hungarian neighborhood centered on the German area of Kleine Deutschland around Avenues A and B and Houston Street. In the early 1900s the Hungarians followed their German neighbors to Yorkville. They settled between 78th Street and 84th Street in the vicinity of Second Avenue. The Hungarian neighborhood, like Hungarian history, alternated between passionate romantic outbursts and resignation. It was like the moody music of a gypsy violin. It was a fistfight in a basement bar followed by a solemn mass at St. Stephen's.

Little Hungary was a land of gray walkups and hanging fire escapes, enlivened by a beehive of social clubs. Over cards and cigars, socialists and monarchists fought their political wars. Though Hungarian Yorkville didn't have the Hapsburg grandeur, it had shops as colorful as those in old Budapest, selling Hungarian wines (*egri-bikavar*) and garlicky Hercz, Pick, and Drossy salamis and *lekvar* (prune butter), from the barrel. The restaurants were appropriately homey in a neighborhood of single men, with curtains and candles and steaming bowls of goulash soup. It took another generation for people to move to the suburbs of Brooklyn.

Just when Hungarian Yorkville looked as though it were becoming Upper East Side anonymous, the old Hungarian stock was renewed by successive generations of refugees following World War II and the abortive Hungarian uprising. Yorkville Hungarians opened their homes and their pocketbooks, and local organizations provided language classes and vocational training. The city's postwar Hungarians, in return, revitalized the cultural life of the community.

They brought books and Hungarian book publishing to Yorkville. Emigré writers formed their own literary circles and even had their own literary controversies. *Free Hungarians,* a monthly with a nationalist stance, was launched in Yorkville in 1956, but its life was cut short by a libel suit from a rival Hungarian publication in 1962. *New Yorki Magyar Elat* (New York Hungarian Life) is the mouthpiece for Yorkville's Hungarian intelligentsia in the eighties.

Hungarian Spice

Hungarian cuisine straddles the German West and the Slavic East. It is wurst and stuffed cabbage, kielbasa (*kolbasa*) and sauerkraut. These literary masters of the bittersweet excel in the sweet and sour, which is sometimes overwhelmed by the sour cream. But the hallmark of Hungarian cooking is paprika—the singular spice that adds zest without disguising natural flavors.

Restaurants

Csarda Restaurant, *1477 Second Avenue (212-472-2892). Monday–Friday 5 P.M.–11 P.M.; Saturday noon–11 P.M.; Sunday noon–10 P.M.*

Csarda is old country inn ambience and unpretentiously hearty Hungarian cooking. The veal or chicken is not lost in the savory paprika and the home fries and onion rings are crisp without being overdone or oily. The waiters and waitresses don't put on airs, they just work hard and care.

Red Tulip, *439 E. 75th Street (212-734-4893). Wednesday–Sunday 6 P.M.–midnight.*

The Red Tulip is very rustic, with trestle tables and chairs like gingerbread, but that doesn't seem to bother the East Side types waiting for a table. The food is Hungarian-rich from the sour cherry soup to the veal goulash to the *somloi galuska,* which combines cake, rum chocolate sauce, and whipped cream.

Mocca Restaurant, *1588 Second Avenue (212-734-6470). Daily 11:30 A.M.–3:45 P.M.; 4 P.M.–10:30 P.M.*

The food is first-rate at the Mocca; superb roast duck with crisp skin and succulent meat. Gypsy violins add flavor on weekends.

Paprika and Prune Butter

The Hungarian shops have the look of yesteryear with smoked meats hanging, and barrels and bags instead of streamlined packaging. There is something old-fashioned about the warm personal service. Hungarian Yorkville once had food shops specializing in everything from soup to nuts and shopping was a daily hunt for the freshest foods. Hungarian variety is a thing of the past and even the Budapest Bakery is not strictly Hungarian.

Paprika Weiss, Importers, *1546 Second Avenue (212-288-6117). Monday–Saturday 8 A.M.–6 P.M.*

Edward Weiss parlayed ten kilos of paprika from Szeged into a Yorkville tradition one hundred years young. Another Edward Weiss runs the show today, minding the endless varieties of paprika and all the different grains, nuts, and herbs. There are also utensils for every conceivable food function for the yuppie gourmets who have moved to the neighborhood. Still, where else in the city can you get *lekvar,* Hungarian prune butter, the old-fashioned way—from the barrel?

Budapest Bakery, *207 West 84th Street (212-628-0721). Monday 8 A.M.–6 P.M.; Tuesday–Friday 7:30 A.M.–7:30 P.M.; Saturday 9 A.M.–7:30 P.M.; Sunday 10 A.M.–5 P.M.*

The Budapest is no longer strictly Hungarian; the new ethnic management (Syrian) has diversified into Levantine *spanokopita* and *baklava,* but the Hungarian strudel is a pure poppy-seed high. The poppy seed is to Hungarian baking what paprika is to the rest of Hungarian cookery.

Tibor Meat Specialities, *1508 Second Avenue at 78th Street (212-744-8292). Monday–Saturday 7 A.M.–6 P.M.*

There is an actual Tibor who smokes all the veal and pork sausage the traditional Hungarian way—with plenty of paprika. His wife, Barbara, has a special relationship with her central European clientele, and she's generous with her samples of salami and black bread. Hungarians from the whole metropolitan area come to Tibor's.

Yorkville Packing House, *1560 Second Avenue at 81st Street (212-628-5147). Monday–Saturday 7 A.M.–6:30 P.M.*

The Yorkville Packing House attracts the best of both Upper East Side worlds, emigré Hungarian and high-rent gourmet. Where else could they find goose liverwurst and smoked goose, or Hungarian potato bread? This Hungarian butcher shop has packaged foods that even food halls like Dean and Deluca haven't discovered.

Place Marks

St. Stephen's of Hungary, *414 East 82nd Street (212-861-8500).*

This Roman Catholic Franciscan Church, named for Hungary's patron saint, still has an active Hungarian parish with a mass said in Hungarian on Sundays and holy days and a Hungarian-language church bulletin. The church entrance has a carved likeness of the Magyar king atop the columns at the entrance. The interior of the church is illuminated by beautiful stained-glass windows behind the altar.

Culture

New York's Hungarian quarter may have decreased in numbers since the early part of this century, but its cultural community still flourishes.

Nepszava, *245 East 81st Street (212-737-9370).*

Nepszava, the old Hungarian-language weekly, is a nerve center of this close-knit emigré community, and it carefully follows the political and cultural tides in a rapidly changing homeland. They publish the latest Hungarian writing, as well as review it.

Puski-Corvin, *251 East 82nd Street (212-879-8893). Monday–Saturday 9 A.M.–6:30 P.M.*

The local literary crowd as well as academic Hungarian specialists come here for the impossible-to-find Hungarian book. Puski has the largest selection of Hungarian books dealing with literature and sociology in the United States, and also publishes some volumes of its own. Hungarian intellectuals come here to talk, to discuss their works in progress, and to make their own prognostications on the current Hungarian regime. Puski is also an informal community bulletin board for upcoming cultural events. Non-Hungarian readers can buy Hungarian cookbooks and more in English.

Hungarian Library, *215 East 82nd Street (212-744-5298).*

A small library with a small collection of books, many of them old if not rare. It's a place where people come to read and perhaps share old memories.

Festivals

St. Stephen's Day is August 20 and is usually celebrated on the Sunday closest to the saint's day. In an earlier age the whole Hungarian community came out for a patriotic parade, but now it's primarily a religious feast followed by a parish picnic.

Hungarian Independence Day is commemorated on March 15. Patriotic Hungarians used to march from their Yorkville community to the statue of their national hero, Louis Kossuth (by the Hungarian sculptor Horvathy), on 113th Street and Riverside Drive. Now they drive to the monument from all over the city to hear speeches and raise their voices for Hungarian freedom and autonomy.

Czechoslovakians

History

Augustine Herman, an experienced surveyor and merchant, was the first Czech to make his mark in the New World. He came over to New Amsterdam in 1643 as an agent for Amsterdam's largest commercial organization, Gabry and Company. While taking care of business, Herman served as an adviser to Governor Stuyvesant and was involved in delicate border negotiations with the British colonies. He made his fortune surveying Maryland for Lord Baltimore, for which he received 20,000 acres of prime land. He planted his estate with tobacco, and called it New Bohemia, in honor of his home region.

Frederick Philipse was another talented Czech merchant. He arrived in the colony in 1647 and was enough of a wheeler-dealer in colonial real estate to create the Philipse dynasty. His granddaughter was so grand she refused the proposal of George Washington. Though early Czech New Yorkers were outstanding successes, by the 1840s there were only 500 Bohemians in the whole city.

The failure of the 1848 uprising in Bohemia led Czechs to seek freedom in New York. These first political exiles were plodding intellectuals and expert craftsmen who shared a fierce belief in something they called free thought. While they had a tendency to be opinionated, the men and women of 1848 laid the foundations for the New York Czech community's spirited intellectual, social, and cultural life.

In 1848, Czech organizational life got off to a flying start with a group named after the revolutionary society *Slovanska Linda*. At that early stage in the life of Czech New York it didn't last long, but it did provide a model for future groups with its library and amateur theatricals and choral society. Two years later, Czech "Forty-eighters" launched the first mutual aid society, *Ceska Spolecnost*.

Finally, in 1854 the CSPS, the Czech Slavonic Benevolent Society, was organized in the city and is still going strong. Many branches of the organization followed and they all embraced causes like abolition and women's rights, but it wasn't until 1897 that the CSPS actually admitted women as equal members.

In a tradition dating back to religious dissenters like Jan Hus, Czech liberal "Forty-eighters" dismissed the conventional dogmas of church and state and favored both political and social freedoms. In 1865, Czech New Yorkers opened their own progressive free school, *Svobodna Skola,* with sixty-five pupils. In 1907 these outspoken freethinkers organized *Svaz Svobodomslnych* (Free Thought), a secular equivalent of a church, with humanistic weddings and funerals.

Czech New Yorkers believed in a strong body as well as a sound mind. They formed gymnast societies called *sokols* where physical training and discipline were combined with a program of character development and Czech nationalism. One Czech-American compared the sokol program with the rigorous code of the Japanese samurai. In 1878 the National Sokol Union joined thirteen groups together in New York. That year the first gymnastic festival took place with sokols from around the country competing. In a 1933 *Sokol Slet,* 2,556 gymnasts participated.

In the 1870s the Hapsburg Empire loosened restrictions on Czech travel and this, coupled with the failure of the sugar-beet crop, triggered a mass movement of peasants to New York City. They were very different from their sophisticated forebears and at least at the beginning identified only with their extended families, villages, and Bohemian or Moravian region.

Newly arrived peasant families did piecework in cramped tenement workshops, rolling cigars and sewing garments at breakneck speed for as long as eighteen hours at a clip. The closeness of Czech families and the self-reliance of their children helped them to work as an efficient economic unit. Jacob Riis, in his exposé of immigrant life, *How the Other Half Lives,* marveled at the strength and equanimity of these working Czech families.

New York Czechs rivaled the Germans as metal workers and competed with the Jews in the needle trades, but they were most heavily involved in making cigars and manufacturing pearl buttons. By the turn of the century, more than 90 percent of Czech New Yorkers were rolling cigars and more than half the pearl buttons in the United States were made by Czechs in the city. The efforts of these indefatigable workers paid off and they were able to leave the deteriorating Lower East Side for model tenements in what would become Czech Yorkville.

Although Czechs never voted as a block, workingmen were class-conscious and politically committed. As early as 1870 the *Delnicky Klub* was established for industrial workers. In 1872 the Czech trade unionists formed a section of the Socialist Labor Party of New York, and in 1893 Czech labor, which refused to socialize with its class enemies, started its own sokol, which came to be called the "Red Sokol."

But New York's Czechs were not all high-minded thinking and intellectual controversy. The industrious and thrifty Czechs liked to sing and dance and raise a glass of pilsner even if the city's Puritans upbraided them for doing it on Sunday. New York's Czechs were very musical; one third of Czech professionals in 1900 proved the proverb *co cech to muzikant* (if he's Czech he's a musician). All the major conservatories in Manhattan had Czech teachers. Even the famous composer of the *New World Symphony*, Antonin Dvorak, directed the National Conservatory of Music in New York between 1892 and 1895. The superb musician and composer Rudolph Friml was the toast of New York in the 1920s, acclaimed for his operetta, *The Vagabond King*.

World War I brought Czech New York together. On May 15, 1916, the Red Sokol and the more conservative Blue Sokol symbolically marched together out of Fort Slocum after eighty-four members of the New York groups enlisted. New York Czechs backed the exiled leader Thomas Masaryk, who was married to a Brooklyn girl and had lectured many times to local Czech audiences. In 1918, Masaryk met with President Wilson and the terms for Czech independence were hammered out before the Versailles Peace Conference.

Immigration restrictions after World War I and a trend toward assimilation had hurt the Czech community. It became more and more diffuse and less self-aware. The economic depression was another blow, closing the city's most important ethnic institutions. Czechs were not adequately prepared to help their homeland when the Munich Agreement became a prelude to a full-scale Nazi invasion.

Just when it looked as though Czechoslovakia would regain its independence after World War II, Stalinists, with the backing of the USSR, staged a coup. There were now new Czech "Forty-eighters" in New York who were victims of left-wing rather than reactionary tyranny. They were more conservative than earlier generations of Czech immigrants and stridently anti-communist. While developing their own organizational base, they were able to enter the American occupational mainstream with their skills as professionals and craftsmen. Czech culture flourished again in the city with groups like the Czechoslovak Society of Arts and Sciences.

Twenty years later, the "Forty-eighters" were joined in New York by the Sixty-eighters, as Alexander Dubcek's democratic reforms and the hopes of the "Prague spring" were crushed by Soviet tanks and armies. The new refugees were more left-wing than their predecessors and less liable to identify with hard-core anticommunist causes.

Many were socialist intellectuals or progressive party apparatchiks. They were distrusted by the new conservative Czech establishment, who viewed them as lacking real conviction or even as unreconstructed communists. Despite the rift in the Czech community, the 1968 refugees added to cultural renewal. Josef Skvornecky, a leader in the group, started an experimental Czech publishing house in New York.

The local Czech community has united behind the country's new democratic regime of 1990. The city's Czechs gave dissident writer President Havel a hero's welcome when he visited shortly after taking office.

Little Bohemia

The Czechs may have started in New Amsterdam, but by the time the Civil War was over they were growing tobacco in the Morrisania section of the Bronx and the Dutch Kill enclave of Queens. The earliest Manhattan Little Bohemia thrived from 1870 to 1905 on the Lower East Side, in close proximity to other Slavic immigrant groups and the large German colony.

Its boundaries were Eighth Street on the north, Third Street on the south, and Avenue A east to the river. The blocks between Third and Fifth Streets on Avenue A were known as the Czech Broadway. The most popular saloon in the area, August Hubacek's, was even well known in Prague. The main Czech Hall, the *Narodni Budova*, was located on East Fifth Street and contained a library as well as a saloon; its public rooms were the site of heated political debates.

The neighborhood also had its own Czech-Slavic Benevolent Society, which achieved its moment of glory when Mayor George Updyke unfurled the future national flag (backwards) at a gala reception in City Hall Park. There were also two transplanted Czech villages, the cigar rollers from Sedlec and the pearl button makers from Zirounice.

By the end of the nineteenth century, Little Bohemia had followed the Czechoslovak cigar stores uptown. It bordered Hungarian and German territory, covering the area between 65th Street and 78th Street and Second Avenue and the river. Czechs were proud of their new neighborhood, the clean and roomy tenements, and the modern buildings housing their organizations.

The showplace of Czechoslovak Yorkville was the new *Narodni Budova* (Czech National Hall), at 335–337 73rd Street, which was completed before the First World War for the grand sum of $250,986. It still stands today, the old splendor missing, along with most of the neighborhood's inhabitants.

The Czech community pioneered low-income housing. On 77th Street they built the six-story Cherokee apartments, which set a new standard with its advanced architectural design. There were balconies, ornamental ironwork, and tiled entryways leading to attractive courtyards. It still retains some of the old charm, though there are very few Czechs to appreciate it.

As Czechs turned from ideology to making the American dream happen in New York, the community began losing its identity and the organizations their membership. Affluent Czechs started moving to Queens and Long Island and though they attempted to re-create Little Bohemia with their own Bohemian Hall in Astoria, it couldn't compete with American social and service organizations.

Czechs also tried to revive Little Bohemia in Yorkville by resettling successive generations of political refugees there. But cosmopolitan Czech arrivals looked beyond ethnicity for their personal satisfactions and viewed assimilation as their passport to financial and career success. Even the Czech intellectuals of the sixties who came to New York to escape literary repression congregated around American universities.

The Crossroads Cuisine

Czech cooking has been described as the crossroads cuisine, a mingling of central European influences from the German to the Magyar to the Slav. Czechs eat schnitzel, goulash, and stuffed cabbage. Like their neighbors in New York, the Hungarians, the Czechs are connoisseurs of goose and duck, which have the place of honor in their restaurants. Lately, with diet cuisines in style, Czech eating places are disappearing one by one.

Vasata, *339 East 75th Street (212-988-7166). Tuesday–Saturday 5 P.M.–11 P.M.; Sunday noon–10 P.M.*

Vasata is an Old-World inn with dark, low-beamed ceilings and white stucco walls. Color is provided by fresh flowers on every table and bright Czech ceramics. The roast duck is the house specialty unless it is October and there is game such as leg of venison, wild goose, or pheasant. The *palacinty,* the Czech dessert version of a bliny, filled with apricot jam or crushed walnuts and brown sugar and covered with powdered sugar, is the perfect way to end an evening at Vasata.

Place Marks and Powder Towers

It is ironic that despite the strenuous Czech efforts to make organized freethinking a viable alternative to organized religion, the only reminders of the flourishing Czech community are churches.

Jan Hus Presbyterian Church, *351 East 74th Street (212-288-6743).*

The Jan Hus Presbyterian Church is named for the Czech martyr of the reformation. It is a real landmark church for the Czech community, with its bell tower modeled on the Powder Tower of old Prague. The church always played an active part in the life of the community. In the days of immigrant Czech Yorkville, it acted as a settlement house where people could learn English and become familiar with alien customs and traditions. Jan Hus houses a theater and various community service groups, and has a wide choice of self-improvement programs.

St. John Nepomucene, *411 East 66th Street (212-734-4613)*.

In this Roman Catholic Church a mass is said every Sunday in Slovak and it is well attended. The outside of the church is brick neo-Romanesque and classical; the inside has the feeling of a village sanctuary, dimly lit with the triptych of St. Cyril and St. Methodius almost floating in the background.

The Scandinavians

Introduction

The Scandinavian countries—Norway, Sweden, Denmark, and Iceland—have similar cultures and speak related languages. At different times they have conquered one another or been joined in confederations. Finland has its own unique folkways and speaks a language similar to Hungarian. It has been occupied by other Scandinavian nations and Russia.

The Danes came to New York first as explorers under the Dutch flag. The Swedes were the first to gain fame in the city. The Norwegians were the largest Scandinavian group to emigrate to the city, and the Finns were the last to come in any numbers. The Scandinavians as a group have made a contribution to the city in shipping and construction out of proportion to their population.

History

Danes

Two of the first ships sent by the Dutch to explore the waters around New Amsterdam harbor and the Hudson River were commanded by Danish captains named Block and Christiansen. Block lost his ship in a fire, but built another one with the help of friendly Indians and made his own early version of the Circle Line Tour, discovering Block Island in the process. He sailed back to Holland with Christiansen, carrying a cache of valuable beaver pelts. Their voyages encouraged Dutch commercial investment and colonization. In 1636 the first Danish family went to live in New Amsterdam. Like later generations of Danish New Yorkers, the Jansens quickly assimilated to the dominant culture and took the Dutch name Van Breestede. They were followed by a Thomsen, who became a Van Ripen, and an Andriessen, who switched to Van Buskirk.

The next two Danes to arrive, in 1639, did more than change their names. Jonas Bronck became one of the largest landholders, buying five hundred acres from the natives for odds and ends including two rifles, a barrel of cider, and six gold coins. He was a successful tobacco planter and when duty called, he helped Governor Kieft negotiate peace with the Indians. At a time when drinking and brawling were favorite pastimes, he collected the colony's largest library. His former lands are now a part of the borough bearing his name, the Bronx.

Bronck's friend and fellow Dane, Jochem Pietersen Kuyter, gained title to four hundred acres in Harlem, but he became famous for his battles with the local Dutch officials. As a member of the Board of Twelve Men, he petitioned the authorities in Holland and was instrumental in the recall of Governor Kieft.

Danes readily adapted to the colony under British rule. They learned English and educated their children in English schools. Unlike their experience under the Dutch, they were free to establish their own Lutheran church, which was built on Broadway and Rector Street in 1704. Life was so comfortable in Anglo-Saxon New York that they gradually discarded their distinct identity.

Danish emigration to the city in the era of the young republic was a succession of isolated individuals. Danes may have helped found New York's first Scandinavian Society in 1844 but they remained a negligible part of the organization and the community.

In 1863 Prussia's devastating defeat of Denmark resulted in a loss of 40 percent of its territory. The war, combined with industrial decline and the rising population on scarce rural lands, led to increased emigration. Between 1867 and 1914, three hundred thousand Danes crossed the ocean.

New York City was primarily a place for Danes to get their bearings and maybe make some money prior to the big push into the Midwest. Only a small group of sailors, artisans, and service workers stayed. Danish female domestics were always in demand and made up a large segment of this ethnic population. The Dania Club, which was organized in Brooklyn in 1886, provided a social outlet as well as health insurance and other services.

By the turn of the century the Danish influx changed to mainly middle-class professionals and businesspeople. These self-assured Danes did not need the company of their countrymen to ease the transition to an unfamiliar society. At the very most they clustered around other Scandinavian groups or in the vicinity of Danish denominational churches in the Bronx and Brooklyn. Their sense of identity came from the Danish newspaper *Nordlyset* and organizations like the Danish American Historical Society, which emphasized their unique heritage.

Though few in number, Danes made their mark in the city. Jacob Riis, the muckraking journalist, stirred the social conscience of the nation with his words and pictures. He arrived in New York in 1870 with only forty dollars in his pocket but with a strong sense of justice. By the end of the decade he was a leading New York journalist and social critic and a spokesman for the settlement-house movement. His series in the *Evening Star,* which graphically detailed the suffering and squalor of the city's immigrant population, led to the enactment of New York housing laws. Theodore Roosevelt once referred to him as ''the best American I have ever known.''

Niels Poulson made his reputation as one of Brooklyn's leading businessmen in the early part of this century. As head of the Hecla Iron Works, he was responsible for the ornamental flourishes of such New York landmarks as Grand Central Station and the original Penn Station. This public-spirited Scandinavian left a fortune, which today still funds scholarships and Danish cultural exhibitions.

Swedes

Sweden in the seventeenth century was exhausted by military adventures and on the decline. Gone were Gustaph Adolphus's dreams of a gilded empire. Some Swedes hoped to recoup their fortunes in the New World. A colony was established in Delaware and the Swedes even schemed with Peter Minuit to take over Dutch New Amsterdam. There were a few scattered Swedes in the Dutch colony; a party of pioneers helped clear Harlem for farmland and Mons Pietersen, a surveyor, laid out the village of Harlem.

There were only a hundred Swedes in New York in the 1830s, but twenty-two of them got together in 1836 to found an organization called the Swedish Society. It was the first Scandinavian mutual-aid society in the New World and only the second in the whole world. The members were merchants and manufacturers with a real sense of community spirit. In 1837 Swedish Brooklynites formed the first Swedish congregation, Swedish Immanuel Methodist. There was already the Bethel Ship Mission, ministering to Swedish seamen in the Port of New York.

In the middle of the nineteenth century, Swedes were primed for mass emigration. There was a scarcity of fertile arable land and too much political privilege. Swedes doing their military service resented the high-handed treatment they received from young aristocratic officers. Thousands of men, women, and children set off for America with the first stopover at New York. Swedish emigrants went on the cheap, spending twelve to fifteen dollars on steerage in freighters carrying Swedish iron ore. After docking in New York, a few hardy Swedes, usually of the seafaring variety, opted to stay.

In 1850 the Swedish population of the city was only five hundred. But it didn't stop Anders Gustaf Obom from starting the first Swedish newspaper, which ran on and off from 1851 to 1853. Despite their small numbers, Swedish-Americans rallied around the Union colors. They held an officers' ball on April 26, 1861, at which Swedish women presented Swedish volunteers with a silk Swedish flag. The regiment had a full military review on May 25 at Astor House.

Captain John Ericson, member in good standing of the Swedish Society, made the largest Swedish contribution to the Union effort by developing and building the first ironclad warship to run on steam, the *Monitor*. His state-of-the-art steamships, which were constructed at the Greenpoint docks, gave the Union the edge in the battle at sea.

Sweden was in trouble in the 1890s with labor unrest, declining wages, and rising populations in the cities. Swedish emigrants to America went from rural to urban. Some had even participated in the mammoth, three-hundred-thousand-strong, general strike that nearly crippled Stockholm. They headed for New York or one of the big Swedish strongholds like Chicago or Minneapolis. The Swedish Aid Society of New York was formed in 1891 to help these working-class immigrants. In just fifteen years, it placed 20,000 Swedes in new jobs and only eighty-three returned to Sweden.

Swedish workingmen moved to Hamilton Avenue in South Brooklyn or settled in the Swedish section of Sunset Park, along Buttermilk Channel and upper Bay behind the Bushwick Terminal. They were initially ships' carpenters, seamen, and longshoremen. Under the supervision of Swedish engineer Carl J. Mellin, they did pioneering work in the Brooklyn Navy Yard in the early 1900s.

In 1912 Swedish-born New Yorkers numbered over thirty-five thousand. That year the city's biggest parade celebrated the Swedish victory in the 1912 Stockholm Olympics. It was a time of real ethnic pride as the yellow-and-blue Swedish flag preceded the victorious athletes up the avenue. All of Swedish New York turned out, marching with their associations and organizations, wearing blue-and-yellow sashes of the folk costume of their country. Ernie Hjertberg was the hero of the day; he not only coached the champion Swedish track team but was a former trainer at the New York Athletic Club.

Swedish professionals were also drawn to this city of opportunity. In 1888 the American Society of Swedish Engineers was established and its members went on to change the New York skyline. David L. Lindquist was responsible for the new elevators that made the Empire State Building a reality. Gustave A. Sandblom perfected skyscraper steelwork in innovative buildings like New York Life. Werner Nygren made high-rises habitable with heating and ventilation systems for buildings as diverse as the Woolworth Building and Macy's. John A. Johnson cut his teeth as a housing contractor for Swedes in Bay Ridge and went on to be the leading contractor for the 1939 World's Fair.

Public-spirited Swedes got involved in government service. Emil F. Johnson, an analytical chemist from Stockholm, was a city public health inspector from 1895 to 1915 and established a system for ensuring safe milk. Arthur W. Wallander worked his way up from a patrolman on the beat to become the first Swedish police commissioner (under Mayor La Guardia) and a leading fighter against police corruption. Thomas Hoving, a second-generation Swede, served as a very popular parks commissioner under the Lindsay administration and created imaginative events that brought the people back to the parks. In 1977, Joanna Lindlof, a devoted teacher of Swedish descent, became the first woman on New York's Board of Education. Though the declining Swedish population did not make much of an impact as a group, Swedes excelled as individuals.

Norwegians

Norwegians like to think they were the first people to visit America, with the Norseman Leif Ericson arriving from Vinland more than a century before that Johnny-come-lately, Columbus. While that is not undisputed fact, it is clear that Norwegians were among the first peoples to settle in the United States. A Norwegian named Sand was even supposed to have been Peter Minuit's interpreter when he negotiated for Manhattan. Early New Amsterdam had its share of Norwegian sailors and carpenters, and a Norseman named Arent Andriessen supervised the Dutch colony's first shipyard.

In 1825, the sloop, the *Restauration,* was the first Norwegian ship with Norwegian passengers to reach New York. The ship was smaller than the *Mayflower* and not made for transatlantic travel, but the brave Quakers on board risked their lives in their quest for religious freedom. It turned out that their ship violated New York law by carrying too many passengers, but a generous New Yorker came to their rescue, putting up a bond and successfully petitioning President Adams to waive their three-thousand-dollar fine. The landing of the *Restauration* is still commemorated by Norwegian Americans on October 9.

A scattering of Norwegians settled on the New York waterfront in the 1830s and 1840s. Even in that early era it was said that you could draw a crowd of Norwegians by going to the harbor and shouting the Norwegian salutation: "Svedisker Norveisk Mand." It was a seafaring community with many temporary New Yorkers, but people were starting to put down roots, like Fredrik Wang, who ran a popular tavern frequented by the Norwegian community.

The numbers of Norwegians emigrating to New York became significant in the middle of the nineteenth century. In no time they were the largest group of Scandinavians to settle in the city. Many were responding to the unemployment brought about by the change from sailing ships to steamships. They were hard-hit by the cuts in crew size and the closing of Norwegian shipyards. Many simply jumped ship in the New World for the higher wages and work opportunities.

The Agder region, on the south coast of Norway, lost a large portion of its maritime population during this period. There were cases of captains who departed for New York with whole crews. It was commonplace to have American ships completely manned by Norwegians. These newcomers to the city received practical support and spiritual assistance from Norwegian missions that represented a whole variety of Christian denominations.

By the turn of the century a growing Norwegian population was putting down roots in Brooklyn, first in Park Slope and later in Bay Ridge. It was the largest urban concentration of Norwegians in the United States. Along its tree-lined streets there were Scandinavian-style bakeries, groceries, and restaurants. Norwegian was spoken in the bars and boardinghouses, and resounded from the church pulpits.

As in the past, these urban Norwegians were primarily involved in maritime employment. They worked the coastal and transatlantic ships, tugs, and barges, and even crewed on luxury yachts. They were involved in the construction of docks and ships and provisioned ships as chandlers. Thousands of Norwegians went to work in the new shipyards of Staten Island and eventually called "the island" home.

These highly skilled workers had a strong sense of their own value and were highly independent. They were avid supporters of unions and at one time 60 percent of all Norwegian laborers in the metropolitan area belonged to labor organizations. For many, the union took the place of the Norwegian church and national fraternal organizations.

New York's Norwegians were enthusiastic joiners. They were members of local churches and missions. They formed village associations called *bygdelags* and Norwegian lodges. In 1905 the *Det Norske Nationalforbund* became the umbrella organization for Norwegian groups in Brooklyn and Manhattan. In less than a decade, the Norwegians of greater New York boasted forty separate organizations.

The most successful aggregation was the Norwegian Club, which acted as a forum for important figures from Norway and the Norwegian-American community. The Norwegian newspaper *Nordisk Tidende* stood at the center of New York's Little Norway. Editors like Carl Soyland and Andreas Nilssen Rygg emphasized their common cultural and historical ties. The paper promoted community-wide events like the Norwegian May Festival and campaigned for charities like the Norwegian Lutheran Home and Hospital. The city's loyal Norwegians showed their colors in 1917, volunteering for service in World War I with New York's 308th Infantry. The Sons of Norway were at the forefront of Liberty Bond rallies; Norwegian New Yorkers pledged $6 million in 1918. While fighting for their adopted country, they were avenging the deaths of two thousand Norwegian seamen who perished in the North Atlantic as a result of Germany's unrestricted U-boat warfare.

In New York's postwar building boom, Norwegian workers and business-men made the transition from shipbuilding to housing and public works construction. Many became successful carpenters and contractors. Seafaring Norwegians worked on skyscrapers as riggers, using their knowledge of rope and tackle to hoist huge steel beams. Norwegian engineers from the country's prestigious technical institutes, innovators like Ole Singstad, Olaf Hoff, and Hans Rude Jacobsen, supervised the construction of the city's most impor-tant bridges and tunnels.

In 1925 New York recognized the Norwegian community with the dedi-cation of Leif Erikson Square during the centennial of the landing of the first Norwegian immigrant ship, the *Restauration*. Little Norway was coming of age with a population of 109,000, including 55,000 native born, but its ties to its homeland were still strong.

The Nazi invasion of Norway mobilized the whole Norwegian commu-nity. They donated food and clothing and raised funds for the Norwegian Red Cross and provided jobs and shelter for Norwegian refugees. After the Allied victory generous Norwegian New Yorkers aided in the reconstruction of Norway. This total community involvement kept Norwegian Bay Ridge together long after similar ethnic neighborhoods had disappeared.

Finns

Finns settled in New Amsterdam in the 1630s and 1640s. They were farmers and mechanics, few in number and hardly distinguishable from their Scan-dinavian neighbors. Two hundred years later Finnish "true-believers" passed through the city as part of a Protestant revival group formed around Lars Levi Laestadius.

Finnish seamen started coming to New York before the mass migrations of the 1890s. They generally jumped Scandinavian ships to draw superior

American wages. In the War Between the States, Finnish New Yorkers were actively recruited by the Union navy.

The Finns of the "great migration" were reluctant emigrants. Mainly tenant farmers and landless laborers from the agricultural region of Vaasa Oulu, one third of the males were forced off the land by overpopulation and the expansion of large farms. By 1900 Finnish emigrants were also responding to the increasingly reactionary policies of their Russian rulers who sought to substitite Russian for Finnish and had instituted military conscription.

Determined Finns worked their way from Helsinki to Stockholm and endured the dangers of steerage from Liverpool to New York. They had neither help from a Finnish colony overseas nor the support of their people at home. For their trouble and struggle, they were often the targets of self-righteous clergymen and reporters. They were attacked as traitors and weaklings without scruples or character. The Lutheran Church even refused, at least at first, to accept their overseas marriages as binding.

The Finns of New York were hardly the deserters depicted in the popular Finnish press. Individually and as a community, they were serious and conscientious, weighing their every action. They would not abandon one another nor their national traditions. Though they had no organizational experience in their native land, they were soon banding together in mutual aid societies and lodges.

When immigrant Finns disembarked at Ellis Island, they were met by community representatives. There were Finnish-speaking clergy who provided spiritual support and assisted them in contacting the local Finnish community in Sunset Park. Enterprising women operated six employment agencies at the immigration station to help newcomers find jobs as domestics. Finnish community representatives also directed emigrants to cooperative boardinghouses, where the new immigrants could share cooking, cleaning, and expenses with their compatriots.

In New York, Finnish maids were in great demand and women outnumbered men in the early days of Little Finland. Women were the backbone of Finnish Lutheran and Congregational churches; they formed church societies and played a key part in fund raising. They worked to preserve Finnish culture through their own groups and as auxiliaries of men's organizations like the Knights of Kaleva.

Finnish males, following the example of other Scandinavians, became carpenters and riggers on the city's big construction projects. In the 1890s these Finnish laborers formed socialist societies and workers' leagues like the Imatra Society. The Finns of this time were radical and committed, actively working for left-wing candidates like Eugene Debs, participating in strikes, and demonstrating against antiunion companies and rightist candidates. Later they would be at the forefront of the movement for cooperative stores and housing, which would take the profit away from the middleman capitalist and hand it to the consumer.

Finns from all walks of life joined the Knights of Kaleva, named in honor of the Finnish national epic, the *Kaleva*. As Knights, Finns could celebrate their ethnic identity and keep up Finnish traditions. The lodge also combined medical assistance and burial insurance with plain old Finnish fellowship. Local Finn halls in Sunset Park and Harlem provided the Finnish community with spirited expressions of ethnic pride. There were dramatic readings of the *Kaleva* and folk song festivals and regular appearances of Finnish dance companies.

The New York Finnish community was candid about drinking and its problems. They were very active in the Temperance Union movement and there were many separate Finnish temperance organizations throughout the city, sponsored by Congregationlist and Lutheran churches and socialist groups. They had a full social program to compete with community-wide events where alcohol was served.

The ties between Finns and their native country remained strong, with almost a third of their community accumulating their nest egg and actually returning home. Some of the socially concerned left New York to participate in experimental socialist communities in Soviet Karelia.

Finnish New York suffered from these defections and was even more hard-hit by immigration quotas that put an end to a vital foreign-language culture. Between 1925 and 1929, only 471 Finns a year could enter the country; this figure was raised to only 566 a year until the big changes in the immigration law. Despite this enforced cultural isolation and the pressures of assimilation, Finns had a real bond with the struggling young Finnish Republic in the shadow of the Soviet Union. Finns were particularly proud of their country's gallant defense against the Soviets in 1939 and the fact that they were the first nation to repay their debt to America after the Marshall Plan ended.

Bay Ridge

Directions: BMT RR Train to 77th Street/Fourth Avenue.

Introduction

Bay Ridge, as a part of Nieu Utrecht, was one of the earliest Dutch farm settlements in America in the first half of the seventeenth century. It retained its rural character into the nineteenth century, when the first Norwegian community started to take root. The Norwegians and the other Scandinavians

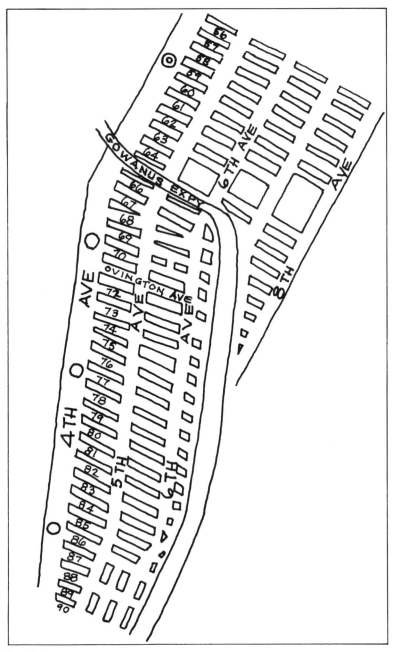

Bay Ridge

who followed them to Bay Ridge favored the area for its open spaces and panorama of the sea. Some said the Narrows, separating Brooklyn from Staten Island, brought back memories of the fjords.

Norwegians had a proprietary feeling for this Brooklyn neighborhood, which spanned Fourth to Eighth Avenues from 54th Street to 90th Street. It was practically a suburb of Oslo. Between 1900 and 1930, the population grew by leaps and bounds, a phenomenon the Norwegians called *Myostkolonien* (the area was maturing like a "sweet Norwegian cheese). In 1930 there were sixty-thousand Norwegians in Bay Ridge, with the overwhelming majority Norwegian-born.

In its prime, Bay Ridge was a slice of Scandinavian life. The buildings were neat and the streets were tidy. Products from Norway and Sweden were on sale in the stores and the signposts and advertising circulars were in Scandinavian languages. People drank aquavit in the bars and ate *lutefisk* at church suppers. They celebrated Scandinavian festivals and civil holidays. In Bay Ridge Christmas was always *Jul*. There were Norwegian and Swedish glee clubs and lodges and charitable organizations. Bay Ridge had its own Scandinavian hospitals, schools, and even an orphan asylum. There was mutual respect between people that sometimes took the form of quiet reserve, and, when the occasion demanded it, free-spirited communal celebration.

World War II and the Nazi occupation of Norway brought the Norwegian community of Bay Ridge closer together. Their concern for friends and family overseas inspired a small-scale cultural revival. But the erosion of this Scandinavian neighborhood was inevitable with the outward movement of more affluent Scandinavian families to Long Island and New Jersey, coinciding with the influx of Italians and other ethnics. Ironically the bridges and expressways that the Scandinavians played such an important part in building spelled the end of their splendid isolation. Though no longer a majority, the Scandinavians are still a presence in Bay Ridge, with their ethnic landmarks and occasional shops.

The Scandinavian Table

The standing joke about Scandinavian eating is that the "Danes live to eat, the Norwegians eat to live, and the Swedes eat to drink." (The Finns are unaccountably left out.) Actually, they have a lot in common in their approach to food, dictated by the climate and terrain and their involvement with the sea.

Throughout Scandinavia, smoked and cured fish from the humble cod to gravlax (salmon cured in sugar, salt, white pepper, and dill) are staples. Hearty root vegetables and dried beans are for soups and side dishes. The long winters are the season for pickled vegetables.

The Swedish smorgasbord, with its endless varieties of herring and endless aquavit toasts, smoked meats, cheeses, and hot-course old reliables like Swedish meatballs, has been adopted by all Scandinavians, with the warmer-weather Danes adding more salads. Sweden's *svart* soup, "black" soup made with goose and pig's blood, has also caught on, though it is not as popular as Norwegian *spekeskinke,* a Nordic version of prosciutto. The very basic ingredients of Scandinavian food are embellished with sour cream and horseradish, dill, and egg yolks. Yellow pea soup with pork and mustard is Sweden's national dish, while the Norwegians are addicted to *fiskepudding.* The Danes are the original herring mavens and the Finns' favorite pudding, *mämmiä,* is made with rye malt, molasses, and bitter orange peel.

Dining

The days of a Scandinavian restaurant row are long past. There is one survivor among the mainly Norwegian restaurants of Bay Ridge.

Atlantic Restaurant, *5414 Eighth Avenue between 54th and 55th Streets (718-438-9348). Daily 9 A.M.–8 P.M.*

The Atlantic looks like a local diner, with a long counter and rotating stools and tables all in a row. But it is brightly painted and has less chrome and mirrors than the typical New York greasy spoon. The waitresses are Norwegian New York; they know the neighborhood and have a joke with their regular customers. The bill of fare, besides hamburgers and fries, includes Norwegian specialties like *fiskepudding* and *middagpølse* (Norwegian baloney with some spice), with prune pudding and rice porridge for dessert.

Bakeries

The Scandinavians are inventive when it comes to breads and other baked goods. It takes real genius to add raspberry filling to a marzipan cake. Their lineup of breads include a dark sweet raisin bread, Norwegian rye, Danish pumpernickel, Swedish *limpa* flavored with anise and molasses, and Norwegian *lofse athin,* flat bread made from potatoes. For Christmas they add citrus peel to a raisin loaf and call it *Jul kage.*

Scandinavian bakeries used to be Brooklyn fixtures and gave the city its favorite breakfast pastry, the Danish. Bay Ridge still has a matching set of Scandinavian bakeries.

Olsen's, *5722 Eighth Avenue between 57th and 58th Streets (718-439-6673). Monday–Saturday 6 A.M.–6 P.M.*

The bakery may be Norwegian, but it has the best buttery fruit Danish, sweeter and less doughy than the commercially produced variety. The king of breads here is *mellambrod,* a sour-rye wheat bread that is both tart and rich as cake. In this changing area Olsen's has added items like cupcakes and brownies that cannot compete with their Scandinavian treats.

Leske's, *7612 Fifth Avenue between 76th and 77th Streets (718-680-2323). Tuesday–Friday 6 A.M.–7 P.M.; Saturday 6 A.M.–6 P.M.; Sunday 6 A.M.–3 P.M.*

The bakery has been serving the Bay Ridge community since 1916. No one remembers if the original owner was Dutch or Swedish, but the latest one is a German with a thorough command of Scandinavian baking. On weekends Norwegians and Swedes come from Northern New Jersey and the Island to buy *kneip* (wheat bread), Danish pumpernickel, and sweet Christmas bread, which they make all year round. They make different varieties of Danish, including the pretzel-shaped *kringle* and the cruller-shaped *stang,* which is filled with custard.

The Scandinavian Gourmet

The neighborhood Scandinavian markets with their own smoked sausage called *polse,* Norwegian *spekeskinke,* and *lutefisk* (codfish cured in brine) are now a rarity in Bay Ridge. Lingonberry jam and Swedish rye crisp are no longer on every grocer's shelf. There are a couple of Swedish food outposts that cater to the old Norwegian community and the new gourmet trade.

Fredericksen and Johansen, *7719 Fifth Avenue between 77th and 78th Streets (718-745-5980). Monday–Saturday 9 A.M.–6 P.M.*

This store sells quality and ranks with the best meat markets in Manhattan but it is much more. Fredericksen and Johansen's is for all the hard-to-find culinary Scandinavia, such as *morpølse* (a sausage with a touch of thyme enriched by lamb), Scandinavian blood sausage, Danish pickled goose, and *graddost* (cheese made with goat's milk). The shelves of this gourmet establishment also contain Toro packaged *fiskesuppe,* Bjelland sardines, and Stabburet liver paste. The Fredericksen and Johansen catalog makes shopping easy.

Mike's Delicatessen, *524 86th Street (718-680-2555) and 9510 Fifth Avenue (718-238-5200). Monday–Saturday 8 A.M.–10 P.M.; Sunday 9 A.M.–8 P.M.*

These neighborhood delis are down-to-earth and friendly spots for relaxed browsing. There are fresh herrings and lingonberries, and in the canned-goods section you can find King Oscar fishballs and Stabburet reindeer meat in gravy. Special Scandinavian cooking paraphernalia is also sold.

Nordic Delicacies, *6906 Third Avenue (718-748-1874). Monday–Saturday 9 A.M.–6 P.M.*

Nordic Delicacies is one take-out that delivers home cooking. It was started by two Bay Ridge women in love with authentic Norwegian cooking, who decided to share it with the whole neighborhood. Their biggest successes are their daily specials. If it's Monday it must be *kjøttkaker* (Norwegian meat-balls); Wednesday is *komper* (potato dumpling); and Thursday is *lapskaus* (a beef hash with onions and potatoes). Buy early before they sell out.

Norwegian Gifts

In the long dark Scandinavian winters when people are housebound, handicrafts like knitting and crewelwork flourish.

Signes Imports, *5906 Eighth Avenue between 59th and 60th Streets (718-492-5004). Tuesday–Friday 10 A.M.–5 P.M.; Saturday 10 A.M.–3 P.M.*

Signes carries traditional handmade sweaters with traditional patterns at prices machine-made sweaters cost. Though everything is individually crafted, there is a certain sameness about the ski sweaters and cardigans.

Norwegian Inheritance

Norwegian clubs no longer blanket the neighborhood but the ones that remain are energetic boosters of Norway and Norwegian-Americans.

Norsemen's Federation, *New York Chapter, 358 87th Street (212-680-4530).*

This Norwegian fraternal organization does more than socialize, though it does that very well. It works hard to make the Norwegian young people in and out of the neighborhood aware of their roots.

Nordisk Tidende, *8104 Fifth Avenue (718-238-1100).*

This Norwegian-language newspaper has been publishing since 1891. It has all the news of Norwegian Bay Ridge that is fit to print, plus what is going on in Norway and the latest about Norwegian visitors to the city. The paper is a cultural lifeline for older Norwegians. The only concession it has made to the times is a page in English.

Norwegian Day Parade

On May 17, Norwegians from the metropolitan area make a pilgrimage to the old neighborhood to reaffirm their ethnic identity and explore old associations. It is a patriotic celebration marking the day Norway received its democratic constitution—a Norwegian Fourth of July without fireworks. It started in Brooklyn in response to another Norwegian milestone, when the country declared its independence from Sweden in 1905.

The parade moves down Brooklyn's Fifth Avenue from 90th Street to Leif Ericson Park at 66th Street. The marchers represent a wide array of organizations, from the avuncular Sons of Norway to the dignified Norwegian Society of America. Young and old move along the avenue in brightly embroidered peasant costume—vests and knee britches and billowing skirts and aprons. There are floats of Viking ships with bearded men waving cardboard swords and blond Norwegian beauties throwing flowers to the spectators. A Miss Norway is crowned, getting a far more enthusiastic reception than the speeches made by Norwegian dignitaries. After the parade Norwegian families can be seen strolling through the neighborhood, reminiscing about the old block and visiting personal landmarks.

Sunset Park

Directions: BMT RR or N for 45th Street/4th Avenue.

Introduction

The Finns staked out their claim to Sunset Park, Brooklyn, taking its name from the park bounding the Gowanus Bay. The heart of Finntown covered 40th to 45th Streets and Fifth to Ninth Avenues. Skilled in the building trades, the Finns created a charming area of neat frame houses. They also built the first cooperative housing in the city, which Mayor O'Dwyer said were "twenty-five years ahead of their time." These neat four-story brick apartment houses are still standing in all their glory.

Before the Gowanus Expressway forced out Finnish homeowners and Robert Moses's idea of progress put an end to a neighborhood, Finntown was a bustling ethnic enclave with cooperative stores selling Finnish foods and handicrafts and a host of Finnish centers and halls. Sunset Park had a half dozen saunas where hardworking locals could relax and unwind in the dry heat of this Finnish institution. There were Finnish restaurants that turned meat loaf into a delicacy with sour cream pastry, and made crayfish something special with dill, vinegar, and beer. Midsummer's eve they lit bonfires in Sunset Park and on *Kaleva Lepos* they celebrated in Imatra Hall, singing ancient songs and reciting from their epic, the *Kaleva*.

After World War II, the aging Finnish community could no longer support its network of organizations, and its labor and temperance groups were out of step with the times. Most of the Finns moved out of Finntown, preferring Finnish communities in warmer climes like Lantana and Lake Worth, Florida. But five thousand Finns stayed on, and active second- and third-generation Finns continue to maintain the Finnish heritage in a neighborhood where more Spanish is spoken than any Scandinavian language.

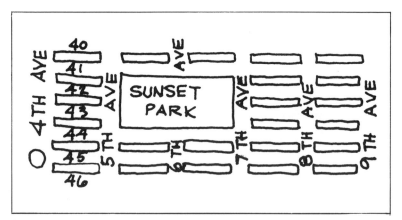

Sunset Park

Landmarks of Little Finland

Imatra Hall, *740 40th Street between 7th and 8th Avenues (718-438-9426).*

The Imatra Society (named after a legendary Finnish waterfall) was formed in 1891 to defend the interests of Finnish workingmen and support working-class causes. It was to provide health and death benefits for Finnish labor along with education and social activities. Finnish culture was a part of its program; the society had its own library, offering "edifying" lectures, and encouraging Finnish singing and study groups.

In 1902 the Imatra Society of Brooklyn joined with thirty-two other similar groups to establish the American Finnish Workers League to back the labor movement. The Imatra Society also started publishing their own politically slanted paper, *New Yorkin Uutiset,* which was edited by the idealistic Matti Kurikka, who founded a Utopian socialist community in the British Columbian wilderness. The group was ideologically left and partisans of strong unions.

As time passed, the organization's predominantly working-class character changed and the newspaper became more mainstream. The organization accepted members representing every class and political view in the Finnish community. The Imatra Hall was now friendly Finns gathering in the Imatra Bar or game rooms, or the whole of Finntown coming out for a Finnish holiday celebration.

Most Imatra Hall traditions haven't changed, though the Society has had to accept associate members who are not of Finnish descent to keep the organization's Sunset Park identity. The hall offers regular appearances of Finnish singers and bands and dancers and has its own Finnish dance fetes in its social hall or in the Imatra gardens. For the midsummer's eve summer solstice celebration there is traditional Finnish dancing, eating, and drinking, and a giant bonfire in their big backyard.

Imatra Hall has seen better days, but its current leadership keeps this old rambling wooden monument together and talks about major fund raising and full-scale rehabilitation. In 1992 they plan a big Finnish blowout for the 100th anniversary of the Imatra Society.

Alku Toinen Finnish Cooperative Apartments, *816–826 43rd Street.*

Alku Toinen Finnish Cooperative Apartments was the city's first cooperative, built in 1916. The building represented a fresh start for many of its Finnish occupants, who literally built the place. The building's name, appropriately, means "beginning." In this true cooperative the actual residents of the building shared the costs of construction and maintaining the property with no middlemen making a profit. The building still has plenty of Finnish tennants.

Finnish Sauna

The sauna is a three-thousand-year-old Finnish tradition connected to pre-Christian religious rites. In Finland it was the custom to build the sauna even before building the house. This ancient heat bath, made by heating rocks to high temperatures, still has an almost mystical significance, part purification rite and part exhilarating penance. More prosaically, it is a way of sweating out a hangover and keeping clean. Finnish sauna enthusiasts rub themselves with steel brushes and whack one another with birch branches as a type of massage. People also socialize in the sauna, solving the world's problems while dousing the rocks with water that rises in burning clouds of steam. It is a place where Finnish businessmen negotiate and politicians make deals. As one Finnish wag insisted, "We just keep on pouring the water on the rocks until they say yes." Sunset Park's last remaining sauna is in Imatra Hall.

═══════ Manhattan Smorgasbord ═══════

The Groaning Board

Before New York turned its sophistication on food, Scandinavian food was smorgasbord restaurants with all-you-can-eat buffets on Manhattan's tourist route. They were fun but no big loss in the taste department. The replacements are superior.

Old Denmark, Inc., *133 East 65th Street (212-744-2533). Monday–Saturday 9 A.M.–5:30 P.M.*

There is a red sentry box outside; inside there are Hans Christian Andersen toy soldiers. Old Denmark gives that feeling of fairy-tale Copenhagen. The front of the shop is Denmark gift items: canned ham, wooden toys, and silversmith jewelry. In the back there is the buffet, a small-selection *koldtbord* (literally "cold table"), the Danish smorgasbord. Old Denmark has a loyal luncheon crowd and they get the personal service.

Nyborg and Nelson, *153 East 53rd Street (Citicorp Center) (212-223-0700). Monday–Friday 11:30 A.M.–9 P.M.; Saturday, Sunday noon–6 P.M.*

The restaurant-cum-Scandinavian deli counter is supposed to look functional and hi-tech but it just looks bare. The proof is in the eating here. The authentic Scandinavian cuisine attracts the Swedes, Danes, and Norwegians from nearby consulates and information offices. There are open Danish sandwiches (sm˘rrebr˘d) and tasty smorgasbord salads supplemented with *pølse* and main dishes like loin of pork stuffed with prunes and apples from Denmark.

Aquavit, *13 West 54th Street (212-307-7311). Monday–Friday noon–2 P.M., 5:30 P.M.–10:30 P.M.; no lunch Saturdays.*

Aquavit is expense-account territory with prix fixe luncheons and dinners that are only reasonable if someone else is paying. The restaurant is named for the potent Scandinavian liquor, which is drunk ice cold with lager chasers. Genuine aquavit is on the drink list, but most of the food is only quasi-Scandinavian. The gravlax is a stunning exception.

Scandinavian Style

Scandinavian clothes in the past have been mostly reindeer sweaters and hiking boots. Things are changing.

Marimekko, *7 West 56th Street (212-581-9616). Monday–Wednesday 10 A.M.–6:30 P.M.; Thursday 10 A.M.–8 P.M.; Saturday 10 A.M.–6 P.M.*

Marimekko has made the leap from designer sheets to designer dresses. The fabrics are still brightly colored and contemporary, while the designs are classical and comfortable. The ready-to-wear is expensive, but there are fabrics on sale for the creative. There are also children's clothes, toys, and accessories.

In Scandinavia, working in wood is the hallowed tradition and the wood of choice is pine. Almost all houses are made of wood and even brick dwellings are frame houses with brick skins. In the rural villages of Scandinavia, furniture-making was and is a high art. Swedish *allmoge,* or country style, is highly respected in all of Scandinavia. The practical Scandinavians took to modern design, where form follows function, and combined it with their devotion to natural materials. The Swedish modern that lends itself to small city apartments may be Finnish, Danish, or Norwegian.

Wim and Karen's Scandinavian Furniture, *319 East 53rd Street (212-758-4207). Monday–Wednesday, Friday 10 A.M.–6 P.M.; Thursday 10 A.M.–7:30 P.M.; Saturday 10 A.M.–5 P.M.*

Wim and Karen Samson's collection of Scandinavian furniture is for every room in the house. The furniture, whether teak, oak, or pine, is made to fit into small city spaces. They have a complete line of wall units that are Nordic solid. The store has the right accessories, lamps, and ceramic pieces for Scandinavian designs.

Norsk, *114 East 57th Street (212-252-3111). Monday–Wednesday, Friday 10 A.M.–6 P.M.; Thursday 10 A.M.–8 P.M.; Sunday noon–5 P.M.*

Norsk has a large showroom but this popular store can get very crowded. The furniture is light and airy for middle-of-the-road American tastes. There are plenty of plain wood bunk beds, chests, and conversation nooks. The prices are also suitable for that first apartment or a student's room.

Scandinavian Design, *127 East 59th Street (212-755-6078). Monday–Friday 9:30 A.M.–5:30 P.M.*

For those with decorators, Scandinavian Design offers a modern environment created with track lighting and economical furniture design. The New York apartment is approached as a whole by the store's knowledgeable staff.

Scandinavian crafts are more than the cottage industries of the countryside. They work in sophisticated mediums like porcelain and glass. They make fine china and flatware and deep etched crystal and sculptured glass. Scandinavian companies like Arabia, Orrefors, Kosta Boda, and Royal Copenhagen are world renowned.

Royal Copenhagen Porcelain, *683 Madison Avenue at 61st Street (212-759-6457). Monday–Saturday 9:30 A.M.–5:30 P.M.*

This sleekly elegant showroom has a wide selection of contemporary porcelain, silver, and crystal fit for a Danish queen. Their Georg Jensen silver is a modern classic.

Gallery Nilsson, *138 Wooster Street (212-431-0050). Monday–Saturday noon–7 P.M.; Sunday noon–5 P.M.*

Swedish glassblowers, like Swedish furniture makers, keep things simple. Everything at Nilsson's from bowls to glasses are hand-blown one-of-a-kind or limited editions. They work with one- and two-man companies that are influenced more by the creative urge than the bottom line.

Place Marks

It is not surprising that Scandinavian monuments begin at the Battery, where Scandinavian seamen made so much history.

There is a bronze statue of the Swede John Ericson, the designer of the first ironclad man-of-war, the *Monitor,* which helped win the Civil War.

The Customs House on Bowling Green has a fresco on the domed ceiling depicting another Scandinavian named Ericson, Leif Ericson, who is supposed to have landed in America.

The seafaring tradition combines with the staunch evangelical religious tradition in the seamen's churches in midtown Manhattan, which have become gathering places for the Scandinavian community after the partial disintegration of Scandinavian neighborhoods in New York.

Norwegian Seamen's Church, *245 East 49th Street (212-319-0370).*

The Norwegian Seamen's is readily identifiable by the large Norwegian flag hanging in front of it. Inside, young volunteers make the Norwegian seamen feel at home and greet the stray Norwegian tourist who happens in. There is a library at the entrance with models of Norwegian liners and pictures of Norwegian sea captains. The main room, a flight down, has a glass ceiling that captures every ray of sunlight; and folk arts are displayed on the wall. Norwegian and Norwegian-American groups meet here.

Swedish Seamen's Church, *5 East 48th Street (212-832-8443).*

The exterior of the building, with its granite stonework and leaded windows, is properly ecclesiastical, and the public rooms are rustically trimmed with wood imprinted with passages from the Bible. The tone of the room is not at all solemn, and above on the mezzanine there is an exhibit of Swedish abstract art. There's a library and up-to-date Swedish papers, which are devoured by Swedish tourists along with the waffles that the church ladies serve.

The Scandinavian Inheritance

Scandinavian organizations and institutions preserve America's Scandinavian past through art, education, and cultural exchanges.

The American-Scandinavian Foundation, *127 East 73rd Street (212-879-9779). Monday–Friday 10 A.M.–5 P.M.*

The American-Scandinavian Foundation is a truly cross-national group deeply involved in educational exchanges and cultural interchanges both here and in Denmark, Iceland, Sweden, Norway, and Finland. They sponsor scholarships and award literary prizes. Their New York headquarters is not just an office; upstairs there are two large rooms that exhibit Scandinavian art—paintings, sculpture, and whatever else will travel.

The American Scandinavian Society of New York, *245 East 49th Street (212-751-0714).*

The movers and shakers in Scandinavian (mostly Norwegian) New York congregate here to celebrate their people's achievements in the United States and in their homelands. They have lectures and meetings and sponsor exhibits. They raise money to preserve the Scandinavian past in New York's present.

Scandia Festivals

St. Lucia Day

St. Lucia Day is a special feast day that Swedish Vikings brought back from Sicily in the Middle Ages. It is dedicated to a young virgin named Lucia who was very virtuous and holy—too virtuous and holy for her pagan suitor, who stabbed her after she refused to marry him and gave her dowry away to the poor. At least that is one version of the story.

St. Lucia Day, which takes place every Dec. 13, is a festival of lights with some resemblance to the pagan Scandinavian rites that celebrated the end of the dark days of winter and the reemergence of light from the underworld.

In the St. Lucia festivities, the youngest girl in the Swedish household dresses as St. Lucia, in white robes and a red sash with a crown of candles adorning her hair. In the middle of the night she wakes the rest of the family, singing the hymn of the Queen of Light, and serves them special St. Lucia sweet saffron current buns. There are three toasts with potent Swedish glugg before dawn, and then a heavy Swedish breakfast.

The St. Lucia tradition is carried on by New York's Swedish community. Every year the city's Swedish churches rent a hall to accommodate the hundreds of people who want to bring in the St. Lucia year. Recently over a thousand have attended this celebration, which freely mixes Christian solemnity and Norse gaiety. It begins with a stirring procession of young Swedish women dressed like St. Lucia, slowly walking up the aisle two by two. They climb the stage and break into the hymn to the Queen of Light of Norse legend. For an hour they intersperse Christmas carols with traditional Scandinavian songs.

This important holiday rates a formal invitation-only dinner at the residence of the Swedish consul, which includes Nobel Prize–winners on its guest list. The Swedish-American Chamber of Commerce holds a December 13 wingding every year at the Waldorf Astoria, with a special St. Lucia Queen chosen from the Swedish community.

The Irish

Introduction

The Irish of New York started out Protestant, but once poor Irish Catholics emigrated to New York in significant numbers they thought it was more "society" to be called Scotch-Irish, and the New York Irish became the Catholic Irish. The Irish are New York's prototypical rags-to-riches story. They came with the clothes on their back and starvation gnawing at their bellies, and in a generation they were running the city. They were the cops and they were the firemen and they were the mayors or the Tammany powers behind the throne. Nowadays the American-born Irish are as likely to be financiers and businessmen as policemen and firemen. But the story of Irish immigration isn't over. There is a whole new group of Irish immigrants, as eloquent and independent as the last batch, who are fighting different battles and making their own successes.

History

The first Irishman to set foot on what would become New York was John Coleman, an able-bodied crewman aboard Henry Hudson's *Half Moon*. John lost his life in a dispute with the Indians and became the first Irishman and white man to be buried on Coney Island.

The Irish played an important part in New York from the time it became the property of King Charles II in 1664. Governor Thomas Dongan, a

Catholic and Irish nobleman of Limerick, gave New York its first city charter. In his charter, which was later rescinded, he recognized liberties that were later included in the Bill of Rights.

Both Protestant and Catholic Irish gained positions of prominence in commerce and government in colonial New York and both Protestant and Catholic Irish welcomed the American Revolution and the opportunity to strike back at unfair British rule. Even Sir Henry Clinton, a loyalist to the core, had to admit that the Irish were the best soldiers on either side. By the beginning of the nineteenth century, the city's Irish were taking sides in the political battles between another Clinton heading the Federalists and a new political organization, Tammany Hall.

The American Revolution inspired another revolution on the Emerald Isle. The British were able to crush this uprising, creating the first of a long line of Irish political refugees. They were intellectual men of action who brought their abilities to the city. Thomas Addis Emmet was one of the leading conspirators in the failed 1798 revolution. He escaped to New York to become a power in city politics and an ardent backer of Jefferson. In 1812 he became the Attorney General of New York.

The city's early Celtic population was very lace-curtain—merchants and professionals and capable craftsmen. They had a newspaper called *The Shamrock* and their Society of St. Patrick rivaled the English St. Andrew's Society. They were divided by religion and united by their Irish identity. Their charitable organizations benefited both Protestants and Catholics. In 1826, New York's united Irish community was large enough to swing the city to Andrew Jackson in a presidential election.

But the city's "carriage-and-four" Irish were soon to be joined by the Irish poor. They were attracted by stories of full larders and meat every day and fat pay envelopes. They were tired of a homeland where they weren't allowed to hold property or worship their own God. They were tired of the brutal tax collectors and soldiers and the humiliating privileges of an alien nobility. Rural Ireland was getting ready to emigrate.

The Irish population rise translated into more political power. They went from being barred from Tammany Hall to nominating an Irish Catholic, Patrick Mackay, to the State Assembly. In 1817 anti-Catholic bigotry still continued and outraged Irishmen broke into the Tammany wigwam that refused to support Thomas A. Emmet for Congress. New York's passage of a law guaranteeing universal white suffrage meant that Tammany politicians like president-to-be Martin Van Buren courted the Irish Catholic population.

These New York Irish built the Erie Canal, which made New York the commercial power it is today and ushered in a golden age. In 1841 Irish Catholic notables like Bishop John Hughes and Congressman Thomas Mc-Keon formed the Irish Emigrant Society under the auspices of the Catholic Church. In New York it was official, Irish and Catholic were one and the same. Over the years the society stopped the abuse of emigrants and provided services for the Irish poor.

Before the biggest Irish famine, in 1845 (there were five Irish potato famines between 1817 and 1848), Irish peasants were squatters on their own national territory. They rented lands that their families had farmed for generations from foreign landlords who extorted large sums for this privilege. The only way the Irish farmers could meet this bill was by planting crops for the British export market and depending on a potato kitchen garden for survival.

The blight that left the potatoes black and rotting in 1845 set in motion a cycle of starvation and death. While freighters were leaving Irish ports for Liverpool packed with produce, human skeletons in the countryside were scavenging for grass and eating dirt. The moderate pace of Irish emigration to New York became a stampede.

Whether Irish emigrants raised the fare for the crossing from a government anxious to get rid of them or from a New York charity, the ordeal was far from over. Ocean travel was still risky and traveling in "Irish berths," below the freight in steerage, had its own dangers.

There was the strain of the endless din in the dark, cramped spaces. Sudden violence was common below decks and there were cases of unprotected women being attacked. If the weather wasn't right the usual eight-week voyage could become a six-month agony. Sometimes provisions were short or spoiled and there was another famine on board. Disease ran rampant in these airless areas. Many Irish died from cholera or typhus before the "coffin ships" reached shore. For some, Irish steerage turned out to be a lot like a slave ship.

The Irishman from "the old sod" was a familiar figure with his brimless *caubeen,* knee britches, flowing cape, and big-buckled shoes, clattering down the gangplank at New York harbor. Before local and federal governments overhauled the immigration process, these naive newcomers were fair game for con men called "shoulder hitters," who sold them counterfeit train tickets, overcharged them for storing or carting their luggage, and steered them to crooked boardinghouses. The unwary Irishman often wound up living in a glorified grogshop on Greenwich Street, where the only thing for free was a plate of loose tobacco. Fast-talking landlords stripped them of their savings and possessions in a few days.

Irish immigrants crowded forty to a celler in decaying Five Points housing and squatted in shantytowns in the wastes of Harlem. They even lived in "dugouts" under the floorboards of cellars, and when they went out to look for work there was the standard "no Irish need apply" in the ads in the newspaper.

Though uneducated, they quickly adapted rural skills to an urban land-scape. They used pure brawn as stevedores and porters, while their knowledge of horses helped them progress from grooms to cabmen and carters. The Irishman who had dug the potato cellars now dug foundations for city buildings. Eventually they proved themselves in the building trades, first as hod carriers, then as bricklayers and masons. Irish women used their domestic skills as housemaids and laundresses and took in sewing.

The Irish famine immigrants were mistrusted for their Catholicism and disdained for their poverty. The *Herald* political cartoonist, Thomas Nast, caricatured them as apes. All the Irish were lumped together with the violent Irish in the Five Points gangs. The Know-Nothing Party in the 1850s pledged to get rid of the Irish and Catholic menace. The Irish fought back, organizing themselves to disrupt Know-Nothing rallies and defeat them at the polls. Their participation in Democratic politics, like their church, became a way of life.

In 1855 Fernando Wood was elected mayor, with Irish voters deciding the outcome. By 1860 one out of every four New Yorkers was Irish. During Wood's administration the immigration station at Castle Garden was opened, allowing new immigrants from Ireland to enter the country unmolested. Representatives of the Irish Immigration Society helped them to contact their families and find employment. Representatives from Tammany did some hiring on the spot and led the new immigrants off to be naturalized so they could vote in the next election.

During Wood's administration the Irish Catholic hierarchy also received permission to build St. Patrick's Cathedral. This impressive sanctuary made it clear that Catholicism was one of the city's major religions and the governing Catholic hierarchy was Irish. The Ancient Order of Hibernians, which was also dedicated to St. Patrick, was founded by Irish New Yorkers in 1853. Since that time it's been doing good work and organizing the St. Patrick's Day Parade and events like the Great Irish Fair.

The Irish were basically rural people facing choices they never had in their villages. Sometimes their passions got out of hand. In July 1863, a group of Irish joined native Americans in a protest against the Civil War draft that turned into one of New York's worst riots.

In the year of the riots there were tensions between the Irish, who were divided on abolition, and New York's established black community. The Irish had no conception of southern slavery, but cheap black labor was a direct threat. Blacks had recently been used to break a bitter Irish longshoremen's strike and bad feeling was running high.

The immediate cause for the riot was the injustice of a new law that allowed the rich to be exempted from the Union draft for a three-hundred-dollar fee.

It was hot, and perhaps agent provocateurs were at work. For three days the New York mob was out of control. Blacks were lynched and the Colored Orphans' Asylum was gutted. But the Irish also saved the day. Archbishop Hughes calmed the mob with words and Irish policemen enforced the peace with guns and nightsticks.

The Irish were of one mind where the Union was concerned and rallied to the colors. Thousands enrolled in the city's militias when the war broke out. Flamboyant Irish fighters went into battle with shamrocks and harps, lots of bravado and gaudy uniforms. Irish soldiers wore Turkish fezzes and red firemen's shirts to the battle of Bull Run. The honor roll of New York's daring Irish forces included the Sixty-ninth Regiment, the Thirty-seventh Regiment, and the Tammany Regiment, led by officers with names like Meagher, Corcoran, and Shields.

Irish immigrants returned to New York after the war American heroes. They were no longer outsiders. They were the core of the city's uniformed professionals, police and fire fighters. Michael Kerwin, who fought for Irish freedom as well as the Union, became police commissioner. The Irish were more than foot soldiers of the Democratic party; they were ward leaders and precinct captains. Honest John Kelly represented his Irish neighborhood in Congress.

New York's Irish were organized labor's rank and file and leaders. They used the talent for organization they revealed in politics to unionize construction workers and stevedores, the skilled and the unskilled. They were past masters of the fine art of negotiation. The Irish labor leader, Peter J. McGuire, went national helping to found the American Federation of Labor and earned the right to be known as the "Father of Labor Day."

In 1871 Boss Tweed, the city's most flagrant grafter, had his comeuppance and Honest John Kelly became the first Irishman to head Tammany. Honest John was a boxer and an actor and a volunteer fireman. He also invented the Tammany machine, the chain of command from block captain to district leader, that won elections. He initiated the Irish political succession, which was only broken by Carmine DeSapio in the 1950s.

Richard Croker was Kelly's political heir and was also a former volunteer fireman and fighter. He made a fortune as coroner and parlayed himself into a position as head of a finance committee that didn't keep any books. Croker had champagne tastes and retired to an estate in Ireland to raise racing horses.

Charles Francis Murphy succeeded Boss Croker in 1902. He was a ball player and the proprietor of four taverns that doubled as Tammany political clubs. He ruled Tammany for twenty-two years and kept politics out of the police department, the schools, and the judiciary. When Murphy died, city politicians lamented that "the brains of Tammany lie in the Calvary Cemetery."

When the Irishman William R. Grace, founder of Grace Lines, was elected mayor of New York in 1880, the ordinary Irish man and woman were still struggling to make ends meet as laborers and maids and living in the run-down tenements of Hell's Kitchen. Some of the kids strayed, breaking and entering in the West Side railroad yards and drifting into gangs like the Knuckle Dusters and the Dead Rabbits. While Irish politicians controlled Tammany, Irish thugs controlled the rackets on the West Side.

But the Irish were also joining the ranks of the respectable super-rich. Thomas E. Murray was one of the first of the Irish tycoons. He started out as a lamplighter in Albany, but this Irish Edison had a real scientific genius and was soon earning patents for circuits, switches, and dynamos. While garnering wealth for his inventions, he managed the Brooklyn Edison Company. Murray died just months before the stock market crash, leaving an estate worth well over ten million.

Murray's daughter Anna married a man with as much energy and wit as her father. James Francis McDonnell was a canny Wall Street trader who had started the high-flying firm of McDonnell & Byrne. He vowed he would make a million before he married and another million for each of his fourteen children. He kept his word. The McDonnells knew they had arrived when they joined dynasties with the Fords and it was Henry II who converted.

Although the Irish were rarely associated with "trade," before Gristede and D'Agostino became household words in New York, a Butler from Kilkenny had a lock on the grocery business. All his stores, which at one point numbered 1,100, were painted green and his fortune in green amounted to thirty million in predepression dollars. Butler loved the racetrack and eventually bought his own, Yonkers. In lieu of allowances, the squire gave his children tips on the races.

In 1916 New York Irish rich and poor backed the Easter Rebellion in Ireland. When the rebellion failed and the British executed the uprising's gallant leaders, the Irish community held demonstrations and special masses were said in the churches. Despite their feelings against Britain, loyal Irish New Yorkers volunteered for the forces in World War I and the Fighting Sixty-ninth, under the command of "Wild Bill" Donovan, was one of the first units to see action in Europe. In the peace following World War I, Ireland at last became Eire, the Irish Free State.

While New York's personable Roaring Twenties Irish Mayor, Jimmy Walker, was making headlines with Broadway showgirls, another Irish New Yorker, Al Smith, fought the good fight for the presidency of the United States. Eventually both left public life but the New York tradition of Irish officeholders and Irish political kingmakers continued.

The new Irish politicians were following their constituents to suburban Brooklyn, the Bronx, and Queens. The last Irish mayor was a Brooklynite named O'Dwyer. He went from walking a beat in Brooklyn to the Brooklyn District Attorney's office and took off time from city government during World War II to be a general. In 1974 a former Brooklyn congressman named Hugh Carey became the governor of the state. An intelligent and effective negotiator, he was instrumental in saving the state and the city from bankruptcy.

Ed Flynn of the Bronx became the city's Democratic political leader after the death of Charles Francis Murphy and he gained national political stature advising Roosevelt in the 1932 presidential election. In 1960, history repeated when Bronx Democratic leader Charles C. Buckley helped propel John F. Kennedy (for a time a resident of the Bronx) into the presidency.

Patrick Moynihan, a New York Irishman who went from the slums of Hell's Kitchen to a professorship at Harvard, was a member in good standing of Kennedy's inner circle Camelot. After the assassination of the great Irish hope, he divided his time between academia and appointive politics. He ultimately ran for elective office and became New York's Democratic senator through the 1970s and the 1980s. His rise reflected the success of the New York Irish community, which was now overwhelmingly white-collar and professional.

Despite Irish political power the new immigration law of 1965 severely limited Irish access to the country at a time of unemployment and economic stagnation. In the words of one New York Irish immigration activist, it was "immigration or die."

The laws have hardly changed but the Irish are still coming to New York in the 1980s. While living under the strain of being an "illegal" immigrant, they work hard in the building trades and service industries and create communities in the Bronx and Queens where hurling and rugby are the sports and a fiddler plays at dances.

========== **Bronx Irish** ==========

Bainbridge
Directions: IRT-Lexington 4 to Mosholu Avenue.

Introduction

The Irish were among the earliest immigrant groups to cross the Harlem River into the Bronx. They glimpsed this scenic playground for the rich while building High Bridge and the Harlem Railroad. It reminded them of the

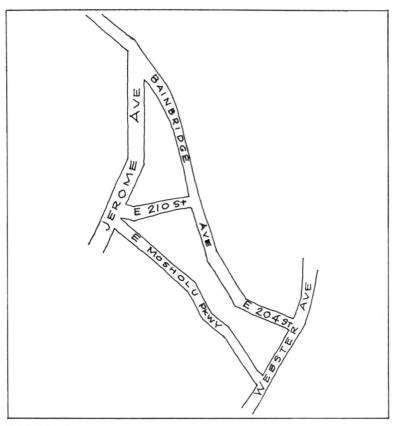

Bainbridge Avenue

meadows and bays of another time and place and they became nineteenth-century commuters.

While wealthy neighbors like the Lorillards built bigger mansions and bred horses, the Irish of Morrisania and West Farms agitated for paved streets and adequate drainage. They wouldn't stop at anything, even annexation to the dreaded Manhattan. In 1874 the city absorbed 12,317 Bronx acres and thirty-three thousand people, and in 1895 it took the other 14,500 acres.

The Irish enjoyed their Shangri-La with its thousands of acres of park land (Croton, Claremont, and Van Cortlandt) and convenient industrial zones. But the extension of the El to West Farms created a real estate boom that changed the face of the Bronx. Now thousands of the new immigrants—Italian and Jews—moved into the borough's fully equipped modern housing.

The Bronx Irish, like their Manhattan forebears, had a gift for political organization and in no time they were building a Democratic base second to none. Edward J. Flynn was the leader of the organization built around his Pondiac (an inadvertent misspelling of Chief Pontiac's name) club. A man of intellect and taste, he was hardly the image of the backslapping pol. He was a political kingmaker, Roosevelt's principal advisor in the rough-and-tumble of getting elected. He also championed Robert Wagner's first candidacy for mayor.

His chosen successor, Charles A. Buckley, was single-mindedly political. A bricklayer and a boxer in his youth, as Bronx Democratic leader and congressman he was a tough infighter. Like Flynn, Buckley played an important role in national politics. Buckley's well-timed endorsement provided John F. Kennedy with the momentum to win the Democratic presidential nomination. When Buckley lost his seat in Congress in 1962, it was more than a personal defeat—it marked the end of the Irish era in Bronx politics.

Although the Irish are long gone from Mott Haven, Melrose, and Hunt's Point, the latest batch of Irish immigrants are making Bainbridge in the Bronx their home. They have come from Cork, Kerry, Limerick, Dundalk, and Donegal to this corner of the Bronx to find work, and if not a pot of gold, a more secure future.

The area where they have rented apartments and begun to raise families was once a solidly Jewish part of the largest Jewish neighborhood in the city. After World War II the majority of these Bronx Jews, like the majority of Bronx Irish, opted for the suburbs of New Jersey and Long Island and exchanged a neat brick apartment house for the sanctuary of a frame one-family with a patch of lawn.

Bainbridge is just north of New York's modern "burnt-out district," the South Bronx. But a sense of community has kept out the drugs and violence. People know one another and look out for their neighbors. Crime is not a runaway problem, though some Irish in Bainbridge who do not look forward to a visit from Immigration and Naturalization might hesitate about reporting a burglary.

Many of the hundred thousand or more Irish-born of Bainbridge must struggle with immigration problems. Unlike their ancestors, their only chance to enter the country is "to bend the rules." They come as tourists. Later they get jobs in the city's "off the books" economy. The men find occupational anonymity in construction gangs; the women work informally as waitresses and baby-sitters.

Like the spunky Irish of the past, the Bainbridge immigrants are making real efforts to help themselves. They have formed the IIRM, the Irish Immigration Reform Movement, to campaign for changes in the immigration law. The group also provides advice and support, helping local "illegals" deal with problems relating to their status, from health care to finances. They meet regularly in the dance hall in Gaelic Park.

The Bainbridge Avenue neighborhood follows Bainbridge Avenue in the Northern Bronx from 210th Street near the Montefiore Hospital and makes its way downhill till it turns east on 204th Street and ends at Webster Avenue. Bainbridge Avenue and 204th Street are the spine of the neighborhood—the place for shopping and socializing. At 3266 Bainbridge Avenue, between Van Cortlandt Avenue and 208th Street, there is a Valentine-Varian House, a historic reminder of an earlier ethnic group.

The housing in the area ranges from brick mansions with front gardens (on Bainbridge between 210th Street and the Reservoir Oval) to six-story apartment houses with fire escapes to frame houses sided with shingle. Off the Reservoir Oval there is a park and a playground. The neighborhood rubs shoulders with some of New York's worst slums and some of the city's best parkland.

Irish Pubs with Entertainment

—The Pubs—

The Irish pub of Bainbridge is no throwback to yesteryear trading on memories of an Ireland that no longer exists. It is not interested in bringing in tourists with sawdust and plaster leprechauns. The pubs are the kind that are currently on the streets of Kilkenny or Kildare. The jukebox is not all Danny Boy Irish. There is traditional Irish music along with the latest Irish rock from groups like U-2 and the Pogues.

The decor, if you can call it that, is informal shirtsleeves relaxation. One has a street sign from Dublin and another Guinness mirrors. The pubs have a preference for natural wood on the walls and on the facades. The long wooden bars are works of art; booths or tables in most cases are merely afterthoughts. The memories of home are in bottles or on tap: Guinness, Harp, Bulmer's, Woodpecker cider, and Jameson Irish whiskey. The conversations with rolling cadences and the ringing laughter are all about the present and tomorrow. On weekends and special occasions there are Irish singers and Irish bands or videos or cable hookups of Emerald Isle sporting events. There are pool tables where the guys play snooker as well as eight ball.

—The Music—

Irish traditional music isn't "When Irish Eyes Are Smiling," which was actually written by an American named Ernest Ball. There is a whole songbook of Irish classics known as "seisuns" (sessions) that the singers of Ireland have passed on from generation to generation.

In Bainbridge they sing songs about life and death, joy and melancholy. They sing about love's longing and the longing for a drink. They sing about Ireland's tragic history and a punch-up at a country fair. The Bainbridge bands usually include some combination of accordions or melodeons, tin whistles, pipes, flutes, fiddles, guitars, and banjos. Although similar to American folk music, Irish music takes itself less seriously and has a lilt and surer step-dance rhythm.

Irish rock in the sixties was Van Morrison-Boomtown Rats, English rock and roll, and American rhythm and blues. The new sound of Irish rock is more experimental; groups like Enya and Hot House Flowers interweave country, jazz, and Irish traditional with the latest rock sounds.

Bars with music (never any food) are always opening up but the good ones are there forever. Opening time is generally 8 A.M. Monday to Saturday, noon on Sunday, closing at 4 A.M.

Village Pub, *3207 Bainbridge Avenue (212-652-9829).*

The mural behind the bar is a beauty, with Celtic crosses and Irish castles. John Flynn is the genial host and a dead ringer for the Sam Malone character on TV's "Cheers."

Friday to Monday, there is traditional music. On Friday evenings there are lines as customers cash their paychecks.

Innisfree, *3178 Bainbridge Avenue at corner of 207th Street (212-655-2748).*

Light wood finished inside and out. Innisfree is favored by the sporting crowd. Every night there are videos of the latest Irish hurling and football matches. The weekend means mostly Irish rock music beginning on Friday. The Guinness and Harp are on tap.

Roaring Twenties, *366 East 204th Street (212-655-8337).*

The Roaring Twenties cannot be missed, with the windmill blades on the front. There are more Irish-Americans than recent immigrants. It alternates between Irish rock and traditional "seisun" Sunday and Monday nights. There are also music and sports videos from Ireland. The pool table gets a lot of attention.

McMahon's, *357 East 204th Street (212-655-6726).*

McMahon's is older and more low-key than some of the other Bainbridge pubs. The entertainment is old-fashioned Irish tenors from Thursday to Sunday with sports videos direct from Ireland on Monday nights. The Guinness and Bulmer are on draught.

Sarsfield's, *320 East 204th Street (212-655-9233/9102).*

Sarsfield's is large, with a big carved mahogany bar and wainscoting on the walls and antique ceiling fans. There is an additional row of bar stools at the counter on the wall. The jukebox is almost all Irish and English rock. The crowd is young and single. There's a pool table in the back and Guinness stout and Guinness gold (lager) on tap.

Irish Food from Blood Pudding to Soda Bread

Ireland is rural and the fare is simple straight-up country table. Irish shoppers in the old country fill their string bags with potatoes, leeks, cabbage, bacon, country sausage, and Irish soda bread. New York Irish have to settle for cooking traditions in cans with some major exceptions.

The Irish cakes and pastries are not overly sweet or rich, although Irish bakers generally use double cream rather than whipped cream in their fillings. The Irish prefer plain cakes with raisins, nuts, and ginger to seven layers with fruit fillings and thick icing. Even Irish wedding cakes are usually standard fruitcakes with a thin layer of white almond paste icing.

Eddie's Delicatessen, *3165 Bainbridge Avenue (212-655-7784). Daily 7 A.M.–11 P.M.*

Eddie has a shrine in the window surrounded with small American flags. It is dedicated to the Yankees, with yellowed newspaper clippings that tell the story of a dynasty from the Babe Ruth Yankees to the Casey Stengel Yankees. Eddie has Irish products with brand names like Erin. He has blood pudding (frozen) and genuine Irish bacon and sausage.

Oval Park Delicatessen, *281 East 204th Street (212-881-4146). Daily 7 A.M.–11 P.M.*

The Oval Deli has the most extensive selection of Irish foods in the Irish Bronx. It has McCann's oatmeal and Erin soups and every Irish jam in creation. It has a full line of Irish meat products, including black and white blood pudding, Irish sausage, and Irish bacon. There are fourteen newspapers from the counties of Ireland to take home with the authentic food.

Traditional Irish Bakery, *3120 Bainbridge Avenue. No telephone. Daily 6:30 A.M.–6:30 P.M.*

The best Irish baking in the city. It has scones, Irish Soda bread, porter cake with almond icing, and a carrot cake with the crunch of nuts. The ''barm brack,'' which straddles the line between fruit cake and raisin bread, is very special. The Bainbridge branch of the Traditional has tables where you can enjoy the baked goods with coffee. The colleens behind the counter are helpful and will take the time to explain the mysteries of Irish baking.

Irish Gifts

The best Irish gift shops are in Manhattan, where they are a novelty, not a part of everyday life. Most in Bainbridge are card shops with a few framed mottoes in Gaelic.

The Celtic Connection, *282 East 204th Street (212-231-1210). Monday–Friday 10:30 A.M.–7 P.M.; Saturday 10:30 A.M.–6:30 P.M.; closed on Sunday except around Christmas and St. Patrick's Day.*

The Celtic Connection covers Irish culture with books by greats like James Joyce and upcoming writers like the handicapped poet Christy Brown. They have hard-to-find Irish music tapes on cassettes and compact discs. Their gift items include bibs in green imprinted with Irish Princess, green shamrock coffee mugs, Irish knit ties, and Irish glassware.

Woodlawn

Directions: IRT-Lexington Avenue 4 to Woodlawn, take BX 34 bus in front of station to Katonah Avenue.

Woodlawn is bordered by Woodlawn Cemetery on the south, Van Cortlandt Park on the west, the Bronx River Parkway on the east and Yonkers to the north. Although it is physically isolated, it is a real extension of the Bainbridge area. The Woodlawn residential area supports the Bainbridge businesses. Woodlawn is a quiet single-family-house suburb of the Bainbridge Broadway.

The Woodlawn neighborhood has had a middle-class character for most of its history, from the time Washington and his army stopped using the Hyatt Homestead as an ammunition dump. It has seen a succession of English, German, Irish, and Italian families. The new Irish immigrants have revitalized the area.

Katonah Avenue is Woodlawn's main street. It has its own pubs and shops.

Fireside Pub, *4272 Katonah Avenue (212-655-9516). Monday–Saturday 8 A.M.–4 A.M.; Sunday noon–4 A.M.*

The Fireside is dark as a cave, with beer signs providing the only glow. It has live music from Thursday to Saturday and groups like Erin's Ghost

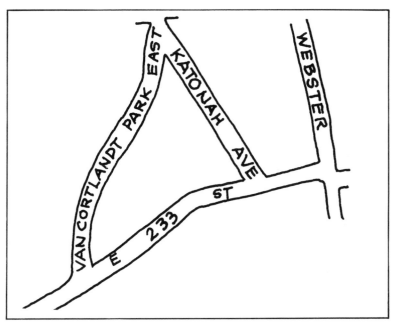

Woodlawn

directly from County Cork. The Guinness on tap goes great with "the best burger in town."

Traditional Irish Bakery, *4268 Katonah Avenue (212-994-0846). Monday–Saturday 5 A.M.–6:30 P.M.; Sunday 6 A.M.–1 P.M.*

Woodlawn has its own outlet of the Traditional. It is smaller than the Bainbridge branch and some of the Irish treats are sold out by noon.

Tri-Eddy's Deli, *4345 Katonah Avenue (212-324-4649). Monday–Saturday 8:30 A.M.–10 P.M.; Sunday 9 A.M.–9 P.M.*

Tri-Eddy's is a small deli with a large variety of Irish products. It has farm-fresh Galtree cheese, Irish bacon, sausages, black pudding, jams, cookies, and sandwich spread. Behind the counter there are shamrock Irish pride T-shirts and tickets to the latest closed-circuit sports events from the motherland.

The Sporting Life

The Irish have a strong sporting tradition and have been champions in American sports ranging from boxing to tennis. New York's Irish, especially the new immigrants, still participate in the fast-paced Gaelic games through sports clubs and associations. These amateurs bring a full-tilt enthusiasm to hurling and Irish football that is often missing from big-money professional sports.

Hurling has been played in New York Irish leagues since the middle of the nineteenth century. It's similar to field hockey, except that players can carry the ball downfield balanced on their sticks. Players score by hurling the ball under or over a crossbar. Hurling is a series of strategic fast breaks requiring plenty of stamina. Women's hurling (*camogie*) is also popular in New York.

Gaelic football is similar to soccer and rugby and as fast a game as Irish hurling. The ball in this brand of football, besides being kicked, can be dribbled and punched with a fist to get it downfield and into a net smaller than a soccer goal. The punching part can lead to impromptu boxing.

Gaelic Park Sports Center, *240th Street and Broadway (212-548-9568).*

Directions: IRT-Broadway 1 to the end of the line at 242nd Street and Broadway.

Irish hurling and Gaelic football are regular Sunday events at Gaelic Park. There are leagues for all ages and levels of proficiency. The teams have loyal followings and Cup Matches decide which is number one. The Gaelic Park Center is used for community benefits, and community organizations like the Irish Immigration Reform Movement hold meetings here.

════ Queens Irish—Woodside ════

Directions: IRT-Flushing 7 to 46th Street.

Introduction

Woodside is an old Irish working-class community. It was originally named by a newspaper man named John Kelly in the days before marsh and woodlands were replaced by warehouses, light industry, and semidetached houses. In the 1920s the Irish joined the German, Jewish, and Italian ethnics following the IRT line out of Manhattan into Queens. After World War II, Woodside had a real Irish flavor, with Irish papers on the newsstands and pools for Irish football in the bars. In the heyday of organized labor, the mainly Irish Local 6 of the International Typographical Union built the Big Six Towers in Woodside, a huge cooperative complex that was occupied

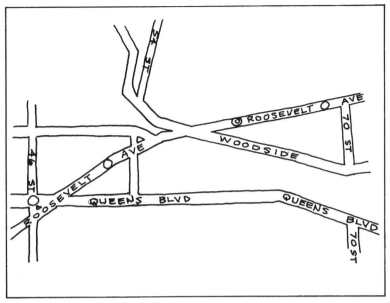

Woodside

predominantly by Irish families. Irish affluence and Irish retirement led to a movement out of the neighborhood. Just when it looked as though Woodside was becoming completely Oriental and Hispanic in the 1970s and 1980s, fresh Irish immigration revived the aging Irish enclave.

The Pubs

The Woodside Irish no longer dominate the blocks but they are definitely wearing the green in the bars and clubs scattered throughout the neighborhood.

Opening time is 10:30 or 11 A.M. during the week and noon on Sunday. Closing is 4 A.M. unless otherwise specified.

Farel O'Toole's, *70th Street and Queens Boulevard (718-478-6655). Restaurant closes 10:30 P.M. during the week and 11:30 P.M. on the weekend.*

Farel O'Toole's is big, very big, with five hundred or so turning out for its closed-circuit showings (on four TV screens) of Irish sporting events like the All Ireland Hurling Final. Weekends this pub/restaurant has rock music for its mostly young crowd. There is not much nostalgia for Irish cooking. When O'Toole's tried to serve real traditional boiled bacon with cabbage instead of corned beef and cabbage there were no takers. Sundays there is an Irish brunch with Irish bacon, blood pudding, sausages, and soda bread. Sometimes there's hurling in the back on Sundays starting at 9 A.M.

The Irish Cottage, *54-20 Roosevelt Avenue (718-429-9426).*

The Irish Cottage is where the young Irish immigrants go for disco. It has a large dance floor and tries hard to have what manager Pascal McMahon calls a "touch of class atmosphere." The barmaids and waitresses from Donegal and Monaghan have more than a touch of the blarney.

Bliss Tavern, *45-50 46th Street (718-729-9749).*

The Bliss accommodates both old neighborhood Irish and the new immigrants. Their music policy is strictly traditional, Wednesday through Saturday with a lone singer/guitarist, or a quartet of two guitars, piano board, and drums. The drink is also strictly Irish with Guinness, Harp, Bulmer's, Bailey's Irish Cream, and potent Irish coffee. The bar food sticks to hamburgers with an occasional bow to corned beef and cabbage.

Sally O'Brien's, *45-52 46th Street (718-729-9870).*

Sally O'Brien's is a cheerful pub with music every night but Tuesday. Mondays are crowded; that's when the Irish papers arrive and are picked up by the neighborhood people. There are occasional Irish sports videos.

* * *

If Woodside Irish are looking for Irish crafts and gifts they take a trip to Irish Imports, which has all the world-respected Irish names in crystal and china.

Irish Imports, *54th Street and Roosevelt Avenue (212-476-0633). Monday–Saturday 11:30 A.M.–7:30 P.M.; Sunday 11:30 A.M.–5 P.M.*

The Irish ladies who run the shop are patience personified as other Irish ladies try to choose between Donegal china and Beleek or Duiske glass and Cavan crystal. The merchandise ranges from Aran sweaters and Beleek crystal to green sweatshirts and framed Gaelic mottoes. The Irish music is traditional and modern and the imported foods are Irish and English. They encourage browsing.

═ That Old Gang of Mine (Manhattan) ═

The Old Neighborhoods

The Irish at one time or another have lived in nearly every neighborhood in the city. They struggled out of a Lower East Side slum called Five Corners in the early years of the nineteenth century only to find later generations living in a hellish Hell's Kitchen on the West Side of Manhattan between 30th Street and 57th Street. In both neighborhoods a century apart they had gangs that terrorized the city. In the nineteenth century there were poor Irish squatters in Harlem and at the turn of the century there were working-class Irish just north of German Yorkville. The last Little Ireland in the city was near the Bronx divide in Inwood and Marble Hill, the last vestige of Manhattan on the north shore of the Harlem River.

Place Marks

Directions: IRT-Lexington Avenue 4, 5, 6 to Brooklyn Bridge. IRT-7th Avenue 1 to Cortlandt Street

Police, Firemen, and Pols

The Civic Center

It is officially called the Civic Center, though most New Yorkers refer to it by nearby street names, Foley Square or Center Street. This collection of imposing public buildings, which make up the Civic Center, is a testament to the Irish who governed the city for more than a century. In their Irish homeland they weren't allowed the most rudimentary legal rights; in New York they built modern temples to administer justice.

North of City Hall, the core of the Civic Center is Foley Square at the junction of Duane, Lafayette, Pearl, and Center Streets. The area has gone through a number of changes from the time it was sixty feet under water and surrounded by the Lippensard swamp.

The English called it the Collect, and while tanners polluted its waters, the first paddle-steamer was tested here. In 1800 it was filled and drained as part of a relief project, then turned into a recreation site. The property was abandoned by the city to the slumlords when it started to sink. The Collect became the squalid habitation of last resort for freed slaves and Irish immigrants. Respectable citizens considered it a den of crime and demanded its demolition. A later generation of Irish turned it into one of the most architecturally impressive parts of the city.

Foley Square

Foley Square was named for an influential Irish politician named Thomas F. Foley. Working behind the scenes from his saloon, he pulled the strings to get Al Smith the nod for governor and stop Hearst from winning a seat in the U.S. Senate. The square is the location of two Corinthian-columned courthouses of grand dimensions. The U.S. Courthouse designed by Cass Gilbert is a thirty-two-story office tower with the classical impact of a Greek temple. It has fifty-foot columns and is topped by a gold pyramid. On the northeast corner of Pearl Street the County Courthouse rises like another Greek epic. The building's finely proportioned portico, three columns deep, holds aloft heroic representations of Truth, Law, and Equity.

Tombs

The infamous "Tombs," the Criminal Courts Building and Prison, is below the classic courthouses at 100 Center Street. Its morbid nickname relates to an earlier prison on the same site that looked like a pharaoh's tomb. Today's Tombs, despite its associations with crime and punishment, is an impressive Art Deco structure with towers of Babylon and cast-aluminum detail. Temporary detention has been shifted to Riker's Island.

Police Headquarters

New York's Police Headquarters dominates Police Plaza just opposite Foley Square. It's a red brick-and-cement block with a grid of small windows. This is one of the more recent additions to the Civic Center, circa 1973. On the south side of the plaza is the Rhinelander Sugar House Prison Window Monument, a small bit of history salvaged from a sugar warehouse of the eighteenth century, where Revolutionary War patriots were imprisoned.

Law enforcement in New York owes a large debt to the Irish. Throughout the years the police and the cop on the beat and later, the cop in the patrol car were practically synonymous with the Irish. As early as 1815, an Irishman named John McManus headed the New York police. By the time of the mass immigrations of the 1850s, the force was almost solidly Irish-born. The highly praised Irish police chief of that time, John A. Kennedy, went on to become the superintendent of the nation's main immigration station at Castle Garden.

In 1895 a New York Irish police inspector became a national celebrity for his ability to crack difficult cases. He also rose to the rank of police commissioner. A New York Irish woman, Mrs. Ellen O'Grady, became the first female deputy commissioner in 1918. Although the office of police commissioner is no longer an Irish sinecure, the Irish still represent a significant portion of the force, especially at the higher levels of captains and inspectors.

Police Academy Museum, *235 East 20th Street between 2nd and 3rd Avenues (212-477-9753). Monday–Friday 9 A.M.–3 P.M. Closed on weekends and holidays.*

The museum traces the history of the New York Police Department through police equipment and uniforms. There are early and unusual weapons and modern SWAT team gear and the nuts and bolts of emergency services. The Police Academy itself is on the guided tour.

Firehouses

The firehouse and fighting fires is an important part of the Irish New York experience. In the first half of the nineteenth century the majority of New York's volunteer fire companies were manned by the Irish. In that early era of fire fighting, companies raced one another to the scene of a fire and fought to be first at the hydrant. The companies were like fraternities with whimsical names like Old Maid's Boys, Fly by Nights, and Dock Rats. They were devoted to their horse-drawn engines, which they washed and polished all day and gave pet names like Hope and Honey Bee. Dousing fires created a big thirst and each company had a steward assigned to keep the drink flowing. The volunteer fire company with its deeds of daring was a real source of satisfaction for the city's dispossessed Irish. With a sense of pride, they wore the brilliant uniforms of their companies in citywide parades. When New York's firemen were put on the city payroll, the courageous Irish were the core of this efficient city service.

Firehouse Company No. 31 at 87 Lafayette Street, a block from Center Street, looks like a French Renaissance chateau. It's all towers and turrets and dormers and decorative crests. Now defunct, when it was built in 1895 it was state-of-the-art fire-fighting technology with automatic latches to release the horses at the sound of the alarm.

Fire Department Museum, *278 Spring Street (212-691-1303). Monday–Friday 10 A.M.–4 P.M. Closed on weekends and holidays.*

There is a whole fleet of fire engines from 1820 to the present along with antique and modern fire equipment. Paintings and drawings illustrate fire-fighters at work and at home in the firehouse.

St. Patrick's, New and Old

New York's Irish had a special regard for their priests, who stood by them in times of persecution and suffering and guarded with their lives Irish national traditions. Priests endured the great potato famine with their parishioners and followed them into exile, sometimes with a price on their own head for refusing to obey the British authorities.

When the British barred Catholic education, Irish parish priests started secret "hedge schools." In New York it was natural for the Irish clergy to lead the Irish community. Their greatest leader was Archbishop John Hughes, who guided the development of New York's Catholic Church during the critical years of mass Irish immigration.

John Hughes was already a bishop when he arrived in New York in 1838. He also possessed an indomitable will and the administrative skills that Irish politicians brought to Tammany Hall. From the beginning in 1839 he fought for Irish-Catholic justice, demanding a fair share of the public school society funds controlled by the Protestant establishment. When he was denied what he believed was his community's due, he started his own parochial school system.

In the 1840s, when thousands of Ireland's destitute landed in New York, he worked tirelessly for their welfare. He was a founder of the Irish Emigrant Society and brought over the Sisters of Mercy from Ireland to help immigrant women find employment. In the days when nativist Protestant mobs threatened Catholic churches and even burned down a cathedral in Philadelphia, he pledged in a typical rousing speech that the city would burn like "another Moscow" if anyone touched a single church. In another example of his powerful oratory, he stopped a raging mob in its tracks during the Civil War anti-draft riot.

The archbishop's greatest labor of love was St. Patrick's Cathedral, which he considered a monument to the New World's Catholics "worthy of the Catholic religion and an honor to this great city." Irish Catholics, who were routinely vilified and attacked for their religion, would have the most noble house of worship in the city.

The first St. Patrick's Cathedral still stands at the corner of Prince and Mott Streets. It was an impressive sanctuary when it was completed in 1809. St. Patrick's was America's second Gothic Revival church and was executed by the distinguished architect, Joseph Mangin. A fire in 1866 did substantial damage to its front, which could not be remedied by thorough reconstruction.

The Cathedral of St. Patrick's on Fifth Avenue between 50th and 51st Streets was designed by the foremost architect of the day, James Renwick, Jr., who happened to be a Protestant. The dimensions of this house of worship were and are spellbinding. Its twin 330-foot Gothic towers and arched doorways dominate Fifth Avenue like no other building. The church has nineteen bells that still call the faithful to worship. Inside, a brilliant geometric rose window lets in the shimmering light above a great organ with nine thousand pipes. Flickering candles light along the north and south aisles in front of the statues of saints and the Holy Mother. Above the altar are the "galeros," the hats of all the cardinals who have served St. Patrick's. St. Patrick's Cathedral Rectory, 460 Madison Avenue between 50th and 51st Streets (212-753-2661).

Political Saloon to Restaurant/Pub

The public house of Ireland was transformed into the Irish neighborhood saloon. It was the New York Irishman's private club, a place to enjoy the company of his peers and forget about his problems. Like the leather-armchair clubs of New York society, the Irish saloon was a pathway to political and employment contacts and a source of invaluable advice and information. In the sawdust precincts of some local saloon, the awkward Irishman from the other side learned how to fit in. The Irish saloon was also the home of the free lunch, where for the price of a beer a hungry workingman could feast on meat and potatoes. The Irish saloon keepers had stature in the community. They were frequently politically connected and, in times of difficulty, openhanded. The saloon was a neighborhood institution where people celebrated weddings and birthdays, and political questions were settled over the bar.

In the age of standardization the Irish saloon became the chain Irish bar. Hundreds of identical bars bore the names: Grants, Blarney Stone, Clancy's, White Rose, and Smith's. The heir to the Grant fortune even kept the political connection alive when he let Tammany elect him mayor. The only thing left of the old free lunch was a table with pickles and onions. The bars' working-class patrons were given good cheap lunches straight from a steam table. The lines formed for a corned beef, roast beef, fresh ham, or Virginia ham sandwich or plate and side orders of baked beans, mashed potatoes or home fries, and cabbage. There were long bars with light provided by neon beer signs and Four Roses and Fleischman's bar specials for singles and doubles. The glasses had bottoms as thick as two fingers and the bartenders were brisk and professional and came equipped with brogues. If the talk flagged there was always the jukebox and later television. McAnn's is the last of this breed.

The Irish saloon has changed with the times in Manhattan. The emphasis is more on food and ambience. The sophisticated city Irish have turned their backs for the most part on traditional Irish fare and have opted for steaks and chops and American ideas of Irish cooking. The Irish food in the typical restaurant/pub is represented by dishes like shepherd's pie (minced lamb in a mashed potato crust), fish and chips, steak and kidney pie, and corned beef and cabbage. Still the Irish breakfast with Irish bacon or Irish sausage has caught on as a popular Manhattan brunch.

Irish bar classics like Costello's have gone yuppie power lunch and dinner, and P. J. Clarke's, Irish playwright Brendan Behan's favorite, now takes reservations. Despite all the changes, Irish restaurant/pubs are alive and well in Manhattan and the pub crawl hasn't gone out of style. The best place to begin is in the granddaddy of them all, McSorley's Old Ale House.

McSorley's Old Ale House, *15 East 7th Street near Third Avenue (212-473-9148). Daily noon—1 A.M.*

Before 1970 the bar was filled with old Irishmen with hacking coughs and big thirsts and young NYU students staring at all the old Collier brothers clippings on the walls. Women weren't permitted entry in those days and the onion on the liverwurst burned like jalapeno peppers. Now only the college students are left along with the sawdust on the floor. The bar is still a wonderful relic and nothing can ruin the Guinness.

Tommy Makem's Irish Pavilion, *130 East 57th Street (212-759-9040). Monday–Saturday noon–10 P.M. Closed on Sunday.*

The Irish Pavilion is a sanitized Irish pub where even a temperance society gentleman would feel comfortable. In the front there is a tiny gift shop, 57th Street sleek, selling Aran sweaters and Waterford crystal. They have fine Irish folk music from Thursday to Sunday and sometimes the Irish virtuoso himself.

Glocca Morra, *304 Third Avenue between 23rd and 24th Streets (212-473-9638). Daily 10:30 A.M.–4:30 A.M.*

The Glocca Morra is nothing fancy—just good Irish fun. Wednesday to Saturday at 10:30 P.M. there's an Irish balladeer on the guitar and everybody joins in a freewheeling Irish singsong. This is a neighborhood place and everyone joins in, Irish or not. The hamburgers are the best thing to eat here.

Kinsale Tavern, *1672 3rd Avenue near 94th Street (212-348-4370). Daily 8 A.M.–4 P.M. Restaurant 11 A.M.–1:30 A.M.*

The Kinsale Tavern is one of the artifacts of this superannuated Irish neighborhood, but it still draws what Irish are left and Irish from all around the city. Everything about the bar from the chat to the barmaids is authentically Irish. There is an Irish brunch with Irish bacon, sausage, and blood pudding, but mostly the Irish and the Irish-Americans would rather eat steak.

Eamon Doran, *998 2nd Avenue between 52nd and 53rd Streets (212-753-9191). Daily noon–4 A.M.*

Eamon Doran started out as a typical New York beer-and-shot bar where it was so dark you could barely see the drinks. They added a menu with things like Irish-American corned beef and cabbage and hamburgers. Eventually they moved across the street to larger quarters and now, with a rise in the prices, Doran is a "licensed vintner." The food is still tasty Irish-American, with dishes like Gaelic steak made with good Irish whiskey. Doran also has steak and kidney pie and boiled bacon and cabbage.

Eagle Tavern, *14th Street and Ninth Avenue (212-924-0275). Daily 8 A.M.–4 A.M.*

The Eagle Tavern is a bar that has a feeling of rural wood-beam Ireland. It is relaxed even when the noise level is high-decibel. The people who come here know the Irish traditional music that is played Monday, Friday, and Saturday.

Abbey Tavern, *Third Avenue at 26th Street (212-532-1978). Daily noon–4 A.M.*

The Abbey Tavern is a set designer's idea of a Dublin pub, but that doesn't change the fact that it is pleasant, spacious, and attractive. The crowd at the bar and in the booths is young and upwardly mobile with a few old neighborhood regulars thrown in for good measure. The waitresses are mostly Irish. The Irish-American specialties like the shepherd's pie and the corned beef and cabbage are anemic.

O'Flanagan's, *1251 First Avenue at 65th Street (212-439-0660). Daily 11A.M.–4 A.M.*

O'Flanagan's is a real Irish singles bar with dancing and Irish groups every night of the week. It is crowded and noisy but it doesn't have that feeling of New York anonymity. People come here from Bainbridge, Woodside, and Irish Bay Ridge for a night out. The steak is prime and the Irish stew is rich with tender chunks of lamb and vegetables that haven't lost their flavor.

P. J. Clarke's, *915 Third Avenue at 53rd Street (212-355-8857). Daily 11A.M.–4 A.M.*

The crowd is very 1990 and the conversation very Madison Avenue, but the dark wood and stained glass bring back memories of the 1800s. The burgers are still good in the back room, but don't forget to make a reservation.

Costello's, *225 East 44th Street (212-599-9614). Monday–Friday 11 A.M.–4 A.M.*

Despite the power-lunch types in suspenders, the place still has plenty of old-time atmosphere. It is the beat of many of New York's Irish reporters.

Aran Sweaters and Other Irish Crafts

Manhattan's Irish craft shops prove that skilled Irish craftspeople can compete with the best.

Mattie Haskin's Shamrock Imports, *205 East 75th Street at 3rd Avenue (212-288-3918). Monday–Saturday 11A.M.–6 P.M.*

Mattie Haskin's is unaffected, like a little shop on a side street in Dublin. Everywhere, in no certain order, there are small Irish treasures: hand-knit turtleneck and crew neck sweaters, intricately carved Celtic crosses, and Waterford crystal. There are Irish newspapers and books and canned and packaged Irish foods.

The Grafton Shoppe, *22 East 54th Street (212-826-6511). Monday–Saturday 11 A.M.–9 P.M.*

The Grafton is located in Reidy's, which cannot be missed because it is a vintage freestanding building attached to a tall skyscraper. The shop is teacup-quaint with the prim flower-print look of a Victorian parlor. The Irish sweaters, lace, linen, mugs, and medals are attractively displayed.

The Irish Secret, *155 Spring Street (212-334-6711). Sunday–Wednesday 11 A.M.–7 P.M.; Thursday–Saturday 11 A.M.–8 P.M.*

Decorated in the colors of the Emerald Isle, the Irish Secret has elegant men's and women's clothes in muted tones. The service comes with a brogue.

════════════════ Festivals ════════════════

St. Patrick's Day

The St. Patrick's Day parade and celebration never had much to do with the city's Friendly Sons of St. Patrick, a Protestant association founded in the eighteenth century. The Ancient Order of Hibernians, a very active Irish fraternal and charitable organization, was the guiding force for this Irish day of recognition.

By the middle of the nineteenth century, the Irish had enough political clout to draw a crowd of politicians to this occasion. One mayor, the Honorable Abraham Hewitt, lost an election by refusing to attend the 1880 parade, but most followed the example of the Tammany political hack Mayor A. Oakley Hall, who wore a green tie, coat, and gloves to the reviewing stand.

St. Patrick's Day in Ireland is a solemn commemoration of the saint who brought Christianity to Ireland and a reaffirmation of the faith. In New York it's a no-holds-barred celebration of the Irish identity. The parade march starts at noon at Fifth Avenue and 44th Street, continuing up Fifth Avenue to 86th Street and over to Third Avenue.

March 17, St. Patrick's Day, is New York's day to be Irish. Everyone wears green, including fashionably dressed black mayors, and brogues are busting out all over. There are green carnations and green buttons, and a Kelly green stripe runs up Fifth Avenue. Every year there are a couple of clowns waving shillelaghs or puffing on Irish pipes or dressed like an advertising guy's idea of a leprechaun. School kids from the whole metropolitan area take the day off and try very hard to have a good time. Like others in the crowd busting to let loose, they are sometimes long on enthusiasm but short on spontaneity.

New York's Tammany Irish enjoy a traditional Irish breakfast with blood sausage and Irish bacon and maybe a drop of Jamison. Many attend a solemn mass at St. Patrick's. Afterwards Irish dignitaries with ceremonial sashes and medals mount a reviewing stand with childlike pleasure. St. Patrick's Day is the city's biggest and brassiest parade with the most spectators and the most marchers. Marching band after marching band after marching band strides up the avenue. Cardinal Hayes High School follows the Fighting Sixty-ninth and is succeeded by a group of firefighters in dress blues. Along the way some character, not necessarily Irish, climbs a lamppost for a better view. The beat of the parade goes on: one moment it's traditional "Stars and Stripes Forever" and the next it's jazzy "Blues in the Night"; kilted police pipers precede a boys' club band from Harlem. The crowd pauses to applaud a precision drill team and then there's the wink and the smile of the real Irish spirit as a group of elderly Hibernian rebels look as though they are on a stroll.

The Great Irish Fair

Directions: IND B or D to Coney Island stop.

The Great Irish Fair is New York's fun-filled meeting of the Irish clans. More than a million head to Coney Island for this Hibernian celebration on the second weekend of September. The site is particularly appropriate, since it was an Irishman named Patrick Boynton who opened the world's first amusement park in this former Brooklyn wilderness.

The legendary Steeplechase Park looks like new for this yearly weekend event in the first week of September. There are bandstands and spacious food tents and the boardwalk is filled with a lighthearted family crowd. Leading Irish folk singers perform and Irish athletes compete in special sports like Irish hurling, sponsored by the Gaelic Athletic Association. There is also a Colleen Queen with more style and grace than Princess Di. Each year traditional Irish boats race to Sheepshead Bay.

The fair is organized by the Ancient Order of Hibernians, the same folks who organize the St. Patrick's Day Parade. It is sponsored by private companies, like Stroh's Beer and Aer Lingus, and restaurants in Brooklyn like Peggy O'Neil's (8121 Fifth Avenue, 718-748-1400) have the food-tent concessions.

═══════════Irish Arts and Culture ═══════════

The Celtic tradition of the spoken and sung word is also a New York tradition. George M. Cohan applied it to the Broadway musical and Eugene O'Neill, in his tragic dramas (often dealing with Irish families), applied it to the Broadway stage. Some of New York's best writers have been Irish journalists. The late Jimmy Cannon, Pete Hamill, and Jimmy Breslin can say more in fewer words, whether in daily journalism or their more ambitious works, than writers who work out of ivory towers.

Irish culture is supported by bookstores and organizations.

Irish Books and Graphics, *90 West Broadway (212-962-4237). Monday–Friday 11 A.M.–5 P.M.; Saturday noon–5 P.M.*

Irish Books and Graphics has all the Irish books that can't be found anywhere else. It has books in Gaelic and rarities that have been translated from Gaelic into English. This bookstore annually stages an Irish-language short-story contest with an award for the winning entry. The shop also carries Irish prints, engravings, and maps.

The Irish American Cultural Center of New York, *1560 Broadway at 47th Street (212-391-1120).*

This group, made up of influential Irish union leaders, businessmen, and politicians, supports the whole spectrum of Irish-American culture. They are particularly active in fostering Irish-American cultural exchanges and Irish education. In the past they have had scholarship funds.

The Irish Arts Center, *553 West 51st Street (212-757-3318).*

The Irish Arts Center has classes in every aspect of Irish culture: dance, music, the Gaelic language, and Irish history. They are available at a nominal charge for members. The Irish Arts Center has an accomplished acting company, and leading Irish writers and directors have involved themselves in their productions.

The American Irish Historical Society, *991 Fifth Avenue at 80th Street (212-288-2263).*

The American Irish Historical Society has an extensive library of documents, letters, books, and newspapers dealing with the Irish experience in early and present-day America. It is all housed with infinite care in a grand Fifth Avenue mansion. The society has its own speakers bureau.

The Italians

History

Columbus may have discovered America, but Giovanni da Verrazano, an aristocratic Tuscan, was the first to see New York. He admired the natural harbor and appreciated the native hospitality, but he did not claim it for his sponsor, Francis I, King of France.

The real Italian presence in America began with the American Revolution. Filippo Mazzei played an important role in the fight for liberty. He was a friend of Jefferson, and his political thought influenced the Declaration of Independence. The British military authorities in New York jailed this revolutionary firebrand and he was forced to escape to France, where he wrote the first history of the American republic.

Throughout the nineteenth century, New York attracted Italy's own revolutionaries and political liberals. Lorenzo Da Ponte was one of the first. In 1805 he arrived to begin a new life at fifty-six. This Renaissance man had already been a revolutionary conspirator, and had written librettos for Mozart. Da Ponte was appointed the first professor of Italian at Columbia University and was instrumental in founding the Italian Opera House.

Giuseppe Avezzana was one of the leaders in the failed Piedmontese uprising. This soldier of the Italian Revolution found a safe haven in New York before he joined Mazzini and Garibaldi in an attempt to capture Rome. During his New York exile he ran a successful wholesale business on Pearl Street.

In 1835 an amnesty released twenty Italian freedom fighters from the dungeons of the Austrian Empire. New York warmly received the exiles and most decided to stay. Though they were a small group, they gained prominence in the business and cultural life of the city. Felice Forest became a professor at Columbia, a leading cultural commentator, and finally American Consul of Genoa. His friend, Louis Tinelli, made a fortune as a pioneer in the silk industry and bankrolled Italian freedom.

The year 1848 was a time of promise for the Italian revolution, but by 1849 the forces of reaction had triumphed and another generation of disappointed Italians sought asylum in New York. Giuseppe Garibaldi, the famed man on a white horse and the leader of the Red Shirts, was forced to contemplate the defeat of his Roman republic in Rosebank, Staten Island.

Italians living in New York before the Civil War were not all notable men of action but many had talent to spare. Italian musicians and opera singers entertained in society drawing rooms, and the works of Italian painters and fine cabinetmakers filled the best New York salons. The portrait painter Joseph Fagnani, who painted the crowned heads of Europe, made a fortune in America doing touched-up likenesses of New York's Four Hundred.

A small population of Italian barbers, bakers, tailors, and organ grinders were also struggling to make a living in the city. They lived in a northern Italian colony near the notorious Collect. New York's Italian elite provided them with a night school and a library to improve their English and learn about Italian culture.

Before the mass Italian migrations, most New York Italians, rich and poor, hailed mainly from the northern region of Liguria. This New York community was large enough to support its own newspaper, *L'Eco d'Italia,* first published by G. P. Secchi de Casali in 1849. They were patriotic enough to form the Italian Guard as part of the New York Militia under the command of the veteran of the Italian revolution, Marquis de Sant'Angelo.

Public-spirited Italian New Yorkers made an impact on the Civil War that was far out of proportion to their numbers. They formed their own volunteer Italian legion, staffed with crack Italian officers. A second New York Italian regiment, the Garibaldi Guards, was led by the Italian silk-industry millionaire Lieutenant Colonel Louis Tinelli, but was not completely manned by Italians.

The city's brashest and most flamboyant Civil War hero was also Italian. Count Luigi Palma di Cesnola was a courageous cavalryman with a hair-trigger temper who was resented by his superiors but commanded the loyalty of the enlisted men. He always led the charges of his unit, the Fourth Cavalry, into battle. At Aldie he was nearly killed and captured, but he lived to fight another day, leading the Fourth in the critical battle near Malverne Hill. Twenty years later he would receive the Congressional Medal of Honor. In the meanwhile, he made his mark as a diplomat, amateur archaeologist, art collector, and the director of the New York Metropolitan Museum of Art.

In the Gilded Age of the 1870s, Italian immigration increased at a rapid rate. Whether from north or south, these new immigrants were poorer and less educated than earlier arrivals. They were mainly peasants. Artists and artisans were succeeded by pick-and-shovel laborers. Some Italian civic leaders like newspaper publisher Secchi de Casoli actively discouraged these immigrants from coming. They believed that these lower-class Italians would damage the Italian image.

Italians, especially those from the poorer south, had no choice but to emigrate. Conditions in Italy were steadily becoming more impossible. Both the taxes and the population were rising while the soil eroded and the crops failed. Earthquakes and other natural disasters made things even worse. Southern Italians left their villages unwillingly. Although they planned to return, leaving was in itself an admission of failure.

New York's streets of gold were sometimes a shock. The urban squalor of Mulberry Bend was very different from the poor Mezzogiorno (south), even if the house in the old country had a dirt floor and no chimney. The decaying buildings of the Bend were damp and airless with forty families packed into five old wood-frame houses. The yards and alleys never saw the sunlight.

Despite the scrub brush and soapsuds, these slums were breeding places for disease. One neighborhood where Italians were dying from TB was called "lung block." The new arrivals had to deal with this unfamiliar and intimidating urban environment, usually without any English or even basic literacy. Sometimes they were also exploited by a labor boss called a "padrone" who used his superior knowledge of all things American to overwork and underpay them.

These *contadini* (peasants) brought a code and a communal feeling that outweighed their cultural disadvantages. They moved in with family and friends, duplicating supportive village ties in the New World. The streets of New York's Little Italy were reassuringly divided according to extended families, villages, and regions.

Southern Italians had the security of custom and social institutions in this alien city. They helped each other find work and shelter. Their sense of family honor enabled them to sacrifice for others in time of need. In the changing world of New York's urban jungle, Italian family relationships were stable. Divorce was rare and children took care of their parents.

A generation of southern Italians built New York's subways and streets and sewer system. They dug the tunnels and ditches, poured the concrete, and laid the pipe. It was backbreaking labor making a modern city. Their children would have the luxury of joining skilled trades or getting an education and becoming professionals. Italian immigrants were workers; they weren't interested in politics that smacked of Old World deceit and intimidation.

The Italians were comfortable in a world of personal face-to-face relationships; mutual aid societies and village associations were usually local groups, an extension of the vertical villages where families and *paesani* lived. The padrone who hired the southern Italian labor and acted as the go-between with the bosses may have taken a big percentage of the wages, but his face was familiar and he spoke the same dialect.

Southern Italians were handicapped by a lack of English and little education but they weren't the narrow suspicious immigrants of the tabloid stereotypes. They were learning quickly to help one another as a group. As early as 1883 Manhattan Italians joined groups from Brooklyn and Hoboken and Newark to raise money for the victims of the earthquake at Ischia. A year later a larger New York–New Jersey confederation raised funds for the city's Italian poor.

The Society of Italian Immigrants was formed in 1901, bringing together American progressives, the Italian community, and the Italian government to deal with the underlying causes of Italian-American poverty. Though Italian welfare groups weren't on the scale of other immigrant nationalities, Italians weren't on the public rolls or dependent on public charities.

Gino C. Speranza, as secretary of the Society for Italian Immigrants, urged the construction of a building to lodge new arrivals. In 1908 the society's spacious five-story building provided clean rooms and Italian cooking at a fair charge. Dr. Antonio Stella, a pioneer in public health, investigated the health problems of Italian New Yorkers with the aid and support of the Italian government. His findings led to the establishment of a clinic in the city in 1910.

Italian New Yorkers, though more concerned with work than with international politics, patriotically supported America and their Italian homeland in World War I. Some Italian reservists even crossed the sea to rejoin their units. New York's Italian neighborhoods were scenes of rallies and parades, American bond drives, and collections for the Italian Red Cross.

Two hundred thousand Italian-born Americans were now settled in the five boroughs of New York. The majority were Manhattanites and a quarter were Brooklyn *paesani;* the remainder were spread throughout the other three boroughs. Counting second-generation Italians in the city, they were 420,000 strong.

Italians were starting to come of age politically. They were losing their distrust of American politics that had been fostered by Old World feudalism. Tammany took note and began to back Italian political leaders and candidates. Michael Rofrano was Tammany's eyes and ears in the Lower East

Side's Italian districts. In 1912, 60,000 Italians in East Harlem elected the first Italian, Salvatore Cotillo, to the State Assembly. He would become one of New York's many Italian State Supreme Court judges.

But it was a freewheeling, independent Republican at odds with the Tammany machine that finally put Italians on New York's political map. His name was Fiorello La Guardia and though he was not the typical immigrant Italian, he reflected Little Italy's hopes and aspirations.

La Guardia's family came from the north of Italy; his mother was a Triestina of Jewish descent. He was born in New York City, brought up in Arizona, and raised in the Episcopalian faith. He developed his strong social conscience working as an interpreter on Ellis Island. In 1916 he became the first Italian-American to be elected to Congress, serving his Italian East Harlem district for a decade with time off to earn medals in World War I.

In 1933 La Guardia became the ninety-ninth mayor in New York's history. In his twelve years in office he won the support of all New Yorkers interested in good government and reform. The flamboyant "Little Flower" was always in the public eye, whether smashing slot machines with an ax or fighting a tenement fire or reading the funnies on the radio. He saved the city with a "No more free lunch" philosophy, and by the end of his watch he could take credit for sixty new parks and expanding the whole public housing system.

While La Guardia was making his name in politics, Generoso Pope was becoming the most powerful Italian businessman in the city. He came to New York from Southern Italy with only ten dollars in his pocket and in less than twenty years was the city's first Italian millionaire. Pope owned *Il Progresso,* the most popular Italian-American newspaper, and sat on the board of banks, but he made his millions supplying sand and gravel for the city's big construction projects like the New York subway.

New York's Italians had their own Italian sports heroes. In 1936 Joe DiMaggio took over center field for the New York Yankees. A figure of grace and power, the image of the Yankee Clipper, he won the Most Valuable Player award three times and his record for hitting safely in fifty-six games has never been broken. Having a DiMaggio in the local limelight made Italian immigrants feel less alienated. He was an inspiration for Italians to excel.

Though the city's Italians were making great strides, they were still objects of prejudice, employment discrimination, and immigration restrictions. In response, Italian New Yorkers came together in a spirit of ethnic pride and proclaimed an Italian identity that transcended their village and region. They joined the Sons of Italy en masse and supported the city's Italian *prominenti* in erecting statues to Italian national heroes like Garibaldi.

Though Mussolini appealed to Italians' pride in their past, he eventually alienated Italian New Yorkers with his foreign adventures; when war came, they enthusiastically rallied behind the Stars and Stripes. Former Mussolini supporters like Generoso Pope disavowed the dictator, admitting the error of their ways. The New York Italian community mobilized to buy $49 million worth of war bonds.

World War II disrupted traditional Italian-American life. Italian women left their insulated communities to work in war industries and began to question traditions and customs. Italian men came back from the war with new American dreams. For some it was time to move out of the neighborhood and get a white-collar career on the G.I. Bill. The postwar prosperity had its own momentum and Italian New Yorkers became upwardly mobile.

In politics Italian Democrats didn't have to petition Tammany. They were Tammany. Carmine De Sapio became the Manhattan leader in 1949. From the start he cut the party's connections to organized crime and wiped out obvious patronage abuses. De Sapio had style and intelligence, and Bronx leader Ed Flynn said he was the "first Tammany man since Murphy I can sit with and not have to talk to out of the side of my mouth."

In 1949 there was a three-way race for mayor involving four Italians. There was the Regular Democrat Ferdinand Pecora, the independent renegade Democrat Vincent Impelliteri, the Republican Edward Corsi, and the notorious radical Vito Marcantonio. Impelliteri ran on his record as a crusading prosecutor and his refusal to take orders from Tammany. "Impy," as he was known, won handily.

Italian communities were closer than other ethnics. Transplanted Italian villages shared traditions and a common history. But despite a determination to preserve their neighborhoods, the demolition ball and the siren song of the suburbs led to an exodus from the inner city's Italian enclaves.

The sixties were a time of change. Italian families were smaller and the Italian husband was no longer the unquestioned patriarch. The grandchildren of Italian laborers were moving up. There were Italians in the staid merchant banks of Wall Street and even on the boards of the stock exchange. Ralph De Nunzio was director of Dreyfus Offshore Trust and served as vice-chairman of the board of the New York Stock Exchange.

The world of New York media was their oyster. Grace Mirabella was the New York fashion phenomenon who edited *Vogue,* and Gay Talese was pioneering the "new journalism" in the *New York Times.* Jerry Della Femina was making people laugh in Madison Avenue's most imaginative ads and founded an agency that would advise presidents.

Though many Italians were very visible in positions of high status and authority, they were still routinely categorized as criminals, part of an international Italian crime conspiracy. Exposés about the Mafia sold papers and political crusades against the Mafia got people elected to office. In too many instances Italians were depicted in films and television as gangster heavies or ignorant buffoons.

On June 29, 1970, over fifty thousand Italian-Americans came to New York's Columbus Circle to celebrate Italian-American Unity Day. Everywhere there were Italian flags and green, white, and red bunting and big buttons with catchy Italian pride slogans. Italian New Yorkers who had never attended a rally in their lives were here to express pride and anger. Some of the speeches were emotional harangues, but there was a real sense of warm Italian togetherness.

In the era of black power, many thought the time had come for Italian ethnic affirmation. Italian groups like the Sons of Italy organized letter-writing campaigns and boycotts. In the universities there were calls for Italian studies along with black and Puerto Rican studies. Taking a leaf from other activist ethnics, Italians formed groups like Americans of Italian Descent (AID) to fight group defamation and the Italian American Civil Rights League to aggressively pursue "Italian Power." A new generation of Italian New York politicians, including future vice presidential candidate and Congresswoman Geraldine Ferraro, made Italian-American rights a national issue.

In the 1990s New York is a city of a million Italian Americans. They can point to Italian Governor Mario Cuomo and Italian Senator Alfonse D'Amato and Italian judges and Italian district attorneys and Italians on the stock exchange and Italians in the boardrooms. The community knows it has arrived.

════════ The Old Neighborhood ════════

Mulberry Street

Directions: IRT-Lexington Avenue 6 to Canal Street.

Introduction

Before the mass Italian migrations to Little Italy in lower Manhattan, the Mulberry Street area was already a byword for urban decay. It was an Irish ghetto ruled by street gangs with housing going back to the Revolutionary War. The Mulberry Bend block was the worst in the area, no more than a series of wood-frame hovels without drainage or sanitation.

The southern Italians who came to Mulberry Street in the 1880s and 1890s were forced to live in "eight by ten rooms" in tall brick tenements in which

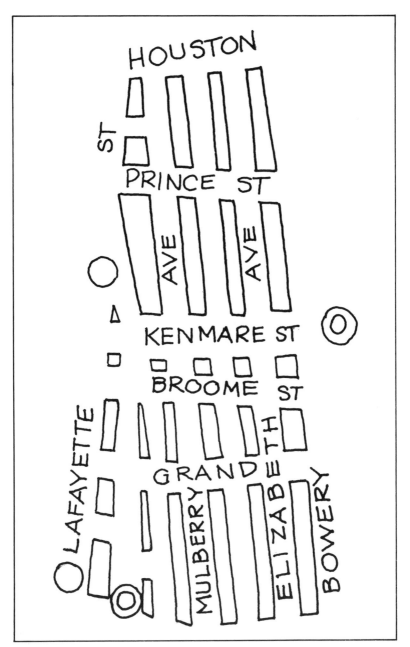

Mulberry Street

windows and ventilation were scarce. These "dumbbell tenements" were built so close to one another that the rear apartments never saw daylight. The Italians of the Mulberry Street area were 40,000 strong. They were packed into seventeen short blocks in a neighborhood that had no public baths and no playgrounds and only three public schools. Diseases like TB ran rampant in these "lung blocks." Fires were a constant hazard.

Despite the crowds and congestion, Italian neighborhoods were alive with activity. Peddlers in front of ash barrels and carts shouted and touted day-old bread and secondhand clothes, while housewives with lace shawls bargained hard with vendors for meat, fish, or vegetables. Men with handlebar mustaches lounged in front of storefront village associations and social clubs or took careful aim on the *bocce* court in a busy park. Long lines led to Italian banks, where people were sending remittances to the old country. On saints' days everyone joined the colorful processions with the movable shrines and the uniformed bands. Mulberry Street Italians were developing a sense of community.

While the men of Mulberry Street labored on city construction projects or worked for Italian building contractors like the Paterno brothers, the women worked in the garment industry and were important supporters of the International Ladies Garment Workers Union.

The unofficial mayor of Little Italy was James March (Antonio Maggio), who recruited construction gangs for the railroad and was the Republican Party's man in the neighborhood. Paul Kelly (Paolo Vaccareli) got out the vote for the Tammany machine and later became a vice president of the International Longshoreman's Union.

By 1915 the Italians of Mulberry Street started moving out of the neighborhood. They moved to northern Manhattan, where they established a large Little Italy in East Harlem, and over to the Bronx. They moved to the Brooklyn areas of Red Hook, Williamsburg, and Greenpoint, where they found work on the docks. They represented less than half of the population of the Lower East Side neighborhood.

But there was still a vital Italian culture in Little Italy, with Shakespeare in Italian and Italian marionette shows. There was even Italian vaudeville. When the movies became the art form of the masses, there were Italian movie theaters. The Festa of San Gennaro was as much a cultural celebration with music and singing and traditional foods as a religious commemoration.

By the end of World War II, second- and third-generation Italians could no longer totally identify with all the "old ways" and were looking for the acceptance that comes with Americanization. They longed to live in green one-family house suburbs instead of tenement walkups. Little Italy was fated to become an ethnic enclave of the old, who still had that Italian attachment to their geographical home.

Today the Italian population of Little Italy is about 5,000 and still declining. The young families are mostly Portuguese or Chinese. The neighborhood itself is getting smaller as an expanding Chinatown crosses the Canal Street border. Still, Mulberry Street has succeeded in maintaining its Italian identity from Houston Street to Canal Street.

While a lot of the Italian locals have deserted to suburbia, Italian businesses have stayed behind, along with the tourists. Little Italy's restaurants, gift shops, food stores, and cafés exist for the tourist trade. They have in the process been modified to mainstream American tastes. There aren't enough Mulberry Street *paesani* to keep all the prices moderate and all the food authentic.

The tourists from the outer boroughs and out of town don't seem to mind. Little Italy is a feeling, a wholehearted delight in food and wine and friends. The street scene is spirited, especially during the summer when white wrought-iron furniture blocks the sidewalks and diners sigh with satisfaction as if they were seated in an Italian garden instead of breathing in the fumes of Mulberry Street gridlock.

Little Italy al Fresco

Little Italy's Italian restaurants don't pretend to be gourmet. Their clientele isn't interested in subtlety. The portions are big, the sauces are unadventurous—not too much garlic or seasoning—and the service is warm and obliging. In this Americanized Italian cuisine regional cooking is irrelevant. The pasta sauces of choice are *carbonara* (a white sauce with cream and bacon), *Alfredo* (with heavy cream and cheese), *Bolognese* or *ragu* (a red sauce with meat), and an all-purpose *marinara* (tomato sauce).

The authentic cuisine of the south, which uses olive oil instead of butter, stints on cream, is lavish with tomatoes, and prefers vegetables like eggplant to T-bone steak is a thing of the past. Stuffed pastas like *cannelloni* (a pasta tube filled with ricotta cheese and flavored with meat) and *lasagne* (sheets of pasta layered with meat sauce) are popular in the Mulberry Street neighborhood. The meat, fish, or fowl can be prepared in a number of ways from Milanese to Francese, but there is a preference for *parmigiano* (covered with melted Parmesan cheese) with a thick topping of tomato sauce. Everything is drowned in the sauce as if to give the customers more for their money.

Benito's The Original, *174 Mulberry Street (212-226-9171).*
Benito's II, 163 Mulberry Street (212-226-9012). Daily noon–11 P.M.

Benito's I was so small—tables on top of one another—they had to open another one. The *mozzarella in carozza* (in carriage), the Italian version of a cheese melt, and the pepper stuffed with vegetables, real tastes of the south, are best.

Paolucci's, *149 Mulberry Street (212-925-2288). Monday, Tuesday, Thursday, Friday noon–10:30 P.M.; Saturday, Sunday noon–11 P.M.*

Paolucci's is gaudy chandelier and gold-trim Little Italy. The simple but well-prepared dishes like the manicotti, lasagne, and the veal *pizzaiola* are served in the Federalist splendor of the nineteenth-century Van Rensselaer mansion.

Umberto's Clam House, *129 Mulberry Street (212-431-7547). Daily 11 A.M.–6 A.M.*

Umberto's is for late-night hunger pangs. The pictures of the celebrities (Cher, Frankie, and Johnny) on the walls are the restaurant bona fides. The clams are all right and the linguine in hot sauce is not so hot, but the *scungilli* (conch) in the hot sauce calls for a second order.

Il Cortile, *125 Mulberry Street (212-226-6060). Daily noon–1 A.M.*

Il Cortile is northern *prominenti* Italian, a restaurant for unhurried four-course dinners. The interior is formal and the waiters know when to anticipate. The *linguine pescatore* with shrimp, mussels, and clams in the shell is a seafood dinner in itself.

Luna, *112 Mulberry Street (212-226-9683). Tuesday–Saturday noon–2:30 P.M., 5:30 P.M.–8:45 P.M.*

With only twelve booths, Luna is long lines and long waits. The restaurant is from the good old days when New Yorkers never heard of *pesto,* and *penne* was something to write with. It is a spaghetti and meatball and sausage kind of place where everything comes *parmigiano.*

Patrissy's, *98 Kenmare Street (212-226-8509). Monday–Friday noon–11 P.M.; Saturday, Sunday 1 P.M.–11 P.M.*

Patrissy's is Little Italy not too far from the maddening crowds. But the dining room is spacious and formal and the waiters don't have to shout to be heard. Patrissy's features a plate called the "Contadino," an Italian-American invention that is a contadino (peasant) dream with potatoes, onions, and mushrooms combined with filet mignon, chicken, and sausage.

Cafés and "Pasticcerie"

The Italian café is the right dessert ending to Little Italy dining. Linger over espresso spiked with Sambuca or Amaretto and a custard-rich *sfogliatelle* (thin layers of pastry filled with sweetened cream) and watch the other tourists watching you. The cafés come in all sizes, from banquet big to shake-hands-with-the-next table. Like everything else in Little Italy, the pastries aren't afraid to be obvious; they're richness and sweetness in overdrive.

Café Biondo, *141 Mulberry Street (212-226-9285). Daily noon–2 A.M.*

Café Biondo is cathedral ceilings and high windows that create a feeling of space in this intimate room. The capuccino comes frothy, with the barest touch of cinnamon, and the espresso is rich enough to be spiked with Sambuca. The *cannoli* with fresh custard and crisp pastry are standard Italian *pasticceria* that are well above standard.

Caffè Roma, *385 Broome Street (212-226-8413). Daily 8 A.M.– midnight.*

Caffè Roma is where the Italians in Little Italy go for their capuccino and cheesecake. Afternoons, old men in button sweaters and nonpower suspenders sit around the ice-cream-parlor tables under the big chandelier munching on *pignoli* cookies and nursing their espressos.

Ferrara's, *195-201 Grand Street (212-226-6150). Daily 8 A.M.– midnight.*

Ferrara's is so big that it should be impersonal, but isn't. Its pastries may be mass-produced but they still manage to taste homemade. Ferrara's special coffee roasts and chocolates are available with twenty-one kinds of dessert in its sleek on-the-premises shop.

Pasta Makers and "Salumerie"

Little Italy before the wars had specialty stores for every variety of Italian food. There were *latticini* for dairy and cheeses, *salumerie* for smoked meat and sausage, and fresh pastas came from the pasta maker. The food shops in Little Italy now are fewer in number and more eclectic. The food shopping is one-stop.

Alleva Dairy, *188 Mulberry Street (212-226-7990). Monday–Saturday 8:30 A.M.–6 P.M.; Sunday 8:30 A.M.–2 P.M.*

The white tile floor and the provolone hanging from the pressed tin ceiling are reminders that Alleva is almost a century old. Rows of rare and common imported Italian cheeses—delights like smoked mozzarella with pepperoni, fresh mozzarella with prosciutto, and *manteche,* mozzarella wrapped around a ball of butter—line the display cases.

Di Paolo's Dairy, *206 Grand Street (212-226-1033). Monday–Saturday 8:30 A.M.–6:30 P.M.; Sunday 8:30 A.M.–2:30 P.M.*

Di Paolo's is so unassuming, who would know it's bursting with small treasures? Its gorgonzola cheese is so special that it makes you forget rich desserts.

Italian Food Center, *186 Grand Street (212-925-2954). Daily 8 A.M.–7:30 P.M.*

The Italian Food Center is just an old-fashioned Italian grocery with a new-fangled name. There's a deli counter where people line up during the lunch hour for hero sandwiches. The shelves are filled with family-size cans of olive oil, boxes of imported pasta, and specialty items like the Motta *panettone* (Italian fruit cake).

Piemonte Homemade Ravioli Company, *190 Grand Street (212-226-1033). Tuesday–Saturday 8:30 A.M.–6 P.M.; Sunday 8:30 A.M.–4 P.M.*

Piemonte has the familiar spinach pasta and lasagne as well as the more novel *calamari* pasta, made with squid ink. It has the flat noodles of the north and the hard, eggless macaroni of the south. The round and square ravioli come filled with meat and cheese as do the *tortellini* and the *cappelletti.*

Italian T-shirts and Novelty Spaghetti

Every tourist strip has its souvenirs and Little Italy is no exception. The gift and souvenir shops are mostly of the button and T-shirt—it's all for a laugh—variety. There are examples of Italian kitsch that even a mother couldn't love and not much Italian craftsmanship.

Carosello Pentagramma Italiano, *119 Mulberry Street (212-925-7253). Daily noon–10 P.M.*

Il Pentagramma has statues of Italian heroes, saints, and men playing cards. Some are for a shrine, most are for a rec room. The lamps and ceramic stands are so extreme the tourists can't stop staring. Customers are treated like family.

Forzano Italian Imports, *128 Mulberry Street (212-925-2525). Daily 10 A.M.–midnight.*

Forzano is the source for Italian imports from hardware to cooking utensils. It has the most extensive collection of Italian records and cassettes in the city. The store is large enough to browse around without being approached by a salesclerk.

Italian Feste

The Italian *festa* is a set-piece celebration in every Italian village. It is a universal religious rite and the affirmation of a very specific regional heritage. It is the saint's day of a neighborhood. The *feste* in Italy were ancient rituals sanctioned by both civil and spiritual authorities. They were dedicated to the saint (or the Virgin Mary), to whom a locality or village was consecrated.

Church of the Most Precious Blood, *113 Baxter Street (212-226-6427).*

The mass for New York's most spectacular *festa,* San Gennaro, is held in this simple sanctuary. The shrine of San Gennaro has a place of honor in the front of the church. When the church was consecrated in 1891 the parish was Italian in religious traditions and spirit. Now there is not even a regular mass said in Italian. The Most Precious Blood refers to the blood of Christ, but it also has special significance for San Gennaro, whose blood was recovered as a relic and miraculously liquefies on September 19, the date of his martyrdom.

Festa San Gennaro

San Gennaro was the bishop of Benevento when the Emperor Diocletian declared war on Christians in 305. He was arrested and tortured but would not recant his faith. The proconsul had him thrown into a burning furnace, but by a miracle he came out unscathed. This patron saint of Naples has been called upon to intercede in fires, plagues, droughts, and other natural disasters.

The feast of San Gennaro is New York's most popular *festa.* Every September the stately bronze and silver bust of the Bishop of Benevento, San Gennaro, the parton saint of Naples, passes through the crowded streets of Little Italy to the accompaniment of local bands as theatrical as any New

Orleans marching band. The movable shrine is the object of prayers and is showered with bills of all denominations. It's a spiritual homage and a sentimental return to a simpler ethnic past.

For seven days, visitors to Mulberry Street—temporarily renamed Via San Gennaro—gorge themselves on sausage heroes, *calzone, scungilli,* and *calamari,* or any of the Chinese, Filipino, or Greek dishes that have been added to the *festa* menu in recent years. There are rides and games of chance and shooting galleries with stuffed-animal prizes. Every year there are those who say San Gennaro is getting too commercial but it's only getting bigger and better. Anyone with an aversion for crowds should take a detour.

The Italian Village

Directions: Ind D or F to West 4th Street.

Introduction

Little Italy south of Washington Square Park in Greenwich Village was the site of the city's first Italian parish, which was established in 1866. Before immigration was blocked by World War I, it was the third largest Italian neighborhood in Manhattan.

As Italians became Italian-Americans, many moved out of the Italian village. But thousands stayed with a new sense of solidarity based on the neighborhood instead of their Old World connections. They dropped out of *paesani* associations and joined local chapters of the VFW and local social/athletic clubs.

The Italians emulated their Irish fellow Catholics and built church halls and gyms and started vocational schools. They joined the old Irish political organization and elected their own man, "Bashful Dan" Marinelli, as district leader. He was succeeded in 1943 by Carmine De Sapio, who would become head of the city's Democratic Party.

After World War II, middle-class Americans and Bohemians started moving into this convenient New York neighborhood. They were outsiders generally ignored by the Italian community, but they gradually changed the character of the neighborhood. In 1961 an aspiring politician named Ed Koch took the Democratic leadership away from Carmine De Sapio.

The rents in parts of the Italian Village have stayed low and parts of the neighborhood, around Sullivan and Thompson Streets from Bleecker Street to Spring, have stayed Italian. The neighborhood is aging and there are few young families. There are few Italian young men hanging out on the corners or Italian housewives hanging out of the windows.

The neighborhood still has its Italian ethnic sights and sounds. On warm nights South Village Italians, including Old World widows in black, sit

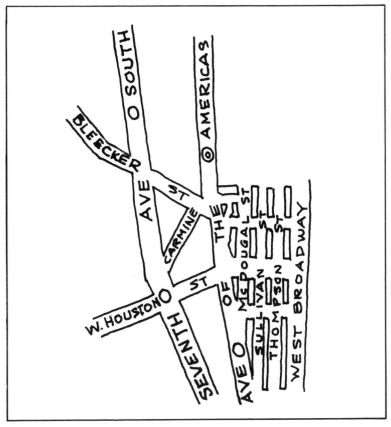

The Italian Village

outside their tenements talking in dialect and watching the SoHo types with their haircuts of the month. There is still the pasta maker and the old Italian parish and the Italian bakery with brick ovens. It is also *risorgimento* time in the South Village. Luncheonettes are being transformed into "Casa de Cafés" and the restaurants are going *al fresco*. The Italian Village is going up-market.

South Village Cucina

The Italian restaurants in the South Village are in most cases less frantic than the ones in the other downtown Little Italy. The restaurants have their share of out-of-towners but they also have neighborhood followings that keep their food honest. The portions are a proper size and there is enough time between courses to be sociable. The menus have their original touches and their gimmicks. The main restaurant drags are Sullivan and Thompson Streets.

Cucina Regionale, *208 Thompson Street (212-475-9021). Daily 4 P.M.–11 P.M.*

The restaurant is Keith Herring graphics and a young crowd; the bill of fare is a sampler of pastas from around the world. The exotic pastas like the one from Trentino, *Capellini Bassano del Grappa,* made with apples and *grappa* (a potent grape liquor), usually taste much better than they sound.

Rocco Restaurant, *181 Thompson Street (212-677-0590). Daily noon–11 P.M.*

Rocco doesn't put on any airs. It's the old tile floor, pressed-tin-ceiling type of place. It delivers real southern Italian food. The veal cutlet Siciliana with eggplant and mozzarella is a regular specialty of the house that gets repeat business.

Il Bocconcino, *168 Sullivan Street (212-982-0329). Daily noon–11 P.M.*

The restaurant is plastered with pictures by the owner, Gilberto Petrucci, whom the press once called the King of the Papparazzi. He runs the restaurant with the same dedication that enabled him to capture celebrities on film in compromising situations. His *rigatoni* in artichoke sauce is light and as refreshing as the Italian Raffo beer.

The Bleecker Street Market

The food stores in the Italian Village are an assortment that would gratify an exacting Italian chef. Shoppers come from all over Manhattan in pursuit of some of their special products. The butchers, bakers, and pasta makers are mostly on Bleecker, where pushcarts once were the rule.

Faicco Pork Stores, *260 Bleecker Street (212-243-1974). Tuesday–Thursday 8 A.M.–6 P.M.; Friday, Saturday 8 A.M.–7 P.M.; Sunday 9 A.M.–2 P.M.*

Coils of hot pepperoni and fennel and cheese sausages are displayed like choice sirloins. In the sausage department there are also dry-cured sweet

Italian sausages (a pepperoni with less bite) suspended from the ceiling. Center cut pork chops take center stage stylishly flecked with fennel.

Ottomanelli's Meat Market, *281 Bleecker Street (212-675-4217). Monday–Friday 6:30 A.M.–6:30 P.M.; Saturday 6 A.M.–6 P.M.*

Success and a chain of unremarkable restaurants haven't taken away the Ottomanelli edge. It sells the young baby veal that makes for a tender scaloppine. October at Ottomanelli's means venison and wild boar sausage.

Porto Rico Importing Company, *201 Bleecker Street (212-477-5421). Monday–Saturday 9:30 A.M.–9:30 P.M.; Sunday noon–7 P.M.*

Shoppers come from all over the city to buy Porto Rico's special coffee blends. They have two types of espresso roast, Italian and French, both outstanding. There's a choice of espresso makers and a tea section for the noncoffee drinkers.

Raffetto Ravioli, *144 West Houston Street (212-777-1261). Tuesday–Saturday 8 A.M.–6 P.M.*

Ravioli—round and square, cheese and meat—is a small part of this pasta storehouse. Besides the standard pastas, Raffeto has small squares of *quadrucci* for soup and the tiny *conchigliette* (small shells), that really hold the sauce. They have the right Arborio rice for al dente *risotto.*

Rocco's, *243 Bleecker Street (212-242-6031). Daily 8 A.M.–midnight.*

Rocco's is the New York source for *panettone,* the Genovese version of fruit cake with a hint of anisette and fennel. The bird's nest here is flaky and light, with just a dusting of powdered sugar. Rocco's is less expert when it comes to layer cakes and rich pastries.

Zito & Sons, *259 Bleecker Street (212-925-9803). Monday–Friday 6 A.M.–6 P.M.; Saturday 6 A.M.–4 P.M.; Sunday 6 A.M.–1 P.M.*

The Bleecker Street Zito is a 1925 brick-oven original and it shows it. It is the yardstick for all other Italian bakeries in the city. The breads studded with bits of prosciutto and olives don't need anything in the sandwich.

The Saints of the South Village

St. Anthony's Church, *163 Sullivan Street (212-777-2755)*.

St. Anthony's was the first American-Italian parish church, and it has the cornerstone from 1866 to prove it. The church still impresses with its Gothic facade of arches and stained-glass windows, especially at night when it's lit up. The church is losing its predominantly Italian character and no longer has a regular mass in Italian.

—St. Anthony's Festa—

St. Anthony of Padua is very popular in Italy and a patron saint of many villages. The *festa* of St. Anthony commemorates the saint as the patron of the South Village neighborhood where the New York Italians had their first parish. Before Cardinal John McCloskey brought Italian Franciscans over to open St. Anthony's in 1866, local Italians had been holding their services in the basement of an Irish church.

The Feast of St. Anthony of Padua is an eleven-day tribute to one of the founders of the Franciscan Order. St. Anthony, like St. Francis, was a gentleman of wealth and position who embraced a life of poverty and service. The image of this saint, associated with good fortune and recovery of lost objects, is carried in a grand procession from St. Anthony's on Sullivan Street on the last day of the *festa,* June 15.

The *festa* is smaller than the nearby San Gennaro but there are enough sausage and *zeppole* stands and games of chance to keep the tourists occupied and the church coffers filled.

—Our Lady of Carmine Street—

Our Lady of Pompeii Church, *25 Carmine Street (212-989-6805)*.

When Francesca Cabrini first came to America to serve the Italians of New York, she was assigned to the parish of Our Lady of Pompeii, where she helped parishioners cope with the problems of a strange country and taught teenage girls embroidery. There is now a shrine in the Church of Our Lady of Pompeii dedicated to the first American saint, St. Francesca Cabrini, who did so much to help Italian-Americans by opening hospitals, schools, and orphanages.

The church still has Italian masses on Sundays and holidays at 11 A.M. and its own *festa*. It had tried for a number of years to hold a *festa* in honor of their Neapolitan patron, Our Lady of Pompeii, but the inclement October weather eventually put an end to it. Now they hold the *Festa Italiana*.

—Festa Italiana—

The *Festa Italiana* is a celebration of the Italian religious tradition and Italian customs. It takes place during ten days in July from the twentieth to the thirtieth, when Carmine Street is the site of Italian food stands, games of chance, and children's rides. Our Lady of Pompeii is opened to the general public with guided tours and special masses. The Our Lady of Pompeii band entertains the crowds.

East Harlem

Directions: First Avenue bus M15 to 116th Street.

Introduction

In its prime, Italian East Harlem was one of the largest Italian neighborhoods in America. It went from 100th Street to 116th Street from Third Avenue to the East River. The neighborhood had a strong sense of its Italian village past. The streets in Italian Harlem were divided into the regions of Italy. Natives of Piacenza occupied 104th, 105th, and 106th Streets. The Sicilians settled on 107th Street. Naples and Salerno were represented on 109th Street and 110th Street. Benevento took over 111th Street and 112th Street. The Barese lived on 117th Street and 118th Street.

The wide thoroughfare of 116th Street with its neat row houses was reserved for the *prominenti* of the neighborhood and was sometimes called Doctor's Row. It was the home of the wealthiest Italian businessmen, lawyers, doctors, and pharmacists. The Italian workingman came here for advice in dealing with the city bureaucracy.

The streets of early Italian East Harlem were also divided into villages: the inhabitants of San Fratello in Sicily made 107th Street in East Harlem their destination when they traveled to the New World; the immigrants from Polla in Salerno transplanted their village to 110th Street. They eventually carried over their village *festa* for Our Lady of Mount Carmel in the 1880s. This pattern repeated itself all over East Harlem and village associations proliferated.

First Avenue was the main shopping street and pushcart market. All the foods from home were available here: Italian butchers sold tripe, brains, and tongue; Italian dairy stores, *latticini,* sold fresh mozzarella and ricotta; fresh pasta was offered for sale every day. There were separate restaurants for the different regional cuisines.

The East Harlem neighborhood had a strong sense of independence. It chose and elected its own leaders without the help of Tammany. In 1912 it put Salvatore Cotillo into the State Assembly. When La Guardia couldn't get

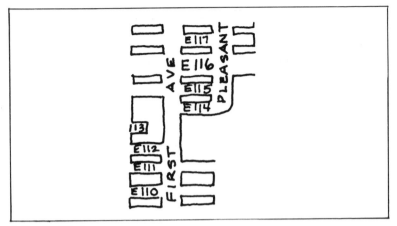

Italian East Harlem

elected congressman in Democrat-controlled Mulberry Street, he moved up to East Harlem and became a congressman in 1917. La Guardia was succeeded by Vito Marcantonio, who continued La Guardia's crusade for the poor and represented East Harlem even when it ceased to be Italian.

One of the neighborhood's most active citizens was Leonard Covello. He was a prominent member of political and cultural committees representing the neighborhood. He was the principal of Benjamin Franklin High School from 1937 to 1957 and was instrumental in adding Italian language cultural courses to the public school curriculum.

With each new American-born generation, Italian East Harlem changed dramatically. The neighborhood became more cohesive and people were more aware of their Italian identity. They dropped the village dialects and mixed Italian with their English and English with their Italian, coining words like *stritto* for "street." The old men still played *bocce,* but the kids played stickball and stoopball and flew kites from the roofs.

In the 1940s and 1950s, affluent Italians deserted the area by the thousands for the detached houses and backyards of the Bronx, Brooklyn, and Queens. Although they were escaping escalating crime, violence, and addiction, they left with regret. Each year the former residents, now numbering more than a thousand, return to the old neighborhood to relive their memories at the Feast of Our Lady of Mount Carmel.

East Harlem, Italian Harlem is almost a memory. Only the rare Italian outpost remains. It's hard to believe that once upon a time around the turn of the century it was an urban replica of Italy. Father Rofrano, the priest at Our Lady of Mount Carmel, says there are about twelve Italian businesses left in the area but that's including plumbing suppliers and a body repair shop.

Italian Harlem's Last Stands

Morrone & Sons, *324 East 116th Street (212-996-3638). Monday–Saturday 7 A.M.–5 P.M.; Sunday 7 A.M.–1 P.M.*

The bakery has a forlorn look on all-Hispanic 116th Street. During the week it's mostly empty, with maybe two elderly ladies comparing ailments near the entry. Most of its business is the commercial restaurant trade. The breads straight out of the coal oven are winners, especially the spicy prosciutto and the yeasty Calabrese.

Rao's Restaurant, *455 East 114th Street at Pleasant Avenue (212-534-9625). Monday–Friday 7 P.M.–10 P.M.*

Rao's has the reputation, the limousine clientele, and the three-month wait for reservations. The southern Italian food is better than ordinary and the ambience is a change from the Four Seasons, but is it really worth all the fuss?

Andy's Tavern, *2257 First Avenue at 116th Street (212-410-9175). Monday–Thursday 4:30 P.M.–9 P.M.; Friday, Saturday 4:30 P.M.–10 P.M.*

Andy's Tavern is not exactly gracious dining; it's a neighborhood bar that looks like a neighborhood bar. But Andy's is all about food and any of the oldtimers in the neighborhood will back that up. Andy's owner is the chef who made Rao's a restaurant legend. He works magic with any scaloppine or veal chop, pasta or risotto.

Our Lady of Italian Harlem

Church of Our Lady of Mt. Carmel, *449 East 115th Street (212-534-0681).*

The Church of Our Lady of Mt. Carmel was revered as a religious sanctuary for its replica of the village of Polla's Lady of Mount Carmel and the Christ Child, which became an object of prayer and the medium of miracles. Pope Pius X recognized the value of this statue by donating two emeralds to the crowns of the Virgin and Child. The church had an active rectory and a school that helped the immigrants make the transition to American life.

But the church's days of glory are over. The Puerto Ricans in the neighborhood go to Spanish parishes and the church ministers to a small aging population. It has many more funerals than Confirmations.

Festa of Our Lady of Mt. Carmel

The Feast of Our Lady of Mt. Carmel is celebrated in both Italian East Harlem and Little Italy in the Bronx between July 6 and July 17. The East Harlem feast was initiated by immigrants from Polla, a village in the province of Salerno in southern Italy noted for its violin virtuosos.

In New York these natives of Polla started out as pick-and-shovel laborers but were soon proprietors of popular restaurants. They formed a society in 1883 under the auspices of the church, vowing to continue the Polla tradition of the veneration of Our Lady of Mount Carmel. It began with a paper image of Our Lady and a handful of people in a courtyard on 110th Street. By the beginning of the twentieth century, it had become a religious event that attracted thousands of pilgrims from around the country.

In its heyday, the East Harlem feast attracted half a million. The streets were practically impassable in the days leading up to and following the July 16 procession of the crowned Virgin. Today only a remnant of this once-proud Italian neighborhood follows the Holy Mother up and down the streets of East Harlem and the big band that leads the parade has dwindled to fewer than ten pieces. Most of the celebrants are Haitians, who also venerate Our Lady of Mount Carmel, and they provide their own music, chanting prayers to a Caribbean beat and repeating Mary's name.

Surrounding the church are the food stands offering sausages and zeppole, games of chance, and even small amusement park rides. But in this feast the carnival spirit doesn't intrude upon the solemnity of the occasion.

═══ Neighborhoods at Mid-Passage ═══

Belmont

Directions: ITR-Seventh Avenue 2, or IRT-Lexington Avenue 5 to White Plains Road. BX12 bus to Arthur Avenue and Fordham Road.

Introduction

Italians call this Little Italy in the Bronx Arthur Avenue or Belmont. It was originally part of an area called Fordham Manor on land that had belonged to the Lorillard estate. Irish and Germans settled here in the 1890s; the Irish worked for the local millionaires, the Germans farmed small truck gardens. The Italians came to know Belmont first-hand from building its streets and subway lines.

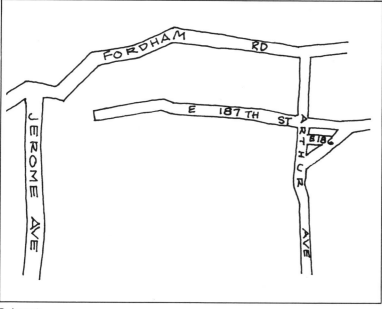

Belmont

The Italians who moved to this practically rural area were natives of Sicily, Calabria, and Campania. Many came by way of East Harlem, lower Manhattan, and south Brooklyn. They eagerly occupied the small frame houses of the Irish and set about planting trees and cultivating flowers and bringing relatives from overseas. In 1906 a storefront mission became the foundation for the Italian parish of Our Lady of Mount Carmel. In 1930 the census counted 27,500 Italian-Americans in Belmont.

Belmont was a vital community with large families and a warm Mediterranean feeling. There were bustling streets filled with pushcarts, Italian specialty shops, *bocce* in the park, and family picnics at Orchard Beach. The kids raised pigeons and played American games like Johnny-on-the-pony and ring-a-levio till they joined their hard-working fathers in the serious backbreaking business of making a living. It was a world of mutual respect and personal pride where a man gave his all for his family.

After World War II and the postwar boom, upwardly mobile Italians followed the new expressways into Westchester and Long Island. They were tired of apartment living and weren't interested in the neighborhood's aging wooden houses. Although their numbers were bolstered by later immigrations from southern Italy, by 1970 over five thousand Puerto Ricans were living in this Bronx Little Italy. In another ten years Belmont was merely an Italian enclave in an area that was mostly black and Hispanic. Many in this old neighborhood still do business and communicate mainly in Italian. Mass is still said in Italian and there are Old World processions in honor of Saint Anthony and Our Lady of Mount Carmel. Italians play cards in their own social clubs, read Italian newspapers, and listen to records on the Italian hit parade. An equally large group in this community are more American-oriented and mainstream in their tastes and preferences. Both groups celebrate with equal enthusiasm an Italian triumph like Italy's world soccer cup victory.

Though bordering one of the most dangerous areas in the city, this stable Italian enclave is considered by such authoritative sources as the *New York Times* to be one of the safest sections of the city. It is more than just one neighbor looking out for another; community organizations like the Merchants' Association provide unity and support. In a changing city, this is one neighborhood that seems able to maintain its equilibrium.

Arthur Avenue Eating

The restaurants in the Bronx's Little Italy more than hold their own with the Manhattan originals. Fancier than the tile-on-the-floor, plastic-tablecloth Italian restaurants, they still have the unaffected warmth of the old neighborhood. The service is personal and off-handedly friendly and the food doesn't compromise with mainstream American tastes. Even the humble *calzone,* pizza, or *pasta e fagiole* (pasta and beans), gets special treatment. The ingredients are high quality and the preparation imaginative.

Mario's, *2342 Arthur Avenue (212-584-1188). Tuesday–Saturday noon–10:30 P.M.; Saturday, Sunday noon–midnight.*

Mario's was a location in the film *The Godfather* and for a while curious Manhattanites traveled to the Bronx. The food is deftly prepared and draws the neighborhood Neapolitans. The *insalata di mare,* the seafood antipasto of mussels, octopus, squid, and shrimp, is the freshness of the sea.

Dominick's, *2335 Arthur Avenue (212-733-2807). Wednesday– Monday noon–10 P.M.*

Dominick's is no menus and off-handed service and shouting across tables. It's bustling and good-natured and the payoff is excellent food. The *putanesca* clings to the fettucine with the sharpness of the anchovies, capers, and olives, and the *osso bucco* (veal shank) is a giant knuckle of meat practically falling off the bone in a rich thick *pomodoro* (tomato) sauce.

Amici's, *566 187th Street (212-364-8250). Tuesday–Friday 11 A.M.–11 P.M.; Saturday, Sunday 11 A.M.–midnight.*

Amici's is leisurly dining, the relaxed hum of conversation, and a concerned and Old World–courteous staff. The cooking is the classic south with plenty of garlic and no stinting on the olive oil. The meat and fish are first quality from the neighborhood.

Roma Luncheonette, *636 187th Street (unlisted telephone). Monday–Saturday 11 A.M.–9 P.M.*

Walk into Roma's and you are in the middle of a conversation; the TV keeps playing and everybody keeps talking. The soups are the thing here and they have specials every day. The *zuppa fagiola* (bean soup) and *lenticchie* (lentil soup) are thick with overtones of garlic and *pancetta* (Italian bacon).

Espresso and Sympathy

On Sundays families still observe the traditional promenade, strolling along Arthur Avenue and 187th Street. Some push baby carriages or hold the hands of small children and all are wearing their Sunday best. After the strolling, there's the café-sitting and a *torta,* dripping sweetness, a strong espresso, or a capuccino sprinkled with chocolate.

De Lillo Pastries, *606 East 187th Street (212-367-8198). Daily 8 A.M.–7 P.M.*

De Lillo is friends and neighbors greeting one another and getting down to the serious business of *cafe panna* (with homemade whipped cream) and a large slice of Italian cheesecake. The rich homemade *gelato* and *spumoni* fit right into this ice-cream-parlor setting.

Egidio, *622 East 187th Street (212-295-6077). Daily 7 A.M.–8 P.M.*

During the day the line forms at the bakery counter in front. The mini pastries (bite-sized *cannoli* and *amaretti*) are a favorite to bring when visiting the relatives in Canarsie. The kids in their neat parochial-school uniforms line up for *gelato* cones.

Caffè Margherita, *673 East 187th Street (212-364-8910). Daily 8 A.M.–8 P.M.*

The Caffè is al fresco in the summer and in the open Italian way locals bring their own lunches and enjoy a Margherita *caffè freddo* (iced coffee) and the sun. There is a mural inside of Neptune cavorting with the Nereids that is pure café primitive.

Artuso's, *670-678 East 187th Street (212-367-2515). Daily 7 A.M.–9:30 P.M.*

Artuso's is located in a big contoured building that from the outside looks like a modern banquet hall. Rich layer cakes revolve in vertical glass cases, and long display counters show off the bird's nest, *cannoli,* and *sfogliatelle* (pastry leaves layered with rich custard). Despite their size and on-the-premises wholesale bakery, Artuso's has not lost the personal touch.

Shopping Arthur Avenue

In Belmont, shopping is no one-stop experience, it is a round of specialty shops: butcher, baker (one for bread and one for pastry), fishmonger, deli, dairy, and pasta maker. For some unexplained reason, the gift shops also sell fresh-roasted Italian-style coffee.

Arthur Avenue Retail Market, *2344 Arthur Avenue (212-367-5686). Monday–Saturday 8 A.M.–5 P.M.*

In 1940 the streets of Arthur Avenue at 186th Street were a pushcart bazaar, selling everything from fresh mozzarella to espresso machines. Mayor La Guardia did not want Italian New York to have an old-fashioned pushcart image, and was convinced that pushcarts weren't very sanitary. So he had the Arthur Avenue Retail Market built to house the local vendors.

Forty years later Mayor Koch and a small army of Democratic office-holders rededicated the market after a six-hundred-thousand-dollar facelift. Even the Italian Consul was on hand to make a speech. The market is all brick and as sturdy-looking as a small armory. Inside, high-quality meats and cheeses attract the most discriminating Italian shoppers in the city. The produce is plentiful and more economical than in Manhattan markets. The market is at its busiest on weekends, but the trade is very steady since locals keep up the Italian practice of shopping daily.

While the market is mainly a produce market where artichoke hearts, eggplants, and radicchio are staples, it also has delis, groceries, and a café in the back.

—Pasta Makers—
Borgatti's Ravioli & Noodle Company, *632 East 187th Street (212-367-3799). Monday–Saturday 9 A.M.–6 P.M.; Sunday 8 A.M.– 1 P.M.*

Borgatti's deals in the obscure and the hard-to-find, like *macherroni alla chitara,* a cross between dense dry and light fresh pasta cut on a device that resembles a frame with *chitara* (guitar) strings. And it sells carrot, spinach, and tomato noodles.

The Pasta Factory, *686 East 187th Street (212-295-4857). Daily 9 A.M.–6 P.M.*

The Pasta Factory prides itself on using extra fancy durum wheat enriched flour, whole-milk ricotta, and first-quality Romano cheese in its pastas plain and stuffed. The round cheese ravioli is so good it doesn't need sauce.

—The Bread and Cookie Bakers—
Terranova Bakery, *691 East 187th Street (212-733-3827). Daily 6 A.M.–7 P.M.*

The Terranova family brings the same expertise to baking bread as they do to making pasta at the Pasta Factory. They make prosciutto bread and olive bread—winter breads in Italy—year round.

Madonia Bakery, *2348 Arthur Avenue (212-295-5573). Monday– Saturday 7 A.M.–6:30 P.M.*

Madonia's cookies are plain and buttery good and their breads are crusty enough for the neighborhood's best restaurants. The semolina bread, which comes in small, medium, and large, is perfect for heroes.

—The Italian Groceria—
Tino's Salumeria, *609 East 187th Street (212-733-9879). Monday–Friday 7:30 A.M.–6 P.M.; Saturday 7 A.M.–6 P.M.; Sunday 7:30 A.M.–1 P.M.*

The only problem with Tino's is that they are always so busy. The Italian cold cuts include the fine Bolognese mortadella and the *cotechine* (a three-inch sausage) made with pancetta.

Marchese Grocery, *Arthur Avenue Market (212-933-2295). Monday–Saturday 7 A.M.–6 P.M.*

Past the produce to the left, Marchese's grocery offers real buys for the experienced shopper. Many items like the extra-virgin Apulio olive oil (equal to the best Tuscan) are half the price of Manhattan's Italian food emporiums.

Calandra Cheese Shop, *2314 Arthur Avenue (212-365-7572). Monday–Saturday 9 A.M.–6 P.M.*

Calandra is always looking for new cheeses, imported and domestic, to satisfy their demanding customers. Samples are given out to help the customers decide. They carry a full line of imported Argentinian cheeses.

—Italian Meat and Fish—

Arthur Avenue Poultry Market, *2356 Arthur Avenue (212-733-4006). Tuesday–Thursday 9 A.M.–5 P.M. Friday–Saturday 8 A.M.–5 P.M.*

The market is barnyard-noisy with cage upon cage of chickens, pigeons, and rabbits. Shoppers pick and choose as though they were at an ASPCA kennel and their dinner comes fresh-killed.

Calabria Pork Store, *2338 Arthur Avenue (212-367-5145). Monday–Saturday 7 A.M.–7 P.M.*

The Calabria looks like a smokehouse with all the meats hanging from the ceiling. It packs country-thick Calabrese sausages that come studded with peppercorns and bits of garlic.

Tim's Meat Market, *600 East 187th Street (212-733-3637). Monday–Thursday 8 A.M.–5:30 P.M.; Friday 7 A.M.–6 P.M.; Saturday 6:30 A.M.–5 P.M.*

Tim's is an Old World butcher shop selling whole baby lambs and goats to Old World customers. They stock unusual cuts: heads, hoofs, and intestines.

Frank Randazzo's Sons Fish Market, *2340 Arthur Avenue (212-367-4139). Monday–Thursday 7 A.M.–6 P.M.; Friday 5 A.M.–7 P.M.; Saturday 7 A.M.–6 P.M.*

The Randazzo's curbside stand-up clam and oyster bar catches the eye. Nearby there are mountains of ice and nests of seaweed for crabs, squid, eels, and swordfish.

—Italian Gifts—

Cerini Coffee & Gifts, *660 East 187th Street (212-584-3449). Monday–Saturday 9 A.M.–6 P.M.*

Among the aromatic mounds of Italian roast coffee waiting to be ground, there's an odd collection of gaudy statues, crystal chandeliers, silver trays, and espresso machines. In the middle of this unusual assortment, a line of wedding favors pops out. It's fun rummaging through Franco Cerini's attic.

Costanza's Gifts, *624 East 187th Street (212-364-8510). Monday–Friday 7:30 A.M.–6 P.M.; Saturday 7:30 A.M.–5 P.M.*

The coffee is the main attraction. The lamps, china, crystal, and statues look as though they are laid out for a jumble sale.

—The Culture Corner—

Enrico Fermi Cultural Center, *610 East 186th Street (212-933-6410). Monday 10 A.M.–6 P.M.; Tuesday, Wednesday noon–8 P.M.; Thursday noon–6 P.M.; Friday 1 P.M.–6 P.M.; Saturday (winter only) 10 A.M.–5 P.M.*

Belmont's Italians are extremely proud of their heritage. The Enrico Fermi Cultural Center was established to maintain that cultural tradition of Michelangelo and Verdi and Enrico Fermi. It's one of the city's main resource centers for information about the Italian-American experience and has an extensive library of books in Italian. The Center is dedicated to the Nobel Prize–winning physicist, Enrico Fermi, an Italian immigrant, scientific innovator, and humanitarian.

Our Lady of Arthur Avenue

Our Lady of Mt. Carmel Church, *627 East 187th Street (212-295-3770).*

The Church of Our Lady of Mt. Carmel dominates East 187th Street between Hughes and Belmont Avenue. Inside the neo-Gothic structure, the Virgin of Mt. Carmel, parton saint of the community, benignly watches over her "children." Regular masses are said in Italian and confessions are heard in Italian. The church is the focal point of the annual feasts of St. Anthony and Our Lady of Mt. Carmel.

Festa of Our Lady of Mt. Carmel

The Belmont Feast of Our Lady of Mt. Carmel started in 1906. It was block after block of decorations, bands playing dramatic Italian music, and climactic fireworks.

The procession starts at 5:30 P.M. on the Sunday after the July 16 saint's day. Members of the parish surround the statue of Our Lady of Mount Carmel and adorn it with flowers and scapulas. Male members of the church carry the Madonna on her alter. The women's sodality leads the procession, followed by a small band, who in turn are followed by the priests and church officials. Some women and older men crowd around the statue, at times touching it and crossing themselves. Most walk beside it and behind for the two hours it takes to traverse the whole neighborhood.

Meanwhile the younger people are crowding around the stands that sell all kinds of Italian delicacies and trying their luck on the wheels of fortune. It is more animated than the Manhattan *festa* but it's sometimes tough to navigate the narrow streets and impossible to park.

Festa of St. Anthony

St. Anthony of Padua is honored in the Bronx as well as Manhattan. The celebration of the Feast of St. Anthony lights up 187th Street from June 5 to June 15. The street carnival of food stands, music, souvenirs, and rides starts every night at 6 P.M.

Bensonhurst and Italian Brooklyn

Directions: IRT-Lexington Avenue 6 to Canal Street. Change to the IND N to 16th Avenue.

Introduction

Cornelius van Werkhoven, a functionary for the Dutch West India Company, got this future part of Brooklyn in a swap with the Indians. He called it New Utrecht in honor of the old Dutch city. In 1783 this area stood four-square behind the American Revolution, erecting a liberty pole at what is today 83rd Street and 18th Avenue.

The neighborhood retained its Dutch character into the nineteenth century and there is still a Dutch Reformed church dating from 1828 in a bucolic churchyard on 18th Avenue. Some of the most prestigious Dutch families in Brooklyn were members of the congregation.

Bensonhurst got its name in 1887 from a family called Benson who owned a square mile of farmland in New Utrecht. Shortly afterwards they subdi-

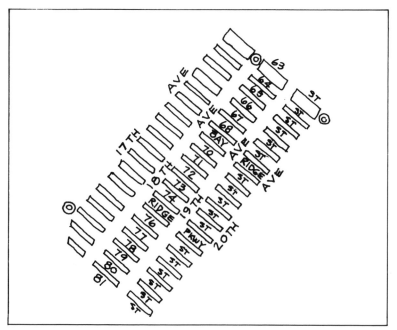

Bensonhurst

vided their holdings, opening them up for settlement. By the turn of the century Bensonhurst was a thriving resort.

The construction of the BMT subway line brought a new population of Jews and Italians making their way out of Little Italy and the Lower East Side. They moved out of the tenements into sturdy brick and stucco two-family houses, but they still carried the closeness and warmth of the old community. Life was the extended family and local institutions like the candy store and the corner grocery.

While the Jewish portion of Bensonhurst has declined, with only a remnant concentrated around Bay Parkway, the Italian presence is strong. They make up the majority of what the City Planning Department Calls Bensonhurst, an area bounded by 14th Avenue on the northwest, 61st Street and McDonald Avenue on the northeast, 26th Avenue on the southeast and Gravesend Bay on the southwest.

Today Bensonhurst has the flavor of a New York Italian neighborhood circa the 1930s and 1940s. Italians fresh off the boat from Sicily or Argentina mingle with first- and second-generation Italo-Americans. Newcomers nostalgically cling to the stand-up espresso bar and the sit-down card-playing social club, while the old guard belongs to the Rotary and enjoys a sirloin with a side order of pasta.

Bensonhurst's main drag, 18th Avenue, has a split personality. There are bakeries, cafés, and restaurants that are Old World authentic alongside made-in-New York Italianate pizza parlors and restaurants. Tastes and ingredients change with time in Brooklyn but the feeling of the grand Italian opera, dramatic and joyful, stays the same. The tenors strut and the sopranos preen.

Bensonhurst Nights Out

Bensonhurst is still a believer in home cooking; the eating ritual keeps families together and besides, the food is better. On the cook's night off (and that may mean Father), there are nights out in Bensonhurst restaurants.

Randazzo's Steak House and Restaurant, *7222 18th Avenue (718-234-9125). Sunday–Thursday 11:30 A.M.–11:30 P.M.; Friday, Saturday 11:30 A.M.–1 A.M.*

Randazzo's serves choice New York sirloins and *Mezzogiorno* (southern) pastas with rich back-to-basics *putanesca* (anchovies, capers, garlic, black olives, tomatoes) and *amatricana* (bacon, hot peppers, tomatoes) sauces. The chicken *scarpiello,* thick with garlic bits in olive oil, and the veal *rollatine picante* are Italian alternatives to the sixteen-ounce steak.

Gambero & Rosso, *7016 18th Avenue (718-259-1858). Tuesday–Sunday noon–11 P.M.*

Gambero and Rosso are the surf part of the Bensonhurst turf. The devil gets his due with their house special, lobster *fra diavalo.* Stick to seafood when it comes to the pastas, white or red *alle vongole,* clam sauce, and the mixed seafood.

Espresso with and without Music

The café/espresso bars of Bensonhurst are out of the Italian immigrant past or Italian modern. They are definitely not Italian local color for the tourists.

The tables are filled with young Italian immigrants at their ease, making their points in musical Italian and punctuating their speech with an Italian semaphore of the hands. The tables are filled with older men—less laid-back, excitedly mixing metaphors in Italian and English. They are retired from the construction trades and small businesses. The espresso has a strength only found in Italy, like the bonds between the friends who meet in the cafés regularly.

On weekends the cafés are a family affair and there is music and Sambuca or Amaretto or a scotch on the rocks to toast the weekend. The Italian pastry is consumed and enjoyed with thorough gusto. There is an illusion of being in Italy that is not self-conscious or sentimental.

The cafés have conventional groups playing rock with Italian and American lyrics, but there are also traditional musicians and singers. There are slow serenades, frantic tarantellas, and whispered lullabies played on a concertina, *chitarra battente* (small guitar), shepherd's flute, and tambourine. The music is so infectious you don't have to know the steps to get up and dance.

Caffè Mille Luci, *7123 18th Avenue (718-837-7017). Monday–Saturday 5 P.M.–midnight.*

The café sparkles with its mirrors, pale stucco, and smart chandeliers. This is urban Italian that never hits a false note. The crowd is young and more Italian than American, taking their espresso in the morning with a sweet roll. A sunken floor separates the elegant Il Grattino restaurant from the Caffè itself. Weekends there is music and, though jackets and ties are in order, the mood is relaxed.

Café Giardino, *7403 18th Avenue (718-256-5611). Daily 8 A.M.–midnight.*

The charming young woman behind the espresso bar doesn't know a word of English, but somehow she makes herself understood to the occasional non-Italian speaker. She has no problem either making a foamy cappuccino or filling a cannoli on the spot, or the shell doesn't get soggy. On weekends, when there is music, a back room is opened up.

Caffè Vesuvio, *7704 18th Avenue (718-259-2436). Daily 24 hours.*

Most of the activity at Vesuvio is at the small Italian coffee bar. After work people drift in and out or hang out with an espresso, a spumoni, or a Budweiser. They talk about *calcio* (soccer) or the city's mayoral race. The place has character and a folk-art Vesuvio that looks like it's on the verge of erupting.

Gran Café Italiano, *6917-6921 18th Avenue (718-232-9759). Daily 24 hours.*

The Gran Café is a New York Italian social club without any membership cards. Everyone knows everybody else and this cross-section of older Italians feels at home. The decoration mixes prints of saints with sensitive eyes and hunting-trophy antlers. The sign behind the bar advertises their homemade *granita di caffè* and *granita di limone* (coffee ice and lemon ice).

Bensonhurst Shopping

Shopping for Italian food in Bensonhurst is not strictly a matter of running down the right store. Specialty stores abound, but the all-Italian influence means that any grocery or food store, even if it's a chain supermarket, is going to sell Italian products that are usually reserved for a Manhattan gourmet shop. The Italian-born citizens of Bensonhurst are familiar with made-in-Italy products and they keep the local merchants up to the mark.

Trunzo Brothers Meat Market, *6802 18th Avenue (718-331-2111). Daily 8 A.M.–7 P.M.*

Trunzo's was once a meat market but now it is an Italian supermarket. There are floor-to-ceiling multiliter cans of imported olive oil and box upon box of pasta in every shape and size. There's a butcher counter with Italian scaloppine cuts, *braciole,* chops, and *rollatini* (veal rolls), ready for the saucepan, and a counter with nothing but sausages.

Bari Pork Stores, *7119 18th Avenue (718-837-1257). 2351 86th Street (718-449-5763). Monday–Saturday 8 A.M.–7 P.M.; Sunday 8 A.M.–2 P.M.*

Bari leads with its pork sausage: milk, hot, fennel, and cheese, and follows up with some fine dairy: fresh ricotta and mozzarella, and a good assortment of grating cheeses.

Bakeries in Bensonhurst have adopted the American practice of mixing bread and cake.

Alba, *7001 18th Avenue (718-232-2122). Monday 8:30 A.M.–5 P.M.; Tuesday–Saturday 8:30 A.M.–9 P.M.; Sunday 8:30 A.M.–7 P.M.*

Alba is four generations of expert pastry chefs. They fill the *cannoli* while you wait (for maximum freshness) and sell rich Sicilian *cassata* and *zuppa Inglese*. Sometimes they serve coffee to their regular customers.

Villabate Bakery, *7117 18th Avenue (718-331-8430). Daily 7 A.M.–9 P.M.*

Angelo is in charge of the *panetteria* and Emanuele is in charge of the *pasticceria.* Angelo is a master of semolina breads, long and crusty, and soft, high, and round with sesame seeds. Emanuele is a master of *tartufo,* the chocolate truffle cake.

Belvedere, *7304 20th Avenue (718-232-1814). Daily 7 A.M.–7:30 P.M.*

The Belvedere is slightly off the Bensonhurst track but it deserves mention for its extraordinary proscuitto bread with nuggets of peppery prosciutto and its *friselle* with slivers of almonds.

Bensonhurst is fresh pasta country and the two storefronts that make it for the neighborhood are as busy as bakeries.

Queen Ann Ravioli & Macaroni Inc., *7205 18th Avenue (718-256-1061). Tuesday–Saturday 9 A.M.–6 P.M.; Sunday 8 A.M.–2 P.M.*

In the front there is every conceivable configuration of pasta, fresh, dry, and in-between, and in back Renato Anticone and his crew are making it happen in a giant steel pasta machine. The stuffed shells with spinach and ricotta are in a case along with the ravioli and the manicotti.

Pasta Fresca, *6518 11th Avenue (718-680-7193). Monday–Saturday 8 A.M.–7 P.M.; Sunday 8 A.M.–5 P.M.*

The city's finest pasta maker has a small closet of a store practically in Borough Park. Celebrities like Dom DeLuise and Sophia Loren have been known to take the long trek for his secret recipe ravioli and tortellini and special smoked mozzarella.

Bensonhurst Gifts

Bensonhurst is a young immigrant Italian neighborhood. It is a neighborhood where weddings are more important than VCRs. The 18th Avenue main street has more bridal shops with names like the Wedding Coach and European Bridal Favors than restaurants. Gift shops that have disappeared from other areas thrive. They peddle everything for a wedding and all the accessories for the first apartment.

The stock runs the gamut from bud vases to meat grinders, and there are displays of fine china that rival Bloomingdale's. Up-to-the-minute Italian top ten hits are available in records and cassettes.

All Occasions Gifts, *7115 18th Avenue (718-232-1332). Monday–Saturday 10 A.M.–6:30 P.M.*

Four Seasons Gifts, *8612 18th Avenue (718-232-5330). Monday–Saturday 10 A.M.–6:30 P.M.*

S.A.S. Italian Records Inc., *7113 18th Avenue (718-331-0539). Monday–Saturday 10 A.M.–9 P.M.; Sunday 10 A.M.–8 P.M.*

Festa of St. Rosalia

Santa Rosalia was the fourteen-year-old daughter of a prince. She was a devout young woman with special powers. She dedicated her life to God and helping the poor. Despite her vows, her father still insisted that she marry into another princely family. When the day was set she went to a grotto to pray, a miracle happened, and her soul was lifted to heaven.

The Feast of Santa Rosalia, which begins on August 30, is an annual week-long event. Arthur Avenue from 67th Street to 75th Street on 18th Avenue is strung with colored lights and ladies from the church auxiliaries and local merchants serve delicious Italian specialties to neighborhood celebrants and visitors. The *festa* is sponsored by the St. Rosalia Society.

Court Street Nostalgia

Directions: IND F to Carroll Street.

When the Italians began vacating Little Italy in Manhattan, south Brooklyn was a convenient destination. The area was called Red Hook in the early 1900s, an anglicization of the Dutch *Roode Hoek,* which referred to seventeenth-century cranberry bogs. Today the neighborhood comprises Red Hook and two gentrifying historic districts, Carroll Gardens and Cobble Hill.

In colonial New York a small part of the vast Remsen estate was sold to a shipbuilder named Jackson and converted into a dry dock. In 1801 the Navy bought the dock and it became the Navy Yard, employing thousands of people. In the Civil War it was the major supply base and debarkation point for the Union forces.

By the time the Italians started coming, Red Hook was the site of huge grain storage facilities and one of the country's main transshipment points. It provided thousands of jobs on the docks for longshoremen and in the Navy Yard plants. World War II brought the Navy Yard and Red Hook its boom years.

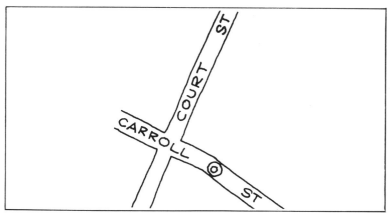

Court Street

The trend toward containerization meant a loss of jobs for the Italians of this neighborhood. The Queens-Manhattan Expressway, which cut a swathe through the area, meant the loss of homes. The city planners renamed portions of Red Hook Carroll Gardens and Cobble Hill to get rid of the waterfront roughneck stigma, and start the process of gentrification.

Italian holdouts have seen all the changes and they just shake their heads. Some Italian commercial outposts have held their ground on Court Street.

Mastellone's Market, *299 Court Street (718-522-6700). Monday–Thursday 8 A.M.–7:30 P.M.; Friday, Saturday 8 A.M.–8 P.M.; Sunday 8 A.M.–6 P.M.*

They have workmanlike fresh sausages and pancetta for cooking and the best extra-virgin cold-pressed olive oil in the nieghborhood.

Caputo's Bakery, *329 Court Street (718-875-6871). Monday–Saturday 6 A.M.–7 P.M.; Sunday 8 A.M.–6 P.M.*

The breads that run out the quickest are the crusty semolina and the grainy wheat bread. The cheese horn pastries filled with ricotta and grated citrus rinds have won the new neighbors over to Italian *pasticceria*.

Pastosa Ravioli Company, *370 Court Street (718-635-0482). Monday–Wednesday, Friday, Saturday 9 A.M.–6:45 P.M.; Thursday 9 A.M.–7:45 P.M.; Sunday 9 A.M.–1 P.M.*

Ray Vivola is a newcomer to the block; he has only been here eleven years. His strong suit is his stuffed pasta: cheese tortellini, ravioli, and manicotti stuffed with both mozzarella and ricotta.

Little Italy Uptown

Introduction

The Upper East Side of Manhattan is the site of a high-style, high-cachet Little Italy. The Italians who live and work here are prosperous and international. They live in the city but are not necessarily of it. These high-status immigrants occasionally came on assignment for Italian corporations and stayed for the financial opportunities. But generally they were experienced entrepreneurs eager to profit from New Yorkers' fascination for things Italian. Their sophisticated boutiques and restaurants were the phenomenon of the 1980s.

Spaghetti Splurges

Before New York put on gourmet airs, northern Italian food was *fettucine Alfredo* (in heavy cream and butter via a famous Roman restaurant), but now it goes so far north Scandinavian salmon is a standard dish on the menu.

The up-market restaurants have definitely made New York diners more familiar with Italian geography and the culinary regions of Tuscany, Emilia-Romagna, and Lombardy. They have also reaffirmed Italian eating etiquette. Forget about the simple assortment of appetizers and entrees; the new roster of dishes includes antipasto hot and cold, shellfish or stuffed vegetables to open the appetite; *primi piati* (first plate) soup or pasta or risotto to alert the taste buds; *secondi piati,* fish or fowl or meat with *contorno* (side dish of vegetables) for the grand climax; and rich desserts or fruit for a rough or smooth landing.

Though some restaurants claim to be strictly northern, they aren't being technical about it and avoid the heavy meat dishes that characterize the north, opting for the trendy light cuisine that a city of joggers craves.

Le Madri, *158 West 18th Street (212-727-8022). Monday–Friday noon–3 P.M., 6 P.M.–10:30 P.M.; Monday–Saturday 10:30 P.M.– 12:30 A.M. special pizza and salad menu.*

One of the newer trendies, where advance reservations are a necessity. Le Madri follows Italy's *trattorie* in having a wood-burning pizza oven in addition to the latest high-profile pastas on the New York-Italian hit parade.

For pasta with a difference, try the buckwheat noodles with potatoes, sage, and taleggio cheese.

Il Nido, *251 East 53rd Street (212-758-0226). Monday–Saturday noon–2:30 P.M., 5:30 P.M.–10:30 P.M.*

Il Nido is a New York town house transformed into a Tuscan farmhouse. The restaurant does magical things to basics like spaghetti Bolognese and *saltimbocca* (literally "jump into the mouth," but actually veal layered with prosciutto and cheese). The wine list has Italian wines that travel.

Nanni, *14 East 46th Street (212-697-4161). Monday–Friday 11 A.M.–3 P.M., 5:30 P.M.–10:30 P.M.; Saturday 5:30 P.M.–10:30 P.M.*

Nanni is always busy but the service is quite attentive. The regulars order *capellini al Nanni* with a cream sauce of mushrooms and prosciutto, followed by a luscious stuffed veal chop combining Fontini cheese, prosciutto, and dry porcini mushrooms.

Primavera, *1578 First Avenue at 82nd Street (212-861-8608). Daily 5:30 P.M.–midnight.*

Primavera is lace curtains and white linen tablecloths and professional flower arrangements. The staff is black-tie formal. The food would be very good at any price and Primavera's are high. The ingredients are fresh garden and prepared to order. There are surprises like baby goat that is moist and tender without being gamey.

Sette Mezzo, *969 Lexington Avenue between 70th and 71st Streets (212-967-7850). Monday–Friday noon–2:30 P.M., 5 P.M.–midnight; Saturday, Sunday 5 P.M.–midnight.*

Always busy, Sette Mezzo's fare is less exotic than standard. The old favorites like linguine *alle vongole* (with white clam sauce), and veal Milanese are what draw the Upper East Side clientele, who call three days ahead for reservations.

Trastevere, *309 East 83rd Street (212-734-6343). Daily 5:30 P.M.–11 P.M.*

It sounds like a gimmick, putting the scampi or scaloppine side by side with the salad, but the tastes work together. The restaurant is dark and the seating is tight, but customers are treated like family and don't seem to mind.

Gourmet Stops

Designer Italian food shopping with all the high prices and pretensions is a citywide phenomenon. In these emporiums the ingredients of a hearty dinner are elevated into art objects, bottles of olive oil are put on pedestals. There is Vivaldi in the background as New York's food cognoscenti go into raptures over squid ink linguine.

Dean & DeLuca, *560 Broadway at Prince Street (212-431-1691). Monday–Saturday 8 A.M.–8 P.M.; Sunday 9 A.M.–7 P.M.*

This temple to food reopened in 1988 with 7,400 additional square feet of space, even grander and more extreme than the 1977 original. It has eighteen-foot ceilings, Roman columns, and marble floors. There is an espresso bar of Carrara marble for gaping sightseers. The Italian staples olive oil, balsamic vinegar, and porcini mushrooms are surrounded by pretense and overpriced like everything else here.

Balducci's, *424 Avenue of the Americas between 8th and 9th Streets (212-613-2600). Daily 7 A.M.–8:30 P.M.*

Balducci's is a New York Italian success story. Old-timers reminisce fondly about the little Italian vegetable market across the street that had the freshest vegetables and hard-to-get herbs. Today, Balducci's is a food spectacular and the source for the best of Italy. They even have a mail-order service.

Todaro Brothers, *555 Second Avenue between 30th and 31st Streets (212-532-0633). Monday–Saturday 7:30 A.M.–9 P.M.; Sunday 8 A.M.–8 P.M.*

Todaro's was once a neighborhood grocery with its own rich blends of coffee beans, home-made sauces, and an Italian deli counter. The people who owned the store worked there and knew their customers. It's gone gourmet with esoteric oils and flavored vinegars, but Todaro's has kept its Italian identity even it it's lost a bit of its Italian soul.

Manganaro's Groceria, *488 Ninth Avenue between 37th and 38th Streets (212-563-5331). Monday–Saturday 8 A.M.–7 P.M.*

Manganaro's is exhaustive when it comes to Italian foods from pickled *scungili* (conch) to stuffed figs. It carries all the cheeses (table, dessert, and grating), and has more sausages hanging from the ceiling than other places stock in a year. There are breads and fresh pastry and a restaurant in the back. This is one-stop Italian shopping without the piped-in music and the pretenses. Next doot they have their Hero Boy store with six-foot heroes for office parties and the best egg and pepper and sausage heroes in the Big Apple.

Esposito's Pork Store, *500 Ninth Avenue at 38th Street (212-279-3298). Monday–Saturday 8 A.M.–7:30 P.M.*

Esposito's is for gourmets of unusual animal parts: heads, snouts, knuckles, tongues, and tripe, and lovers of sausage with a light touch, whether it is hot or stuffed with cheese.

High-Style Shopping

High Fashion

Italian designers have as much representation in style and price on the Upper East Side as the well-known French names. Each has a unique viewpoint, from the tailored elegance at Armani to the many-hued knits at Missoni to the more extravagant lines at Versace. They're all within steps of each other on Madison Avenue and offer a real overview of what's being worn on the streets of Milan and Rome. All but Krizia have both men's and women's fashions.

Giorgio Armani Boutique, *815 Madison Avenue between 67th and 68th Streets (212-570-1122). Monday–Wednesday, Friday, Saturday 9 A.M.–6 P.M.; Thursday 9 A.M.–7 P.M.*

Krizia Boutique, *805 Madison Avenue between 67th and 68th Streets (212-628-8180). Monday–Saturday 10 A.M.–6 P.M.*

Missoni Boutique, *836 Madison Avenue at 69th Street (212-517-9339). Monday–Saturday 10 A.M.–6 P.M.*

Valentino Boutique, *823 Madison Avenue between 68th and 69th Streets (212-772-6969). Monday–Saturday 10 A.M.–6 P.M.*

Gianni Versace Boutique, *816 Madison Avenue at 68th Street (212-744-5573). Monday–Saturday 10:30 A.M.–6:30 P.M.*

Fashionable Favorites

Salvatore Ferragamo *(Ladies) 717 Fifth Avenue at 56th Street (212-759-3822). Monday–Saturday 10 A.M.–6P.M.*
(Men's) 730 Fifth Avenue between 56th and 57th Streets (212-246-6211). Monday–Saturday 10 A.M.–6 P.M.

Known for shoes that are first in comfort and second in style, Ferragamo customers still manage to step out with elegance. In recent years they have expanded their line to include small leather goods and knit clothing, all with the same conservative polish as their shoes.

Gucci Shops, *683 Fifth Avenue at 54th Street (212-826-2600). Monday–Wednesday, Friday, Saturday 9:30 A.M.–6 P.M.; Thursday 9:30 A.M.–7 P.M.*

The Gucci name is worldwide and its famous double G logo copied extensively. The salespeople breathe rarified air, but the selection of small leather goods is second to none in variety and quality.

Lofty Leathers

Italian shoes and bags are beautifully made of the finest leathers and in the most up-to-date styles. New York is full of stores opened by recent arrivals or branches of shops in Florence and Rome and Milan. They're all expensive, follow the fashion trend of the moment, and offer a dazzling choice. Here are just a few.

Andrea Carrano, *677 Fifth Avenue at 53rd Street (212-752-6111).*
745 Madison Avenue at 65th Street (212-570-9020).
1144 Madison Avenue at 85th Street (212-734-6644).
Monday–Friday 10 A.M.–7 P.M.; Saturday 10 A.M.–6:30 P.M.

Arlene La Marca, *41 East 57th Street (212-759-8588). Monday–Saturday 10 A.M.–6 P.M.*

Beltrami, *711 Fifth Avenue between 55th and 56th Streets (212-838-4101). Monday–Saturday 10 A.M.–6 P.M.*

Bottega Veneta, *635 Madison Avenue between 59th and 60th Streets (212-319-0303). Monday 10 A.M.–6 P.M.; Tuesday–Friday 10 A.M.–7 P.M.; Saturday 11 A.M.–6 P.M.*

Fratelli Rosseti, *601 Madison Avenue between 58th and 59th Streets (212-888-5107). Monday–Saturday 10 A.M.–6 P.M.*

Prada, *45 East 57th Street (212-308-2332). Monday–Saturday 10 A.M.–6 P.M.*

Marion Valentino, *730 Fifth Avenue at 51st Street (212-485-0322). Monday–Wednesday, Friday, Saturday 10 A.M.–6 P.M.; Thursday 10 A.M.–7 P.M.*

Jewels at the Top

Men about town and men about Wall Street buy their ladies baubles at these Italian jewelers. They're Cellini extravagant with precious gems in ornate settings that recall Renaissance splendors. Price is never an object.

Buccellati, *46 East 57th Street (212-308-2507). Monday–Saturday 9:30 A.M.–5:30 P.M.*

Bulgari, *795 Fifth Avenue at 57th Street (212-486-0086). Monday–Saturday 10 A.M.–5:30 P.M.*

High-Style Homes

Portantina, *886 Madison Avenue between 71st and 72nd Streets (212-472-0636). Monday–Saturday 10:30 A.M.–6 P.M.*

Portantina brings the glowing tones and the sumptuous fabrics of Venice to Madison Avenue. There are cushions and shawls and small decorative pieces, all imported from the fabled city.

Pratesi, *829 Madison Avenue at 69th Street (212-288-2315). Monday–Saturday 10 A.M.–6 P.M.*

Pratesi sells linens of quality with the elegance associated with Italy. The printed sheets and duvet covers are not the mass-produced designs that appear at the August white sales, but the prices aren't either.

High-Style Minds

Rizzoli International Bookstore, *31 West 57th Street (212-759-2424). Daily 10 A.M.–10 P.M.*
454 West Broadway (SoHo) (212-674-1616). Monday–Saturday 11 A.M.–11 P.M.; Sunday noon–8 P.M.

Rizzoli's is the source for foreign-language newspapers as well as their special collection of art books from European publishers. Browsing in Rizzoli is second best to a private library.

Place Marks

Museums and Culture

Metropolitan Museum of Art, *Fifth Avenue at 82nd Street (212-535-7710). Tuesday–Thursday, Sunday 9:30 A.M.–5:15 P.M.; Friday, Saturday 9:30 A.M.–8:45 P.M. Contribution, except Friday and Saturday evenings.*

In an era when Italians were considered inherently artistic, Count Luigi Palma di Cesnola was appointed the first director of the Metropolitan Museum of Art. The Count had more to offer the museum than his knowledge of classical art and his experience as an archeologist. He brought to the job thirty-five thousand artifacts of ancient Greece, which he had collected while he was consul in Cyprus. For years his collection was the museum.

The Metropolitan devotes a lot of gallery space to the Italians, from the statues of Roman emperors off the Main Hall to the Joseph Stella painting of Coney Island in the American Wing. Highlights of the Italian Metropolitan include gondola prows, a Venetian ceiling by Dizani, and bronze heads molded by Tiepolo (Galleries 8–14). There are full-fledged Italian masterpieces: a Raphael Madonna, a Botticelli painting of St. Jerome, and a Titian Venus and a Madonna (Galleries 3–9). Cellini, who crafted objects d'art for Renaissance princes, is represented by an astronomical tower clock showing the position of the planets and the signs of the zodiac (Gallery 40).

Garibaldi-Meucci Museum, *420 Tompkins Avenue at the corner of Chester Street, Rosebank, Staten Island (718-442-1608). Tuesday–Friday 9 A.M.–5 P.M.; Saturday, Sunday, and holidays 1 P.M.–5 P.M. Free.*

After Napoleon III destroyed Garibaldi's dream of a united Italy, the exiled warrior mulled over his temporary defeat in the wilds of Rosebank, Staten Island. He stayed a year with an unsung genius named Meucci, making candles in Meucci's workshop.

Antonio Meucci tried to make a living at a variety of businesses, but inventing was his passion. He invented a special glue, a formula for fizzy drinks, and a hygrometer. Twenty years before Bell, he created a crude telephone that he never had the resources to develop. Today his house stands as a reminder of his own thwarted ambitions and the liberator of Italy's sojourn in America. The Garibaldi-Meucci Museum contains a wealth of memorabilia dealing with the lives of these two Italian giants.

Italian Opera in Lincoln Center

The Metropolitan Opera House, *Lincoln Center, Broadway at 65th Street (212-580-9830).*

The Italians gave New York opera. They were the first opera impresarios in the city and the first operas performed—even if the music was by Mozart—were sung in Italian. Lorenzo Da Ponte, who was a librettist for Mozart, was involved in the building of New York's Italian Opera House and the formation of its first opera company. An Italian businessman, Fernando Palmo, lost a fortune trying to attract an American audience to its productions.

For its first season (1883–1884) the Metropolitan Opera chose the Italian conductor Augusto Vianesi, who recruited the best musicians from the opera houses of Venice and Naples for his orchestra. The program of mostly Italian opera was put together by the Metropolitan's director, Cleofante Campinni. Soon its leading singer was the Neapolitan baritone Antonio Scotti. In 1903 another Neapolitan, the tenor Enrico Caruso, took the city by storm and became a national celebrity.

The Metropolitan Opera came of age in 1908, when the demanding and dictatorial Giulio Gatti-Casazza of La Scala became the manager and the legendary Toscanini wielded the baton. Their spectacular production of *Aïda* and a dramatic *Rigoletto* featuring Caruso are part of New York's opera lore.

At the same time, another Italian impresario, Alfredo Salmaggi, was promoting opera for the masses. He staged productions in Madison Square Garden and city stadiums with a twenty-five cent top price for tickets.

Even after Gatti-Cassaza retired in 1935 and impresarios started to have names like Bing, the Italian singers were the leading performers. There were Giovanni Martinelli, Rosa Ponselle, Ezio Pinza, Franco Corelli, and many more. The operas that were the most popular were also Italian: Puccini's *La Boheme* and Verdi's *Aïda*. Today Luciano Pavarotti is opera's heir to Caruso with a celebrity that transcends opera.

The Metropolitan Opera House is Lincoln Center's ten-story wonder, with high marble arches revealing vivid Chagall murals. In the spirit of opera black-tie, it is very grand in gold, red plush, and marble with endless nineteenth-century staircases. On the concourse there is a gallery of the Metropolitan's greatest singers, many of whom are Italian. Busts of the two men who truly built this house of operatic music, Giulio Gatti-Cassaza in bronze and the great Caruso in marble, have the place of honor.

Preserving the Heritage of Dante and Michelangelo

Italian Historical Society of America, *111 Columbia Heights, Brooklyn (718-852-2929).*

The Italian Historical Society has a complete collection of materials documenting the Italian experience in America. But the society's main function is to make Italian-Americans aware of their contributions to the city, the country, and the world at large. It is responsible for monuments in the city honoring Italian notables from Verrazano to Verdi, and joined the Sons of Italy in the preservation of Garibaldi-Meucci House.

The Italian Cultural Institute, *686 Park Avenue (212-879-4242). Monday–Friday 9 A.M.–12:30 P.M.*

The Italian Cultural Institute is housed in a Park Avenue mansion along with the Italian Consulate. The library has books both in Italian and English about Italy. It also keeps up-to-date Italian newspapers and periodicals. There are learned lectures in the upper rooms for those interested in art and culture. The institute awards prizes to Americans for Italian-language writing.

Casa Italiana, *1161 Amsterdam Avenue at 117th Street (212-854-2306).*

Casa Italiana is on the Columbia University campus in an Italian Renaissance piazza created by Italian-American stone cutters. It sponsors art exhibits, concerts, plays, and films. Call for information about upcoming events, which sometimes don't receive their fair share of publicity.

Italian Monuments

In Italy the people erect statues and monuments to their great men and women in the main public piazza and in this way they are close to their past. Dante and Michelangelo and Garibaldi are a constant bronze and marble presence. They are the examples for the future. Italian New Yorkers have adopted this tradition and Italian masters and heroes appear in the parks and on the busy avenues and streets of Manhattan.

Francisco Verrazano, *Battery Park.*

Verrazano in bronze gazes on the sea. He discovered New York before Hudson.

Giuseppe Garibaldi, *Washington Square Park, Greenwich Village.*

Giuseppe Garibaldi stands at attention near an arch dedicated to the father of this country. He galvanized the forces that united Italy.

Christopher Columbus, *Columbus Circle, 59th Street and Broadway and Eighth Avenue.*

Columbus is elevated on a 77-foot granite pedestal. He discovered the New World if not North America.

Dante Alighieri, *Dante Park, Broadway and Columbus Avenue at 63rd Street.*

Dante in bronze is severe and dignified. He made writing in the vernacular respectable and was the author of the *Divine Comedy*.

Giuseppe Verdi, *Verdi Square, Broadway triangle north of 72nd Street.*

Verdi in Carrara marble contemplates his greatest operatic creations: *Aïda, Othello, Falstaff,* and *Leonora.* He was the nineteenth century's most popular composer of opera.

═══ The Secular Festa ═══

Columbus Day Parade

On October 12, 1492, a seaman on the *Pinta* sighted one of the islands in the Bahamas, and Cristoforo Colombo gained immortality as the discoverer of America. Before World War I, Italian community leaders made Columbus Day a celebration of Italian accomplishment. Later, after they won a long campaign to make Columbus Day a legal holiday, it became a way of identifying with America. It was their ethnic rite of passage, a secular *festa*.

New York's Columbus Day Parade follows Fifth Avenue from 44th Street to 86th Street. The crowds along the line of march are large, almost as large as on St. Patrick's Day. There are schoolchildren with Italian Power buttons and union members with signs from their locals and recent Italian immigrants who wear their accents as badges of pride.

The parade begins with the politicians, a contingent that gets bigger and bigger as the Italian population of New York increases. Every year there are floats of the *Niña,* the *Pinta,* and the *Santa Maria,* complete with a beautiful Italian Isabella or a member of the Sons of Italy in tights and a false beard. Marconi has a float and so does Alitalia, complete with a smiling stewardess. There are marchers from the Italian VFW trying to keep in step with a military band and high school kids playing salsa and doing complicated dance steps. The marching bands from all the city's Italian festivals participate. Members of the Dante Alighieri Society sedately walk down the avenue, while the Knights of Columbus move with real conviction. The Italian police and firefighters are represented, and no parade is complete without the Police Department's Emerald Society bagpipers.

The Jews

History

In September of 1654 the *St. Charles* landed in New Amsterdam with twenty-three Jewish passengers who had been rescued from Spanish pirates. The Jews were Sephardic, of Spanish and Portuguese descent. They could trace their ancestry back to Jewish nobility of the "golden age" before the Inquisition.

These grandees of Iberia were an elite, leaders in the arts, the sciences, and finance. Again they were fleeing the *auto-da-fé,* this time from Brazil, which the Portuguese had recaptured from the tolerant Dutch. New York's first Jews arrived with little more than the clothes on their backs. In retrospect these refugees would have the stature of Jewish pilgrims.

Governor Peter Stuyvesant was eager to rid the Dutch colony of these heretics, who he feared would "infect and trouble this new colony." Stuyvesant requested the support of his superiors at the Dutch West India Company, but Dutch tolerance and the influence of Jewish stockholders in the company saved the day. The Jews would stay. They had the company's protection.

The Jews were granted a charter of settlement by the Dutch West India Company in April 1655, recognizing their loyalty to the Netherlands and upholding their basic rights. Stuyvesant was forced to yield, but he continued in attempts to restrict their participation in the life of the Dutch colony.

Stuyvesant tried to bar Jewish religious worship, but the company took the Jews' side and backed their right to have services in their own homes. In

1655, New Amsterdam's twenty-three Jews founded a congregation that they called *Shearith Israel,* the "Remnant of Israel." Shortly afterwards, they were permitted to have their own Jewish cemetery just outside the city walls. Individual Jews tried to secure the full privileges of citizenship. Asser Levy, the proprietor of a popular tavern, refused to pay the "Jewish tax" that exempted him from guard duty. He recognized his duty to protect his community and challenged the governor and the Dutch West India Company to revoke the tax and the exemption.

Another Levy named Moses became the first Jew to hold public office after the colony came under British rule. This wealthy merchant was well known for his philanthropies and was one of seven Jews to contribute to the construction of the Trinity Church steeple.

New York's Jews played a prominent part in the life of British New York. They were leading shopkeepers and major traders who financed their own merchant fleet. They contributed to public subscriptions and joined philanthropic campaigns. Jewish businessmen even had their own "great country seats." But the Jews didn't feel fully accepted until they were allowed their own public house of worship. They built Temple Shearith Israel in 1728 on the site of a old mill in the heart of what is today the financial district.

In the era of the American Revolution, Jewish New Yorkers had an almost religious regard for freedom. They associated the Revolution with their own celebration of the Passover and liberation from the Egyptian Pharaoh. When the Redcoat armies occupied New York, Rabbi Gershom Mendez Seixas, the spiritual leader of Shearith Israel and American patriot, escaped with most of his congregation to free Philadelphia.

Haym Salomon was a member in good standing of Shearith Israel and the "banker of the Revolution." He helped provision the New York militia under the command of Philip Schuyler. Later he became involved in a plot to burn British ships in New York harbor and was imprisoned as an American spy. Released by the British, Salomon arranged the financing that enabled the Revolutionary Army to continue its fight.

At the time of George Washington's presidential inauguration, the Jews of New York and their fellow Jews in other communities took the opportunity to declare their loyalty to the new government in an open letter. Washington replied with a ringing defense of religious freedom and a pledge to the "stock of Abraham."

In the New York of the new republic, Jews were contributing members of society. Mordecai Manuel Noah was a successful playwright and journalist, a prominent Mason, and a major in the state militia. Noah was civic-minded and eager to run for office and at various times served as sheriff and judge of the New York Court of Sessions. He was appointed to such important offices as surveyor of the port of New York and consul of Tunis.

Uriah Phillips Levy made millions in New York real estate, but that was secondary to his commitment to the U.S. Navy. Despite the anti-Semitism of ranking officers he rose from cabin boy to commodore and saw combat in the War of 1812. This Jewish New Yorker was credited with abolishing corporal punishment in the navy. At the end of his career he used his vast wealth to renew a run-down Monticello, creating a national shrine for his hero, Thomas Jefferson.

By the time the first Ashkenazi (German) Jews came to New York in the 1830s, Sephardic Jews could count themselves among the city's banking and business establishment. Socially they held themselves aloof in a small aristocratic circle of Baruchs, Lazaruses, Nathans, Hendrickses, and Cardozos. They valued reserve and thought of themselves as high-minded and cultivated. The German Jews with their queer accents and aggressive manners were definitely not their crowd.

Judge Albert Cardozo disappointed his exclusive Sephardic set when he resigned from the New York Supreme Court bench after rumors of corruption and favoritism. He awarded the majority of lucrative refereeships to members of Boss Tweed's family. His son, Benjamin Nathan Cardozo, was shocked by the loss of family honor. He dedicated his life to regaining that honor and in the process became a respected legal scholar and a United States Supreme Court justice.

The German Jews were too busy creating dynasties to be overly concerned by the chilly Sephardic welcome. The Seligmans started out as peddlers in cotton country but soon opened a string of dry-goods stores from New Orleans to New York. The headquarters of their small retail empire in 1846 was 5 Williams Street, very near the stock exchange where these future merchant bankers would make history.

Joseph Seligman, the oldest of seven brothers and three sisters, was the patriarch of the clan that would earn the title of the ''American Rothschilds.'' His first speculations were in the gold market and he got out fast enough to make a fortune and avoid the panic of 1857. Seligman liked the company of men in power and was an intimate of President Lincoln. He got into international finance bankrolling the Union cause with bond sales in Europe.

Three thousand New York Jews joined New York regiments to fight for the Union. The Jews had their own Brigadier General Philip Jochimsen, who led the Fifty-ninth New York Volunteers, and a Jewish enlisted man, Benjamin Levy, received the Congressional Medal of Honor. A Jewish Brooklynite, Colonel Leopold Levy, died a hero's death at Chancellorsville.

The Lehman brothers, unlike the Seligmans, did their peddling from a horse and wagon. They opened a dry-goods store in Mobile, Alabama, which became the center of their cotton empire. After the Civil War they set themselves up in New York, trading in commodities and becoming the biggest cotton brokers in the country. By the turn of the century they were branching out into investment banking.

The Seligmans were the first of the German Jewish merchant bankers to recognize the profits in railroad investment, but they were soon upstaged by Kuhn, Loeb, and Company and their rising star, Jacob Schiff. This imperious German with a streak of old-fashioned Jewish piety held his own with J. P. Morgan and robber barons like Hill and Harriman. He was on the board of directors of some of the nation's most important railroads.

Some German Jews stuck to retailing. Nathan and Isidore Straus started in glassware and crockery at R. H. Macy & Company and quickly became the proprietors of the two biggest department stores (Macy's and Abraham & Strauss) in the city. New York's Jewish-owned department stores also included Gimbel's, Altman's, and Bloomingdale's.

Despite their accomplishments and their devotion to charitable causes, the German Jews were victims of social discrimination. Joseph Seligman, himself a member of the prestigious Union League Club, was refused accommodation in the fashionable Grand Hotel in Saratoga. By the end of the century this form of social restriction had spread. Jews were excluded from fashionable Coney Island and Manhattan Beach and were forbidden to ride the Long Island Railroad.

"Our Crowd" retreated into itself. It became more insular and laid more emphasis on its German heritage. They spoke German among themselves and sent their children to a New York school modeled on a German *gymnasium*. They embraced German Reform Judaism and worshiped at Temple Emanu-El, the image of a progressive German synagogue.

New York's German Jews socialized with New York's German Jews. They were members of the Harmonie Club and their children prepped at Sachs Collegiate. They occupied mansions on Fifth Avenue and competed for the services of the same French chefs, but the German Jewish style remained calculatedly low-key.

As the first Russian Jewish waves crowded into Grand Street, the last of the great German Jewish dynasties made their fortunes. Adolph Lewinsohn and his brothers used a loophole in the law to import cheap copper and profitably export low-grade copper ore. By the 1890s they controlled most of the country's copper and merged with the Rockefeller interests.

In 1881 German Jews spoke out against the persecution of their fellow Jews in Russia after the assassination of Tsar Alexander II. They hated the pogroms but they also believed that the Russian Jews were backward "Orientals."

Though they were ambivalent about the Russian newcomers, Jewish New York mobilized to help them. They formed the Hebrew Emigrant Aid Society to help them find shelter and jobs. They had an employment office in the Castle Garden immigrant station and a restaurant and a boardinghouse in

Greenwich Village. There was also a temporary shelter in Greenpoint, Brooklyn.

The Russian Jewish emigrants settled at first on the Lower East Side. They were peddlers, they did piecework on sewing machines, and they rolled cigars, They were Russian Jewish furriers and Jews who only studied the Torah, the sacred books. They all endured together the damp disintegrating tenements, the dirt and disease, and the rotting garbage on the street.

Jewish uptown met Jewish downtown in the Lower East Side settlement houses. Social-work pioneers like Lillian Wald helped immigrants adapt to this strange new world with health and educational programs. Often the German or Sephardic Jews who worked with the Russian immigrants (like Emma Lazarus of Statue of Liberty fame) came away from the experience with a strengthened sense of Jewish identity.

In 1896 Jews joined the ranks of the city's most important opinion makers when Adolph Ochs bought the bankrupt *New York Times.* He was interested in objectivity where the news was concerned and in keeping personal views to the editorial page. Dorothy Schiff, the granddaughter of the investment banker, was the next Jew to publish a New York newspaper, the *New York Post.* Her unspoken policy was to combine liberal politics and Broadway gossip.

By 1905 studies showed the Jewish "greenhorns" were moving out of the sweatshops and wearing white collars. Jewish children were reared to strive and surpass their parents. They became professionals, retailers, salespersons, and clerical workers. They were also improving themselves by moving out of lower Manhattan and Brownsville into Yorkville, Harlem, and Williamsburg.

Russian Jews were still the backbone of union militants in the city. From 1909 to 1914 garment-worker unions organized waves of strikes, including the first general strike in the needle trades. Uptown Jews led by the millionaire investment banker Jacob Schiff intervened. Sweatshops were eliminated and labor leaders like Sidney Hillman and David Dubinsky won the right to collective bargaining.

The political activist Jews of New York elected the Socialist Meyer London to Congress in 1910, 1916, and 1920. Morris Hillquit, the militant socialists' antiwar candidate for mayor, ran a remarkably close race in 1917. At the same time, Jewish party regulars like Belle Moskowitz and Joseph Proskauer were advising the future presidential candidate, Governor Al Smith.

New York Jews from the Delancey Street ghettos were singing Irving Berlin's "Oh, How I Hate to Get Up in the Morning" when they went off to war in 1917. Their fighting force was the Seventy-seventh Division, which held the line at Meuse-Argonne. A Jewish Gumpertz and a Kaufman were Medal of Honor winners.

While the war took many Jews out of the ghetto, others used their special talents to take Broadway and Madison Square Garden by storm. The Marx Brothers, Al Jolson, Fanny Brice, George Burns, and Eddie Cantor were headliners in vaudeville and in Broadway revues. Benny Leonard and Barney Ross became world boxing champions. When private colleges had restrictive quotas, City College became the New York Jews' stepping stone to success. Financier and adviser of presidents Bernard Baruch was a City College graduate, and the discoverer of the polio vaccine, Dr. Jonas Salk, also received his first degree from CCNY. Supreme Court Justice Felix Frankfurter went to City College, and literary critic Alfred Kazin did his earliest writing for the college literary magazine.

In the years following World War I, New York's older Jewish families were heavily involved in public service. Herbert H. Lehman deserted his family's Wall Street offices for the political hustings. He became the governor of New York, a U.S. senator, and a member of the War Refugee Board. Another member of the German Jewish elite, Henry Morgenthau, Jr., was Secretary of the Treasury for FDR.

The lives of Russian Jews continued to improve as they moved out in greater numbers to the suburban Bronx and Brooklyn. Their modern housing came equipped with refrigerators and gas ranges! The Chanins, Brickens, and Backers, who cut their teeth on this residential construction, eventually changed the skyline of Manhattan with structures like the Chrysler and Woolworth buildings and the Waldorf-Astoria Hotel.

In the depression, New York Jews struggled like other New Yorkers just to find a job. College graduates took whatever they could get even if it was blue-collar work. Despite their personal concerns, Jewish New Yorkers followed the rise of Nazism in Europe, and through organizations like the American Jewish Committee and American Jewish Congress tried to help their threatened coreligionists.

Though restrictive immigration laws worked against them, some Jewish refugees from Nazism landed safely in Manhattan. They were mostly intellectuals and artists who settled in the city's Upper West Side and Greenwich Village. They included writer Isaac Bashevis Singer and social critic Hannah Arendt. In the 1930s the New School of Social Research was transformed into the University in Exile with a faculty of German political refugees.

Jewish New Yorkers campaigned to aid Britain and enter the war against the Axis powers. They joined the armed forces in record numbers once war was declared. A West Point graduate from Brooklyn, Colonel Mickey Marcus served on the American general staff and was in the thick of it on D-Day. America won the war, but in the midst of the euphoria of victory, Jews came face to face with the horror of the Holocaust.

Jewish soldiers came back to the city to resume their lives with new homes and expectations. They took advantage of the GI Bill to complete their education and train for new careers. They came prepared for the postwar boom. At the same time, HIAS and the Federation of Jewish Philanthropies helped Jewish displaced persons from Europe settle in New York, as they would later help Jewish refugees from the Soviet Union.

In this new era of affluence, Jews voted for more mainstream candidates. A liberal Jewish Republican, Jacob Javits, succeeded Herbert Lehman as senator. In the 1970s the first Jewish mayor to govern New York was the decidedly middle-of-the-road Democrat, Abe Beam. The controversies over Jewish teachers in Ocean-Hill, Brownsville, and the friction between Jews and minorities in Canarsie changed the nature of the Jewish electorate.

Ed Koch was good enough to be the Jewish mayor of the city for twelve years. He seemed to delight in his Jewish identity and was an outspoken supporter of Zionist causes. He was the city's chief administrative officer during the austerity of the budget crunch and also led New York in a time of physical growth and expansion.

══════ The Lower East Side ══════

Directions: IND F to Essex Street, or Second Avenue M15 bus to Delancey Street.

Introduction

The eighteenth-century Lower East Side was bucolic country; the Rutger and DeLancey estates shared the geography. As New York grew commercially, Federal-style residences and row houses appeared on the new street grid, and rich merchants and shipping magnates took title to the Lower East Side. The neighborhood was fashionable.

In the 1850s and 1860s Irish and German immigrants made the Lower East Side their own. The townhouses were subdivided and in some cases more than one family occupied a room. Although poor, the neighborhood produced its Irish political leaders and German manufacturers. Tammany had its wigwam on Chatham and Frankfort Streets.

Many of the Lower East Side Germans were Jews and they had their own Jewish fraternal groups and newspapers. Starting out working class, they became professionals, garment manufacturers, and jewelers. In 1880 the German Jewish colony numbered eighty thousand.

The Lower East Side had another radical change in 1881, when pogroms ignited by the assassination of Tsar Alexander II led to a mass Jewish exodus. The Jews who came in family groups for permanent settlement were running for their lives. They were very different from their German predecessors.

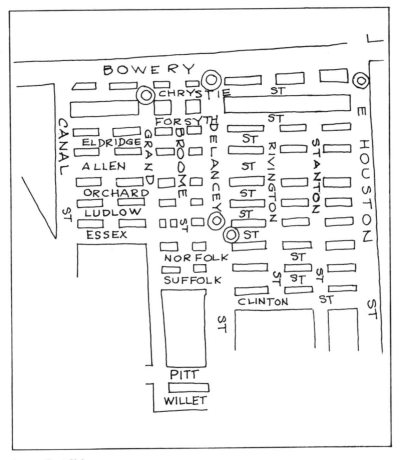

Lower East Side

The men had long beards and fur hats and shabby gabardine coats and the women shaved their heads and wore wigs. In Russia and Poland they were restricted to Jewish areas. They were second-class citizens with limited job and educational opportunities.

The new Lower East Side arrivals became peddlers and graduated to pushcarts or joined the mass-production clothing industry, otherwise known as sweatshops. Peddling was often long frustrating hours with little reward; the sweatshops were low wages and brutal working conditions.

The Lower East Side was more densely populated than London's notorious East End. Over three hundred thousand people occupied the square mile bound by Allen Street, Essex Street, Canal Street, and Broome Street. Russian Jews moved into run-down tenements, where tuberculosis and typhus ran rampant. The rooms had little ventilation and light, and were divided among families. Privacy was nonexistent. The Russian immigrant found no relief on the Lower East Side's streets. They were crowded and unclean and reeked of garbage. Street gangs waylaid the "greenhorns" to extort money or for the fun of pulling their beards. Some young Russian Jews were themselves corrupted by the streets and became criminals and prostitutes.

But the Jews of the Lower East Side were more than equal to the hardships and temptations. They persevered from morning to night, working sixteen- and eighteen-hour days. They learned English and made sure their children were educated. They sent them to the Educational Alliance and to the settlement houses.

Jewish immigrants counted their pennies and did a good deal of their shopping in the cheapest of the cheap, the *Khazermark* (pig market) on Hester Street. Bargain days were Thursdays and Friday mornings right before the Sabbath; everything was bought and sold, new and used and in the final stages of decay. It was a colorful shouting and pushing bazaar where the bargaining was always hot and heavy.

The Lower East Side could be crude but it had a rich cultural life. The writer Hutchins Hapgood proclaimed that "no part of New York had a more intense and varied life than the colony of Russian and Galician Jews who live on the East Side and form the largest Jewish city in the world."

The neighborhood was the scene of heated political debates, head-to-head chess matches, literary lectures, and a slew of self-help programs. There were technical schools, business schools, and language classes sponsored by uptown philanthropists. The German Jewish Educational Alliance taught David Sarnoff, the founder of RCA, to speak English and gave world-renowned sculptor Sir Jacob Epstein—when he was still Jake—his first art lessons.

The Yiddish theater was one of the centerpieces of the Lower East Side, with its Jewish King Lears and Jewish Hamlets. On benefit nights it was pure audience participation, when families came complete with bawling babies to cheer the heroes and hiss the villains. At the end of a Jacob Gordin tragedy there wasn't a dry eye in the house. It was a training ground for Paul Muni, Edward G. Robinson, and young Walter Matthau.

For the price of a cup of coffee or a strong glass of Russian tea, poetry cliques and political factions whiled away the evening. In Levine's on East Broadway or Schreiber's on Canal Street, Jewish intellectuals and sweatshop Lenins argued women's rights, free love, the merits of the latest production at the opera, or the future of socialism. They took on the issues that were discussed in the neighborhood's five Yiddish papers.

The Jews of the Lower East Side refused to depend on German-Jewish charity. They formed *Landsmanschaften''* (mutual aid societies) from their Old World villages and towns. These societies provided a place to socialize with friends and reminisce, and kept alive local religious traditions and built synagogues. In time there were *Landsmanschaften* hospitals and convalescent homes.

In 1903 and 1906 the brutal Russian bloodletting and Jew baiting brought another wave of refugees to the Lower East Side. The Balkan Wars from 1908 to 1914 added Sephardic Greeks, Turks, and Syrians to the Jewish melting pot. By the time World War I exposed European Jewry to further suffering, there were 600,000 strong in the neighborhood.

In America the values of Bialystok or Vilna were turned upside down; prayer and religious study suddenly took second place to the race for survival. Jews moved from the synagogue to the secular and aggressively pursued the American identity. They became true believers in the American dream or ideologues of New World utopias. Unions or Zionism or a home in Riverdale were the answers for a new age in a new country.

The success of Lower East Side social programs, educational programs, organizations, and protests eventually led to the end of a solidly Jewish neighborhood. By the 1920s stridently American Lower East Siders were relocating to Riverside Drive and Central Park West and the Bronx. The next influx of Jewish refugees would ignore the crumbling East Side. These German Jews fleeing from Nazism planted their enclave in Washington Heights.

The Jewish Lower East Side is still more than memories. Jews cling to the neighborhood, too poor or too stubborn to retire to the suburbs of Miami Beach. They walk with slow half steps or the spring of an active old age to the Jewish shops and restaurants that survive mostly on the tourist trade. But increasingly, they are joined by younger Hasidic Jews with families who follow Jewish traditions that go back to eighteenth-century Hungary and Poland.

The Lower East Side's Jewish bazaar is intact, with blocks of stores selling off-price clothes, linens, electronic goods, and china. But the times are changing. Bargaining is common, but by no means across-the-board, and some of the people minding the stores are Indian or Korean.

Lower East Side Nosh

Jewish ethnic cooking is as varied as the lands of the Jewish diaspora, but mainstream Eastern European cuisine characterizes the Jews of New York. It is forthright *shtetl* (village) food heavy on the garlic, onions, and *shmaltz* (rendered chicken fat). Following Jewish dietary laws, meat and dairy are separate and there are always two sets of dishes in strictly kosher homes. Kosher meat is always ritually killed, and pork and shellfish are forbidden.

The Jews of New York take a special delight in their "vorspiese" (appetizers) such as chopped chicken liver (*shmaltz* providing the extra kick) and gefilte fish (chopped pike, carp, and whitefish with carrot adding sweetness). Jewish chicken soup is legendary—with noodles, *kreplach* (a noodle stuffed with meat), or matzo balls (dumpling made of unleavened bread meal). Roast chicken, chicken fricassee, meat balls, boiled beef, potted brisket, and stuffed cabbage are popular main courses; noodle pudding, potato pudding, and potato knishes (in a dough shell) are on the side. The absence of refrigerators in nineteenth-century Eastern Europe made pickled vegetables and smoked meats and fish a necessity. Today pickles, pastrami, and smoked salmon are enjoyed by Jews and their fellow New Yorkers just for their taste. The bagel, a ring-shaped roll that is boiled before being baked, is another Jewish staple that has become mainstream New York.

The Lower East Side's Jewish restaurants are in the tradition of the Jewish mother's refrain *"ess, ess"* (eat, eat). The portions are over the top. Like the Jewish mother, the restaurants are still objects of sentiment to which errant Jewish sons and daughters return regularly. Some of the restaurants still have a built-in floor show—the Jewish waiter. He is the master of the semi-insulting quip and the rude aside. Don't expect bowing and scraping, the service is very egalitarian on the Lower East Side.

Sammy's Rumanian Jewish Restaurant, *157 Christie Street (718-673-0330). Daily from 4 P.M. till very late.*

Sammy's is garlic and onions, Jewish heavy and spicy, and please pass the chicken fat. The two cents plain is on the house, but after the *griebenes,* (chicken skin and onions fried in rendered chicken fat), the stuffed derma, and a big rib steak, Alka Seltzer is more to the point.

Steinberg's Dairy Restaurant, *21 Essex Street (212-254-7787). Sunday–Thursday 6:30 A.M.–6:30 P.M.; Friday 6:30 A.M.–3 P.M.*

The more recent Lower East Side Jews who commute to Yeshivas in Israel have a taste for things Middle Eastern. Steinberg's now serves *felafel* (fried, spiced pureed chick peas), along with the blintzes and lox and cream cheese.

Ratner's Dairy Restaurant and Bakery, *138 Delancey Street (718-674-9406). Sunday–Thursday 11 A.M.–11 P.M.; Friday, Saturday 11 A.M.–midnight.*

When the Jewish Upper East Side shops for bargains on the Lower East Side, it breaks for brunch at Ratner's. The mushroom-barley soup, *kashe var-*

nishkes (wheat groats with noodles), and lox and eggs are what Jewish memories are made of.

Bernstein-on-Essex, *135 Essex Street (212-473-3900). Sunday–Thursday 9 A.M.–1 A.M.; Friday 9 A.M.–2:30 P.M.; Saturday one hour after sunset–1 A.M.*

In 1959 it introduced the kosher egg roll to New York. Orthodox Jews in gabardine, wives and children in tow, dissect the Talmud over kosher egg foo young, beef chow mein, and vegetarian egg rolls. The food is more expensive than the real thing just south.

Grand Dairy Restaurant, *341 Grand Street at Ludlow Street (212-673-1904). Sunday–Friday 5 A.M.–3:30 P.M.*

The once bustling Grand is quiet now, almost diffident. It's austere old men eating *matzoh brei* (unleavened bread scrambled with egg) and gefilte fish and cups of coffee that are mostly milk. The waiters are the Lower East Side leftovers, polite and a little melancholy.

Katz's Delicatessen, *205 East Houston Street (212-254-2246). Sunday–Thursday 7:30 A.M.–11 P.M.; Friday, Saturday 7:30 A.M.–1 A.M.*

The name is Katz's, but that's about the only thing that is strictly kosher. It's an old-style cafeteria where a ticket greets you at the door to be punched as you order. The cold cuts from this landmark deli come dried out and the Coney Island fries are cooked in yesterday's oil.

Jewish Food Markets

The Lower East Side may no longer be a big-city *shtetl* but it still has all the makings for a traditional Jewish meal. It just takes more time to gather them together.

The Essex Street Market, *104 Essex Street (212-254-6655). Monday–Saturday 6 A.M.–8 P.M.*

This enclosed market filled with an array of stalls is a good place to start Lower East Side shopping. There are Jewish-style greens for *schav* (cold sorrel soup) and beets for borscht, which have now been joined by plantains and breadfruit and bean sprouts and bok choy for the latest residents. The meat counters in this international market are no longer strictly kosher; they currently run the gamut from kosher chicken livers for chopping to hot Italian sausage.

Miller's Cheese, *13 Essex Street (212-496-8855). Sunday 9 A.M.–6 P.M.; Monday–Wednesday 9:15 A.M.–6:45 P.M.; Thursday 9 A.M.–9 P.M.; Friday 9 A.M.–two hours before sunset.*

Miller's is fresh farmer cheese with the creamiest curds and special kosher Mehadrin milk. Miller's counterman, if given half a chance, will introduce the uninitiated to creamy kosher dessert cheeses.

Guss's Pickles, *35 Essex Street (212-254-4477). Sunday–Thursday 9 A.M.–6 P.M.; Friday 9 A.M.–4 P.M.*

Sour pickles or half sours from the barrel are part of the romance of the Lower East Side. Guss's Pickles has not gone Hollywood since appearing in "Crossing Delancey"—the wry quips still come free with the pickles.

Moishe's Homemade Kosher Bakery, *181 East Houston Street (212-475-9624). Sunday–Friday 7 A.M.–6 P.M.*

Moishe's is *challah* (braided Sabbath bread) warm from the oven, and sticky (with honey) *teiglach* made from unleavened dough for Passover. The store on Sunday is take a number and wait.

Russ & Daughters, *179 East Houston Street (212-475-4880). Tuesday–Sunday 9 A.M.–6:30 P.M.*

Russ's daughter Ann is still minding the whitefish, pickled herring, and belly lox. Keeping up with the uptown Joneses, there are also beluga caviar and pâté de foie gras at Lower East Side prices.

Yonah Schimmel Knishes Bakery, *137 East Houston (212)-477-2858). Daily 8 A.M.–6 P.M.*

The knishes come fresh and hot and heavy from the dumbwaiter. Yonah Schimmel's knishes cannot be compared with the article sold at hot dog stands. The crust melts in the mouth and the stuffing, whether potato, kasha, or cabbage, is nicely seasoned with white pepper and garlic.

Kossar's Bialystoker Kuchen Bakery, *367 Grand Street (212-473-4810). Daily 24 hours.*

People cross the river and double park for these bagels and bialys. They are harder, more chewy, and less doughy than the supermarket varieties.

Schapiro's House of Kosher & Sacramental Wines, *126 Rivington Street (212-475-7383). Sunday–Thursday 10 A.M.–5 P.M.; Friday 10 A.M.–3 P.M.*

Schapiro's Wines is a city landmark. For generations New York Jews have visited Schapiro's cellars to get a real kosher Malaga with that almost cloying kiss of sweetness.

Jewish Bargains

Shopping on the Lower East Side is a New York Sunday ritual. It goes back to the days before the uptown stores could open on Sunday and the Lower East Side, with its Saturday Sabbath, was the only shopping game in town. But the Lower East Side was more than a way of getting around the blue laws; it offered discounts on brand names that New Yorkers and out-of-towners couldn't refuse.

The Lower East Side was a Sunday spectacular that attracted Upper East Side mink and uptown flash. It was a good-natured, multiethnic, multiracial crowd scene where bargain hunting was the common denominator. The Jewish sellers with Old World accents were more than willing to *hondl* (bargain) even as they insisted they weren't making a profit.

The Sunday ritual is still going strong on Orchard Street, the Lower East Side's Fifth Avenue. From Houston to Division Streets, it still draws the crowds but there is a feeling that something is missing.

The bargains aren't what they used to be. The uptown department stores have their own Sunday openings and constant sales, cutting into the Orchard Street advantage. Top designers like Calvin Klein and Bill Blass no longer manufacture in large quantities; the rising costs and shrinking inventories that provided the source of the Orchard Street bargains are no longer common on Seventh Avenue. These days it's easier to find names in the midprice range, like Liz Claiborne, Evan Picone, and Blassport with large manufacturing runs.

It's best to get an early start to get the best buys. The stores close early in the afternoon as the shoppers disperse. Be prepared to do a lot of walking and stalking. The action around the racks and shelves requires true grit and determination. Most items have a marked price, sometimes open to bargaining, but be ready to pay what the ticket says.

Store hours are set, but more often than not, disregarded. Early closing on Friday and closed on Saturday is not. Otherwise, Sunday to Thursday 9 A.M. to 10 A.M. opening and 5 P.M. to 6 P.M. closing is the rule, not always followed.

Women's Clothing

Fishkin's, *63 Orchard Street, 314-318 Grand Street. (212-226-6538).*

It's always worth a few minutes at Fishkin's to check out the sportswear and separates. The Grand Street store specializes in more casual styles.

Forman's, *82 Orchard Street, 94 Orchard Street, 78 Orchard Street (212-228-2500).*

On Sundays they sometimes have to lock the door to keep the crowd manageable. Forman's usually has a lot of Liz Claiborne and Evan Picone, as well as an ample selection of high-quality, discount-priced coats and suits. Petites should shop at 94 Orchard Street and large sizes at 78 Orchard.

M. Friedlich, *196 Orchard Street (212-254-8899).*

Friedlich's is the store to spy out Italian and French imports, but they don't neglect American sportswear either. It's also possible to find some great buys in coats.

Shulie's, *175 Orchard Street (212-473-2480).*

You go to Shulie's for Tahari's designs. The selection is not quite as up to date as in the Madison Avenue store, but the prices are better.

Women's Lingerie

Well-known-brand lingerie and underwear is easy to find in one or the other of the Orchard Street shops specializing in these items. Some shops have a no-try-on/no-return policy, so it's best to know exactly the brand, style, and size before starting out. The discounts on sleepwear can be large—up to 70 percent—but 20 percent seems to be the rule on undergarments. If one shop is out of stock, another or another might have just what you're looking for.

D & A Merchandise, *22 Orchard Street (212-925-4766).*

A. W. Kaufman, *73 Orchard Street (212-226-1629).*

Lolita, *70 Orchard Street (212-982-9560).*

Charles Weiss, *331 Grand Street between Orchard and Ludlow Streets (212-966-1143).*

Men's Clothing

G & G Projections, *53 Orchard Street (212-431-4530).*
Shirts and sweaters are the reason for shopping G & G. The discount on Hathaway and Christian Dior shirts runs about 30 percent.

Jodamo International, *321 Grand Street at Orchard Street (212-219-0552).*
The styles are a little slicker and high fashion. Most come from Italy, and are usually a year ahead. The store is spacious enough for easy looking.

Pan Am Men's Wear, *50 Orchard Street (212-925-7032).*
Pan Am has a fine selection of American designers with more conservative styles. The discounts are excellent.

Men's Shirts

Victory Shirt Company, *96 Orchard Street (212-677-2020).*
It's up the stairs for 100 percent cotton shirts manufactured by Victory themselves. The prices are very reasonable and the selection of styles impressive.

Men's Underwear

Louis Chock, *74 Orchard Street (212-473-1929).*
You can find most of the well-known brands at Chock's: Calvin Klein, Hanes, Jockey, and BVD are available on the premises and also by mail at discount prices.

Leather Goods—Shoes and Bags

Lace-Up Shoe Shop, *110 Orchard Street (212-475-8040).*
The Sunday lines are an indication that there are good buys to be found in Lace-Up. Top-designer high-style women's shoes—better for looking

at than wearing—are one of the main attractions at heavily discounted prices.

Leslie Bootery, *36 Orchard Street (212-431-9196).*

Women's shoes are on the main and second floors; men's are downstairs. Top-designer brands like Cole-Hahn and Bally sometimes appear on the shelves, but you're more likely to find Reebok's and Clark's sportier models.

Fine & Klein, *119 Orchard Street (212-674-6720).*

There's a vast selection of designer handbags at bargain prices as well as small leather goods. The wallets, belts, and briefcases are a whole lot less than in the uptown department stores.

Linens

One of the best reasons to shop on the Lower East Side is the selection of linens for bedroom and bath. Shops line Grand Street from Forsyth Street to Orchard filled with Fieldcrest and Martex towels, Wamsutta sheets, duvets and their covers, bed spreads, and all the accessories a well-dressed bathroom needs. The prices are well below those at the uptown stores; now and then you can come across a buy that is exceptional.

Eldridge Jobbing House, *90-88 Eldridge Street (212-226-5136).*

Ezra Cohen, *307 Grand Street at Allen Street (212-925-7800).*

Harris Levy, *278 Grand Street (212-226-3102).*

Electrical Appliances

If you need a hair dryer or a toaster or a TV, the Lower East Side is the place to shop. Starting at the lower end of Orchard Street, going along Canal and on up Essex Street, there's a group of stores selling electrical appliances small and large, all at discounted prices—often at 50 percent below list. Not every store has every model; prices vary from store to store as does the return policy. It's best to comparison shop, if you have the patience. Sundays are very busy and the service minimal.

ABC Trading Company, *31 Canal Street (212-228-5080).*

Bondy Export Corporation, *40 Canal Street (212-925-7785).*

Dembitzer's, *5 Essex Street (212-254-1310).*

Lewi Supply, *15 Essex Street (212-777-6910).*

Judaica

The stores are small and dark and sign-posted in Hebrew—the Lower East Side at the turn of the century. There are prayer books and books of Torah commentary and ritual phylacteries and prayer shawls; in a place of honor are the sacred scrolls themselves with silver pointers and velvet covers and shields with the Lion of Judah. Judaica, which also includes rare and antique items used by Jews in earlier centuries, like plates and glasses with Jewish decoration, are found mainly on Essex Street.

Hebrew Religious Articles, *45 Essex Street (212-674-1770).*

Kipab Or, *49 Essex Street (212-260-3252).*

Louis Stavsky, *147 Essex Street (212-674-1289).*

Yiddish Place Marks

While other Manhattan neighborhoods have been gentrified out of existence, the Lower East Side has changed its population but kept a lot of its Jewish character. The story of the Eastern European Jewish immigrants is still revealed in brick and mortar Lower East Side survivors.

Cultural Landmarks

The Educational Alliance, *197 East Broadway (212-475-6200).*

German-Jewish millionaires established the Alliance to Americanize their "less civilized" coreligionists. Besides language lessons, it offered technical training, cultural programs, and business courses. Children could attend Alliance camps or use the gym and take advantage of the showers. Legal aid and pasteurized milk were both available through the wide array of Alliance services.

The Federation of Jewish Philanthropies still runs the Alliance for the benefit of poor Jews, Puerto Ricans, blacks, and Chinese. Its Hall of Fame on the main floor contains photographs of such notable Lower East Side alumni as David Sarnoff, the radio and television magnate, Eddie Cantor, the entertainer, and sculptor Louise Nevelson.

The Henry Street Settlement, *263–267 Henry Street (212-766-9200)*.

While its fine Federalist buildings have been designated landmarks, the settlement house organization is still working to improve the lives of the people in the neighborhood. It continues the programs of its founder, Lillian Wald, a German-Jewish nurse who pioneered social work and preventive medicine at the beginning of the century.

Henry Street has a day-care center, a credit union, homecare for the elderly, employment training, educational programs, and even an art gallery. The exhibits feature the East Village avant-garde and indigenous Rembrandts.

Lower East Side Tenement Museum, *97 Orchard Street (212-431-0233). Tuesday–Friday 11 A.M.–4 P.M.; Sunday, call for times for special programs. Admission charge.*

This museum preserves the authentic tenement, the log cabin of urban life, along with the artifacts of the Jewish families who occupied them. Sunday afternoons there are plays and slide shows dramatizing the immigrant tenement experience. The Lower East Side Conservancy, the group behind the museum, strives to make it a "truly living experience."

Just for Looking

Jewish Daily Forward, *175 East Broadway*.

In its prime, when Abraham Cahan was editor, the *Jewish Daily Forward* stood ten stories tall with the largest electric Yiddish sign in creation. It was the eyes and ears and heart of the Jewish Lower East Side, telling it like it is, whether about garment industry goons or Allen Street prostitutes. The paper gave the uninitiated advice along with left-of-center politics and balanced tabloid sensationalism, literary essays, and quality fiction. Now the signs on 175 are in Chinese.

Independent Kletzker Brotherly Aid Society, *5 Ludlow Street.*

Just off Canal Street are the former premises, not a little worse for wear, of the Independent Kletzker Brotherly Aid Society. At one time there were six thousand of these *Landsmanschaften* representing villages in Eastern Europe. They provided health and burial benefits and a replica of *shtetl* fellowship for poor Jews.

Yarmulowsky's Bank, *Corner Orchard and Canal Streets.*

Yarmulowsky's was tall for its time, with a big clock and the name Yarmulowsky carved above the entrance. It once contained the savings of the Lower East Side, but it failed in 1914 before the days of federally insured bank accounts. Two thousand outraged customers picketed the bank and another five hundred stormed Yarmulowsky's house.

Synagogues

The children of the book took religion very seriously on the Lower East Side and the synagogue was at the center of the community. Since the Jews left the neighborhood, some of their houses of worship have been converted to churches or public buildings; others have been vandalized.

A choice few still have active congregations. East Broadway is still the domain of Jewish Orthodoxy; storefront synagogues proliferate between Jefferson and Montgomery Streets. But in an earlier era Lower East Side Jewish houses of worship were among the most impressive in the city.

Shaarey Shimoyim, *The First American Rumanian Congregation, 89 Rivington Street (212-673-2835).*

Shaarey Shimoyim means the "Gates of Heaven." It was the pride of the Lower East Side, with seating for 1,600. Lately there aren't enough attendees to keep the Gates of Heaven open.

Beth Hamedrash Hagodol Synagogue, *60-64 Norfolk Street (212-674-3330).*

The Beth Hamedrash Hagodol Synagogue is designated a landmark and its attractive Gothic Revival exterior and the evocative biblical murals and carved pews are kept in good repair. It is difficult to believe that it was a Baptist Church in 1852.

Bialystoker Synagogue, *7–13 Willett Avenue (212-475-0165).*
The Bialystoker Synagogue has seen better days but it is still admired for its
fieldstone finish and Federalist details from 1826.

Lower East Side Jewish Festival

The Lower East Side Festival takes place on the third Sunday in June. Jews
and others with a nostalgia for the old neighborhood come down to glimpse
the local color and eat a knish. The local Jewish merchants and restaurant
owners roll out the red carpet and share their memories. There are kosher
food stalls and stands selling Judaica. The East Broadway Educational
Alliance sponsors this exercise in reawakening Jewish identity.

I'll Take Manhattan

Introduction

The Jews are spread throughout the borough of Manhattan from the Jewish
intellectual Upper West Side to the Jewish artist SoHo to the Jewish businessman Upper East Side. Though they aren't a people apart, they have
preserved a Jewish identity. There are neighborhoods in the city where this
identity stands out and places of interest where Jews can renew their sense
of ethnic awareness. At the same time, the Jewish New York experiece has
influenced the rest of the city in everything, from its taste in food to its
approach to art. And the Jew has become so much a part of the city that it is
difficult to know where New York starts and Jewish ends.

There's No Business Like Business
Garment Center

The garment center once spanned 25th to 41st Streets between Sixth (Avenue
of the Americas) and Ninth Avenues and included the fur district, children's
clothes, and men's cloaks and suits, besides women's ready-to-wear. But
foreign imports have taken a big bite out of the business and the center, which
is not sanforized, is shrinking. The companies with designer names are
moving uptown and the small operators are going out of business and being
replaced by Latin and Oriental contractors.

The garment center, from 36th Street to 41st Street between Avenue of the Americas and Eighth Avenue, is still typical New York chaos. While car horns blow and the occasional irate driver vents his frustrations, lines of trucks double-park for pickups and deliveries. The sidewalks are clogged with Dominican and Puerto Rican workers and the occasional Hasid dragging racks of coats or skirts or balancing boxes on a hand truck. In between time they check out the smartly dressed action on the street. Upstairs, in the showrooms of skyscrapers, the companies hold court for out-of-town buyers. The dynamic manufacturer and his protégée on the sales floor are the white-collar offspirng of the Lower East Side sewing-machine operator and cutter.

Eastern European Jewish characters have left the center along with old Jewish hangouts like the Kosher-style cafeteria Dubrow's, to be replaced by Jews with business degrees and pasta joints. But Seventh Avenue (now renamed Fashion Avenue between 36th Street and 38th Street) still has the high-rise showroom landmarks at 498, 500, and 512 built before the Depression.

The Diamond District

The diamond district used to be between the Bowery and Canal Street; a conventional row of jewelry stores was the backdrop to bearded and side-locked Hasids dealing in diamonds. Millions of dollars in gems was traded on the sidewalks with a handshake. The jewlers and the merchants and the cutters eventually followed the well-heeled clientele uptown to their current location on 47th Street between Fifth and Sixth Avenues.

While jewelry stores and jewelry exchanges with individual stalls line both sides of the street offering gold, pearls, and gems in different settings, the diamond dealers in the black suits and wide-brimmed hats conduct their trade in lofts equipped with state-of-the-art alarms and video cameras. Most of the stores offer tourist prices, but perseverance and old-fashioned bargaining can work wonders in the exchanges.

In recent years some diamond district locations have gone Fifth Avenue with fancy facades and lush displays. But the diamond district shopping adventure is all about unset stones produced from folds of white paper and the drawn-out process of making a choice and weighing the stones and agreeing on a price. It is a jewelry bazaar in the middle of modern Manhattan. The Jeweler's National Exchange at 4 West 47th Street is as good a place as any to play let's make a deal.

From Deli to Haute Cuisine

Jewish food is alive and well throughout Manhattan. Jewish deli is New York deli and the bagel is the New York equivalent of the French croissant. While New York's nonreligious Jews have become partisans of French and Italian gourmet cuisines, the city's religious Jews have insisted that haute cuisine go kosher.

Lou S. Siegel's, *209 West 38th Street (212-921-4433). Sunday–Thursday 11:45 A.M.–10 P.M.; Friday 11:45 A.M.–2:45 P.M.*

Lou Siegel's is no longer diamond pinky ring Garment District and beef flanken with a teaspoon of horseradish. The kosher designer suit crowd is more comfortable with the cajun fish.

Diva Dairy Italian, *306 East 81st Street (212-650-1928). Sunday–Thursday 5 P.M.–10:30 P.M.; Saturday 7:30 P.M.–11:30 P.M.*

Diva is authentic kosher Italian with some recipes originating in the Roman ghetto. It's uptown town house luxury dining. The virtuoso dishes include artichokes alla Romana and *rotelle* (pasta twists) with smoked salmon.

Levana, *141 West 69th Street (212-877-8457). Monday–Thursday 5 P.M.–11 P.M.; Saturday (winter only) 8 P.M.–11 P.M.; Sunday 3 P.M.–11 P.M.*

Levana has the fancy presentation of nouvelle cuisine in kosher continental. It even serves kosher venison in a formal dining room with pastel tablecloths.

Fine & Schapiro, *138 West 72nd Street (212-877-2874). Saturday–Thursday 8:30 A.M.–11 P.M.; Friday 8:30 A.M.–9 P.M.; Restaurant opens at 11 A.M.*

The West Side's "between the wars" Jewish refugees were Fine & Schapiro regulars. The stuffed cabbage is just the right blend of sweet and sour, and the boiled beef is better than a French *pot-au-feu*.

Jewish Appetizers Go Gourmet

The appetizer shops uptown are all gourmet flourishes and snob appeal. Everything must be lark's tongue rare and caviar expensive. The trend started when the dull old neighborhood stores started importing the lox from Nova Scotia and calling it nova. The humble bagel was followed by the baguette and the rest is history. Before you know it, they were branching out into walnut oil and balsalmic vinegar and selling espresso machines.

Zabar's, *2245 Broadway at 80th Street (212-787-2000). Sunday– Friday 9 A.M.–6 P.M.; Saturday 9 A.M.–midnight.*

Zabar's is where Barbra Streisand goes when she's looking for a bagel and smoked salmon or a can of caviar. It has 400 kinds of cheese and twenty-two varieties of coffee. It sells more whitefish than all of the stores on the Lower East Side combined. Upstairs in its kitchen appliances department the Cuisinart was introduced to New York.

Barney Greengrass, *541 Amsterdam Avenue between 856th and 87th Streets (212-724-4707). Tuesday–Thursday, Saturday, Sunday 8:30 A.M.–5:45 P.M.; Friday 8:30 A.M.–6:30 P.M.*

Barney Greengrass is what Zabar's used to be before it got pretentious. Greengrass is truly the sturgeon king, as it bills itself, and the smoked salmon and whitefish king as well.

Orwasher's, *308 East 78th Street (212-288-6569). Monday–Saturday 7 A.M.–7 P.M.*

Orwasher's has been creating Jewish designer bread on the Upper East Side since 1916. Their raisin pumpernickel in rolls or bread is particularly delicious.

The Deli Winners Circle

New York's Jewish deli mavens have long argued the merits of their own favorite deli hangouts over the competition. Articles in New York newspapers and magazines have explored the intricacies of fatty versus lean pastrami and the vagaries of different smoked corned beefs. The delis, besides blowing their own horns with battling publicists, encouraged the celebrity trade (which always brings in lots of ordinary people) by honoring them with triple-decker sandwiches. The three winners (in any order) of this ongoing deli competition are:

Second Avenue Deli, *156 Second Avenue at 10th Street (212-677-0606). Daily 7 A.M.–2 A.M.*

In front there is the Yiddish theater equivalent of Hollywood's Grauman's Chinese, with dedications on the sidewalk to Muni, Robinson, and the

Adlers, and many others. The deli is as authentically Jewish as these stars of the Yiddish theater.

Stage Deli, *834 Seventh Avenue between 53rd and 54th Streets (212-245-7850). Daily 6:30 A.M.–2 A.M.*

Max Asnas, the original owner, was funnier than most of the Jewish comedians who did their acts at his tables. He sold out in the 1950s and flopped with a new place called the Star. The Stage today with its high-and-wide deli on rye sandwiches are re-creating the days of the old master.

Carnegie Deli, *854 Seventh Avenue at 55th Street (212-757-2245). Daily 6:30 A.M.–3:30 A.M.*

Leo Steiner made this place with all-green bagels for St. Patrick's Day and Guinness Book of Records frank-eating contests. The deli is the most ecumenical of the bunch, getting most of the out-of-town orders for pastrami on white with mayonnaise.

Place Marks

Jewish Culture

The Jewish Museum, *1109 Fifth Avenue at 92nd Street (212-860-1688). Sunday 11 A.M.–6 P.M.; Monday–Thursday noon–8 P.M. Admission charge, except Tuesday evening. (From January 1991 to December 1992 the Jewish Museum will be housed in the New-York Historical Society, 170 Central Park West, Tuesday–Sunday 10 A.M.–5 P.M.)*

The Jewish Museum mounts exhibits that transcend their Jewish subject matter. There are mulitmedia theme shows and collections of memorabilia from the recent New York Jewish past. George Segal has contributed to their permanent collection a memorable plaster cast sculpture whose subject is the Holocaust.

Yivo Institute for Jewish Study, *1048 Fifth Avenue (212-535-5700). Monday–Friday 9:30 A.M.–5:30 P.M.*

The Yivo Jewish Institute originated in Vilna in 1925 but was moved to New York during the war to protect its precious manuscripts and books. This library, which is open to the public, contains three million photographs, letters, and documents. There are secret Nazi memoranda in their files and material on the Jewish presence in the Far East.

Yeshiva University Museum, *2520 Amsterdam Avenue (212-960-5390). Tuesday–Thursday 10:30 A.M.–5 P.M. Admission charge.*

The Jewish historical experience is depicted through photos, paintings, Jewish folk art, and religious articles. There are ten scale models of the world's most famous synagogues.

The Jewish Theological Seminary, *122nd Street and Broadway.*

The Jewish Theological Seminary is more than a training ground for American rabbis. It is a repository for some of the rarest Jewish books in the world. It has 250,000 volumes, including special finds from the old Cairo synagogue.

Yiddish Theater

Folksbeine Theater, *123 East 55th Street (212-755-2231).*

The heritage of the Yiddish theater is still alive in the Folksbeine Theater. They have kept the tradition for seventy-four years, putting on dramas and musicals in Yiddish. The younger actors sometimes need a bit of coaching, but the words of Sholem Aleichem haven't lost their impact.

The season runs from October to April, but not continually. Check the box office for the complete schedule.

Synagogues

Temple Emanu-El, *Fifth Avenue and 65th Street (212-744-1400).*

Temple Emanu-El is the seat for Reform Judaism in the city; it is thoroughly German-Jewish and ''progressive.'' This Romanesque/Byzantine structure seats 2,500 amid the splendor of its bronze ark, Stars of David, and Lions of Judah.

Congregation Shearith-Israel, *Central Park West and 70th Street (212-873-0300).*

Though this Sephardic Jewish sanctuary only goes back to 1897, the congregation has been in existence since 1654. No one can say New York's Jewish grandees don't do things right—the stained-glass windows are by Tiffany. The congregation still preserves a cemetery in Chatham Square with headstones from the seventeenth century.

Central Synagogue, *Lexington Avenue and 55th Street (212-838-5122).*

The building, built in 1872, has been formally designated a landmark. It is a Moorish Revival structure with bulbous domes rising to a height of 122 feet. The architect, Henry Fernbach, was the first Jew to practice architecture in the city. The original synagogue was on Ludlow Street in the Lower East Side.

Festivals

The Jews of New York use the occasion of the Salute to Israel Parade, which marks Israeli independence, to proclaim their support for the Jewish state and to celebrate their Jewish identity. It usually takes place on the first Sunday in June.

The parade was kicked off in 1965 with a short line of march from 72nd Street and Third Avenue to Fifth Avenue. Two years later, in the critical days preceding the Six Day War, the parade proved itself, drawing over a million spectators registering support for Israel. Today the Salute to Israel parade route follows Fifth Avenue from 57th street to 86th Street with thousands of marchers and professionally mounted floats.

Jewish youth representing Zionist organizations and religious schools (yeshivas) in the metropolitan area make up the majority of marchers. They come in costume representing Jewish pioneers, carry colorful banners, and wear the severe garments of Orthodoxy. These youngsters run the gamut from joyously enthusiastic to solemn.

They are joined by their elders from the Jewish War Veterans, World Zionist Congress, and other Jewish organizations. The ecumenical touch is provided by assorted marching bands from public high schools and groups like the New York Emerald Society bagpipe band.

Though the paraders smile and wildly wave to the crowd in the time-tested fashion, the Salute to Israel Parade is basically a serious affair. The wearing of the six-pointed Jewish star (*Mogen David*) and the showing of the blue and white Israeli flag are testaments of survival in the midst of persecution.

In conjuction with the Salute to Israel Parade there is an Israel Folk Dance Festival and Festival of the Arts. The Israel Folk Dance Institute puts on performances of vibrant Jewish circle dances like the hora that capture the energy of this young nation. Dramatic presentations from the Israeli stage, both in Hebrew and in English, are featured. They usually deal with themes involving the heroic struggles of this new state.

Jewish Brooklyn

Borough Park

Directions: IND B to New Utrecht Avenue/55th Street.

Introduction

Borough Park is the Hasidic capital of Brooklyn, but it was once the Dutch village of New Utrecht with nineteen Dutch families instead of thousands of ultra Orthodox Jews. The Jews and the Italians came to Borough Park in the twenties, following the subway lines and responding to ads to "Build Your House in God's Country." The neighborhood was a neat collection of single-family frame houses and six-story apartment buildings. By the next decade it had a settled-in look with some very impressive religious structures and public buildings.

New highways and a building boom in the 1950s and 1960s accelerated the move out of Borough Park to the Long Island and New Jersey suburbs. The suburban-bound were soon replaced by Orthodox Jews leaving deteriorating areas of Williamsburg and Crown Heights. Many of these observant

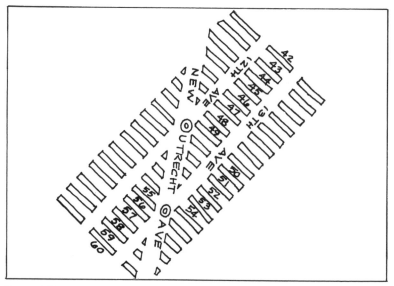

Borough Park

Jews were displaced persons from World War II and the concentration camps. They were apprehensive of big-city crime and racial conflicts, but they were more afraid of the assimilating suburbs and stayed in Brooklyn. Borough Park would become a gathering of the Hasidic clans: Vishnitzer, Pupper, Szigeder, and Krasner.

The Jews of Borough Park have the same side curls (called *payoth*) and the same beards and wear the same uniform of dark suit, dark coat, white shirt, and dark broad-brimmed hat as Hasids in other communities. But the fabric of the suits is more expensive and the jackets hang better; closer inspection reveals cufflinks and Rolex watches. These men have a sleek substantial look, the confidence of the things of the flesh. They are students of the Torah, but they are also businessmen who travel to Manhattan to work in the diamond district and the garment center. The women are Orthodox enough to wear wigs and dress modestly, but they haven't lost a feeling for fashion and color.

The character of Jewish Borough Park is casual. Nobody has to be self-consciously Jewish in an area where gentiles are the minority. The bearded Jewish mechanic in greasy coveralls or the youth in *payoth* riding a bicycle are completely at ease. The women wheel their baby carriages along 13th Avenue, speaking Yiddish so quickly they hardly seem to take a breath, and only stop to window-shop. Old men in dignified homburgs embrace one another near the benches in front of the bank, where the elderly take the sun. In a shoe-repair shop a woman waits for heels, reading from a prayer book. Borough Park is a big Jewish neighborhood; it is a Jewish village in the middle of New York's largest borough.

The main shopping area of Borough Park along 13th Avenue is not *Fiddler on the Roof shtetl*. Aside from touches like the sinks showing in restaurants, this could be Main Street in any middle-class neighborhood. The window displays—even if they are merchandising Jewish ritual objects—are modern and the store fixtures are glossy and new. Most of the restaurants and food shops have a mainstream American look, whether the bill of fare is kosher chow mein or blintzes. There is even Jewish fast food with the neat functional style of a McDonald's.

Borough Park Essing

The Jewish restaurants in Borough Park take pleasure in converting other cuisines to Orthodox Jewish. Eastern European Jewish is old hat. Jewish pizza, chow mein, and yakitori are the wave of the future.

Taam Eden, *5001 13th Avenue (718-972-1692). Sunday–Thursday 7 A.M.–9 P.M.; Friday 7 A.M.–two hours before sundown.*

The Taam Eden looks like a gleaming Greek coffee shop with counter space and booths. But surprise, surprise, the short-order cook and the counterman wear *yarmulkes* (skull caps worn by religious Jews). This dairy restaurant doesn't have to apologize for its baked whitefish or broiled flounder. The eggplant Parmesan isn't Italian but it is delicious.

Kosher Delight, *4600 13th Avenue (718-435-8500). Sunday–Thursday 7 A.M.–9 P.M.; Friday 7 A.M. to two hours before sunset.*

This kosher version of McDonald's, with its French fries, nuggets of chicken, and double burgers is a novelty at first. Kosher Delight is three times the size of the usual Borough Park restaurant and is also three times as loud.

Ach Tov, *4403 13th Avenue (718-438-8494). Sunday–Thursday 11 A.M.–9:30 P.M.*

Almost everyone in the restaurant is a Hasidim in a long black coat. They are all eating the soup of the day, which might be a rich mushroom-barley, followed by side dishes of noodles and cabbage and herring or whitefish salad. Beware of the halibut teriyaki and the sweet-and-sour whitefish.

Mazel Pizza, *4807 New Utrecht Avenue (718-854-3753). Sunday–Thursday 9:30 A.M.–8 P.M.; Friday 9:30 A.M.–3 P.M.; Saturday 8:15 P.M.–midnight.*

The small Yemeni Jewish gentleman at the pizza oven tries very hard to please, but it is clear he doesn't understand a word that doesn't appear on the menu. The *felafel* is better than the pizza.

La Nosheria, *4813 13th Avenue (718-436-0400). Sunday–Thursday 11 A.M.–11 P.M.; Friday 11 A.M.–3 P.M.*

The Chinese menu is endless with chow meins, lo meins, moo goo gai pans galore. It is kosher and heavy on the cornstarch and MSG. The self-service is not at self-service prices.

Kosher to Go

When it comes to eating, Borough Park prefers to eat at home, even if the wife doesn't feel like doing the cooking. The traditional Jewish food is sold in nontraditional takeout. Some of the customers drive in from Jersey and Westchester.

Meisner's Glatt Kosher, *1312 55th Street (718-436-5529). Sunday–Wednesday noon–7 P.M.; Thursday 11 A.M.–8 P.M.; Friday 8 A.M.–1 P.M.*

At Meisner's they never stop slaving over a hot stove and the cooking aromas are total temptation. They make everything Hungarian Jewish, from a simple knish to a cauliflower souffle.

Guttman's, *5120 13th Avenue (718-436-4830). Sunday noon –9 P.M.; Monday–Thursday 2 P.M.–9 P.M.; Friday 8 A.M.–4 P.M.*

The food here is made for the meat-and-potatoes man by a friendly and forceful meat-and-potatoes woman. The Guttman's larder includes sides of pot roast, stuffed veal, mountains of mashed, and oceans of thick gravy.

Mehadrin Supermarket, *5124 12th Avenue (718-435-2678). Sunday–Thursday 7 A.M.–6 P.M.; Friday 7 A.M.–4 P.M.*

Mehadrin is an all-around market, from fresh vegetables to smoked appetizers to dried beans, dried fruit, and nuts. The takeout emphasizes salads—cucumber, eggplant, and salmon.

Jewish Sweets

When Borough Park is invited to dinner they are more likely to bring a pecan coffee ring or a box of sweets than a bottle of wine.

Weiss Bakery, *5011 13th Avenue (718-438-0407). Sunday–Thursday 6 A.M.–9 P.M.; Friday 6 A.M.–one hour before sunset.*

Even on an ordinary weekday it is wall-to-wall Jewish housewives. They wait on line for the *rugele* (small cakes made with cream cheese dough), *babka* (sponge cake), and chocolate layer cakes.

Candy Man, *4802 13th Avenue (718-438-5419). Sunday–Thursday 9 A.M.–7:30 P.M.; Friday 9 A.M.–4 P.M.*

The Candy Man is easily recognizable because it is usually surrounded by children. They eye sweets very seriously, trying to decide between licorice whips or candy buttons or an all-day sucker. For adults there are hand-dipped chocolates from Israel.

The Real Jewish Article

In a neighborhood identified by its dedication to Orthodox Judaism, stores selling articles connected to worship and Jewish ritual are more common than video stores in other ares. The stores are merchandised with imagination and style.

Eichler's, *5004 13th Avenue (718-633-1505). Sunday–Thursday 9:30 A.M.–8 P.M.; Friday 9:30 A.M.–4 P.M.*

The clerks are a little shy if you're not from the neighborhood but very obliging. There are pictures of Hasidic leaders for framing, and pictures of the Wailing Wall. The *yarmulkes* are embroidered and the prayer books are leather-bound.

Kodesh Religious Articles, *5205 13th Avenue (718-633-8080). Monday–Thursday 10 A.M.–10 P.M.; Friday 11 A.M.–3 P.M.; Sunday 10 A.M.–7 P.M.*

Rabbis browse through the aisles looking for the right titles in Hebrew, tugging their beards thoughtfully. The silver *kiddish* cups (silver cups for prayers over the wine) and candelabras are works of the silversmith's art. Besides the serious religious articles, there are snappy framed mottoes like "Stop, it's Shabbos."

Crown Heights

Directions: IRT-Lexington Avenue 4, or IRT-Seventh Avenue 3 to Eastern Parkway/Kingston Avenue.

Introduction

In the seventeenth century Crown Heights was Dutch farmsteads; later it was a part of the vast Lefferts estate. In the nineteenth century the high ground was settled by free blacks and it came to be called Crow Hill. In 1883 the Brooklyn Bridge was built and the area became more developed. On the edge of Crow Hill near Bedford, high-hat Manhattanites occupied plush apartments and even had a branch of the exclusive Union League Club. Frederick Law Olmstead and Charles Vaux, the designers of Central Park, put the finishing touches on the area, with the imposing tree-lined Eastern Parkway.

Even before Crow Hill became Crown Heights in 1916, Charles Ebbets and the McKeever brothers built Ebbets Field. It became the home of the Brooklyn Dodgers and the hub of the neighborhood until the Dodgers went

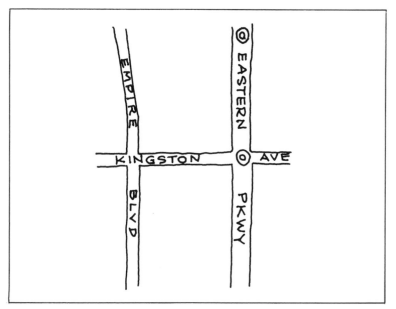

Crown Heights

west and it became a Brooklyn project. Four years later the IRT connected Crown Heights with the rest of the city and the neighborhood developed quickly. It became mostly middle-class ethnics with a professional upper crust on Eastern Parkway.

In the 1960s when panic selling and blockbusting were pushing the white nonreligious Jewish population out of Crown Heights, the leader of the Lubavitcher Hasidic community advised his followers to stay. The Lubavitchers, despite the warnings, prospered and thrived in a new Crown Heights, side by side with West Indians and Haitians. They had the faith of their leader in the future and the large Lubavitcher family spread through the neighborhood.

In Crown Heights he is simply called the Rebbe. Menachem M. Schneerson is the octogenarian Grand Rabbi of Lubavitch. For seven generations his family, from father to son, has passed down this grand Hasidic title. Though a member of a kind of religious royalty, the Rebbe is far from forbidding; he has the innocence of the elect. His pale blue eyes are clear and very striking and his lips are firmly set. His full white beard is the image of benign old age. Many in this committed community of twenty thousand believe that he is the potential *moshiach,* the coming messiah.

The streets of Jewish Crown Heights have the glow of commitment. There are many young men and women in this community of large families. They carry themselves with a sense of purpose. If they are not in Manhattan trying to reclaim nonreligious Jews, they are following the Rebbe's dictums about charity. Their elders also have the words of the Rebbe on their lips; they mill around the Lubavitchers' headquarters as if it were the Temple in Jerusalem.

The streets of Jewish Crown Heights have an unexpected tranquility. After all, this is big-city Brooklyn, not a *shtetl* in eighteenth-century Eastern Europe. Everyone seems to recognize one another and there is an unspoken consideration. The face of Jewish Crown Heights is open. The shopkeepers don't know how to stock their shelves or arrange a window, but they know people by name and always ask about their families. In every store there is a picture of the Rebbe. And the life of the community follows the rhythm of the Jewish calendar, from the penance of Yom Kippur to the joy of Purim.

Lubavitcher Tastes

The restaurants in Jewish Crown Heights are furnished like someone's kitchen, the food doesn't try to rise above hearty, and the food shops seem to take more pains over dietary laws than taste. Jewish Crown Heights is not really about food.

Mermelstein's, *351 Kingston Avenue (718-778-3100). Sunday–Thursday 9 A.M.–9:30 P.M.; Friday 9 A.M.–4 P.M.*

The Orthodox diners eat with the intensity they bring to their *bruchas* (blessings). The stuffed pepper and stuffed cabbage are heavy on the sweet with currants and raisins. The southern fried chicken is the south of Hungary.

Ess & Bentch *(Eat & Pray), 299 Kingston Avenue (718-771-9323). Sunday–Thursday 8 A.M.–midnight; Friday 8 A.M.–two hours before sunset.*

Yeshiva boys with mischievous expressions under broad-brimmed hats sneak in here between classes for a deli nosh. The meat sandwiches can run a little heavy, but the lighter salad sandwiches are a good bet.

Oneg Bake Shop, *425 Kingston Avenue (718-493-2697). Sunday–Wednesday 7 A.M.–7 P.M.; Thursday 7 A.M.–8 P.M.; Friday 7 A.M.–4 P.M.*

The Jewish mother who presides over Oneg has wide smiles for strangers as well as for regular customers. She is particularly proud of the *challah* (a braided egg bread) Oneg bakes for the Sabbath and the holiday honey and sponge cakes.

Kosher Candy, *419 Kingston Avenue (718-778-6037). Sunday–*
Thursday 7:30 A.M.–6:30 P.M.; Friday 7:30 A.M.–3:30 P.M.

This is a vintage Brooklyn sweet shop, only all the candy is made under strict
rabbinical supervision with no animal fat or animal enzymes or milky
product. It's a lot of trouble over jelly beans, pop corn, and *parve* tofutti.

Nosh World, *386 Kingston Avenue (718-363-1920). Sunday–*
Thursday noon–1 A.M.; Friday noon to half hour before sunset.

The meat and poultry are glatt kosher but that doesn't make them more
appetizing. The salads—carrot, eggplant, and beet—are the safest course.

Shabbos Fish Market, *417 Kingston Avenue (718-774-1659).*
Sunday–Thursday 8:30 A.M.–6:30 P.M.; Friday 8:30 A.M.–2 P.M.

The fish is so fresh it's still swimming in the tank. The fishmonger wears a
rubber apron and hip boots.

Religious Gifts

Outside the Lubavitchers' main offices there is a banner in Hebrew proclaim-
ing "We Want Moshiach Now." The Lubavitchers follow the millennial
tradition; they pray for a messiah and more than half expect it. But while they
wait, they endeavor to live worthy lives and follow Jewish traditions. Those
traditions are reflected in some of the more interesting stores in the neighborhood.

Tzivos Hashem, *332 Kingston Avenue (718-467-6630). Sunday–*
Thursday 11:30 A.M.–7 P.M.; Friday 10:30 A.M.–2 P.M.

The *Tzivos Hashem* means the "Army of God." This army is comprised of
the children of Jewish Crown Heights. Tzivos Hashem is a toy store with a
message. The jigsaw puzzles, board games, and Hebrew letter blocks are
Lubavitcher lessons.

Hafmitz Stam, *361 Kingston Avenue (718-744-0900). Sunday–*
Thursday 11 A.M.–7:30 P.M.; Friday 11 A.M.–3 P.M.

Hafmitz Stam supplies Crown Heights with every variety of religious article.
The prayer shawls, *yarmulkes* (skull caps), and Sabbath candelabras are
imports from Israel. There are full-color pictures of the Rebbe appropriate
for framing.

Chassidic Art Institute, *375 Kingston Avenue (718-774-9149). Sunday–Thursday noon–7 P.M.; Friday noon to three hours before sundown.*

Chassidic art is representational and inspirational. There are paintings of the Rebbe and scenes from the Bible; the Lubavitcher commandments are represented in oils.

Lubavitcher Landmarks

The Rebbe's House, *770 Eastern Parkway.*

The Lubavitchers are a world movement. In Israel they have a group that subscribes to the wisdom of the Rebbe and even keeps a model of the Rebbe's Brooklyn house at 770 Eastern Parkway in a place of honor. The house is from the days Eastern Parkway was doctor's row. It's a big brick building with gables and hedges. On Sunday mornings Rabbi Schneerson stands in front of his house and distributes one dollar bills. It's a gesture to promote *tzadek,* charity.

Lubavitcher Headquarters, *784–788 Eastern Parkway.*

The Lubavitcher Headquarters is the nerve center of the Lubavitcher organization. It plans and administers the group's outreach and charitable programs and day-to-day operations. It has its own communications center with a radio transmitter and video facilities. The Hasidim in the neighborhood spontaneously gather around the building during a crisis or a time of special celebration. The building is now in the process of becoming a twenty million dollar shrine.

Williamsburg

Directions: IRT-Lexington Avenue 4 or 5, or IRT Seventh Avenue 3 to Fulton Street. Change to M or J to Marcy Avenue. Take B24 (free transfer) to Lee/Division Street.

Introduction

Williamsburg fans out from the bridge bearing its name to Flushing and Bushwick Avenues. It was part of the original Dutch farm settlement of Bushwick, but didn't have a life of its own until it was surveyed by a Colonel Williams in 1810. By the middle of the nineteenth century it was a luxurious resort attracting high society and the robber barons from Commodore Vanderbilt to William C. Whitney. In 1903 the Williamsburg Bridge made this attractive corner of Brooklyn accessible to the immigrant masses. Hotels were replaced by congested tenements.

Jews, Poles, and Italians poured out of the Lower East Side to cross the bridge and populate Williamsburg. But it turned out that they exchanged one set of slums for another. The city tried to redevelop the area by building costly public housing. At the time, people marveled at the Williamsburg Houses and favorably compared them to housing on Park Avenue. Still, the neighborhood decline continued and the old ethnics deserted Williamsburg for the suburbs after World War II. The Satmar, a sect of Hasidic Jews from Hungary, stepped into the breach. They now share the area with Hispanic arrivals.

The Satmar, whose name derives from the Hungarian village of Satu Mare (St. Mary), are the Orthodox of the Orthodox, strict constructionists of an exacting Torah. Their food is under the strict supervision of Hasidic rabbis and must be glatt kosher; their clothes, when not manufactured by one of their own, are taken apart and tested for shatness (impurities), and even corpses are given a ritual bath before burial. They do not practice any form of birth control. Unlike other Orthodox Jews they have deep antipathy toward Israel, a secular state that they believe has interfered with the spiritual plan of the redemptive messiah.

The Williamsburg Jews live like their Old World ancestors. They have their own theocracy with the Rebbe, the holy man and ultimate authority. There are rabbinical courts that mediate disputes and enact punishments. Many in the community devote their lives to prayer and study, while radio, television, and even some Yiddish newspapers are forbidden. Their spirituality is reflected in their austere dark coats and jackets and the black

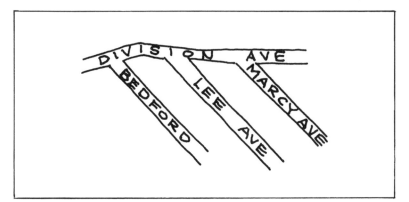

Williamsburg

homburgs they favor. In the middle of Brooklyn these remarkable people live a slow otherworldly existence out of another century.

The main street of the Satmar village is Lee Avenue. It is where the mothers wheel the carriages and the communal buses leave for the diamond district. The stores, like everything else in the neighborhood, are stripped of decoration that would be frivolous. The signs are in Yiddish and English and very direct. There are nineteenth-century touches like little girls wearing long dresses with high collars and woolen stockings and bearded men in top hats and Chesterfield coats. There are paradoxes along the avenue.

On the surface the Jews of Williamsburg are solemn and severe, a sort of Brooklyn Jewish puritan in black gabardine, the image of formal rectitude. But the men and women of Williamsburg can unbend, especially in the company of playful children. There is a real capacity for joy that comes out in their holiday celebrations, a smile under the dignified display. It is a place of paradoxes: young men with sidelocks and old faces and old men with beards and young faces.

Strictly, Strictly Kosher

The Satmar are finicky when it comes to judging whether a place serving food conforms to dietary laws. but when it comes to eating their tastes are simple. The rabbinical seal of approval has a more prominent place in restaurant windows than the daily specials.

Landau's Glatt Kosher Deli, *65 Lee Avenue (718-782-3700). Sunday–Thursday noon–10 P.M.; Friday noon to one hour before sundown.*

This Jewish deli may never make a list of New York's ten best, but its thick-cut brisket sandwich on fresh seeded rye cannot be equaled for twice the price in Manhattan.

Itzu's, *45 Lee Avenue (718-384-8631). Sunday–Thursday 5 A.M.–6 P.M.; Friday 5 A.M.–1 P.M.*

This is a genuine Satmar hangout with Yiddish banter and table-hopping. There is the smell of cheese and potato blintzes frying in butter and when these beauties come to the table they get a dollop or two of sour cream or applesauce.

The food shops are pure pandemonium on Friday morning before the sundown Sabbath and on the eve of a holiday. Satmar men and women compete for the salesclerks' attention to get the really best for the family table. At other times the shops are forlornly empty.

Flaum Appetizers, *40 Lee Avenue (718-387-7934). Sunday–Thursday 8:30 A.M.–6 P.M.; Friday 8:30 A.M.–2 P.M.*

The people at Flaum run their business like a public trust, warning you off one item and urging another. The smoked salmon can compete with the yuppie appetizer shops on the Upper West Side of Manhattan at a fraction of the price.

Sander's Kosher Bakery Shop, *159 Lee Avenue (718-387-7411). Sunday–Thursday 6:30 A.M.–9 P.M.; Friday 6:30 A.M.–4 P.M.*

Sander's takes a special delight in the large twisted fragrant Sabbath *challahs* (egg bread) and holiday baked goods like the *hamantaschen* (three-cornered pastries for Purim filled with prune preserves).

The Rebbe's House

Congregation Yetev Lev D'Satmar, *554 Bedford Avenue.*

This synagogue is not only a place of prayer, it is a Torah (the first five books of the Old Testament, sacred to the Jews) study house and a social center. The Satmar pray with a fervor that can only be compared with Pentecostal Christians. It is pure exaltation, bending backwards and forwards as they pray, almost shouting, to the Creator. The stiffness that the Satmar sometimes show totally disappears in Torah worship.

The Festival of Simchas Torah

Satmar has its schools and synagogues on Bedford Street; it is the center of the community's spiritual existence. On joyous Simchas Torah, the holy scrolls of Torah are celebrated as the cycle of the Torah readings begins all over again. Bedford Street is closed off on Simchas Torah night and there is a *Hakafos* (a religious procession). All night long the Satmar dance and chant and clap and sway, transported by the wonder of it all. Simchas Torah usually takes place in October, but it is a movable feast. For exact times contact the synagogue.

Brighton Beach

Directions: IND D train to Ocean Parkway/Brighton Beach Avenue.

Introduction

Brighton Beach in the seventeenth century was just a scrubby section of sand on Konijn Eisland (Rabbit Island) with more long-eared rodents than human inhabitants. In the early part of the nineteenth century it was a popular destination for paddle steamers from Manhattan carrying day-trippers out for the sea and the sun and a picnic. In the 1870s John Y. McKane, a Brooklyn political boss, made some land grants that included Brooklyn's Brighton Beach, and it began to be developed as a resort.

A decade later Brighton Beach had a racetrack, a hotel, and a music hall that attracted big spenders like "Diamond Jim" Brady. It was the Atlantic City of its day with the glamour and the gamblers but also the prostitution and the crime. The resort went respectable in 1909, when racing was banned. The new summer residents were Eastern European Jewish immigrants who stayed in baseboard bungalows.

When the subway expanded to Coney Island in 1920, the summer renters became full-time. Suddenly there were thirty six-story apartment houses where there had been sand. There were many synagogues, some with *mikvahs* (ritual baths) and Jewish social and charitable organizations. During the Depression and the war years, this religious and politically conscious Jewish neighborhood was overcrowded.

After World War II, Jewish refugees from the Holocaust settled in Brighton Beach. Older Jews from Brownsville and Williamsburg came to the community in the 1960s and early 1970s, refugees from crime and decay.

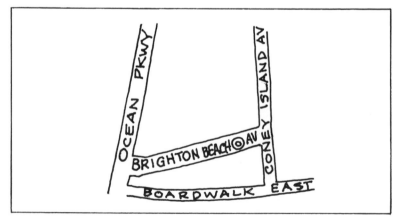

Brighton Beach

But Brighton Beach was still aging and moving south for retirement. There was an epidemic of housing vacancies and some were being filled by unsupervised mental patients. The neighborhood was poised on the edge of decline when emigrants from the Soviet Union saved the day.

These Soviet Jews were part of a protest movement that started in the 1960s and mushroomed after the Israeli Six Day War. They were tired of the restrictions and discrimination that Jews faced in the USSR and wanted to reassert their own Jewish identities. They risked everything to apply for emigration to Israel. The Jews of Silence became refuseniks.

In 1976 the HIAS, the Hebrew Immigration Aid Society, began channeling some of the Soviet emigrants into America. These later refugees were not the committed Zionists of the first waves of Soviet emigration. They were refugees of opportunity, who resented the Jewish quotas in the universities and the shortages of food, clothing, and shelter. The majority of these emigrant families were from the seaside city of Odessa, and Brighton Beach had the charm of the familiar, with its long boardwalk and three miles of beach.

Brighton Beach also had cheap and spacious apartments and plenty of commercial vacancies for aspiring Russian entrepreneurs. The Soviet emigres went about remaking the neighborhood in their own image, with Russian-style stores and signs using Cryrillic letters, and the streets came back to life. Most immigrants thrived in the freer, make-your-own-choices environment. While some engineers, doctors, and lawyers wound up driving cabs, there were Odessa cab drivers who became business successes.

The streets of Brighton Beach have lost the old Jewish neighborhood calm. There is a youthful volatility that is pure Russian. The Russian conversation is excited and the pedestrain traffic is impatient. Younger men and women of the newest immigration outwardly enjoy the materialism of the West with smart clothes and fashionable hairdos. Their unsophisticated elders wear Soviet suspenders and straw hats and brightly printed scarves and shapeless smocks. They are full-figured and have not discovered the American fad for dieting. When they smile in their sheepish way, bits of gold gleam from their mouths.

Borscht without Tears

Russian Jewish cuisine à la Brighton Beach is not quite Russian (at least don't expect the Russian Tea Room), nor is it brisket-and-chicken-fat Jewish. The food is southern Ukraine, a hybrid of the cuisines of Mother Russia and the Central Asian Steppe, maybe kosher but not kosher-style.

The local cuisine, like Brighton Beach itself, is short on subtlety and very obvious—heavy on the onions, garlic, dill, and lemon juice. The food is to be flat-out enjoyed, not mulled over and appreciated. And drink, preferably chilled vodka with orange peel or buffalo grass, is the necessary complement for this Russian-Jewish eating experience. Brighton Beach Avenue is where most of the good eating starts.

Primorski, *282 Brighton Beach Avenue (718-891-3111). Daily 11 A.M.–2 A.M.*

Primorski cooks with a touch of the Caucauses of Soviet Georgia. Circassian chicken in walnut sauce is served Georgian style as a main course. The shashlik (skewered lamb) is moist and tender and the soylanka (lamb stew) has the delightful tartness of Central Asia. There is a very reasonable three-course dinner.

Zodiac, *309 Brighton Beach Avenue (718-891-2000). Daily noon–midnight.*

The Zodiac is a dark eating place done in science-fiction modern. It is more self-conscious than the usual relax-and-unwind Russian-Jewish restaurant. The menu is Brighton Beach standard with a chicken Kiev that is anything but standard.

Kavkaz, *405 Brighton Beach Avenue (718-891-5400). Daily 11 A.M.–midnight.*

Kavkaz is glitter on the ceiling, more mirrors than a locker room, and an open kitchen. Still the food is above average and sometimes original. Lamb chops on a skewer are a real improvement over ordinary shashlik. The hot borscht is perked up with bits of beef and vegetables. The Stolichnaya vodka comes in carafes.

Mrs. Stahl's Delicious Knishes, *1001 Brighton Beach Avenue (718-648-0210). Daily 8 A.M.–6:45 P.M. (Manhattan branch at 146 West 72nd, (212-580-7019). Monday–Friday 8 A.M.–9 P.M.; Saturday, Sunday 10 A.M.–9 P.M.)*

The knishes are even better than Yonnah Schimmel's, with tasty and unusual fillings like sweet potato and spinach in a pastry crust.

The Balalaika Plays On

When the Jews of Brighton Beach celebrate—which is practically every weekend—they celebrate Russian style. The music is fast dance or slow sad, the vodka toasts are nonstop, and the eating is total excess. Nobody is taking a cholesterol count or counting the drinks or even notices how loud the music is playing. While people are enjoying the pleasures of Mother Russia, they are forgetting themselves.

When Brighton Beach's Russian Jewish nightclubs first opened, the people dressed like caricatures of Las Vegas chic and the clubs themselves had crystal chandeliers and cupid fountains. The balalaikas were electric guitars and the sounds were Russian, Yiddish, and American disco. Though the dance floor was hardly the size of the Rainbow Room, spontaneity ruled and at the right moment everyone got up, formed a circle or threw arms over one another's shoulders, and whirled around the floor till the room started listing.

The decor has been toned down and the dancing isn't as passionate as it used to be. A lot of the Russians now dress for success rather than *Guys and Dolls*. But it is still an all-Russian affair with an openness and warmth that is truly exhilarating. At the end of an evening, when the lights dim and the band plays Brighton Beach's unofficial anthem ''Oy Odess,'' there is not a dry eye in the house.

Odessa, *1113 Brighton Beach Avenue (718-332-3223). Daily 8 P.M. until you can't dance anymore.*

The appointments are streamlined and modern, and the dancing is more couples than circles, but Brighton Beach obviously approves of the changes since you still have to wait a month for a reservation. There is one charge for all you can eat and a bottle of vodka for a party of four. The Caucasian chicken, chicken Kiev, and shish kebab just keep on coming and you haven't even put a dent in the chilled Stolichnaya.

The National, *273 Brighton Beach Avenue (718-646-1225). Friday–Sunday 8:30 P.M.–3 A.M.*

The National is as big as a wedding hall and it gets a lot of the Brighton Beach wedding parties. It also gets most of the rubberneckers from Manhattan. The buffet starts slowly with the pickled mushrooms and tongue and works its way through the *pirogen* (small turnovers) and Caucasian chicken to a grand kebab climax. The band is relentless with more special effects than a Spielberg movie and the dancers hardly ever sit down.

From Kvas to Caviar

Brighton Beach Avenue's food shops are at a fever pitch on weekends. The Russian Jews put the same energy into shopping that they put into having a party. And the broad-shouldered *babushkas* (grandmothers) are terrors at the food counters as they maneuver for first place. Though most of the clerks in the stores speak only Russian, it doesn't matter since no one can hear anyone anyway. The big food markets have a range of Russian and Eastern European products that impresses, and it's worth suffering through the crowd scene.

M & I International Foods, *249 Brighton Beach Avenue (718-615-1011). Daily 8 A.M.–9 P.M.*

M & I International Food is Brighton Beach's answer to Dean & De Luca. But instead of having shelves of extra-virgin olive oil and balsamic vinegar, it has miles of garlicky Russian sausage and bottle after bottle of sour pickles. M & I needs two floors and an army of thick-skinned clerks to sell all its prepared foods, cold-smoked fish, fresh produce, sweets and cakes, net bags of garlic, and caviar.

Mos Deli, *411 Brighton Beach Avenue (718-769-2466). Tuesday–Sunday 8 A.M.–8 P.M.*

In front they are selling *kvas* from the barrel (the mildly alcoholic drink of choice for peasants in Dostoyevski novels). It should be avoided, but the cold-smoked chub (herring) is something special and so are their pickled vegetables.

Fish Town, *414 Brighton Beach Avenue (718-332-7445).*

Fish Town is not only a fish store; it is also a pun on owner Gregory Fishilevich's name. If the store isn't mobbed with fish lovers, Gregory is more than happy to explain the difference between Russian cold-smoked (the fish takes longer to smoke and is moister and closer to the taste of Japanese raw fish) fish and hot-smoked fish and maybe plug his Beluga caviar that sells for 20 percent less than the caviar anywhere else.

Russian Samozat

The Black Sea Bookstore, *3175 Coney Island Avenue (718-769-2878). Daily 11 A.M.–6 P.M.*

The young woman at the front desk is either reading a book or matching wits with the local intelligentsia, all of course in Russian. The Russian readers thumb through the Russian books from Paris and the Soviet Union like the place is a library. They have the latest cassettes of Russian rock groups and *samozat* (unofficially printed protest literature) from writers who haven't yet heard of Glasnost.

Aleppo in Flatbush

Directions: IND F to Kings Highway/McDonald Avenue.

Introduction

The El station at McDonald Avenue and Kings Highway divides a modest mainstream Italian neighborhood from one of Brooklyn's most fascinating Jewish quarters. It is Oriental Jewish territory, comprised of old-guard Syrian families and Israeli newcomers.

The Brooklyn Jewish Levant is in the southern section of Flatbush, originally called Midwout by the Dutch and anglicized to Midwood. In the seventeenth century it remained a Dutch-speaking enclave even after the British began to rule. For fifty years after the American Revolution King George III's coat of arms hung in the town hall.

In 1894 Midwood became a part of Brooklyn and by the time the subway linked it to Manhattan in 1920, Horatio Alger ethnics occupied its sturdy brick buildings. It became the preserve of Syrian Jews in the 1940s.

The area's Syrian Jews are proud of their noble pedigree, tracing their ancestors back to the Babylonian captivity and the destruction of the Temple

Aleppo in Flatbush

in 586 B.C. They are mainly of the exclusive Jewish clan of Aleppo (H'alab), the ancestral city of Abraham.

For centuries they were intermediaries between East and West on the caravan routes to the Orient. But their peaceful and prosperous world finally came crashing down amid the conflicts and political changes of the Ottoman Empire. These ancient people of the East were forced to leave Syria for the Lower East Side.

The America of streetcars and sweatshops and tenements came as a shock. They were outsiders in this alien city and had nothing in common with their Eastern European Jewish neighbors. They banded together in Sephardic boardinghouses, making the most of their limited resources.

Eventually the community managed to make its way to Williamsburg, where they were reunited with their families. In the 1920s and 1930s the Syrian-Jewish community settled in Bensonhurst. They built a synagogue and a religious school and opened a dozen Oriental food stores on 20th Avenue. By the 1940s the upwardly mobile Syrian Jews had discovered the new promised land in the area of Midwood in Flatbush.

The Syrian Jews have not been spoiled by success. While making money in imports and exports, especially electronics and clothing, they have not deserted their neighborhood or broken the continuity of their centuries-old community. They are a rarity, a Jewish community without identifiable clothing or physical attributes, that has maintained its customs and traditions.

Brooklyn Jewish Arabs have reached out to help the surviving Jewish communities of Aleppo and Damascus. After the creation of the state of Israel, many Syrian Jews who were at risk were aided by Aleppo-in-Brooklyn. This Syrian-Jewish remnant was assisted in escaping or bribing its way to safety. These refugees and later Oriental arrivals injected new life into the Midwood community.

Aleppo in Flatbush looks substantial—large one- and two-family brick houses, tall hedges, and broad shade trees. It extends from Avenue I and Avenue Y, intersected by Ocean Parkway. It is comfortably suburban, a place for close Sephardic families to stroll along tree-lined streets "to temple." There are houses of worship here representing the Syrian Jewish communities of Aleppo, Damascus, Egypt, and Lebanon, schools, and a large community center.

Today, the Syrian Jews of Brooklyn are being joined by the latest Jewish immigrants from the Mideast. These new arrivals are from Israel and, though the first to come were of Syrian or other Arab Jewish descent, the Israelis who followed are now mostly of Eastern European origin.

Israeli emigrants or *Yoridim* are sometimes considered turncoats by the people they left behind. Still, they continue coming in large numbers, creating long lines for visas in front of the American Embassy in Tel Aviv.

The numbers of Israelis entering New York and the Midwood neighborhood increased after the Yom Kippur War in 1973. They were looking for economic and employment opportunities and they were looking for peace. They represented all layers of Israeli society from manual laborers to big business.

Midwood's *Yoridim* say they will always be Israelis, and the Kings Highway neighborhood displays a direct and matter-of-fact Israeli character and culture. In Midwood, Hebrew is sometimes the spoken language, but it is also clear that these Israelis are opening up businesses and putting down roots.

Jewish Near East Eating

The Midwood Levant is easy to recognize, with signs in Hebrew and Arabic and the aroma of Eastern spices and Israeli *felafel* in the air. The restaurants and the food are more blunt Israeli than subtle Sephardic. The Mid-Eastern *meze* (appetizers) like *baba ghanuoj* and *hommus* are blander with less lemon and garlic, and the meat dishes like the lamb with okra and the *kebbe* (ground lamb with pine nuts) do not have the cinnamon and rose-water delicacy.

While the Oriental Jews have adopted a more low-key American style, the vibrant Israelis retain their unwavering directness and dry humor. The "People of the Book" are nonstop talkers. The restaurants and snack shops are scenes of uninhibited Hebrew conversation.

King Solomon Restaurant, *529 Kings Highway (718-339-0707). Sunday–Thursday 9 A.M.–midnight; Friday 9 A.M.–3 P.M.*

It's not easy to order with the all-Hebrew menu and the non-English speaker behind the counter, but sign language can go a long way. Point to the *shawarma* (the vertical lamb on a spit) and the pita bread or a Middle Eastern omelet steeped in peppers and tomato.

McDaniels, *555 Kings Highway (212-627-9668). Sunday–Thursday 10 A.M.–10 P.M.; Friday 10 A.M.–5 P.M.; Saturday 7:30 P.M.–11 P.M.*

McDaniels is the kosher McDonald's of Kings Highway. The recent Sephardic arrivals who opened McDaniels add Oriental spice to their fast food. They serve pizza that could pass for *lamajhan* and Middle-Eastern *bourek* (a cheese pie) under the name *calzone*.

Dates and Spices

On Kings Highway near 4th Street there are a host of stores catering to Syrian Jewish tastes, selling bulgar (cracked wheat), Arab yogurt called *leban,* and produce like eggplant and artichokes. The stores have not put on the American gloss; they have a homey look with handwritten signs, uncategorizable shelves, and improvised fixtures. On Avenue M and Avenue U there are assimilated Syrian small businesses from butchers to jewelers that are indistinguishable from American.

Kosher Korner, *492 Kings Highway (718-645-2466). Sunday–Thursday 8 A.M.–8 P.M.; Friday 8 A.M.–6:30 P.M.*

The Kosher Korner is a Middle Eastern supermarket. It has everything the atmospheric Arab Jewish groceries have up the street plus convenient self-service shopping. In the back there is a fresh-ground Turkish roast coffee and in the front a comprehensive assortment of dried fruits, grains, and nuts. Syrian foods have joined the twentieth century, with frozen *bourek* and *lamajhan.*

Mansoura Pastry, *515 Kings Highway (718-645-7977). Sunday–Thursday 9 A.M.–6 P.M.; Friday 9 A.M.–5 P.M.*

The pastry from *baklawa* to the *knifeh* is Arabic Alleppo. There are Arabic flatbreads to be complemented by Mansoura's full line of *mezes,* which are prepared fresh and are the best in the neighborhood. The courteous owner looks Levantine but there is Brooklyn in his voice.

Phoenicia, *551 Kings Highway (718-645-2466). Sunday–Thursday 7:30 A.M.–8 P.M.; Friday 7:30 A.M.–6 P.M.*

Phoenicia is a neighborhood grocery with a Middle Eastern flare. There are shelves of canned goods from Israel and local Arab wholesalers, zip-lock bags of spices, dried fruit, seeds, and nuts, and open containers of olives and pickled vegetables. The gray-haired proprietor, who speaks Arabic to his scurrying employees, and the incense of cardamon and cinnamon create a feeling of faraway places.

The Greeks

History

New York's first Greek Consul General claimed Columbus was a Byzantine nobleman named Dispatsos. Although this was never substantiated, there is documentation that at least one sailor in Columbus's crew, John Griego, was Greek. The Consul General, John Botassi, when not creating history or moonlighting as the representative for the Ralli Brothers Import and Export Company, did his best to discourage his countrymen from settling in New York in the early part of the nineteenth century.

Despite official warnings, Chriastos Tsakonas came to New York in 1873. Convinced that New York was the land of opportunity, two years later he went back to Greece with the purpose of bringing out five compatriots. For his efforts this first Greek immigrant to New York has been called in local annals the "Columbus of Sparta."

Greek immigration to New York and the whole United States grew slowly, despite the pressure of an increasing population dependent on a relatively small amount of cultivatable land. It finally took off when Greek agriculture was devastated by the decline of its chief cash crop, the humble currant. In twenty years, one fifth to one quarter of the Greek labor force emigrated. This large-scale flight began in Sparta and swept through neighboring Arcadia and the whole Peloponnese before becoming a mass movement in central Greece, Crete, and the islands.

Fighting in the Balkans and the revolutionary activity in the Ottoman Empire spurred Greek-speaking populations in Constantinople and Anatolia to follow. Greek immigration was also encouraged by the exertions of enterprising Greek steamship agents who canvassed customers from Alexandria to Constantinople.

The majority of Greek arrivals, who came from rural areas, still gravitated to the cities. They preferred the urban feeling of being close to people. The farms in America were too spread out from one another for the gregarious Greeks. Most of these Greek immigrants were male—95 percent were men in the peak years between 1899 and 1910—but they quickly returned to bring back other members of their family and get married. The first Greek New Yorkers settled in the South Bronx and along Eighth Avenue between 14th and 15th Streets in Manhattan; later they went to live in lower Manhattan, Hell's Kitchen, and Washington Heights.

The earliest generation of Greek New Yorkers came as *padrone* labor; they were indentured for an indefinite period, usually three or four months, to the *padrone* who provided the passage and show money to meet immigration requirements. In Greece, land was mortgaged as a guarantee that the new New Yorker would not renege on this debt. There were many abuses under this system, with some very young or very naive immigrants working years for a *padrone* for practically nothing.

Greeks fresh off the boat usually found work as dishwashers, flower sellers, or bootblacks. Dishwashing was dirty, low-paying, backbreaking work, but it was the first rung on the ladder to owning your own restaurant. In New York, Greek involvement in the restaurant business led to the saying, "If two Greeks meet, they start a restaurant." The Greeks were active in the wholesale and retail flower business, and the new immigrant often wound up on the street peddling flowers that were not good enough to be sold in stores. Shining shoes was considered by Greeks to be demeaning work even if the owner of the shoestand was a fellow countryman, and it was very hard work with a fifteen-hour day norm.

In 1894 the first daily newspaper in Greek, the *Atlantis,* was started in New York buy Solon Vlastos. Although it defended the interests of the Greek-American workingman and fought the abuses of the *padrone* system, it was royalist and conservative in its outlook toward Greek national politics. *Atlantis* didn't have any competition until 1915, when Demetrios Callimachos launched *Ethnikos Kiryx* (National Herald), a newspaper that was antiroyalist and supported the Panhellenic policies of the Greek Republic leader, Venizelos. Now the political debates that raged in New York's *kafeneia* (Greek coffeehouses) were out on the newsstands.

The rivalry between the Royalists and the Republicans reflected regional differences between Greeks, which eventually split the local community. There were separate social organizations and even separate churches representing the two points of view. World War I made it even more volatile, with Venizelos backing the Allies and King Constantine calling for neutrality.

Ultimately Greek-Americans laid aside past political affiliations to pull together for their adopted country. The Greek community sold over ten million dollars in U.S. War Bonds and over sixty thousand Greeks served in the American army in World War I. Greek New Yorkers faced another sort of political problem after the war, resulting from a wave of antiforeign sentiment. Greek-Americans were the victims of unprovoked attacks and calculated business boycotts. In 1921 the Johnson Act was passed, reducing Greek immigration to one hundred a year. Greeks responded to this bigotry by strengthening both their American and Greek identities. They formed AHEPA, the American Hellenic Educational Progressive Association, in New York in 1922. Its purpose was to promote Americanization, English-language education, and American values. The American Progressive Association, which was established in New York the following year, took the opposite tack, calling for the preservation of the Greek language and Greek customs among first- and second-generation Greek-Americans.

Both of these approaches proved successful. Greek New Yorkers made the leap from blue collar to white collar in one generation. Greeks now have one of the highest percentages of professionals—doctors, lawyers, and engineers—of any immigrant group, and while they have acquired affluence and social prestige they have kept their ties with their ethnic past. In New York alone there are sixty associations dedicated to the traditions of particular Greek villages, islands, or regions. New York's eleven Greek day schools make sure that the special Greek identity continues into the future.

In 1965 a new immigration act was passed, altering the restrictive ethnic quotas. At the forefront of the movement to change the old law were old-line Greek organizations like AHEPA and APA and new Greek politicians like Paul Sarbanes and John Brademas and successful businessmen like Tom Pappas and Spyros Skouras. The new law ushered in a new wave of Greek immigration, which is still continuing. The new immigrants, whether Athenian professionals or dispossessed Cypriots, have revitalized New York's established Greek community. It has created a "Little Athens" in Astoria and a new sense of national pride in second- and third-generation Greek New Yorkers.

In 1974 conflicts in Cyprus and the defacto partition of the island led to a Greek Cypriot exodus. One of their prime destinations was New York. Many left with just the clothes on their backs and required special social services. Groups were formed like the Hellenic American Neighborhood Action Committee to cope with the immigrants' problems. They were instrumental in the implementation of bilingual education programs and speeded the delivery of conventional aid and supplementary benefits. They acted as a liaison between the non-English-speaking immigrant and the city government.

Astoria: Little Athens

Directions: BMT N to Ditmars Boulevard.

Introduction

Astoria is Old World Greece in Queens, Little Athens, north of Long Island City and across the East River. The faces are Mediterranean, the gestures are expansive, and the accents are rapid-fire Greek. The aroma of dark Greek coffee drifts through the streets, along with the wail of tape-deck bouzouki. Young couples café-sit over rich Greek pastry, and family groups promenade till after midnight. In a nightclub the size of a small stadium, members of the Association of Samos get up to do the *zeibekiko*.

This fifteen hundred acres in northeast Queens wasn't always an ethnic enclave. When William Hallett first took title in 1654, it was a beech forest on a riverbank without even an Indian. Governor Peter Stuyvesant didn't need much persuading to sign the land over. For the next 175 years it

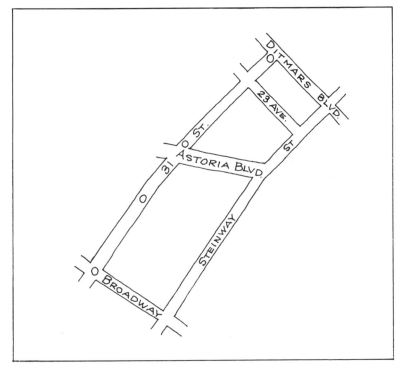

Astoria: Little Athens

remained undeveloped, a sleepy summer resort for rich Manhattanites, named Hallett's Cove in honor of its founder.

In 1839 New York's richest man, John Jacob Astor, overpowered local opposition to have Hallett's Cove incorporated as a town under his own name, Astoria. He went on to transform it into a prosperous ferry port doing a thriving trade with Manhattan. In no time the picturesque forest became lumber and the fragile summerhouses substantial mansions. Remnants of its opulent past still remain on 27th Avenue. The frame of the Greek revival Remsen House stands at 90-26 27th Avenue; across the street at 90-29 is Renaissance revival Wayt House.

By the turn of the century the area had lost its cachet and Italian and Irish immigrant families from Little Italy and Hell's Kitchen were moving in. With its rustic village green and attractive detached houses, it was a real contrast to the tenements and teaming streets of Manhattan. In 1927 the first Greek families came to live in Astoria. They declared their intentions to stay and build a community by laying the foundation for the Greek Orthodox church, St. Demetrios. This magnificent domed Byzantine edifice is still standing on 31st Street and boasts the largest Greek Orthodox congregation outside of Greece.

After World War II, returning veterans from Astoria were looking for a change and bypassed the old neighborhood to move farther out into Queens and east to rural Long Island. Astoria seemed secondhand and faded. Local industries were leaving and stores were staying vacant. The old ethnic communities had lost their verve.

Astoria was a working-class area on its way to becoming a slum, but in 1965 new life was breathed into the neighborhood with the passage of an amended immigration act that enabled thousands of Greek immigrants to enter the country. The new Greeks were drawn to Astoria by the already existing Greek community and its relatively suburban atmosphere. At least it was free of high rises. In a flurry of activity, old buildings were renovated and new buildings were constructed. New businesses that catered to the special needs of the community opened up one after another.

The new immigrants were primarily professionals from Athens whose skills were needed in the United States; the relatives of the old immigrants from the villages in the Peloponnese, central Greece, and the islands; and war refugees from Cyprus. Whether the arrivals were middle-class and modern, or working-class and traditional, or Cypriots speaking a strange dialect, they were welcomed with open arms by Astoria's Greeks.

Little Athens is always growing, but at the present time its borders are Ditmars Boulevard to the north, Broadway to the south, 31st Street to the west, and Steinway Street to the east. The Greek population within this rectangle is estimated at eighty thousand. It also contains eleven Greek Orthodox churches, countless two-family brick houses, and an assortment of restaurants, "tavernas," Greek nightclubs, coffeehouses, and exotic groceries.

Astoria's Times Square and crossroads is the intersection of Ditmars Boulevard and 31st Street, steps away from the Ditmars Boulevard subway stop, twenty minutes from Manhattan. To get a feel for Little Athens, promenade 31st Street, which is just under the elevated train track. Afterwards, walk up Ditmars Boulevard left of the subway station to Steinway Street and follow 23rd Avenue, making a complete rectangle turning back up to 31st Street.

Eating and Drinking

Restaurants and Tavernas

The terms *restaurant* and *taverna* have virtually lost their meaning in Astoria and are used interchangeably. A *taverna* in Astoria is just as likely to be an expensive restaurant with music as a standard, reasonably priced eating place with barrel wine and simple village fare. The distinction in Astoria's restaurants are more about the owner or the cook's place of origin in Greece or Cyprus than words like *psitaria* (grill) and *taverna*.

Since Astoria's restaurants basically cater to a Greek population, the Greek food is unequaled in authenticity by restaurants found in other parts of the city. The food is basic and hearty, depending on olive oil, oregano, garlic, and lemon for its singular flavor. Lamb is the meat of choice, whether in a stew or mixed in a layered *moussaka* (the Greek lasagna), or stuffed with cheese Corfu-style.

The Greeks are purists where meat is concerned and have a preference for grills, *souvlaki* on a spit or *brizoli* (chops). The cheese of choice for the Greeks is sharp, pungent feta, which is enjoyed in *horiatiki,* or village salad. The Cypriots like *haloumi,* which is often served fried as an appetizer or *meze*. The *mezedakia* is a collection of small dishes like *taramosalata* (a spread of fish eggs), *tzatziki* (yogurt mixed with garlic and cucumbers), *keftedes* (grilled meatballs), and delicacies like lambs brains. Drink is always accompanied by some kind of *meze*.

Eating out in Astoria is a social occasion. People take their time over food and the conversation is nonstop. Between courses parents and grandparents dandle children, and if there is music and the mood strikes, people get up and dance. Dining, as in Greece, starts late, around 9 P.M., and the restaurant closes when everyone finishes. To find out specific opening and closing times—which are always changing—call in advance.

Salonika Restaurant, *31-17 23rd Avenue (718-728-5829).*

The Salonika is a restaurant for romantic candlelight evenings. There is broiled fish and charcoal grilled *oktopodi* (octopus). One night a week ballad singer Marios Locca provides Hellenic atmosphere.

Taverna Vraka, *23-15 31st Street (718-721-3007).*

This restaurant has been drawing New York's celebrities for twenty years. It's said Onassis came here to listen to the sad songs sung by Lambis Krokydas and John Nikas. Governor Cuomo's assistant drops in for the *sheftali,* a highly spiced lamb sausage. It tries to look rustic but it's too New York for a true *taverna.*

Zygos Taverna *22-55 31st Street (718-728-7070).*

A display of rich tavern food, featuring lamb with *youvetsi* (small rice shaped pasta), *moussaka,* and stuffed tomatoes, entices almost at the door. Walk farther in and there's a whole lamb and coils of *kokoretsi* rotating over a blazing fire. The open kitchen encourages sturdy appetites. The room is darkened like a traditional *taverna,* the decor smart and understated.

Nea Hellas, *31-15 Ditmars Boulevard (718-278-7304).*

Nea Hellas is an unpretentious place with simple food (*doner* and shish kebabs and mile-high Greek gyros) and inexpensive prices. There is counter service, but most of the time the stools are filled with regulars passing the time with the convivial owner, John Spridakas. The back dining area has a primitive mural of Greek carousers straight out of an Athenian *taverna.*

Zacharoplasteia

A *zacharoplasteion* is a café cum pastry shop. The *zacharo* in *zacharoplasteion* refers to sugar and the pastries are extremely sweet. Two of the most popular, *baklava,* a phyllo pastry filled with pistachios, and the *loukamades,* a donut variation, are served swimming in honey. The *floghera* is rich with egg custard. The Greek version of espresso also comes *gliko* (very sweet), *metrio* (moderately sweet), and *sketo* (unsweetened). The *zacharoplasteion* is a place to make an art of doing nothing. It's a place to talk and let the world go by.

Lefkos Pyrgos, *22-85 31st Street (718-932-4423). Daily 7 A.M.–1 A.M.*

Called the White Castle for the famous tower in Salonica, the original home of a past owner, the shop is open and cheerful, adorned with Greek travel-poster art. A big part of the clientele is male and Old World. They hang out at the front tables. Lefkos Pyrgos is known in the Astoria community for its *koulourakia,* a kind of Christmas cookie.

Nights Out

The music is hypnotic. Combining the harmonies of bazouki, clarina, and violin against a field of insistent rhythm, slow or fast, mournful or happy, it makes a Greek dance. For Greeks it's *kefi,* that feeling of bubbling joy and high spirits that starts the feet moving. Greek dancing as old as the pagan rites is still alive in the nightclubs of Astoria.

Greek dances are generally put in two categories: the *pedecto* is quick and involves jumping, hopping, and leaping; the *syrto* is slow and involves pulling and dragging steps. The dances are often done in groups, in lines, or in open circles. Three of the most popular are the *haspaiko, tsamiko,* and *syrtaki.* Both the *haspaiko,* the slow and moody butcher's dance, and the *tsamiko,* the whirling acrobatic handkerchief dance, require practice, but the light and bouncy *syrtaki* can be learned in minutes. In Astoria's nightspots, they are all performed every evening, sometimes to the accompaniment of breaking plates.

Crystal Palace, *31-01 Broadway (718-545-8402). Daily 11 P.M.–1 A.M.*

The Crystal Palace is often filled with private parties. The owner, Paul Calamaras, talks about people dancing till dawn and literally covering the floor with money for the musicians. The dancing here is exceptional and it's a favorite place for new immigrants. Check ahead because it's often closed for private parties.

Grecian Cave, *31-11 Broadway (718-545-7373). Monday–Saturday 10 P.M.–4 A.M.*

There's a psuedo Las Vegas stage show with whey-faced belly dancers of indeterminate nationality. Many of the drinks come in tall glasses with ornamental umbrellas. The club seems to cater to bachelor parties and visiting firemen.

Stani, *290-21 23rd Avenue (718-728-4966). Daily 11 P.M.–4 A.M.*

Stani bills itself as the "family nightclub." It's a place where people bring the "kids" and the "kids" chase one another between the tables. Actually it's really a restaurant with a stage show that begins early. It tries hard to be both a *taverna* and a club.

Microcosmos, *21-11 31st Street (718-728-7093). Daily 5 P.M. until very late.*

Microcosmos is Astoria's version of sophistication, hi-tech, and black-on-black elegance. The crowd here is Greek, intellectual, and young. While they play at dissent and rebellion, the resident pianist, Lambis Krokidas, tickles the ivories. On weekends the music policy is more mainstream rock and the chic *boîte* becomes a disco.

Shopping

One of the joys of Astoria is doing a walkabout, Greek-style. Stop in the stores, look in the old-fashioned barrels and bins. Sample some of the foods, try the Kalamata olives or the sharp *mizithra* cheese from Crete, or the *bastirma,* the Greek version of salted beef or that unusual sweet, rose petals in syrup. The proprietors don't really care if you buy, but they do enjoy lively conversation and love to ask questions. Meanwhile, outside there's a sidewalk show. The barest hint of sun brings the old men out with their folding chairs and newspapers to engage in the ancient Greek art of argument. Soon passersby are joining in and people are treating one another to coffee. It's a slice of Greek life without the village fountain and the plane tree.

Expect the unexpected in Astoria's stores. A fruit store has a full line of Greek cheeses and delicacies; a meat market has vegetables and fruit. Gift shops mix Greek daily newspapers with holy icons and country and western records. Shopping in Astoria is just another way of sightseeing.

Kiryakos Grocery, *29-29 23rd Avenue (718-545-3931). Monday– Saturday 8 A.M.–7:30 P.M.*

Kiryakos has the odd, hard-to-find essences necessary for Greek cookery like almond, roses, and tamarind. Its owner, Kiryakos Moutaphopoulos, is proud of his selection of dried beans, from peas to the giant beans of *gigantes*. Some of the spices he claims to have brought from the spice market in Istanbul, where he still has family.

John's Fruit Market, *31-27 Ditmars Boulevard (718-278-0705).*
Monday–Saturday 9 A.M.–9 P.M.

The owner's name isn't John, it's Evangelous Barcus, and very little of his
business involves fruit. It is one of the places to go for the chewy Greek candy
loukoum and nougat. It has barrels filled with feta and Cypriot sheep cheese.
The store has the flavor of the Levant.

Kalamata, *38-01 Ditmars Boulevard (718-626-1250). Daily 8
A.M.–11 P.M.*

This store offers the widest variety of black and green olives and a big
assortment of Attic honeys. The owner, who comes from Volos, says that
the best cheeses come from the mountain area of Metsova and he sells plenty
of them to prove it. The store looks like a standard New York delicatessen
but the stock is very different.

Corfu Center, *22-113 31st Street (718-728-7212). Daily 6 A.M.–
midnight.*

It seems like only a newsstand from the outside but inside, in addition to the
Greek newspapers and magazines, there are tapes of Greek top ten hits and
better-than-average crafts from Corfu, including jewelry and knits.

Kentrikon Astorias, *31-12 23rd Avenue (718-721-9190). Monday–Saturday 10 A.M.–8:30 P.M.; Sunday noon–6 P.M.*

Kentrikon Astorias is a fancy gift shop specializing in the traditional Greek
paraphernalia involved in weddings, christenings, and holidays. Unlike
other ethnic shops, it stays away from mass-produced souvenirs in favor of
authentic handicrafts like village embroidery. There are tape decks of the
latest bouzouki and videocassettes of small-budget Greek movies.

Sevastakis, *22-39 31st Street (718-548-4119). Monday–Saturday
10 A.M.–8 P.M.; Sunday noon–5 P.M.*

The largest selection of imported Greek shoes in the city is here, running the
gamut from sturdy Cretan boots to beautifully executed copies of women's
designer pumps. Artemis Korkidis, the owner, delivers Greek warmth and
charm in addition to patient service.

Manhattan

Introduction

The Greeks never had an exclusive ethnic colony in Manhattan. During the years of mass immigration between 1890 and 1910, numbers of Greeks set down stakes in the West Village near the Washington and Gansevoort Markets, the meat and produce center of the city. It was just the right location for a people who would become heavily involved in the food-service industry. This area, which was known as New York's Levant, also attracted an interesting mix of Egyptians, Turks, Syrians, and Armenians. The streets that lead down to the waterfront were a casbah of exotic spices and exotic dancers, where bargains were sealed over tiny cups of Turkish coffee. But it all disappeared before World War II, making way for the construction of the West Side Highway.

Gansevoort Street is still the southern border of the frenetic New York wholesale meat market, an area of narrow cobblestone streets, nineteenth-century buildings, and twentieth-century traffic. It's worth a sightsee and can be reached by the IRT-Seventh Avenue, getting out at West Houston Street and walking west.

Many Greeks preferred to settle farther north, closer to the excitement and hurly-burly of midtown. They moved into an area straddling Chelsea and Hell's Kitchen between 26th Street and 47th Street, and lived side by side with the neighborhood's large Irish population. They labored in the Eleventh Avenue slaughterhouses and the flower market spreading out from 27th Street. Gradually the industrious Greeks took control of New York's wholesale flower industry and, instead of hefting sides of beef, were serving it in their own restaurants. The Greeks left Manhattan tenements to live in the greener pastures of Queens, Long Island, and New Jersey, but they still make their livelihood in the borough's food and flower businesses.

Since the 1950s Greek Manhattan has gone upscale. A new breed of golden Greeks with names like Onassis, Niarchos, and Livanos took Manhattan by storm with their shipping millions. High-spending and high profits, they are the 21 Club Greeks. Olympic Towers, the gaudy Onassis skyscraper and personal monument, epitomizes the lavish side of the city's Greek experience. Completed in 1974, in time to be christened but not occupied by Onassis, this fifty-one-story high rise, tinted like the tycoon's ever-present dark glasses, dominates the northeast corner of 51st Street and Fifth Avenue. It claims to be the first skyscraper in Manhattan to combine chic shopping, office space and luxury apartments, and the first to have a waterfall, trees, and an open bar in its lobby.

Restaurants

The Greeks, with their rural background, do not claim any native expertise in running restaurants, but the *kafeneion,* which serves snacks as well as coffee, was always a respected village institution where people met to transact personal business and deal with community problems. In the New York environment the *kafeneion* quickly lost its Greek exclusivity and, under the name of "coffee shop," became the New Yorker's favorite spot for eating on the run. They serve large portions of simple foods like goulash or hamburgers "to stay or take away."

Today, as in the past, the coffee shop is the Greek path to success. Beginning as dishwashers, busboys, waiters, and hot dog stand operators, through perseverance and hard work, they now own and manage restaurants. Currently, Greeks are the most important force in Manhattan's commercial food business, from street vendors to king-sized midtown luncheonettes.

The Greek-owned restaurants in Manhattan are too numerous to mention, but a contingent specializes in Greek cuisine.

Molfetas, *307 West 47th Street (212-840-9537). Monday–Saturday 6 P.M.–11:30 P.M.*

The oldest Greek restaurant in Manhattan and considered by many to be the best outside of Astoria. The lamb, whether grilled or minced or in a stew, attracts a celebrity following.

New Acropolis, *767 Eighth Avenue at 47th Street (212-581-2733). Daily 11 A.M.–11:15 P.M.*

The New Acropolis gets the overflow from Molfetas. It has the look of a luncheonette straining to be a grown-up restaurant. The *baklava* and other pastries are the standouts on the menu.

Periyali, *35 West 20th Street (212-463-7890). Monday–Saturday noon–3 P.M., 6 P.M.–11 P.M.*

Periyali can get noisy, but the lamb dishes are worth the decibel level. The fare is simple island food. The *gigantes,* stewed white beans in a light tomato sauce, are outstanding.

Plaka, *165 Bleecker Street near Avenue of the Americas (212-674-9709). noon–midnight.*

Greeks eat here, Greek music is in the background, and the white stucco decor could be in Athens. The adventurous will want to try the marinated octopus.

Z, *117 East 15th Street (212-254-0960). Monday–Friday 11:30 A.M.–10 P.M.; Saturday 2 P.M.–10 P.M.*

A neatly arranged restaurant with red-and-black checked tablecloths, white stucco walls, and painted tiles. The à la carte menu is attractively priced, and includes pita bread sandwiches. Z has a garden for outdoor dining.

Greek Village, *1016 Lexington Avenue between 72nd and 73rd Streets (212-288-7378). Daily noon–10:30 P.M.*

A family *taverna* on the Upper East Side without Upper East Side prices. The *retsina,* Greek resinated white wine, comes in big pitchers and goes well with the grilled lamb combination plates.

Avegerinos, *153 East 53rd Street, Citicorp Center-Plaza Level (212-688-8828). Monday–Saturday 11:30 A.M.–9:30 P.M.; Sunday noon–9:30 P.M.*

An airy restaurant with interior arches giving a feeling of al fresco dining. White walls wonderfully show off an attractive assortment of Greek crafts. The Greek specialties are a blander, less-olive-oil-and-herbs, upper East Side version of the real thing.

Estia, *308 East 86th Street (212-628-9100). Tuesday–Saturday 5 P.M.–11 P.M.*

A familiar and friendly Greek presence on 86th Street from the days when it was almost an all-German enclave. Estia has the typical white stucco Greek restaurant look and a menu that emphasizes kebabs. The music is exuberant and the waiters double as dancers.

Food Shops

Although the Greeks on the West Side of Manhattan are a thing of the past, the Greek flavor survives in some choice shops.

Poseidon, *629 Ninth Avenue near 44th Street (212-757-6173). Tuesday–Saturday 9 A.M.–7 P.M.; Sunday 10 A.M.–4 P.M.*

The premier Greek bakery in the city sells to the top restaurants as well as to the public. The bakers are masters of the savory *tiropita* (cheese pie), *spanakopita* (spinach pie), and *kreatopita* (meat pie), as well as honey-drenched *baklava.* On Greek Easter there are lines for the braided bread with a red egg on top, *Christopsomi.*

International Grocery, *529 Ninth Avenue (212-279-5514). Monday–Saturday 8 A.M.–6 P.M.*

The International has all the spices and herbs needed for Greek cookery. There are strings of red peppers and garlic and bundles of mint and oregano. Freshly made phyllo dough is available for Greek baking. Located near the Port Authority Bus Terminal, avoid browsing during the rush hours.

Chic Shopping

Greek businesses have moved into the luxury end of the Manhattan marketplace. In an international city they have an international following.

Ilias Lalounis, *4 West 57th Street (212-265-0600). Monday–Saturday 10 A.M.–5 P.M.*

The international jeweler to the ultra-rich. The designs are based on Byzantine baubles worn by empresses and patriarchs, all in twenty-two-carat gold with outrageously large precious and semiprecious stones.

George Stavropoulos, *10–12 West 57th Street (212-582-0924).*

The couturier to New York's café society, his glittery evening gowns grace the society pages. He also dresses the wives of the city's top politicians and business magnates. He did the bride and bridesmaids for the former governor's wedding. Stavropoulous designs can be found at Martha's, 475 Park Avenue at 58th Street.

Christatos & Koster, *201 East 64th Street, the corner of Third Avenue (212-838-0022). Monday–Friday 8 A.M.–6 P.M.; Saturday 8 A.M.–noon.*

Caters to the carriage trade, providing flowers for New York Society weddings and coming-out parties. Robert Christatos's flower arrangements are works of art.

The Flower Market

Since the ancients, Greeks have had a special affinity for flowers. Pagan Greeks adorned themselves and their shrines with flowers; flower origins were the subject of classical myth and they were a staple of architectural decoration. In present-day Greece, flowers ornament city terraces and rural gardens. It's still a popular pastime to pick wildflowers on weekends. On May Day the Greeks exchange bouquets en masse and attach flowers to their car antennas.

It was very natural for this nation of flower lovers to turn to the flower business when they came to New York. They got their start as street sellers, buying from the Long Island flower growers at the foot of East 34th Street, and in one generation had their own shops scattered throughout the city. They cornered New York's wholesale flower market.

The wholesale flower market is an assortment of competing businesses between Broadway and Seventh Avenue, on and off 27th and 28th Streets. The area is all awash with color from standard American varieties and wild tropical blooms. Giant plants and even trees fill the storefronts and sprawl across the sidewalk. At 7:30 A.M. it's total frenzy, with a traffic jam of trucks and vans picking up and dropping off. Excitable proprietors bargain with retail florists, voices raised, gesturing to big bundles of flowers. It is a genuine New York scene and the perfume of so many flowers even overwhelms the fabled Manhattan exhaust fumes. Ultimately things settle down for the afternoon retail business, with browsers buying bonsai trees, rubber plants, and shrubs for roof-terrace gardens.

Everyone knows one another in the flower market. Along the streets there are spontaneous exchanges in Greek and a feeling of community. Many of the businesses in the area are fixtures, family owned and operated for decades. Bill's Flower Market, Mutual Cut Flowers, and the People's Flower Corporation have been going strong for decades. But things are starting to change. The Greek flower market founders are no longer the majority, but they still have a sense of continuity. Wholesalers like Peter Hadges of American Cut Flowers maintains: "My father Gus was here forty-seven years ago, and my son John will be here forty-seven years from now."

Bill's Flower Market, *816 Sixth Avenue at 28th Street (212-889-8154). Monday–Saturday 7 A.M.–6:30 P.M.*

Here there's a full array of flowers at prices below those at most retail florists. It also offers a fine selection of miniature rose plants and hybrid tea roses.

People's Flower Corp., *786 Sixth Avenue at 27th Street (212-686-6291). Monday–Saturday 7 A.M.–6:30 P.M.*

People's is worth a look for its hothouse tropical plants. They also make up special odds-and-ends bouquets for the retail market.

========================= **Place Marks** =========================

The Cultural Heritage

New York's Greek culture is not limited to bouzouki bands and *taverna* food. Greek art with its signature of harmony and proportion is on display in the city's chief museums.

Brooklyn Museum, *Eastern Parkway at Washington Avenue (718-636-1378). Wednesday–Saturday 10 A.M.–5 P.M.; Sundays & holidays 1 P.M.–5 P.M. Admission charge.*

Outside the entrance there is a stunning Greek-style frieze depicting cultural figures: Plato, Phidias, Praxiteles, and Demosthenes. Climb to the third-floor auditorium court, where there's a dazzling collection of 150 Hellenic gold ornaments from delicate garlands to jewel-encrusted cups that rival the Vergina find. Fine examples of Greek urns and vessels from the second century B.C. provide an interesting contrast.

Metropolitan Museum of Art, *Fifth Avenue between 80th and 84th Streets (212-535-7710). Tuesday–Thursday, Sunday 9:30 A.M.–5:15 P.M.; Friday, Saturday 9:30 A.M.–8:45 P.M. Contribution, except Friday and Saturday evenings.*

The Metropolitan is the largest museum in the Western Hemisphere and a precious section of its exhibits is devoted to the beauties that were Greece.

The Greek collection is mainly on the first floor. It covers a wide spectrum of Greek art from Cyclidic abstracts dating from the second and third millenniums to delicately tooled bronzes from 800 to 200 B.C. There are rows of idealized busts depicting gods and godessess and politicians, and distinctive grave sculptures like the fallen warrior. Besides an extensive world-class collection of Grecian urns, there is a selection of helmets, ornaments, mirrors, wine jugs, and water jugs.

========================= **Festivals** =========================

Greek Independence Day

Ever since the conquest of Constantinople in 1453 by the mighty Ottoman forces, the Greeks longed for freedom. Some escaped to the mountains of the Mani or Rumeli and carried on a campaign of bandit raids, while others marked time in the employ of the Turks, waiting until when they were strong enough to strike.

In 1821 Alexander Ypsilanti turned on his Turkish overlords and led an uprising among Greeks in several Ottoman provinces. Alarmed Turkish authorities sought reassurances of Greek loyalty and summoned the titular heads of the Greek community, the Greek Orthodox primates. Disregarding the summons, the Greek prelates gathered at the Monastery of St. Laura. On March 25, 1821, Archbishop Germanos of Patras blessed the banners of the Greek revolutionaries and proclaimed a free Greece.

In New York on March 25, a parade honors the heroic struggle of the Greek people to regain their freedom. The parade follows New York's most prestigious thoroughfare, Fifth Avenue, from 59th Street to 49th Street. The crowds lining the streets are not as large as on St. Patrick's Day or Columbus Day, but there is a warmth and enthusiasm not easily equalled.

The parade marshal may be Telly Savalas or Mike Dukakis, a movie star or a presidential hopeful, but it's still a people's parade: Greeks feeling proud and wearing their colors. Blue and white, the colors of the Greek flag, are everywhere. Blue and white bunting adorns lampposts and blue and white buttons say "Kiss me, I am Greek." The not-very-precise drill teams are wearing blue and white and so are the Olympic Airlines stewards and stewardesses in open cars.

It's a time for fancy dress. Men and women in folk costumes pass in review, in black or brightly colored embroidery, an Evzone kilt or an ankle-length Anatolian dress. Some stop to improvise dance steps. Floats with the acronyms of organizations like the Sons of Pericles or the Daughters of Penelope carry members in classical dress. With unforced smiles they throw flowers to the onlookers. There are also the tailored military-style uniforms that the marchers wear with Greek informality. Striding along, they shout remarks to friends and family in the crowd.

The Blessing of the Waters

St. Nicholas Orthodox Church, *155 Cedar Street (212-227-0773). Monday–Friday 9 A.M.–4 P.M.; Sunday 8 A.M.–1 P.M.*

St. Nicholas was Manhattan's first Greek Orthodox church; it was consecrated in 1892. Dedicated to the patron saint of seamen, its original congregants were seafarers. Besides offering spiritual solace, it was a meeting place for immigrants—a source of job information and news from home. Today with its glowing brass chandeliers, somber icons, and dark intricately carved iconostasis, St. Nicholas is an oasis of serenity in the high-voltage financial district.

Every year on January 19 St. Nicholas is the starting point for a grand religious procession. Bearded priests in black robes and high cylindrical hats lead hundreds of the faithful carrying holy icons, Orthodox banners, and standards of the cross through the center of high finance to the Hudson River.

The archbishop stands on the pier buffeted by the winds, makes the sign of the cross, and chants in Greek. He is blessing the water. In honor of St. Helen, mother of the Emperor Constantine, and to commemorate her discovery of the original cross, the archbishop flings a gleaming cross into the dark Hudson. Shivering young men covered with grease leap into the choppy water to retrieve it. A cheer goes up from the watchful crowd as one swimmer suddenly emerges splashing, sputtering, clutching the precious cross. He ceremonially hands the cross to the archbishop, kneels, and is blessed. Pictures are snapped and videos roll for the afternoon papers and the evening news.

The Slavs

Introduction

The Slavs who have settled in New York over the centuries represent different tribes and nations. They span an area of Eastern Europe from the Black Sea to the Baltic Sea and the Carpathian Mountain to the Urals. The Poles, Ukrainians, and Russians have many similarities in language and culture, but throughout their histories they have determinedly defended their individual identities, even when their countries were overwhelmed and conquered. Whatever era they came to New York, whether the Poles in 1830 or the Russians in 1917, these Slavs shared a desire for freedom and national independence. While they adapted to the city and became American, there is something still very personal in their links to their native lands.

Poles

History

Daniel Litscho was the first Pole to gain prominence when New York was still New Amsterdam. During the administration of Dutch Governor Peter Stuyvesant, he attained the rank of lieutenant in the tiny Dutch colonial militia and participated in military expeditions against the Swedes and maverick Patroons. Litscho was also a popular innkeeper with taverns on Pearl Street and Wall Street.

Captain Marcin Krygier also served in the Dutch militia under Peter Stuyvesant. He was elected three times to the prestigious office of deputy burgomaster of New Amsterdam. Krygier commanded the fort that defended the city; it was named in his honor for the great Polish monarch, John Casimir.

Litscho and Marcin Krygier made such a powerful impression on the stolid Dutch governor that Stuyvesant urged the Dutch West India Company to recruit more Polish colonists. Dr. Alexander Curtius was brought to New Amsterdam to start the first high school. Governor Stuyvesant praised this Polish educator for his skill and diligence until he embarrassed the tightfisted governor by demanding the agreed-upon salary.

The American Revolution brought Polish freedom fighters to the forefront of the American experience. They had been deprived of their ancestral lands and ancestral rights by the joint action of Prussia, Russia, and Austria in 1795. They were ready to strike a blow for freedom in the New World.

Casimir Pulaski was promoted to brigadier general over four American colonels even without a knowledge of English. He was admired for his bravery and envied for his command of cavalry tactics. He died courageously in battle, charging the Redcoat cavalry.

Thaddeus Kosciuszko joined the revolutionary forces as an engineer with the rank of colonel. From the beginning General Washington recognized Kosciuszko's importance and placed him under his direct command. He played a major role in the preparation of military fortifications for West Point and Saratoga. On October 13, 1783, the debt owed by the young republic was recognized and Congress granted Kosciuszko the rank of brigadier general.

The Pulaski Skyway and the Kosciuszko Bridge are two New York monuments to these Polish heroes. New York's Polish community and organizations revere both of these leaders and the Pulaski Day Parade is the principal celebration of Polish New Yorkers.

In the 1830s internationally conscious New Yorkers were concerned about Russian and Austrian persecution of Poles. The New York City Council was the first official body in the United States to declare support for the Polish uprising of 1831. Forming a committee in Clinton Hall chaired by Columbia President William A. Duer, New Yorkers pledged to support Polish freedom.

New Yorkers were the first to offer the outnumbered Polish freedom fighters asylum. In 1834, 234 Polish exiles arrived at the port of New York on Austrian ships. They were welcomed with speeches by city luminaries like writer James Fenimore Cooper. Albert Gallatin, a former secretary of the treasury, organized a committee to aid the proud refugees, who were soon contributing members of New York society.

Despite their lack of English, these extraordinary Poles gained prominence in many fields. Samuel Brilliantowski and Robert Thomain became successful physicians; and a pioneer woman in medicine, Marie Zakrzewska, founded the New York Infirmary. In the arts, Eustachy Wyszynski became a leading painter and his compatriot Adam Kurek joined the brass section of the New York Italian Opera and became a recognized composer.

These Polish patriots laid the foundations of Polish communal and cultural life in the city and the country as a whole. In 1842 Ludwik Jezykowicz, a staunch Polish cleric, chaired the Association of Poles in America. The same year Paul Sobolewski and Eustachy Wyszynski founded the first Polish periodical, *Poland, Historical, Literary, Monumental and Picturesque*. The Polish Slavonian Literary Association was established in 1846. The Polish community launched the newspaper *Echoz Polski* at the time of the Civil War.

Politically conscious Poles rallied to the Union cause and eagerly enrolled in the city's Garibaldi Guards and the Fourth Cavalry. The Polish military man, Alexander Raszewski, organized the Thirty-first New York Infantry; Joseph Smolinski led a cavalry regiment.

Wladimir Kryzanowski was a Civil War hero on the scale of Pulaski. He volunteered only two days after war was declared and in no time made colonel and took over the Fifty-eighth Regiment. He was cited numerous times for bravery and was specially singled out for his exploits during the Battle of Bull Run. President Lincoln nominated him for the rank of brigadier general. After the war he made a career of government service, finally retiring to New York City to use his influence on behalf of a new influx of Polish immigrants.

The immigrant Poles of the late nineteenth century and the first decades of the twentieth were very different from their aristocratic forebears. They were peasants with a reverence for the land and little understanding of geopolitics. They had the strength of character to stand firm against Russian and German efforts to undermine their Polish language and customs. They guarded their Polish identity. But Polish pride by itself could not deal with the problems of starvation and disease and the threat of military conscription, and they were forced to leave for America.

Polish peasant life centered around the family, the church, and the ancestral village. In America the Polish community revolved around the family, the church, and the neighborhood. But many Poles came to New York with the firm intention of returning to their ancestral villages after they had earned enough money to buy land and a house. Whether they returned or not, they still passionately believed in the Polish proverb that "a man without land is a man without legs."

The Poles who came to New York in steerage were not accorded the same cordial welcome as the freedom fighters. Like other peasant immigrants, they faced prejudice and discrimination and had no choice but to accept some of the harshest menial work in the city. The tough Poles cleaned the stills in the Brooklyn refineries, removing solid residues in Sahara heat. They labored in Brooklyn's iron foundries, inhaling noxious fumes while handling scalding buckets of molten iron.

Polish labor, despite its Old World conservatism, demanded its rights. Poles were active in the wave of strikes that erupted in Brooklyn plants in 1907, 1910, and 1917. Independent Polish workers picketed a Brooklyn sugar refinery when they were forced to work on Easter Sunday and walked out of a Bayonne factory where a foreman had made slurs about their nationality. Some militant Poles joined radical groups and were deported during the "Red Scare" of the twenties.

America's enterprise society inspired Polish-Americans. They opened all kinds of businesses from big-city banks to local dry-goods stores. But for the Polish-Americans it wasn't "business as usual." Polish merchants had a close, almost paternal, relationship with their customers and the community. They performed extra services like translating papers and documents and even helped customers find jobs. Polish businessmen put their profits back into the community.

While the Polish immigrants weathered trials and triumphed through determined effort, they never lost sight of their conquered motherland. In New York and Brooklyn they belonged to patriotic Falcon Societies, where they prepared themselves for the national struggle. They practiced gymnastics and fencing and discussed strategies for independence. Polish New Yorkers representing every strand of opinion from radical to monarchist formed coalitions, calling upon the world to grant Poland self-determination.

At the start of World War I Ignatz Jan Paderewski, one of the world's leading concert pianists, became the spokesman of the Polish freedom movement in an impassioned concert tour that combined Chopin and politics. He galvanized national support and helped convince an undecided President Wilson to embrace Polish freedom.

New York's staunch Polish community went even further with young men volunteering for action in a fighting force under the command of the Polish coalition leader, Jozef Haller. Haller's "Blue Army" even recruited soldiers for the American army in 1917. By the end of the war a higher proportion of Poles had died on European battlefields than any other American ethnic.

Stunned by the horrors of battle and depressed by postwar political wrangling, returning Poles were eager to get back into ordinary American life. Many had given up the idea of settling permanently in Poland. They had become New Yorkers. Later they were disappointed and angry at restrictive emigration laws that barred their families and friends from joining them.

New York's Poles were very conscious of their Polish identity. In their own communities on the Lower East Side, in Williamsburg, and in Greenpoint, Poles celebrated the Polish homeland in dance groups, glee clubs, and Polish societies. In their parochial schools overseen by Polish nuns, second- and third-generation Poles learned the rudiments of the Polish language and the basics of Polish culture.

High Polish art from theater to concert music also thrived in the city. Stephen Mizwa, a Polish-born, Harvard-educated academic, founded the Kosciuszko Foundation in New York in 1925 to encourage Polish creativity and Polish studies. He hoped that his organization would foster American cultural links with a resurgent Poland. At the local level first- and second-generation Poles formed fine-arts clubs.

New York's Poles needed more than cultural pride to cope with the human tragedies brought on by the economic depression of the 1930s. The closeness of the community and their willingness to help one another, providing credit and even shelter to those in need, kept neighborhoods afloat. In the political arena, they supported Roosevelt's relief and welfare measures and voted the Democratic ticket, though they received little in patronage for their efforts.

As prosperity returned, Polish New Yorkers' concern shifted to Eastern Europe, where Nazi threats against Poland materialized in a devastating Panzer invasion. *Nowy Swiat,* New York's leading Polish newspaper, mobilized the metropolitan area's Polish population who bought bonds, gave blood, and participated in newspaper and scrap-iron drives.

The newspaper's publisher, Maximilian Wegrzynek, organized the National Committee of Americans of Polish Descent, KNAPP, to fight Soviet involvement in the liberation of Poland. Later his group joined with others in a united front, the Polish American Congress, to defend Poland from Soviet domination.

World War II and the Yalta Agreement, which gave the USSR de facto control over Poland, increased the number of Poles seeking refuge in New York. There were intellectual emigrés like Oscar Halecki, who established the prestigious Polish Institute of Arts and Sciences in the city in 1941. There were members of Poland's defeated government like the exiled minister of education, Waclaw Jedrzejewicz, who became the executive director for the Josef Pilsudski Institute of America, established in New York in 1943.

But the majority of new Polish immigrants were DPs, displaced persons, and veterans of special Polish army units and groups of partisans. They came in family units with the intention of making a new life in America. The lobbying efforts of KNAPP and the passage of legislative acts and presidential directives made their entry possible. They brought new life and flavor to the Polonias of New York.

The *General Black* was the first ship to land in New York with this precious human cargo in 1948. The Polish refugees of World War II called themselves the Black Generals in honor of this special ship. They included such notables as Dr. Zbigniew Brezinski, who went from Columbia's halls of ivy and the chairmanship of the Trilateral Commission to become President Jimmy

Carter's chief foreign policy adviser and chairman of the National Security Council.

While Polish New Yorkers have gone from success to success and made the leap from blue-collar respectability to white-collar affluence, they have not forgotten their homeland. They have continually sent food and medicines and money to help their people struggling under the tyranny and incompetence of the Soviet satellite regime. In recent years Polish New Yorkers have even directly supported democratic *Solidarnosc* and its leader, Lech Walesa.

Greenpoint

Directions: IND E or F to Queens Plaza. Change to G to Greenpoint Avenue.

Introduction

Greenpoint, the city's largest Polonia, is across the East River in Brooklyn. It is so close to Manhattan it offers some spectacular views of the skyline. But for the Polish people of Greenpoint, Manhattan is simply a place to work. Their hearts are in their own close-knit community.

The Dutch purchased Greenpoint from the Indians in 1630. A fertile forested area with underground springs and a meandering creek, it was earmarked for farmsteads. For centuries Dutch and English families plowed and planted its fields.

In the nineteenth century Greenpoint went industrial. The shipyards came first. It was ideally suited for shipbuilding with its central coastal location. At the foot of Cayler Street, the ironclad warship, the *Monitor,* was built for action in the Civil War.

In the Gilded Age following the Civil War, Greenpoint was noted for the "five black arts": printing, pottery, gas, glass, and iron. There were also oil refineries on the waterfront. Despite the black smoke of industrial chimneys, the Irish, German, and old American families who resided here created a small-town community in the middle of Brooklyn.

Greenpoint struck a nice balance; there was no room for rundown slums or opulent mansions. Working- and middle-class Greenpoint lived in neat brick row houses and attractive brownstones. These neo-Greek and Italianate structures still line Kent Street off Greenpoint Avenue, which has been described by the *New York Times* as "one of the city's better and more completely preserved nineteenth-century streets."

The most exuberant chapter in Greenpoint's history began in the late nineteenth century, when Poles began streaming in to work in the area's

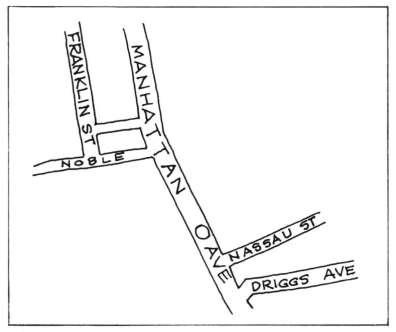

Greenpoint

ironworks and oil refineries. Poles who had emigrated to Brooklyn from lands under German, Russian, and Austrian domination banded together to re-create their national institutions in a free America.

They built Roman Catholic churches like St. Kostka's, and in their Polish parishes reenacted their age-old Slavic rituals. Our Lady of Czestochowa, the Black Madonna, was a source of spiritual unity. In their parish schools they preserved their Polish language and in their fraternities and social clubs they kept alive Polish music and dance. Polish solidarity revealed itself in mutual benefit societies like the Polish National Alliance of Brooklyn, U.S.A.

Greenpoint was a strong, stable neighborhood with well-maintained houses and a thriving commercial area. But it was not politically powerful, and a large part of Polish Greenpoint was bulldozed to make way for the Long Island Expressway. Other ethnic enclaves did not survive the wholesale destruction of parts of their communities in the name of progress, but Polish Greenpoint rallied. New Polish immigrants from overseas were a source of new vitality.

Greenpoint forms a rectangle with Manhattan Avenue and Franklin Avenue bordering east and west and Noble Street and Greenpoint Avenue bordering north and south. It is a neighborhood where landmark row houses alternate with small shingled or aluminum-sided single-family houses. Greenpoint's restaurants and shops have the intimacy of someone's living room, while the neighborhood's churches have the grandeur of Old World Warsaw. Its strong character comes from its people, who have the romantic idealism of their aristocratic antecedents and the forthright honesty of their peasant forebears.

Manhattan Avenue is the main shopping street of Greenpoint and has a large number of Polish businesses and specialty stores among the standard American shops. At the beginning of Nassau Avenue, the area undergoes a change. A border has been crossed and the street becomes an all-Polish main drag. It's a Polish scene of fair faces and flowered patterns and broad-shouldered men with Lech Walesa mustaches. The people have an earnestness when they speak: they are believers.

Hearty Eating

Polish food is not for the fastidious or faint-hearted. It is rich and heavy with heaping portions of sour cream and pork and more than a touch of dill and a hint of garlic. This hearty cooking sticks to the essentials: cabbage and dumplings and a pastry called *pierogen* stuffed with cheese or potatoes or minced meat. A real peasant cuisine, it doesn't have any prejudices against pig's knuckles or tripe, and the humble smoked sausage, *kielbasa,* is Poland's national dish.

Polish restaurants with richly satisfying portions, the forthright flavors of Eastern Europe, and modest 1950s prices are the rule in Greenpoint, Brooklyn. The eating places are usually no-frills with proverbial "eat off the floor" cleanliness. The service is warm and personal; customers are treated like long-lost relatives. There's not much gloss but a lot of heart.

Manhattan Corner, *631 Manhattan Avenue (Unlisted telephone). Daily noon–9:30 P.M.*

Manhattan Corner calls itself a luncheonette, but it's really an old-fashioned cafeteria. The prices are rock-bottom and the portions are huge. Don't look for decoration; the world-class Polish eaters provide the ambiance. There are thirteen soups to choose from, including white borscht and pickle soup and unusual *pierogen* pastry, stuffed with mushrooms and sauerkraut.

Polska Restaurant, *136 Greenpoint Avenue (718-389-8368). Daily noon–9 P.M.*

Three strapping Poles at the counter knock off plates of cheese *pierogen* and follow up with giant pig's knuckles and mashed, all washed down with brown beer. At the Polska, eating is serious business and there is still room for strawberry and blueberry blintzes before blowing a kiss to owner Jadwiga on the way out the door.

Polish & Slavic Credit Union, *138 Greenpoint Avenue (718-937-4356). Tuesday–Thursday, Sunday 9:30 A.M.–5:45 P.M.; Friday, Saturday 9 A.M.–8:45 P.M.*

Senior citizens, the men in caps and the women in kerchiefs, grab their trays and take bowls of thick soup with hunks of black bread and sit down. This is cafeteria eating with the clatter of plates and trays and people trying to shout above the noise in Polish. This is no ordinary kielbasa house; the credit union that subsidizes this cafeteria provides financing for a good portion of the housing in Greenpoint.

Henryk's, *105 Norman Avenue (718-389-6859). Daily noon–8:30 P.M.*

Henryk's may have plastic tablecloths and flowers but those are the only things that are artificial. In the back there are high-pitched ''conversations'' over the cooking, while the man minding the register has across-the-room chats with his neighbors. Henryk's has a way with cabbage—sweet and sour in soup, or stuffed with ground pork, veal, and beef and rice.

Polski Dinners, *192 Nassau Avenue (718-349-2449). Daily 12:30 P.M.–10 P.M.*

The owner of Polski is a recent immigrant and born-again New Yorker who has put pictures of the Brooklyn Bridge and the New York skyline on the restaurant wall. As an appetizer to a superb Polish pork chop or sautéed chicken livers you may have a short speech on the virtues of American democracy.

Continental Restaurant, *11 Nevel Avenue, at Driggs Avenue (718-383-2768). Monday–Friday 3:30 P.M.–10 P.M.; Saturday, Sunday 2 P.M.–1:30 A.M.*

The entrance to the Continental, with its anonymous door, looks like a ''Joe sent me'' speakeasy. The Continental has a busy front bar and a back room with a polka beat on Saturday and Sunday. The cold Polish vodka with buffalo grass complements the plates of sour tomatoes and pickles and the platters of roast chicken and crispy fried veal cutlet.

Shopping Polonia

Though Polish Greenpoint is more than a generation old, it has kept its Polish character. The neighborhood is Polish tastes and Polish styles. The stores are Polish immaculate and simple with maybe a Solidarity poster or a picture of the Virgin of Czestchowa for inspiration.

The Poles have not quite gotten the knack of western consumerism. They know their local merchants by name and shopping is personal and social. The stores help people connect with their culture. Brightly colored ceramics and carvings and flower fabrics are an affirmation of Polish identity.

Kielbasa has pride of place in Greenpoint. In groceries and butchers it hangs from the rafters over the counter to tempt the unwary shopper. But there are other surprises in the neighborhood's food stores. There are Polish hams and every variety of sausage, black peasant breads, and pickled vegetables. The shopkeepers know their customers and inquire about the family before taking an order. No one is in a hurry.

White Eagle, *600 Humboldt Avenue (718-389-2214). Monday–Friday 7 A.M.–noon.*

Following the mass at St. Stanislaus, an assortment of nimble elderly communicants cross the street for a Polish cheese or chocolate *babka* (a plain cake a little less sweet than a Danish). White Eagle's major business is wholesale, so they close their doors when they are finished baking. Catch them early.

Sikotski & Winski, *603 Manhattan Avenue (718-383-8132). Monday–Saturday 9 A.M.–6 P.M.*

The counterman at Sikotski & Winski is surrounded by a curtain of hanging kielbasa and Polish charcuterie, and by customers anxious for their kielbasa fix. Late in the afternoon, after the bins of Polish black bread and pumpernickel are sold out, friends drift in like it's an open house.

Steve's, *104 Nassau Avenue (718-383-1780). Monday–Saturday 7 A.M.–7 P.M.*

There was no voting but somehow Steve's has won the title of number one in kielbasa. Steve's deserves it, both for the quality of his products and the patience and good humor of everyone who works there. The kielbasa doesn't overdo the garlic or the fat. They put the same goodness in a kielbasa cold cut called *krakowska* that makes a very unusual sandwich.

Nassau Meat Market, *121 Nassau Avenue (718-383-3476). Monday–Saturday 8 A.M.–8 P.M.*

The Nassau Market believes variety is the spice of Polish sausages. In addition to the old reliable kielbasa, Nassau has dried *kabanosa* sausage, Polish hot dogs called *mysliwska,* veal sausage, and Polish headcheese.

Zakopane, *714 Manhattan Avenue (718-389-3487). Monday–Saturday 10 A.M.–7 P.M.; Sunday noon–5 P.M.*

The wood carvings that line the shelves of Zakopane bear no resemblance to souvenir-shop junk. They are painstaking replicas of man and nature. The subjects, such as a mountain stag or a peasant dancer, reflect rural life. The shop also has some fine examples of Polish Easter eggs and peasant embroidery. The blue and clear crystal gleams like expensive jewelry. Mr. Strug, who presides over this handicraft kingdom, charges very reasonable prices.

Turysta Travel, *107 Nassau Avenue (718-383-4010). Monday 9 A.M.–8 P.M.; Tuesday–Saturday 9 A.M.–7 P.M.*

Turysta is not your typical travel agent selling cruises to the Caribbean. While it does a land-office business in airline tickets and travel packages to Poland, it is equally involved in money transfers and the shipment of clothes and medicine to the homeland. This travel agent is a lifeline for many Polish families who depend on the aid of relatives in Greenpoint.

Place Marks

—The Cultural Heritage—

The FFA Gallery, *16 Clifford Place (718-383-8932). Hours vary according to show. Call.*

The FFA exhibits the latest work of the more adventurous Polish and Polish-American artistic spirits. The shows are superbly mounted in an unconventional gallery setting. Don't expect traditional realism. These Polish artists are visionaries in form and content. But even in their neon sculptures and minimalist statements there are images of Mother Poland.

Centrum Ksiask Polskiej, *Polish Book Center, 140 Nassau Avenue (718-383-3501). Monday–Friday 11 A.M.–7 P.M.; Saturday 10 A.M.–6 P.M.*

The Polish bookstore is more than a bookstore, it's the informal cultural headquarters of a community, where people can find out about the latest Polish concert, recital, or exhibition. At the Centrum, Polish intellectuals discuss the subtleties of *Solidarnosc* and its relations with the past Communist regime and its future. The shelves of the Centrum are devoted to Polish classics by Lem and Woldt and the literature of the Polish freedom movement. There is a selection of recorded Polish music.

Polish National Alliance of Brooklyn, U.S.A., *155 Noble Street (718-389-4704).*

The PNA started as a fraternal group with a mission to advance Polish culture and the Polish nation. Its members volunteered to fight for a free Poland during World War I and condemned the World War II peace that left Poland in the Soviet orbit. PNA has provided scholarships for students studying the Polish language and culture and has provided grants for Polish schools.

—The Pope's Church—

In times of defeat and tyranny the Church has kept the Polish national identity alive. The Poles have repaid it with a special devotion. Polish faith is an integral part of Polish life; it's fatalistic and still believes in miracles. The Church and the parish are the tangible center of that existence. The Poles of Greenpoint in the past called their neighborhood St. Stan's after their parish church.

St. Stanislaus Kostka Church, *607 Humboldt Street (718-388-0170).*

The eminence of St. Stanislaus Kostka stands out among the small neat one-family houses of Greenpoint. Every day there are Polish masses and every day candles are lit in front of the shrine of the Polish national patron, Our Lady of Czestchowa. In 1969 Cardinal Karol Wotjtyla visited St. Stanislaus and blessed the congregation. The parishioners of St. Stanislaus have not forgotten that day and the dignity and gentle humanity of the cardinal from Krakow. They honored this man who became the first Polish pope by naming a square near their church between Broome and Humboldt Streets Pope John Paul II Square.

Polish Musical Exchanges

Poland has a great musical tradition that partakes of the classics of the court musician and the folk songs of the peasants. The music is the spirit and the dances of the Polish people. It is the intensely romantic polonaises and mazurkas of Chopin and the accordion and clarinet accompaniment to polkas. It is the soaring exhilaration of the warrior and the death knell of the defeated. Paderewski, the most complete piano virtuoso of the twentieth century, was able to capture the paradoxical moods of the Polish people. Halka, Poland's national opera, presents it with drama and choruses, ballet and mazurkas.

Though the local Polish community has in the past been at odds with Poland's commissars, this had not prevented cultural exchanges. A month usually did not go by without a performance of some first-rate performing troop from Poland like the Silesian Opera Company or the Rzeszowiacy Song and Dance Ensemble. Cultural exchanges have intensified under the new popular government. Classical and folk, mazurka and highlander's dances, the entertainment comes highbrow and traditional. Announcements of the latest events and tickets are usually available at the Polish Book Center.

Manhattan Renaissance

Introduction

Polish Manhattan is more than memories. The old neighborhood on the Lower East Side is clearly on the upswing. Each time the native Poles took to the streets to protest—in Warsaw in 1956, in Poznan in 1968, and in Gdansk in 1971—they voted the only way they could—with their feet. After each protest, more political refugees came to New York and settled on the Lower East Side.

Though the renewed Polish presence in Manhattan has not been recognized by the rest of New York because of their neighborhood's Ukrainian character, Poles have a growing community life that goes beyond the neighborhood. They have their own restaurants, where Polish immigrants casually coexist with East Village eccentrics and artists. They have their own churches, where the older generation of the Polish tradition stands side-by-side with the bright young Poles of possibility.

Like the Poles who first came to New York in the early part of the nineteenth century, these post–World War II political refugees are intellectually sophisticated. Many are writers, historians, and artists. They are not the folk art and polka types; they are into experimental writing and modern art. The new Polish immigrants have their own literary circles and artists' support groups.

The Polish Café

They look like unpretentious and informal luncheonettes. When a Polish coffeehouse tries cozy decorative touches it winds up looking like an older woman with too much makeup. The only decorations that work are a *Solidarnosc* poster or a picture of the Polish pope. The Polish coffeehouses live a double life; they get the local trade of post-hippies, college students, and tourists, and they have their regular Polish coteries who treat the coffeehouses like social clubs.

The food as in all the other Polish restaurants in the city, is rich Polish soups, stuffed cabbage and peppers, and their own versions of Hungarian goulash and Austrian schnitzel. There are blintzes and *pierogen* and potato pancakes for snacks and side dishes.

Leshko Coffee Shop, *11 Avenue A (212-473-9208). Daily 6:30 A.M.–midnight.*

Leshko is the coffee shop that gets tourists, whether they are uptowners checking out the neighborhood's remaining galleries or Polish sightseers from Port Washington taking a peek at Paderewski in Tompkins Square Park. The blintzes are exceptional, whether filled with cheese or fresh fruit.

Lillian's, *23 Avenue A (212-677-4710). Monday–Saturday 8 A.M.– 8 P.M.; Sunday 10 A.M.–4 P.M.*

Lillian's is one moment a group from the Polish artists' support group and the next some kids from New York University. The best things on the menu are the boiled beef and horseradish and the lamb flank that falls right off the bone.

Bruno's, *200 Second Avenue between 12th and 13th Streets (212-777-9728). Daily 7 A.M.–11 P.M.*

Bruno's is roomier than the other Polish places, but it has to be big to hold the bearded, expansive owner. Bruno's is always breaking in new counterpeople from the other side, so sometimes you have to listen hard and speak slowly. The white borscht is chock-full of good things like kielbasa.

Jolanta, *119 First Avenue between Seventh Street and Avenue A (212-473-9936). Daily 10 A.M.–midnight.*

Jolanta is where Jerczy Kosinski comes for *flaczki* (tripe soup). The food is the most authentically Polish in the neighborhood.

Christine's, *438 Second Avenue at 25th Street (212-684-1879). Daily 8 A.M.–10 P.M.*

Christine took the exotic out of Polish cooking and made it an everyday thing all around the town. Christine's became a chain without sacrificing quality, but the Lower East Side Christine's is the only one with the Polish atmosphere. For a fast lunch break, have a meat *pierogen* with the top-of-the-line red borscht, thick with cabbage and just a hint of tomato.

Polish Purchasing

New York's cosmopolitan Poles have no problems dealing with American supermarkets and American tastes. But sometimes they hanker for kielbasa or the full-bodied flavor of a Polish beer.

B & C Meat Market, *111 First Avenue at Seventh Street (212-677-1210). Monday–Saturday 7 A.M.–7 P.M.; Sunday 10 A.M.–5 P.M.*

The B & C is mostly Polish imports, from canned hams to jars of Polish pickled vegetables and Polish imported beer. But the Polish kielbasa and *kabanosa* that dangles from the ceiling is homemade from one of those secret recipes that gets passed on. B & C tries to be ecumenical; it also carries some Ukrainian products.

Manhattan's Polish Eagles

The eagle of Polish culture flies all around Manhattan from trendy downtown to the palmy Upper East Side. The cultural institutions are conservative and glossy and avant-garde and struggling. Some have stood the test of time and others are hanging on. The Polish audiences are mainstream and folk-art and elitist and experimental. The more recent arrivals look upon culture as a liberation while older Polish-Americans view it as a tradition. It is the Polish newspaper and church and an artist's support group.

Polish Artists' Gallery, *19 Irving Place (no telephone). Call Polish Institute for information on current showings.*

The Polish Artists' Gallery has twice-a-month shows of Polish artists who are mainly new to America. It is all modern but the mediums change: there are paintings, sculpture, collage, tapestry, and modern ceramics. The Artists' Support Group is associated with the gallery. It helps Polish artists adjust to the competitive world of American Art.

Polish Institute of Arts and Sciences, *208 East 30th Street (212-686-4164). Tuesday–Thursday 10 A.M.–4 P.M.; Saturday 11 A.M.–4 P.M.*

The Institute was started in the dark days of World War II to preserve a Polish culture that seemed threatened by Hitler and his minions. It soon broadened its agenda to include the Polish-American experience. It has its own publications and library.

Nowy Dziennik, *21 West 38th Street (212-354-0490).*

In English the name of this paper is the Daily News, and it does have that in terms of both the local and national Polish-American community and the Polish nation. The paper tries not to be divisively ideological, but it makes no bones about being pro-Solidarity and has even raised funds for the organization. It supports all the community's cultural events involving Polish and Polish-American musical and dance groups. It backs Polish galleries and even local choirs.

Kosciuszko Foundation, *15 East 65th Street (212-734-2130). Monday–Friday 9 A.M.–5 P.M.*

The Kosciuszko is Polish-America's most important cultural resource center. It has an excellent gallery of paintings, traditional and modern, and a fine collection of Polish photographs. The library of the foundation includes over a hundred thousand documents and thousands of books in Polish and English. The organization has sponsored concert series (the Chopin masters Witold Malcuzynski and Artur Rubinstein) and commissioned a sixteen-part film series on the Polish contribution to America. It awards scholarships to individuals of Polish descent and has an annual Chopin music scholarship.

Place Marks

St. Stanislaus Church, *101 Seventh Street (212-475-4576).*

The congregation of St. Stanislaus is primarily Polish-born. There are three Polish masses on Sunday and one daily. The Sunday masses bring together a young, vital Polish community; on weekdays it's mostly older women in black. The church has many statues and paintings, but Our Lady of Czestochowa is the focus of attention. Currently the church is involved in a big drive to collect money to erect a bronze likeness of Pope John Paul II.

Patriots in Red and White
Pulaski Day Parade

On the Sunday closest to October 5 Polish New York comes out to pay tribute to a great Polish-American hero of the American Revolution, General Casimir Pulaski, and their own national identity. It is one of the year's most spectacular parades. A typical Pulaski Day lineup includes forty-five floats and fifty marching bands. The parade follows Fifth Avenue from 26th Street to 52nd Street.

The Grand Marshal, usually representing some important Polish-American organization, leads the march, smiling and waving to enthusiastic crowds. Polish-American leaders follow on foot and in limousines. Many are dressed to the nines in top hats and morning coats with sashes in red and white, Poland's national colors. The parade pauses on the stairs of St. Patrick's to greet the cardinal. Flowers in the shape of a cross are solemnly placed in front of the cathedral.

In a moment the mood of the parade is lighthearted: a polka band begins to play on a red-and-white float and soon dancers in high boots and embroidered vests are whirling down the avenue. The long line of march picks up the polka beat as Polish cops and firemen and choirs and high school students pass along Fifth. The newly crowned Queen of Polonia on the Royal Polonia float holds her scepter aloft as her subjects clap and whistle. Another band picks up a military beat and the mood changes as old men in old uniforms—the uniforms of World War II partisans—step lively up the avenue. There are Polish-American Legionaires and Veterans of Foreign Wars and marchers in Revolutionary War uniforms. Even the Polish visionary, Copernicus, in a plumed hat and tights, makes an appearance on a float.

══════════ Ukrainians ══════════

History

Ukrainians are characterized by a deep loyalty to their homeland. Even centuries of foreign domination have not destroyed their sense of national identity. Their forebears brought Christianity to the eastern steppes and governed democratically during Europe's dark ages; the Kievan Republic was a lengendary center of culture and learning. For Ukrainian New Yorkers it is still a sacred inheritance.

The first modern Ukrainians to land in New York sailed with the Russian fleet between 1862 and 1863. Some of these anonymous sailors jumped ship, never to return, while others went back to relate the wonders of the city to wide-eyed peasants. New York seemed like a dream to these people who were denied their land, their language, and their religion.

An adventurous clergyman named Ahapius Honcharenko took an unscheduled sabbatical from his religious studies in Athens and arrived in New York in 1865. After traveling throughout the country, supporting himself teaching Greek, he settled for a time in lower Manhattan in the heart of what would become the Ukrainian community.

In the 1870s, despite government efforts to prevent them from leaving, Ukrainians crossed a continent and an ocean, settling mainly in the mining and industrial areas of the Northeast and the Midwest and the urban area of Manhattan. The majority—Ruthenians, Carpatho-Russyns, and Galicians— were from the western part of their nation. At the outset, most wanted to return to the Ukraine to buy land and begin families.

The bribes of steamship agents and rural poverty forced Russian government authorities to open the way to mass emigration. Families mortgaged their lands and pawned their possessions to pay the passage. Young men who were eager to avoid lifetime military service deserted their villages and the women followed. Between 1877 and 1899 hundreds of thousands were America-bound.

In New York the mainly male population lived four to six to a room in boardinghouses on the Lower East Side between the German and Jewish enclaves. They energetically set to work to pay their passage and relieve the burdens of the people they left behind. They were barbers, bricklayers, tailors, and day laborers. The women who joined them took jobs as domestics and cleaned offices at night.

Ukrainian New Yorkers established a whole network of organizations. Some were connected to Greek-Catholic or Orthodox Ukrainian churches like the St. Raphael Ukrainian Immigration Society, which helped Ukrainian New Yorkers find jobs and shelter. Regional associations like the Lemko Brotherhood Society provided a place where people from the same area could socialize and also offered health and burial insurance. Proud Ukrainians generally refused public relief; the Ukrainian National Association aided the sick and the needy. Women's groups, such as the Ukrainian Women's League, preserved Ukrainian traditions and folk arts.

In 1917 the Tsarist state was overthrown and at last, after centuries, the Ukrainians won independence. They declared a free Ukraine on January 22, 1918, but its existence was brief. Russia and Poland quickly carved it up according to the terms of a 1921 treaty. New York's Ukrainian community closely followed the fortunes of their country and offered support. Local Ukrainian groups demonstrated for Ukrainian freedom and protested deportations and state-sponsored famine and murder.

By 1919 New York was the site of the largest metropolitan Ukrainian community. It was split between the Lower East Side from Third to Sixth Streets and the Upper East Side in the vicinity of 72nd Street. The Ukrainian community on the Lower East Side even sent one of its own, Stephen Jarema, to the New York State Assembly. There was also a scattering of Ukrainians in Williamsburg, Brooklyn, and the Bronx.

During World War II Ukrainian freedom fighters were the victims of Nazi and Soviet brutality. There were mass Ukrainian executions after the German surrender. New York's Ukrainian population raised money and mobilized politically to save thousands of Ukrainian displaced persons.

In 1948 the Ukrainian Resettlement Center was established in the city. Many Ukrainian newcomers who were processed through the center were highly qualified academics, clergy, professionals, and intellectuals. They added new luster to the New York Ukrainian cultural community.

Ukrainian New Yorkers were given official recognition by the state and city government in 1955. The occasion was the anniversary of Ukrainian independence, which had been declared on January 22, 1918. In his proclamation Governor Averell Harriman commended Ukrainian New Yorkers as a "proud and freedom-loving people" while Mayor Robert F. Wagner praised "their matchless faith and courage." For the first time in the history of the city, the Ukrainian flag flew above City Hall.

Little Ukraine

Directions: IRT-Lexington Avenue 6 to Astor Place, or Second Avenue M15 bus to 8th Street.

Introduction

Little Ukraine lays claim to a corner of New York generally called the East Village, bounded by Fourth Street and 14th Street, Avenue A and Third Avenue. The Ukrainians don't seem to have too many problems coexisting with the hippie leftovers, working-class Hispanics, and the elderly vestiges of other immigrant groups. Although the neighborhood only numbers thirty thousand Ukrainians (a steep decline from seventy-five thousand in less than a decade) it still retains its national character in shops, restaurants, and cultural landmarks.

The history of Ukrainian New York is an account of the rich civic life of the Little Ukraine. In 1905 Peter Jarema ushered in a dynamic new era in Ukrainian New York by organizing the United Ukrainian Organizations of New York City to promote Ukrainian activities. In the same year, Ukrainian New Yorkers founded St. George's Ukrainian Catholic Church, the spiritual

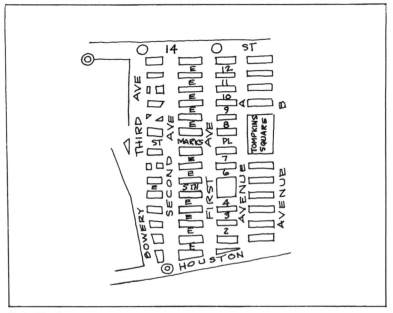

Little Ukraine

and social hub of the community. The church's school sustained Ukrainian New York, instructing succeeding generations in the Ukrainian language and traditions.

The Little Ukraine was the culture capital of Ukrainians in America. It was the home of the first Ukrainian theater and music hall, which was launched in the twenties, and the first gymnastic society. In 1932 the Surma Book and Music Company, which is still going strong on Seventh Street, sponsored a program of Ukrainian music that was carried on eighteen radio stations around the country. Ukrainian New York even had its own film company, which released two films in Ukrainian in 1936. In the same year, Professor Alexander Koshetz directed the Ukrainian Mixed Choirs of New York in their Carnegie Hall debut.

Ukrainian New Yorkers, while celebrating their own culture, never lost sight of their people overseas. There were always new committees and protests in the Little Ukraine to make the world aware of the suffering of the Ukrainian people. In the 1930s Ukrainian groups attacked the Polish pacification of the western Ukraine and the Stalinist famine and genocide. Through the Organization for the Defense of the Four Freedoms, which was founded in the 1940s, Little Ukraine continued to fight the Communist exploitation of their homeland up through the present.

After World War II, Little Ukraine was inundated with displaced persons from Europe. They were determined survivors, trained professionals, and eager young students, the nucleus of the neighborhood's Ukrainian renewal. In 1946 the Self-Reliance Association of American Ukrainians was formed in New York City. It not only assisted Ukrainian students, but it also built one of the best Ukrainian libraries in the city.

At the same time, the Shevchenko Scientific Institute was established to aid Ukrainian scientists. The arts thrived; the Ukrainian Literary Art Club and the Ukrainian Chorus were both organized in 1949. The Ukrainian Academy of Arts and Sciences was the crowning achievement in this era. In 1950 the Academy was organized in New York to sponsor the study of Ukrainian subjects. It had a library of twenty thousand books and its own prestigious academic journal dealing with Ukrainian history, literature, and social sciences.

In 1955 the Ukrainian-American community celebrated their golden anniversary. It was a time to take stock and to appreciate the solid accomplishments of Ukrainian New York's organizations and associations. Marking this occasion, Dr. Alexander Sokolyshyn wrote the *Golden Jubilee Book Commemorating Organized Ukrainian Life in New York*. It looked forward to another fifty years of group solidarity and progress.

In the next decade the Ukrainians struggled to maintain their community as the flower people moved in and the Ukrainian Lower East Side became the East Village. Though the conservative Ukrainians could hardly approve of the new Bohemian life-styles, their art galleries and dance clubs helped the neighborhood thrive commercially.

While the neighborhood stabilized, the Ukrainian's strong organizational base kept the community active and vital. The area's museum, world-famous choir, and Ukrainian shops and festivals flourished. Ukrainians were able to provide social services for a growing elderly population. Even people who had left the Lower East Side stayed close to and supported the community.

Ukrainian Bigos Tastes

Ukrainian cooking is heavy Slavic from the breadbasket of the Soviet Union. The potato defers to wheat groats (*kasha*), and wheat flour *verhenyly* dumplings (stuffed with meat or cheese) are the Ukrainian ravioli. The Ukrainians eat plenty of beef, but they have a preference for pork and it sometimes stands alone with rice in stuffed cabbage (*holubsti*) and stuffed peppers. They make a rich meat loaf (*zayac*) out of ground pork with veal for flavor. They are partial to bacon (*bochok*), which is served marinated as a meaty main dish. Like the Poles, Ukrainians are mad about kielbasa (*kobasa*), which they enjoy coarsely ground. Ukrainians also slice it up and add sauerkraut for a favorite national dish called *bigos*. Ukrainian cuisine is not heavily seasoned; a dollop of sour cream is the favorite condiment.

Ukrainian restaurants are plain and fancy—a simple coffee shop with counters and formica tables or a formal dining room with chandeliers and white tablecloths. Whether the restaurants cater to the original locals or the latest hip group of outlanders, they share the Ukrainian sense of hospitality. They haven't learned to be urban brusque. On Sundays, after mass at St. George's and a stroll, Ukrainian families pile into the neighborhood's restaurants for an old-fashioned Sunday dinner.

Veselka, *144 Second Avenue at 10th Street (212-228-9682). Monday–Friday 7 A.M.–1 A.M.; Saturday, Sunday 7 A.M.–4 A.M.*

Veselka is East Village ambience and Ukrainian food, and is usually crowded with the latest counterculture bunch against a post-modernist backdrop of whooping Indians on the wall. They still sell the Ukrainian paper from a stand in front and sell out the meat *pierogen*.

Ukrainian East Village Restaurant, *140 Second Avenue between 9th and 10th Streets (212-529-5024). Daily noon–11 P.M.*

The Ukrainian is located in the Ukrainian National Home. The restaurant is dimly lit and formal for Ukrainian family evenings out. Broad-shouldered Ukrainians, awkward in their Sunday suits, squire their gray-haired ladies, and there are often three generations at a table. Suburban Ukrainians make expeditions here for the lean *krakiewska* sausage and the veal with the special stuffing.

Odessa Coffee Shop, *117 Avenue A (212-473-8916). Daily 7 A.M.–midnight.*

Odessa is where the old Ukrainian chess players—the ones who use to play in Tompkins Square Park—come for coffee. Talking gives people an appetite, and thoughts soon turn from chess to cheese blintzes. Ukrainian school kids drop in for poppy-seed pastries.

Kiev Restaurant, *117 Second Avenue (212-674-4040). Daily 24 hours.*

The Kiev is Ukrainian food around the clock. Its thick meal-in-a-dish soups from mushroom barley to borsht are standouts. The Ukrainian style Schnitzel with a side order of kasha swimming in onion sauce is a real treat.

Pysansky and More

Ukrainians are proud of their handicrafts. They are more than a tradition; these folk arts are a part of the present. The colorful geometrics of Ukrainian *kilims* and Easter eggs are the centerpieces of Ukrainian households.

For Ukrainians the egg is the symbol of life and renewal. In pagan times there was a spring festival where Ukrainians danced at first light in honor of the sun and spirits. They painted eggs as offerings with special geometric designs and cosmic patterns of the rooster and the sun. These magical eggs in Christian times became associated with Easter and the resurrection of Christ and were blessed by priests on Easter mornings. The art of the Easter egg, *pysansky,* is passed on from generation to generation in the Ukrainian East Village.

Surma "The Ukrainian Shop", *11 East 7th Street (212-477-0729). Monday–Friday 11 A.M.–6 P.M.; Saturday 11 A.M.–5 P.M.; Sunday 11 A.M.–2 P.M.*

Surma started out in the Ukrainian music business. It still has Ukrainian sheet music and records of the Dumka Choir and thirty-string banduras. Surma now needs the tourist trade and has branched out into embroidered peasant blouses and vests and Ukrainian inlaid boxes and carving.

Arka, *26 First Avenue between 1st and 2nd Streets (212-473-3550). Daily 10 A.M.–6 P.M.*

Arka is a study in red and white in pottery, fabrics, and embroidered blouses. There are assortments of carved wooden plates, Ukrainian greeting cards, and Ukrainian cassettes.

Ukrainians are adamant that their foods are unique in taste and texture and though outsiders may not be able to tell the difference between a Ukrainian sausage and kielbasa, East Village Ukrainians will accept no substitutes. Some local food shops cater to their preferences.

New First Avenue Bakery, *121 First Avenue at 7th Street (212-674-5699). Monday–Saturday 6 A.M.–7 P.M.*

The bread covers the Eastern European waterfront with a fine pumpernickel that goes well with spiced Ukrainian sausage or kielbasa. The Ukrainian style *babka* with cheese is what the local ladies have with their tea.

Kurowycky Meats, *124 First Avenue between 7th and 8th Streets (212-477-0344). Monday–Saturday 8 A.M.–6 P.M.*

Three generations of Ukrainian butchers prepare spiced dried Ukrainian sausage and a sausage heavy on the garlic and caraway seeds. Their smoked meats have a reputation that attracts limousines from out of the neighborhood, but the Kurowyckys like it where they are. Their customers are familiar faces.

Ukrainian Choral Music

Ukrainians are fanatics when it comes to their choral music. The saying goes that when two Ukrainians meet they start another choir. The Ukrainian choir has the range of a symphony orchestra with intricate and precise harmonies. Sometime the choirs are joined by symphony orchestras, but usually the traditional bandura (a thirty–sixty-string instrument between a guitar and harp) provides the accompaniment.

The Koshetz choir of the independent Ukraine Republic introduced Ukrainian choruses to a wider American audience in the twenties. The leading members of the choir remained in New York after the Soviet takeover of the Ukraine and became involved in New York choirs, which gained a reputation for being the best in the country.

The Dumka is the leading Ukrainian choir in New York. It has performed at Lincoln Center and given concerts to mark milestones in the Ukrainian community. The choir's repertoire includes Carpathian and Cossack folk music and specially written choral music with Ukrainian lyrics and harmonies. The Dumka considers music their first language.

Ukrainian Place Marks

Ukrainian Museum, *203 Second Avenue (212-228-0110). Wednesday–Sunday 1 P.M.–5 P.M. Admission charge.*

The museum is an intimate journey into the folk arts and folkways of a people. The exhibits of painted Easter eggs, ceramics, and embroidered peasant costumes capture a naive delight in color and a sophisticated sense of form. There are special exhibits dealing with the significant and the rare, from icon covers to illuminated manuscripts. The staff is obviously involved and gladly answers any questions.

Ukrainian Institute of America, *2 East 79th Street (212-288-8660). Call for information on special events.*

Voldymyr Dzus, the inventor of the industrial fastener, founded the Ukrainian Institute of America in 1948. It was to be a repository for Ukrainian artifacts and arts and crafts and a center for the study of Ukrainian culture. In a magnificent Gothic Revival mansion, it houses Ukrainian religious relics, examples of Ukrainian embroidery and Easter eggs, and a gallery of Ukrainian portraits and sculpture. The institute also sponsors Ukrainian concerts and symposiums.

St. George's Ukrainian Catholic Church, *33 East Seventh Street (212-674-1615).*

The sanctuary of St. George's Church is a copy of a Carpathian Uniate church. Though a Catholic house of worship, it has icons like an Orthodox church, a massive dome, and sixteen remarkable stained-glass windows. The church plays an important part in organizing community-wide events like the Ukrainian festival, while the church school keeps Ukrainian culture alive.

Ukrainian Festivals and Festival Makers

May 17 is a great day for the Ukrainians, marking the conversion of their nation to Christianity. The whole Manhattan Ukrainian community—probably numbering around thirty thousand—crowds 7th Street between Second and Third Avenues to enjoy national dishes like stuffed cabbage and borscht and admire Ukrainian Easter eggs and embroidered peasant blouses. There are many older Ukrainians who return to the neighborhood on this day. Their eyes shine with recognition and memories. Grandchildren and even great-grandchildren are in tow.

In the afternoons limber Ukrainian folk dancers in high boots and embroidered blouses go through their acrobatic paces. A special mass is held on Sunday at St. George's Ukrainian Catholic Church, the sponsor of this festival.

════════════ Russians ════════════

History

The Russians who made it to New York City were frequently political refugees. In 1905, when the first workers' revolution failed, a spellbinding orator named Leon Trotsky escaped with his family to Brooklyn. When Leon Trotsky, Lenin, and company defeated the tsar and sent the provisional government packing in 1917, Alexander Kerensky, the leader of that government, turned up in New York.

Russian writers, artists, and composers escaping Czarist or communist oppression also found a refuge in the city. The daring composer, Igor Stravinsky, after arriving in New York, was able to cross the boundaries of melody. The Russian emigré ballet master, George Balanchine, who came to New York in 1932, was the first to choreograph ballets to Stravinsky's music breaking the conventional story format.

After World War II, Russian writer Vladimir Nabokov lived in New York between stints in universities. Using his second language, English, he changed the ground rules of the modern novel.

In the years of the Cold War before détente and *glasnost,* defecting or exile were the only ways to emigrate. New York's ballet benefited from these unconventional arrivals. Rudolph Nureyev was not only the leading dancer with the American Ballet but he was the toast of New York nightlife with frequent appearances at Studio 54. Mikhail Baryshnikov, with his acrobatic leaps, was a New York Ballet matinee idol. He was also a serious choreographer who wasn't afraid to experiment as dance-master of the American Ballet.

Russian emigrés who settled in New York also included generals and foot soldiers of the White Army, with a strong attachment to the old order. There was a whole raft of Russian aristocrats who formed their own organization where they could spend their time looking up genealogies and reminiscing about the czar. These Romanovs and Obolenskys married into notable New York families and became outstanding members of the city's café society.

The Russians who came to New York were not the same kind who labored in the mines of Pennsylvania. They were rich enough not to need a neighborhood or they had the intellectual skills to rapidly assimilate. Russian New York was the Russian Orthodox Church with masses that lasted longer than a double feature, the odd Russian restaurant, and the curio shops with exquisite antiquities.

Borscht or Bust

Russian cuisine is the haute cuisine of the Slavs. It is the same food that the Poles and Ukrainians eat, but with the touch of a French chef. The Russian buckwheat blini that wrap the caviar are Russian crêpes. The Russian *pierogen* stuffed with meat are Russian brioches. Chicken Kiev, lightly breaded and fried and wrapped around a cube of butter, delicately brings out the taste of the chicken breast. Beef Stroganoff, with the tenderest strips of beef flavored with mushrooms and sour cream, is almost tart on its delicate bed of white rice.

The Russian Tea Room, *150 West 57th Street (212-265-0847). Daily 1:30 P.M.–4 P.M., 4:30 P.M.–9:30 P.M.*

The Russian Tea Room once was a Russian restaurant but nowadays is a theatrical landmark. In the interim, the food hasn't improved but the prices reflect the new clientele. The beef Stroganoff is still the best in the city, but it's not easy to appreciate when you're sitting in your neighbor's lap.

Russian Samovar, *256 West 52nd Street (212-757-0168). Tuesday–Saturday noon–3 P.M., 5 P.M.–11 P.M.*

The Russian Samovar is all about food and not looking at the people at the next table. The not-to-be-missed specialty is the *pojarski* cutlet, ground veal and chicken rolled and sauteed and served with kasha.

Kalinka, *1067 Madison Avenue between 80th and 91st Streets (212-472-9656). Daily 11 A.M.–9:45 P.M.*

This East Side establishment is neat and narrow with the expected folk-art accoutrements. The restaurant does provide some lighter variations on the rich Russian fare. It is strong in the smoked salmon and caviar department and the blinis almost float to the table.

Catering à la Russe, *315 West 54th Street between Eighth and Ninth Avenues (212-246-6341) Monday–Saturday 10 A.M.–7 P.M.*

The shop is way off the beaten track and modest in appearance, but where else can you get Russian food to go with authentic Russian accents? Some of the food, like the chicken Kiev, doesn't lend itself to reheating but the salmon *koubiliaca* (salmon in a pastry crust with onions and mushrooms) and *pierogen* and blintzes are excellent to prepare in the microwave. It caters to West Side Russophiles.

The Glory of Russia—Past and Present

A La Vieille Russie, *781 Fifth Avenue at 59th Street (212-752-1727). Monday–Friday 10 A.M.–5 P.M.; Saturday 10 A.M.–4 P.M.*

The show window of this exquisite shop displays some of the jewels that might have belonged to the Russian aristocracy before the Revolution. At Easter they set out some of the fabulously crafted enameled and jeweled eggs made by the Frenchman Fabergé for the Russian nobility, just a hint of the opulence that was.

Eduard Nakhamkin Fine Arts, *1070 Madison Avenue at 81st Street (212-734-0271). Monday–Saturday 11 A.M.–5 P.M.*

Russian poster art is a thing of the past. The Russian avant-garde dazzles the New York masses at Nakhamkin's gallery. The painters who show are living and working in Russia as well as in Paris and New York.

The White Russians Are Coming

The White Russians are traditionalists. They live in a gossamer memory of vast estates and country houses. It is the Russia of white nights and balalaika music, of bowing peasants and diamond Fabergé Easter eggs. The Tsar is the lynch pin of this world and the Russian Orthodox Church is its spiritual center.

St. Nicholas Patriarchal Cathedral, *15 East 97th Street (212-289-1915).*

The Russian Orthodox church's giant onion-shaped domes tower over the neighborhood like some Arabian Nights fairy tale. Inside, the icons with their religious figures in stylized poses also seem Oriental. The great chandeliers are simply spectacular. The masses in Russian are long but the ritual is moving. The St. Nicholas boys' choir is special.

Russian Nobility Association of America, *971 First Avenue at 52nd Street (212-755-7528).*

The library is all about genealogy, a thousand volumes in all. It is the place where old Russian aristocrats go to polish their coats of arms. It is also the seat of the Russian Nobility Association of America, which keeps track of old Russian families in the States like a college alumni department.

The Arabs

Introduction

New York's Arab community is a rich microcosm of the whole Arab world, representing many nations and religious affiliations united by a common Arab language and culture. Arab New York encompasses the traditions of Muslim and Maronite, Yemenite and Syrian. It is the Lebanese and Palestinian fresh from the barricades and the engineer or doctor from Egypt or Iraq. In New York's most recent American Ethnic Parade the Arab contingent represented twenty-two nations, from North Africa to the Near East and from the Atlantic Ocean to the Indian Ocean. While the Syrians and Lebanese have far outnumbered other Arab immigrant groups in the past and are still the most influential segment of the Arab community, the latest Palestinian arrivals have infused the community with a new sense of Arab identity.

History

The first Arabs to make the long journey to New York had only a vague sense of nationality but if put to it, they considered themselves Syrian, whether they came from the wealthy Melkite quarters of Damascus, the mountain strongholds of the Lebanese Shuf, or holy Jerusalem. The overwhelming majority were Christians, who for more than a millennium of Muslim rule had maintained their religious identity.

They were devoted Eastern Rite Catholics of the Maronite or Melkite Communion or Syrian Orthodox. There was a significant minority of Muslims and the Druse of Lebanon, who subscribed to many Islamic beliefs and had their own esoteric holy books. All of these groups shared a deep loyalty to the family, a feeling of tribe that positively influenced their overall behavior and approach to an alien culture.

The situation of Syrian Christians and, to a lesser extent, their Muslim neighbors changed with the fortunes of the Ottoman regime. One moment Christians were the privileged intermediaries of the spice route and the next they were infidels squeezed by a heavy head tax. Rich or poor, they were at times vulnerable to the petty persecution of the authorities; but generally, in line with the laws of the Koran, they were treated with respect as a "protected" people.

In 1860 the competition for scarce land in Lebanon led to the massacre of thousands of Maronites and Melkites by a Druse army. The Western powers reacted immediately to the violence by pressuring the Turkish sultan to institute a more autonomous regime in Lebanon under a Christian administrator. This new government, under the sponsorship of the European powers, ushered in a period of economic growth and the expansion of Western culture from 1861 to 1915.

In some areas of Lebanon and Syria, agriculture had become too dependent on cash crops and foreign imports, and large landholders were able to enlarge their holdings at the expense of small farmers. In an atmosphere of rising expectations, immigration became the solution for economic problems.

Following in the footsteps of their adventurous Phoenician ancestors, Syrian-Lebanese set their sights on the New World. An advance group of merchants from Damascus, Beirut, and Jerusalem journeyed to the Philadelphia Centennial Exposition in 1876 and sent back glowing reports of commercial success. The response was immediate and overwhelming; young Arab men, eager to make their fortunes and serve their families, crossed a continent.

This first wave of Arab emigrants were mostly Christian. They were helped at every stage of the way from Cyprus to Marseille to Liverpool by local Syrian-Lebanese communities. In New York at Ellis Island, Najib Arbeely, the Immigration Bureau's Arab interpreter, was a one-man information service. He assisted Arab newcomers in contacting their families or their religious communities and counseled the uninitiated about employment opportunities.

After the Syrian-Lebanese emigrants disembarked at the Battery, it was only a short walk to the Arab hubbub and bazaar on Washington Street. They were warmly welcomed by relatives or friends from their villages. The new arrivals, who often thought their stays would be temporary, were anxious to get started. They intended to work hard, spend little, save some dollars, and return home to buy land or finance a business.

In the formative years of Little Syria the inhabitants were mainly male. They lived together in bachelor boardinghouses, saving on expenses and sharing the cooking and cleaning. They helped one another find jobs or get into business and exchanged precious bits of information about home.

Once they had some scraps of English and a handle on American customs, the majority took up the peddler's pack. Though peddling was the preserve of Greeks, Jews, and Armenians in their homeland, more than 90 percent of these mainly agrarian Arabs were peddlers prior to World War I.

New York was known to the Arabs as the "Mother of Peddling Communities." Local Syrian merchants provided the goods, usually local handicrafts or imports from the Mideast. At first the peddlers sold crosses from the Cedars of Lebanon and rosaries from the Holy Land, but later they branched out into such exotica as silk handkerchiefs, embroidered kimonos, and lace shawls. These Arab peddlers traveled alone or in pairs and scrupulously avoided competing with one another.

For Arab New Yorkers, peddling proved to be the quickest path to cultural assimilation and material success. Peddlers traveling crosscountry had a crash course in things American and the American language. They were able to develop their entrepreneurial skills and powers of persuasion on farm people in rural backwaters, while earning the necessary money to establish secure businesses.

The gradual collapse of the old Ottoman order and an unending series of brush-fire wars put added pressures on the peoples of Syria. There were confiscations of food and supplies, and the burden of taxes became unbearable. In 1908 the government of the Young Turks threatened their subject populations with military conscription.

Many Syrian-Lebanese left their ancestral lands for freedom and survival. In the decade preceding World War I almost one quarter of the population deserted the rugged country of Mount Lebanon. But Arab New Yorkers were not cut off from their homeland and many returned regularly to help build and rebuild churches and hospitals. They supported poor family members and assisted others to emigrate. Many Christian Arab women now joined their husbands and fathers in the city.

New York City became the unofficial capital of the Syrian-Lebanese community. Washington Street was a Levantine market with animated vendors selling exotic spices, Oriental rugs, and gold bracelets. There were tables gorgeously inlaid with mother-of-pearl and scimitars of Damascus steel. In the cafés men in fezzes drank tiny cups of Turkish coffee and sat on cushions, smoking hookahs and playing backgammon.

Hundreds of Syrian men, women, and children filled apartments between Washington and Greenwich, Rector and Carlisle Streets. Merchants established Middle Eastern import and export houses and entrepreneurs opened small garment factories specializing in silk embroidery. Some of the more successful Arab businessmen like Saleem Malouk were even able to move uptown to Fifth Avenue mansions and become patrons of the arts.

The New York casbah became the model for all Arabic-American communities. It had three churches and six newspapers and organized the first Arabic-American Association in the country, which assisted Arabs to learn English and get an education.

Arab success was no accident. Syrian-Lebanese were impelled to succeed by a need to win honor and status for themselves and their families. The American get-rich-quick ethic meshed with Arab values like generosity, hospitality, and munificence. Coming from a society where people were frequently jockeying for position, the Syrian-Lebanese were prepared to compete for the rewards of wealth. They were determined to work hard and sacrifice for the source of their identity, the family.

But the Arab people who kept classical learning alive during the Dark Ages had interests beyond mere money. The earliest leader of the Arab intellectual community was Dr. Joseph Arbeely, who reached New York in 1881. He had been involved in translating the Bible into Arabic and recognized the importance of the Arab linguistic heritage.

His sons founded the city's first Arabic newspaper and laid the foundation for the whole Arab press in America. The two most powerful organs in this highly sectarian community were *Al-Hoda,* which represented the Maronite point of view, and *Murrat-ul-Garb,* which was the voice of the Orthodox. In 1910 *Al-Bayan* (The News) began publication, concerned with issues involving the Muslim and Druse communities.

New York was the center for an experimental Syrian literary movement that was creating Arabic equivalents for modern Western forms like free verse. Kahlil Gibran, the renowned author of *The Prophet,* was the leader of *Al-Rabitur al-Qalamiyya* (the Pen League), a circle that included writers like the Arab Walt Whitman, Ameen Rihani, who wrote with Whitmanesque energy and verve. The Pen League attacked the literary status quo and encouraged the publication of new Arabic writing.

Arab men and women increasingly dressed American and their actions were no longer strictly limited by parental authority. Women without head-scarves (even Christian women wore scarves in their villages as a matter of modesty) were even involved in the world of work outside the home. Syrian-Lebanese married Americans and immigrants from European countries and some gradually lost their Arab identity.

In 1905 there was a pitched battle in the narrow streets of Little Syria between traditionalists and the forces of Americanization. Five people were injured in the fifteen-minute "pistol-knife" fray that embarrassed the whole

Syrian-Lebanese community. Najeeb Malouf and Syrian Orthodox Bishop Hawaweeny tried unsuccessfully to mediate the dispute.

But the New York Arabic community was able to unite in the face of old-fashioned American bigotry. In January of 1909 a Lebanese named Costa George Najour was refused citizenship on the basis of the Asian exlusionary rule and Arabs were officially classifed as nonwhite. Arab New Yorkers and the local Arab press went into action, raising over a thousand dollars to appeal the case, and Najour was finally granted citizenship.

Following World War I and the years of accumulating capital, the Arab peddler was replaced by the Arab store owner. The community gained a new stability, which was not even threatened by the movement of Syrian-Lebanese away from the old Little Syria near the Battery to a new ethnic enclave in Brooklyn. Arabs increasingly went retail, opening dry-goods stores, grocery stores, and fruit and vegetable stands.

While some Arab New Yorkers eagerly assimilated, there was a reawakening of cultural identity in the New York Arab community. The Maronite Arabs began to view themselves as a special people, the descendants of Phoenician empire builders. This Lebanese national pride was encouraged by a new political entity in the post–World War I Middle East. The Maronites believed that the Greater Lebanon Mandate, which was controlled by the French, was their own nation.

After another world war the whole map of the Middle East changed again and the city's Arabs could now point with pride to the state of Lebanon. The majority could trace their bloodlines back to the mountaineers of this new land. They also found it easy to identify with such a cosmopolitan country with its long-standing French-Maronite connection. Soon it became the rule to add the Lebanese national identification to the names of local organizations. The notion of Lebanese nationality was so pervasive that even New Yorkers of Syrian Christian descent referred to themselves as Lebanese.

The Hart-Celler Immigration Act of 1965 opened the doors of New York to Arabs from different geographical areas and segments of society. New immigration quotas based on professional skills instead of race or national origin enabled educated elites throughout the Arab world and many more Muslims to emigrate to the city. Engineers and physicians from Egypt and Iraq found employment and economic opportunity. Like the early Syrian-Lebanese peddlers, many who had previously studied in the United States, also took American brides.

The 1967 Arab-Israeli War increased the flow of Palestinian refugees, who had been emigrating to New York in significant numbers since the end of the Arab-Israeli War in 1948. They were very different from other recent arrivals. The Palestinians were politicized and really committed to their Arab identity.

Many Arab New Yorkers rallied around these refugees, believing the time had come to assert their ethnic pride. Arab-American university graduates convened in 1968 to map a strategy to improve the Arab image. New York's Arab churches and organizations inaugurated classes in Arabic and Arabic culture. The Eastern Federation of American Syrian Lebanese Clubs even sought a voice in American foreign policy. Arabs from Lebanon, Yemen, Egypt, and Palestine were united and committed to a Pan-Arabic identity.

Atlantic Avenue Neighborhood

Directions: IRT-Seventh Avenue 2 or 3, or IRT-Lexington Avenue 4 or 5 to Borough Hall.

Introduction

Atlantic Avenue between Henry and Clinton Streets is the Main Street of the Arab community, not only of New York but of the whole country. This Brooklyn commercial area is the Arabs' sentimental home: it is the place to find Arab food, Arab music, Arab books and newspapers, and Arab cultural artifacts from rugs to worry beads.

Here the Arab presence that is usually so diffuse becomes an actual part of the city. Among their own people and Atlantic Avenue's spice market and bazaar, Arab-Americans can live their identity. Atlantic Avenue is more than a street, it is a state of mind.

In another age Atlantic Avenue, where it today meets with Clinton Street, was the crest of a hill called Cobble Hill. During the American Revolution the British army retook this high ground, which George Washington had used as a vantage point to watch the movements of the Redcoats. For all their trouble, the British eventually used Cobble Hill as an evacuation point.

Though Atlantic Avenue never reached the elegant heights of its close neighbor, Brooklyn Heights, it did provide pleasant housing for Irish immigrants on the move. Later it attracted Scandinavian residents who were employed at the Navy Yard at Red Hook. Italians from southern Italy and Spaniards from Galicia in northern Spain were next to occupy Atlantic Avenue.

In 1892, while Washington Street's Arab neighborhood was still growing, Arabs started to leave its dark, poorly ventilated buildings for comparatively spacious Atlantic Avenue housing. It was a convenient area to choose, the first stop on the Fulton Ferry leaving Battery Park.

The numbers of new Arab immigrants quickly increased as married Syrian men began bringing over their wives and children, and more young, ambi-

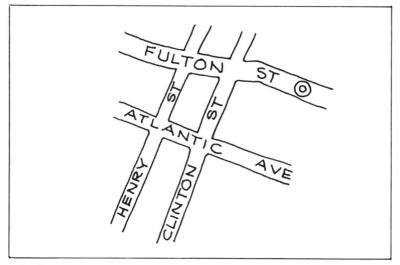

Atlantic Avenue

tious Arab men were attracted to the city by the constant flow of overseas money orders. Soon there was a need for the immigrant communities to expand but the Washington Street neighborhood was hemmed in by the development of commercial buildings for the financial district. In 1940 work on the Brooklyn Battery Tunnel bulldozed Manhattan's Arab neighborhood out of existence, making Brooklyn's Atlantic Avenue the community's center.

Through the efforts of enterprising Atlantic Avenue merchants like the Sahadis and the Malkos and Moustaphas, the retail businesses on the block prospered, and Syrians and Lebanese were soon moving out of apartments above the stores to the landmark buildings of Cobble Hill and Brooklyn Heights. There was a solid community life of families, churches, and village associations.

American politics were foreign to a people who related to others on the basis of blood ties and religion rather than geographical closeness. In 1932 Lebanese and Syrians could not gain the recognition of Tammany, and a local Democratic club voted Republican. Despite the Depression the Arab colony was able to spread out to expensive period houses in Park Slope and nearby Prospect Park.

At the end of World War II, Atlantic Avenue was the scene of wild celebrating in honor of V-E Day and the independence of Lebanon. In 1948 another war between the Israelis and the Arabs brought displaced Palestinians to the neighborhood around Atlantic Avenue; the later 1967 Six Day War added West Bank Arabs with Jordanian passports to the influx. Syrian and Lebanese community leaders tried to keep tensions with their Jewish neighbors to a minimum by forming the Salaam (peace) Club in 1970.

In the late 1960s Yemeni Muslim refugees began leaving their partitioned nation to create their own enclave on Atlantic Avenue. They were welcomed by established Yemeni families like the Almontasers, who had owned a number of popular Atlantic Avenue restaurants.

The civil war in Lebanon was a cause of great concern and renewed Lebanese emigration to Brooklyn. The Atlantic Avenue Lebanese (and Lebanese throughout the whole Metropolitan area) have worked hard to integrate these refugees into the community and have continued to send relief to their war-weary homeland. Meanwhile the Arab colony has continued its Brooklyn hegira to the more suburban Bay Ridge on Shore Road.

Dining

Arab cooking is simple. The ingredients are fresh and natural. Lamb, yogurt, bulgar (cracked wheat), rice, pine nuts, dried apricots, grape leaves, lemons, okra, string beans, chick-peas, squash, and eggplant are the essentials of the Arab kitchen. Garlic, lemon, cloves, cinnamon, coriander, cardamon, thyme, mint, and rose water provide the aromatic flavors. The food is hot-weather light and the tastes are subtle.

Among the Arabs, eating is more than satisfying hunger; it is a social occasion and an opportunity for hospitality. The *mazza* is an Arabic selection of appetizer-like dishes shared by a group with pita bread and good conversation. *Hommus* (mashed chick-peas with garlic, lemon, and sesame oil) and *baba ghanouj* (broiled eggplant mashed with garlic, lemon, and sesame oil) are typical cold *mazza,* while felafel (fried chick peas puree) and *kibee* (fried or broiled lamb mixed with yogurt, bulgar, and pine nuts) are popular hot *mazza.* Christian Lebanese whet the appetite for more dishes with Arak, an anise-flavored liquor that burns going down, usually mixed with ice and water.

In the Magreb of North Africa they add a little heat to the food in the form of hot peppers; couscous (semolina grains) replaces cracked wheat as the grain of choice. For the favorite dish of this region, the couscous is steamed in a special pot and covered with stewed meats and vegetables served with their juices and harissa, a hot flavorful sauce.

In Syria and Lebanon stews are made with lamb and a single vegetable, mainly string beans, okra, and squash. The squash is also stuffed with chopped lamb and rice. Touches of rose water, mint, and cinnamon bring out rather than overlay these basic tastes. Broiled meat in the Arab world is the basic lamb kebab cooked on a spit.

Atlantic Avenue's restaurant row offers mostly authentic tastes of the Middle East for an essentially Arab clientele and the yuppies and literary types from Brooklyn Heights. Many of the restaurants represent three generations of Syrians or Lebanese, while others are owned by more recent arrivals.

Adnan, *129 Atlantic Avenue (718-625-2115). Daily 11 A.M.–11 P.M.*

Adnan is run by the Yemeni family Almontaser and is a fixture on Atlantic Avenue. It goes back to the days when the only way to woo customers was to modify the native cuisine to Western tastes and call it Continental. The staff tries hard but the crepes and kebabs don't mix.

Tripoli, *6 Atlantic Avenue (718-596-5800). Daily noon–midnight.*

Tripoli is Lebanon before the bombs went off. The restaurant is friendly and free-spirited. It's couples, extended families, and men-only meetings with laughter and banter over *mazza* and Arak and wine from Lebanon. The stuffed zucchini and the Arab lamb stews, *bamia* (okra), and *loubia* (string beans) are satisfying without being at all heavy. The wooden booths carved in arabesques, the ornate balcony off the bar, and the colorful mural of Lebanon keep up the mood of an Arabian Nights party.

Bourock, *172 Atlantic Avenue (718-624-9614). Monday–Friday 2 P.M.–midnight; Saturday, Sunday noon–midnight.*

Bourock means "flying horse" but it hardly takes off. It is down some stairs and unpretentious. The kebabs and *mazza* are very straightforward with none of the unexpected spice flights of fancy. The flying horse is more for a snack than a leisurely meal.

Yemeni Café, *176 Atlantic Avenue (718-834-9533). Daily 8 A.M.– 10 P.M.*

The Yemeni Café is just what the sign says. It is a real old-fashioned Arab café where Arab men, mostly new immigrants in ill-fitting suits, while away the hours over thimbles of coffee and Cokes. The occasional interloper is politely ignored.

Moroccan Star, *205 Atlantic Avenue (718-643-0800). Daily 11 A.M.–3 P.M., 5 P.M.–10 P.M.*

The couscous is chockful of vegetables with a whole soup bowl of juice per portion. The couscous *merguez,* made with the delectable Moroccan lamb sausage, is the couscous star. The waiters try to please while never losing their sense of humor.

Arabic Brick Oven

On weekends, returning Arab sons and daughters from Jersey and the Island double-park along Atlantic Avenue to get Syrian bread (they never call it pita) and stock up on spinach and meat pies and maybe sweet syrupy *baklawa.*

The Arabs actually invented bread; their paper-thin bread *macouk* was first prepared over a hot stone. The Arab flat breads come in many varieties: wheat, white *swimson* (sesame), and *zahta* (lightly covered with thyme, sumak, sesame seeds, and olive oil).

Arab pastry has a certain sameness, lots of variations on phyllo sheets and semolina flour, crushed walnuts and pistachios and honey or a sugary syrup. But nothing is better with strong Turkish coffee. (The Turks named it, but it is another Arab original.) The cookies are simplicity themselves, rings and circles of dough with and without nuts or sesame.

Damascus Bakery, *195 Atlantic Avenue (718-855-1456). Daily 8 A.M.–7 P.M.*

The big commercial producer of Syrian flat breads. People come here to buy breads in quantity. The *zahta* is so good it doesn't need any accompaniment. The individual date cakes and the *kanafe* (looking like General Mills shredded wheat drenched in syrup) are two excellent old standards and the *fatir bil ishta* is the wonderful thing that happens when phyllo meets custard.

Near East Bakery, *143 Atlantic Avenue (718-875-0016). Tuesday–Saturday 9 A.M.–4:30 P.M.; Sunday 9:30 A.M.–1 P.M.*

This bakery is worth the basement crowds in confined spaces. The three-cornered meat pies made with chopped lamb and onions and the spinach pies made with spinach and onions are nonparallel finger food. The crunchy phyllo bird's nest filled with green pistachios with a hint of rose water and topped with syrup is too rich to be believed.

Mini-Bazaars

Arab food shops on Atlantic Avenue and its side streets are mini-bazaars. Arab food in cans and packages are a very small part of the show. From seeds to nuts, from olives to coffee, things are sold loose from vats, sacks, or

apothecary jars. Arabs like their foods fresh. Shopping Arab-style takes time
and a lot of looking and on weekends usually a wait on line.

Like the bazaar, the Atlantic Avenue shops deal in diversity. Even in a
small grocery-sized store Middle Eastern coffee makers compete for space
with music tapes, canned chick-peas, jars of pickled turnips, Turkish camel
saddles, Moroccan brass trays, and anything else the proprietor thinks he or
she can sell.

Sahadi Importing Company, *187 Atlantic Avenue (718-624-
4550). Monday–Saturday 9 A.M.–7 P.M.*

Sahadi is the longest-running shop on the avenue, having started out in the
original Washington Street Arab neighborhood. The inventory of Arab
foods, crafts, and manufactured goods is endless. There is more than one
kind of anything, whether it is halvah, loose tea, brass coffee grinders, or
backgammon boards, and everything an aspiring belly dancer could possibly
need. The spice and herb selection is a miniature Mideast spice market.
Sahadi even sells canned Arab food under its own label.

Oriental Pastry and Grocery, *170 Atlantic Avenue (718-875-
7687). Daily 10 A.M.–8:30 P.M.*

This combination grocery/bakery makes its own pastry and supplies all the
ingredients for do-it-yourself Arab bakers. There are Arab cookbooks available for beginners.

Arab Music Connection

Rashid Sales, *191 Atlantic Avenue (718-852-3298). Monday–Saturday 9 A.M.–7 P.M.; Sunday noon–7 P.M.*

There are cassettes and Arab records in other stores but nothing to compare
to Rashid. It covers everything from Egyptian classical to Algerian rock. The
people at Rashid's know their stuff and are willing to give the customer the
benefit of their knowledge. Rashid's sponsors three and a half hours of Arab
music every week on WFUV-FM (89.5) and WSOU-FM (90.7).

Arab Religious Life
Arab Churches

When the Arabs were under the rule of the eight-hundred-year Turkish
Ottoman Empire, the leaders of their churches acted as intermediaries with

the Ottoman officials and rulers. The churches were a kind of nation and the church hierarchy had considerable secular power. Even in the twentieth century, Brooklyn Lebanese and Syrian Christian churches are a prime source of individual identity. These churches have an important social role and perform charitable functions that other ethnics have handed over to secular groups.

Our Lady of Lebanon, *13 Remsen Street (718-624-7228).*

This Maronite house of worship is in the landmark church that originally housed the Congregational Church of Pilgrims. An 1845 Gothic Revival structure, it has some unusual details like doors from the luxury liner *Normandie* and a piece of Plymouth Rock in its tower. Father Abdullah is the spiritual leader of this large congregation, which includes many recent refugees from the civil war in Lebanon. The church helps in any way it can to find jobs and housing for these new Americans and send aid overseas to their beleaguered community. On Sunday at 11 A.M. the church holds a mass in Arabic.

"Mahrajan"—the Arab Party

The first *Mahrajan* (an Arab celebration of self, combining both picnic and party), was held in Bridgeport in 1930. This affirmation of identity through food, music, and dancing soon spread to New York and Brooklyn. In the early days it was a fund-raiser for churches and groups. The churches are still the main sponsors of these events, but they are all-Arab happenings crossing denominational lines. Families come together and strangers share in this appreciation of the Arab heritage. The music is loud and lively and the dancing is spontaneous, as are the smiles.

Brooklyn's premier *Mahrajan* is held in the churchyard of Our Lady of Lebanon on the first weekend in June. Admission charge.

The Arab Mosque

Masjid Al Farouq, *552–554 Atlantic Avenue between Fourth and Fifth Streets.*

There are no minarets in front of Al Farouq. It is in a six-story Art Deco building. The Muslims who attend the mosque are mainly Arabs from the neighborhood but there is also a large number of African-Americans, Pakistanis, and Afghanis. Prayers in the mosque, bowing to Mecca in the East, are not only a vivid act of faith but a demonstration of Muslim brotherhood. Members of the mosque practice charity toward poorer minorities in the community. Since prayers must be spoken in Arabic, instructional classes in the language are given. Members of the mosque also participate in Palestinian relief programs.

Ramadan and the "Id-al-Adha"

Ramadan is a Muslim observance occurring in the spring at the time of the new moon. It is the holiest month of the Muslim calendar and an occasion for fasting and self-examination. Muslims fast during daylight and at sunset break that fast with dates and water like the Prophet Mohammed. Later they have the *Iftar,* the evening breakfast with thick soups and heavy stews which will help them endure the long fast.

Toward the end of Ramadan, worshipers sleep in the Atlantic Avenue mosque. They prepare for the Night of Power, when Mohammed had his revelation and all dreams can come true. Ramadan is ushered out with the *id al fitr,* the festival of fast breaking, with feasting and gift-giving.

In the summer, Muslims celebrate the Feast of Sacrifice, *Id-al-Adha,* commemorating Abraham's sacrifice of a ram in place of his son Ishmael. It is a time of sharing at the Al-Farouq Mosque, when lambs are slaughtered according to a special ritual (in a slaughterhouse) and the greater part is given to the poor. Some call it the holiday of sharing.

The Atlantic Avenue Antic

The Atlantic Avenue Antic is usually on the third Sunday in September. The Antic block party covers the length and breadth of Atlantic Avenue, spanning ethnics from Gallegos to Belizians, but the real festivities are concentrated on the avenue between Clinton and Court Streets. There are portable stages with Arab bands and belly dancers. Arab spectators aren't shy; they hold their hands over their heads, do a few steps, and shake their bodies. The restaurants are doubling as street stands and the smell of barbecuing kebabs fills the air. There is all manner of Arab pastry from *baklawa* to meat pies and all the dishes for a curbside *mazza.* Sahadi even breaks his no-opening Sunday rule for this special day.

════ Little Lebanon in Bay Ridge ════

Directions: BMT R to 77th Street/Fourth Avenue.

The Arabs did not have to leave Brooklyn to relocate in the suburbs; they found them in Bay Ridge. The Arabs are an important presence in a changing

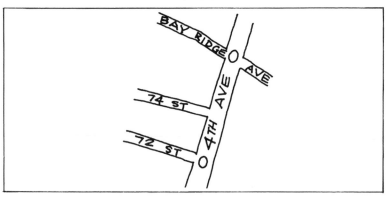

Little Lebanon in Bay Ridge

Bay Ridge. Their foods and flavors add color to the old Scandinavian neighborhood, near the sweeping silhouette of the Verrazano bridge.

Samira's, *6916 Fourth Avenue (718-745-2416). Monday–Saturday 8:30 A.M.–6:30 P.M.*

Samira's bills itself as an international kitchen and its around-the-world menu includes lasagna, paella, and corned beef and cabbage. But its real culinary standouts are pure Middle Eastern. The delicious *loubia* (string beans) and *bamia* (okra) are served on real Syrian rice laced with noodles and pinoli nuts. *Fajwada* is an Arab beans with meat dish that leaves hot Tex-Mex chile in the cold.

King Falafel, *7408 Third Avenue (718-745-4188). Daily 11 A.M.–midnight.*

The King is mainly a takeout and deliver type of place. The fresh vegetarian specialties—the *falafel, hommus,* kebabs *baba ghanouj,* and *foul*—are preferable to the kebabs and *kibee* that are sometimes dried-out and greasy.

El-Manara, *7111 Third Avenue (718-745-2284). Daily 11 A.M.–11 P.M.*

El-Manara is the restaurant where most of the local Lebanese go to seal a deal or to celebrate. The attractive dining area is pastel light and comfortable with pictures of Lebanon. The friendly couple who owns the restaurant create a feeling of family. El-Manara has some seafood plates like *sumki hara* (fish cooked in a spicy sauce with almonds and walnuts) and vegetarian platters like *mjudra* (lentils cooked with bulgar and onions) that are rarely cooked so well in the city.

Manhattan Arab

Introduction

There are almost no traces of Manhattan's Little Syria. St. George's (Melkite) and St. Joseph's (Maronite) are gone. Jabbours, the long-standing Lebanese retailer, has moved to Long Island. The Fifth Avenue Arabs, the importer Mallouk, the silk industry Kiamies, and the Persian rug-dealing Tadross, have disappeared or assimilated. Even the R. G. Haddad Foundation, which provided scholarships for deserving Arab youngsters, is a part of the past.

The new Arab Manhattan has more to do with multinationals and international diplomacy than merchants and churches. The Manhattan Arabs are highly trained individuals, doctors and engineers and respected college professors like Edward Said of Columbia University, not a geographical community. Sometimes they are second-generation Arabs, like special prosecutor Maurice Nadjari, who headed the corruption-busting Knapp Commission.

Restaurants

Authentic Arab restaurants in the city are a rarity. Most of the eating places that claim to be Arab restaurants—whether North African or Middle Eastern—are just taking advantage of the current vogue for *tabouli, hommus,* and *baba ghanouj.* It is fast-food Arab and very bland.

The Cedars of Lebanon, *39 East 30th Street (212-725-9251). Daily 11:30 A.M.–3 A.M.; music starts at 10 P.M.*

Cedars of Lebanon is the oldest Arab restaurant in the city specializing in Lebanese food. The local rug merchants, Armenian, Persian, and Arabic, in the buildings on 29th and 30th Streets keep the cuisine honest. The *mazza* is well prepared, and there are full dinners from lentil soup to shish kebab to milk pudding and Turkish coffee.

Chez Momo, *48 MacDougal Street (212-979-8588). Tuesday– Sunday 5 P.M.–midnight.*

Chez Momo is Algerian food of the first quality. The appetizers like the spicy carrots are Algerian and unusual. The couscous is made with care: the vegetables are cooked to just the right consistency, the lamb and chicken are succulent. There is no liquor license, so it's bring your own. The crowd ranges from champagne to beer.

Sido, Abu-Salim Restaurant, *81 Lexington Avenue at 26th Street (212-686-2031). Monday–Friday noon–11 P.M.; Saturday, Sunday 1 P.M.–11 P.M.*

Sido started out a few blocks up on Lexington with kitchenette furniture, red wallpaper, and excellent Lebanese-style food. The food is still excellent; the surroundings are now white-tablecloth gracious. Their couscous is too refined, but the *kibee,* raw or cooked, is perfect and the *mazza* with hot and cold appetizers, from *hommus* to falafel, is a bargain at any price.

Falafel 'N' Stuff, *1586 First Avenue between 83rd and 84th Streets (212-879-7023). Daily noon–11 P.M.*

The food is Egyptian and there is a mural of pharaohs and Nubian slaves on the wall that also makes that point. The restaurant is modest but good-natured. The Egyptian national dish *foul mudammas* (brown beans with garlic, spices, and oil) is much ado about beans. It is the Egyptian *melokhia* (a leafy green stewed with chicken or lamb) that is the real Egyptian soul food. Fat pita bread sandwiches with *hommus, baba ghanouj,* or felafel and plenty of salad are recommended.

At Our Place, *2527 Broadway between 94th and 95th Streets (212-864-1410). Daily 3 P.M.–11 P.M.*

The owner is an Egyptian who makes it a matter of personal honor to keep his customers happy. The food he serves is across-the-board Middle Eastern from something he calls Egyptian *moussaka* to couscous. His *kanafa* with cheese is the best way to end a meal. Low prices also inspire joy.

Arab takeouts are very common in the city, but most aren't any better than the stands on the street that sell felafel or kebabs with their Italian sausage. The following are exceptions.

Bennie's, *37 Seventh Avenue at 13th Street (212-633-2044). Monday–Friday 7:30 A.M.–8 P.M.; Saturday 9 A.M.–6 P.M. 321 Amsterdam Avenue at 75th Street (212-874-3032). Daily 10 A.M.–10 P.M.*

The owner should be called Dr. Bennie; he's a Lebanese plastic surgeon. He does great things with salads from a simple *khiar b'leban* (cucumber and yogurt) to *muda data* (a mix of rice, onions, and lentils). His hybrid Arab chicken salads could turn the head of a purist.

Ella Wendy, *77 Lexington Avenue between 25th and 26th Streets (212-686-2349/2299). Daily 10 A.M.–midnight.*

Wendy has all the pita sandwiches, including a *foul mudammas* filled with spicy fava beans. The couscous is good when it is freshly prepared. The zucchini *bashmala* (with ground meat and heavy cream) is winning a following.

Arab Nuts

Arabs are natural health food fanatics; they love nuts, seeds, and dried fruits, and yogurt called *leban,* drained through cheesecloth, is their dairy favorite. Arab shops in Manhattan cater to these tastes.

Nader International Foods, *296 Fifth Avenue between 30th and 31st Streets (212-736-1183). Monday–Saturday 9 A.M.–7 P.M.; Sunday 10 A.M.–6 P.M.*

Nader deserves special mention for its fine pistachios and dried apricots and just about every known variety of nut, all in giant containers lining the walls of the front of the store. He also stocks Arab groceries at prices well above the going rate in Brooklyn.

Yes International Food Company, *165 Church Street (212-227-4695). Monday–Friday 9:30 A.M.–7 P.M.; Saturday 11 A.M.–6 P.M.*

The nuts here are freshly roasted, and the prices are the best in Manhattan. It should be avoided early afternoons when the nearby offices break for lunch.

The Fine Art of Belly Dancing

The musicians are not just playing background, they are totally involved. The mustachioed man on the *durbek* (Arab bongos) never misses a beat as the *oud* (mandolin-like instrument) player fingers the strings like a Near East Jimmy Hendricks. All the while, the third man on the *kannon* (zither) smiles beatifically.

The music is hot and rhythmically hypnotic. The woman in her harem costume keeps time with her *zills* (finger cymbals) and the movement of a hip and does a counterpoint to the beat with the graceful motion of her hands and arms. Suddenly she's kneeling and, still keeping time, she leans slowly back and her shoulders touch the floor.

In the days before topless bars and x-rated videos, there was a strip of Turkish and Greek belly dancing joints with names like the Egyptian Gardens on Eighth Avenue between 28th and 29th Streets. It was the most daring show in a town where La Guardia outlawed burlesque. The clubs today are far more sophisticated and expensive and attract couples.

Darvish, *23 West 8th Street (212-475-1600). Wednesday, Friday–Sunday 8 P.M.–4 A.M.*

The Darvish is not too dressed up to have a good time. The dancers and musicians are real professionals, making it look easy and spontaneous. It is a downtown type of place where you can really listen to the music.

Ibis, *151 East 50th Street (212-753-3429). Friday–Sunday 9 P.M.– 4 A.M.*

The club Ibis is a real Arabian Nights' fantasy with lots of glitter and nonstop dancers. The Egyptian food is an added bonus and not cheap. It attracts Upper East Siders looking for something completely different and Arabs who don't need expense accounts.

Arabs in Museums

The American Museum of Natural History, *Central Park West at 79th Street (212-769-5100). Sunday–Tuesday, Thursday 10 A.M.–5:45 P.M.; Wednesday, Friday, Saturday 10 A.M.–9 P.M. Contribution, except after 5 P.M. Friday and Saturday.*

Gallery Three on the second floor is devoted to Asian peoples, and a part of that exhibit deals with the world of Islam. A painting of the Grand Mosque of Mecca is the starting-off point. There are crafts from the Mideast from brasswork to rugs. The ornate dress and jewelry of the women of Palestine and Yemen are on display.

The Brooklyn Museum, *Eastern Parkway and Washington Avenue (718-638-5000). Wednesday–Monday 10 A.M.–5 P.M. Contribution.*

There's a sculpture of the Prophet at the front, among the other great men. The Hagop Kevorkian Gallery on the third floor in room 16 explores the ancient Middle East and the antecedents of the Syrians. There are twelve monumental reliefs from the Palace of Ashurnasirpal II among other impressive artifacts of that age.

New York City's First Mosque

Islamic Center, *One Riverside Drive (212-362-6800).*

The Islamic Center has been the religious meeting place for Arabs in Manhattan. The center conducts prayers five times a day, offers classes in Arabic, and runs a religious school for children. At the time of this writing, it is being superseded by a magnificent dome and minaret mosque on Third Avenue, built with the assistance of the Saudi Arabian government, which should rival St. Patrick's.

The African-Americans

Introduction

New York's African-Americans are Haitian, West Indian, and southern migrant. There are even vestiges of New Amsterdam free men. They all came to the hemisphere on slave ships and did hard time on the white man's plantations. They exchanged Africa for scraps of French, English, and southern plantation culture.

New York has represented a new start for turn-of-the-century southern sharecroppers and West Indians who labored on the Panama Canal and Haitian boat people from the Duvalier seventies. Despite prejudice in the new Jerusalem, they continue to pursue the American dream.

History

Manhattan's eleven original Africans were carried over as chattels on a Dutch merchant ship in 1626. These "Angolans" had greater freedom than the slaves in British colonies; they were legally entitled to hold property and marry and had the right of free movement. Their children could not be taken away from them.

An African slave in early New Amsterdam was not considered very different from a white indentured servant. They were "allowed" to keep their African identity and were not stigmatized by color. In 1644 the original slaves petitioned the Dutch West India Company for their freedom and it was granted. The same year, however, the Dutch legally authorized the slave trade in the colony.

Jansz Van Salee was one black in New Amsterdam who didn't have to petition for his freedom. He was the buccaneering son of a Dutchman who captained a ship for the Ottoman sultan. Jansz married a Dutch woman named Griet Reyniers, and they established a homestead in the present Gravesend. The descendants of their four daughters are in the New York social register.

Most African slaves in New Amsterdam were the property of the Dutch West India Company or belonged to high officials like Governor Peter Stuyvesant who had forty on his Bouerie estate. The ordinary Dutch citizenry were not generally comfortable with slavery and often helped runaway slaves. Even slaveholders as a rule offered slaves "half freedom." Slaves were released from their bond on the condition that they perform agreed-upon labor at agreed-upon times.

Slavery was far stricter under the British, who took over the colony in 1664. Now slaves had no more rights than property. The families of slaves could be broken up with impunity. Slaves who protested or resisted were subject to public whipping and worse. The British viewed slavery as a business; it was a source of high profits and a high priority. The number of African-American slaves more than tripled from 1664 to 1746.

New York City's slaves were skilled craftsmen, coopers and carpenters, glaziers and goldsmiths. They also possessed household skills like spinning, weaving, and cooking. Slaves were hired even out in competition with free labor.

Although the slaves' movements and rights of assembly were restricted by law, these bondsmen and women routinely disobeyed curfews and socialized in forbidden "tippling houses." There were open gatherings where slaves formed relationships. The most disaffected joined gangs of runaway slaves that prowled the waterfront.

A slave insurrection with buildings set afire and ambushed colonists took place in 1712. The aftermath was white panic and black persecution, complete with public burnings. A simple burglary and false accusations of arson led to the burning and hanging of innocent slaves twenty years later. A woman named Mary Burton was the first false witness to ignite an orgy of recrimination on the scale of the Salem witch trials.

Revolution disrupted slavery in New York. Redcoats and revolutionaries urged slaves to join their forces, holding out the promise of freedom. Blacks worked in the British army's arsenal and served with loyalist irregulars. Thousands joined the rebel militias and as a group were specially cited for bravery. Christopher Greene's black regiment fought with great distinction in the bloody battle of Points Bridge.

The New York Assembly freed the city's slave soldiers in 1781. Four years later, the city's leading citizens formed the New York Manumission Society to work for the eradication of slavery. John Jay was the society's first president and his successor was the leading intellectual light of independence, Alexander Hamilton, whose ancestors from Jamaica may have been African.

Samuel Fraunces was a leading member of the newly free community of this era. His tavern at 54 Pearl Street attracted New York's first citizens, and was the scene of George Washington's emotional farewell dinner for his officers. The city's principal businessmen met in the tavern's long room to organize the first chamber of commerce.

In 1799 slavery in New York was on its way to legal extinction; a law was passed freeing all children born to slaves after July 4, 1799. Males were to be freed at twenty-eight and females at twenty-five. In 1817 every slave born before July 4, 1799, was technically freed. Nevertheless, many New York City slaves were illegally transferred to southern slaveholders in the time it took the law to go into effect.

Black liberation did not mean equality in the first half of the nineteenth century. In 1821, New York's African-Americans were made the target of a restrictive property requirement that made it almost impossible for them to vote. Black citizens were denied access to ''public transport'' and had to pay special licensing fees even for the right to be a carter.

Newly freed slaves were no longer in demand as skilled craftsmen. White workers in the city made sure they were limited to service and menial jobs. Black men now donned the uniforms of coachmen, porters, barbers, or waiters; women were cooks, maids, and laundresses.

Often blacks were forced to settle for inferior housing in crime-ridden neighborhoods. They lived in the damp vermin-infested cellars and the leaky garrets of Five Points. White churches restricted them to the galleries or barred them altogether. Public places like the New York Zoological Institute refused to admit blacks. To top it all off, African-American New Yorkers were prey to petty harassment and assaults.

Blacks vented their anger at these abuses in the pages of the city's first African-American paper, *Freedom's Journal*. The city's free community countered some discrimination by forming their own institutions. They started their own religious denominations, training eloquent clergy and building handsome churches. Thomas Paul in 1809 was the first in a long line of exceptional clergymen at the helm of the Abyssinian Baptist Church. The Reverend Paul Williams, of the pioneering African Methodist Episcopal Zion Church, became one of New York's leading abolitionists.

While black churches were a bulwark for black unity and morale, these activist churches were also a prime target for racist mobs. In July of 1834, in the aftermath of hard-fought city elections, blacks attending an abolitionist meeting at the Chatham Square Chapel were attacked by a proslavery gang. In the course of the next three days, a raging mob of twenty thousand torched black and white churches that vocally supported abolition.

African-Americans did not rely completely on religious organizations and churches. They formed their own labor groups and insurance societies. The first mutual aid society was established by black sailors in 1810. Later there was an American league of Black Laborers, and in 1839, a special association for ship's cooks and stewards. The African Dorcas Society was the first black group to help the infirm and indigent.

Deprived of education as slaves, blacks were very aware of the importance of education. They worked closely with white socially conscious New Yorkers to develop black schools through the New York Society for the Promotion of Education and the New York Phoenix Society. They launched successful literacy programs.

Despite economic and social barriers, blacks were able to make their mark in early New York. James McCune Smith became a respected physician with a prestigious degree from the University of Glasgow. Thomas Downings operated one of the most popular oyster bars, catering to the financial magnets on the Stock Exchange. In the 1830s Thomas M. Jackson was the favored caterer of New York high society. Ira Aldredge even became one of the leading actors of this era, after learning to perform Shakespeare on the stage of New York's Free African Theatre.

New York's African-Americans were influential figures in the antislavery movement. Samuel Ringold Ward, known as the "Black Daniel Webster," inspired many to join the cause of abolition with his fiery rhetoric. He became such a threat to the proslavery establishment that he was forced to flee to England. Frederick Douglass conveyed through his own slavery experience the physical brutality and psychic pain and humiliation of bondage. He was instrumental in building Abolitionist sentiment in the North.

New York's entrance into the Civil War on the northern side did not immediately improve conditions for the city's blacks. Ever the scapegoat, the vulnerable black community of 12,472 became the target for the city's proslavery Democrats and the nation's first disgruntled draftees. In the 1863 Draft Riots, immigrant and native-born Americans lynched blacks, burned down a black orphanage, and chased the whole black population out of their Cherry Street neighborhood.

By the end of the War Between the States, a resurgent black population had gone beyond Lower Manhattan to West Side neighborhoods. They spread through the low-rent Tenderloin, where violence and vice made normal life very difficult. Black New Yorkers, who were city dwellers from colonial times, were able to cope, but they were now joined by more impressionable blacks from the rural South.

Eventually the black elite began to relocate to the brownstones of Brooklyn. These successful lawyers, doctors, and businessmen even had their own version of high society. They called themselves the Society of the Sons of New York. Members had to be accomplished and black, and their exclusive group barred southerners and West Indians.

In 1900 black New York was over sixty thousand strong and rapidly growing. Incidents between ethnics and blacks were on the rise and a precommunity relations police force added to the friction. On August 15, 1900, a knifing led to black and white mob confrontations with police participating as white partisans. For a month, roving bands of white toughs considered blacks fair game.

There were fair-minded white New Yorkers like Mary White Ovington, who worked with black educator W. E. B. Du Bois and others to found the National Association for the Advancement of Colored People. Other interracial groups were formed in the city to help create opportunities for blacks, and were consolidated into the National Urban League in 1911.

In ten years fifty thousand black New Yorkers made the move from the Tenderloin to the wide, tree-lined streets of Harlem. They paid high rents for the privilege of decent housing. Overcrowding was inevitable. By the Depression there were two hundred thousand blacks competing for space in Harlem. Although it was the most deprived section of the city, it received the barest minimum of government services. It had only one playground and new school construction was zero.

Mayor La Guardia's heart was in the right place and he was genuinely disturbed by black poverty and illiteracy, but he did little to improve the black New Yorker's situation. Black areas did not benefit from his major construction programs, which changed the face of the city.

He did, however, change the complexion of municipal government by making black appointments. In his administration, Hubert Delaney became tax commissioner and Jane Bolin became a judge. He had Gertrude Ayer hired as the first black school principal in the city.

The Depression devastated black New York resulting in a 50 percent unemployment rate. Black self-help was their only option in an indifferent city. Father Divine's Kingdom provided cheap meals and lodging and opened dry-goods stores and cleaners that employed blacks. Though his divinity was doubtful, he supplied hope. At the same time many conventional black churches followed the example of the Abyssinian Baptist Church in Harlem by offering free meals and shelter, food baskets, and clothes.

Black New York went off to war in 1941 in a segregated force. While their units received commendations, it seemed as if they were more segregated than white prisoners of war. On the homefront in 1943, Harlem was burning. On a hot August night wartime resentments and high rents and employment discrimination led to looting and gunshots. At the end there were five dead and blocks destroyed.

A year later, with the creation of a Harlem congressional district, Adam Clayton Powell, Jr., a young city councilman and minister of the Abyssinian Baptist Church, became Harlem's national representative. The election of Mayor William O'Dwyer in 1946 led to many citywide black political appointments. J. Raymond Jones, the Harlem Democratic leader, became a housing commissioner, and Rev. John M. Coleman of Brooklyn became the first black to sit on the Board of Education. In 1953 blacks had another first with Hulan Jack elected Borough President of Manhattan.

At the same time that African-Americans were entering New York's political mainstream, they were joining New York's sports teams and becoming genuine sports heroes. Jackie Robinson was the first black player to break the "color line" on the Brooklyn Dodger's ballteam. Soon the Giants' Willie Mays was competing with white Mickey Mantle for the title of the best all-around player in baseball.

Between 1940 and 1960, one and a half million white New Yorkers left the city. The black population, which had previously been concentrated in Bedford-Stuyvesant and Harlem, spread out through the other boroughs into Morrisania, the Bronx, central Brooklyn, and southern Queens. Black New Yorkers established new power bases and centers of influence.

In 1963 the civil rights movement in the South was changing attitudes throughout the country. Martin Luther King, Jr., had made the elimination of Jim Crow a moral crusade. There was an effort to wipe out the effects of bigotry, North and South. In Harlem HARYOU-Act was founded and funded by the federal government to create black pride and break down the cycle of dependency.

Racial tensions came to a head in the long hot summer of 1964, and there was a repetition of the Harlem riots. Raised black expectations were not being fulfilled. The assassination of Martin Luther King, Jr., in 1968 led to more riots in Harlem and Bedford-Stuyvesant. A city seeking racial justice elected fusion candidate John V. Lindsay mayor. Black New York votes were crucial to his election.

The Lindsay years were a time of racial confrontation. The black community of Ocean Hill-Brownsville in Brooklyn struggled with the white teacher's union for control over their children's future, and white parents in Canarsie blocked black children from being bused to their schools. Blacks lobbied for a Civilian Review Board and made continual charges of white police brutality. It was the age of Stokely Carmichael and the Black Panthers.

It was also the age of Shirley Chisolm, a dynamic black congresswoman from Brooklyn, who was nominated at the Democratic convention for president, and Percy Sutton, an eloquent Harlem politician, who many believed would be the next mayor. In another arena, writer Claude Browne stirred white consciences with his ghetto memoir, *Manchild in the Promised Land.*

In 1977 the city was racially divided over a scattered sight public housing project in Forest Hills, and Edward Koch beat out Harlem assemblyman Herman Farrel and Mario Cuomo for mayor. Though Koch couldn't win any popularity contest in the black community, he made some ground-breaking African-American appointments, including Police Commissioner Benjamin Ward and Board of Education Chancellor Richard Green. In 1990 a fastidious African-American Marine named David Dinkins went from Manhattan borough president to mayor, uniting a racially divided city in the process.

Harlem

Directions: IND A to 125th Street/Frederick Douglass Avenue, or IRT-Seventh Avenue 2 or 3 to 125th Street/Lenox Avenue.

Introduction

Harlem is the heart of African-American New York. Black hip begins here, its styles and trends sweeping through the city and finally capturing a whole nation. From ragtime to rap, Harlem is in a state of perpetual Renaissance.

Harlem's first inhabitants were native Americans in lean-tos on the banks of the Harlem River. Their reservation would have fit the grid from 110th Street to 125th Street. In 1658 Dutch settlers gave the natives a dispossess and incorporated the village of Nieue Harlem. The soil was rich and the high ground was easy to defend.

A few years later black slaves raised the Nieue Harlem real estate values, constructing ten miles of road from New Amsterdam to Nieue Harlem. In the late eighteenth century New York gentry, whose names are now on street signs—Morris, Hamilton, DeLancey, and Beekman—built their summer houses in the wilds above the present 140th Street.

In 1837 a railroad running down Park Avenue divided East and West Harlem. While West Harlem attracted the ''carriage trade,'' East Harlem became a blighted area of shacks and squatters with pigs rooting through the garbage. The arrival of the El trains on Second and Third Avenues in 1879 attracted industry and more working-class immigrants to East Harlem. The other Harlem was still reserved for the wealthy: successful German and German-Jewish businessmen and manufacturers bought and built big homes in the area.

At the beginning of the twentieth century, the IRT line along Lenox Avenue opened Central Harlem to middle-class commuters. The building

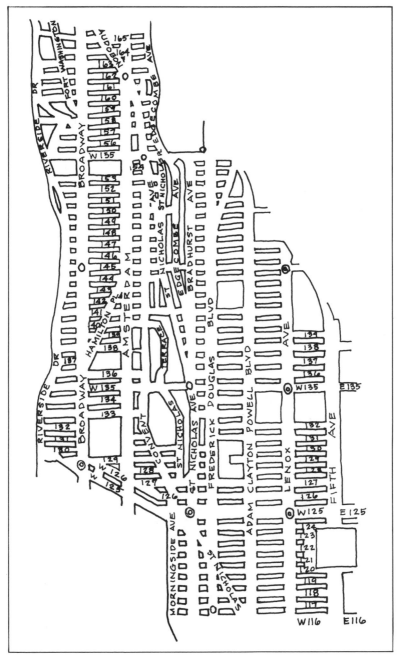

Harlem

boom was on: there were luxurious row houses and the most up-to-date apartment units. But when the demand fell short and landlords were caught holding the bag, a smart black realtor, Philip Payton, came to the rescue.

For developers who would rent to his people, he promised top-dollar rents and efficient management. The first blacks to move uptown were relocated from their homes on the site of the future Penn Station. Thousands of African-Americans fled the substandard housing of the Tenderloin, Thompson Street, and San Juan Hill for the suburban comfort of Harlem. Rural migrants from the South and West Indian emigrants headed straight for Harlem. Harlem had a mystique.

Harlem was the main chance, the new black Jerusalem. Black churches joined their congregations in the exodus. In the 1920s black creative juices produced the Harlem Renaissance and America listened. Claude McKay, Jean Toomer, and Zora Neale Hurston were the literary lions, while Duke Ellington, Bessie Smith, and Fletcher Henderson made beautiful music, blue and red-hot. James Weldon Johnson was the Renaissance man: writer, composer, musician, and philosopher of the black experience. Marcus Garvey preached the new gospel of black self-sufficiency, a world of their own making.

Black capitalism boomed. Lillian Harris started out selling pig's feet out of a baby carriage on 125th Street. She was uneducated, but an astute businesswoman who put her profits in Harlem real estate and retired in luxury to Southern California. William Felton made his fortune in Harlem by inventing the automatic car wash. He built a seven-story building to house his enterprises. Madame J. C. Walker devised her own black hair treatment, which earned her millions and an estate in exclusive Irvington-on-the-Hudson.

Meanwhile, whites came slumming to whites-only clubs like Connie's Inn and the Cotton Club, where they were entertained by black bands and singers and the famous ''high yellow'' girls of the chorus. The ''New Negro'' of the black literary set was the weekend spree of the Roaring Twenties.

There was a burgeoning black bourgeoisie and the sense of a black future when the 1929 Depression postponed the Harlem dream. The glamour and good times gave way to a reality of discrimination and poverty.

During the 1920s black Harlem more than doubled in population from 83,248 to 203,894, with double the density of the rest of the city. Greedy white landlords had subdivided a neighborhood into a slum. And even white businesses that survived on the black trade wouldn't employ blacks.

Black institutions like the Abyssinian Baptist Church tried to rally the people with their social programs and economic campaigns. Rev. Adam

Clayton Powell and his son, the charismatic Rev. Adam Clayton Powell, Jr., offered hope and action and provided crucial leadership. Though riots came with the 1940s, there were also successful black boycotts of white merchants and a black borough president named Hulan Jack.

The Rev. Adam Clayton Powell went to Congress in the 1940s and was a powerful congressional committee chairman during much of the 1960s. It was the era of Malcolm and Martin, and Harlem was inspired by the civil rights movement and the drive for black power. Martin Luther King, Jr., led civil rights marches up 125th Street while Malcolm X spread the message of black pride in the Audubon Ballroom on 166th Street. Both died for their beliefs and Harlem erupted. Hopelessness combined with crime and the epidemic drug rise turned Harlem into a Manhattan tragedy.

But Harlem was not about to give up the ghost. A new, more-commercial Harlem stylishly struts its stuff on 125th Street. There is the skyscraper State Office Building and even that elegant dowager, the Hotel Theresa, has become a gleaming office tower. Percy Sutton, a former candidate for mayor, is putting his efforts into a Harlem economic revival, while another Harlem favorite son, David Dinkins, after a hard-fought election, has become New York's first black mayor.

The artists and writers are returning to their uptown roots from the hothouse world of SoHo and the Village. Young black professionals are restoring Harlem's grand residences or are moving into that neighborhood's new luxury apartments. Visitors, especially those from Europe, are less careful about venturing into Harlem, and there are even bus tours with predictable guidebook patter. Harlem is working its way back to another Renaissance.

Soul Food and Soul Singers

Good Eating

The black cuisine that came up from the South and flourished in Harlem is soul food. It is food without pretenses, hearty and full-bodied like a blues singer's shout. The ingredients are the staples of sharecropping country: pig's feet and spare ribs, black-eyed peas and collard greens. The emphasis is on cooking talent that can turn a scrawny backyard chicken or bony catfish into a delicacy. There is an art to black southern pan gravies and crusty breading and the barbecue sauces that burn. Even the bread made from corn meal tastes like cake. Good soul food spans the whole of Harlem from Harlem Central to Sugar Hill.

Sylvia's, *328 Lenox Avenue between 126th and 127th Streets (212-996-0660). Monday–Saturday 7:30 A.M.–10:15 P.M.; Sunday 1 P.M.–7 P.M.*

Sylvia's is South Carolina soul in the cooking and down-home hospitality. The funky be-yourself feeling is a relief after all of New York's restaurant pretenses. It's homey with its winter wonderland mural and pictures on the wall. The jukebox, from rap to synthesizer soul, and the sit-down comedy of the regulars at the counter are the round-the-clock floor show. Sylvia and her kin also have regulars dropping by from Tokyo and Paris for the meaty ribs with pepper and spice and the cinnamon sweet potato pie. The main dishes, fried or barbecued, with the collard greens and yams, are almost too ample to finish.

La Famille, *2017 Fifth Avenue between 124th Street and 125th Streets (212-722-9806). Monday–Friday 11:30 A.M.–11:30 P.M.; Saturday 4 P.M.–11:30 P.M.; Sunday 1 P.M.–9:30 P.M.*

La Famille is dress-up soul with white linen tablecloths and wood paneling. The weekends are to see and be seen at La Famille. But don't try to be Continental when it comes to the menu—stick to the Southern-style braised short ribs and black-eyed peas with grainy corn bread.

22 West, *22 West 135th Street between Lenox and Fifth Avenues (212-862-7770). Daily 8 A.M.–12:30 A.M.*

22 West has the feeling of an informal Harlem open house. From opening to closing, you can choose whatever you want, from ham hocks and black-eyed peas for breakfast, to grits, ham and eggs, and biscuits for dinner.

Wilson's Bakery & Restaurant, *1980 Amsterdam Avenue at 158th Street (212-923-9821). Daily 6 A.M.–9 P.M.*

Harlem is fried chicken country, from fast-food franchises to closet-sized take-outs. Everyone has their unbeatable secret recipe, so why not go into business? Wilson's easily wins any fried chicken competition; the breading is light and slightly spicy, and the bird isn't swimming in the shortening. A bakery counter is conveniently near the entrance for a sweet potato pie or coconut cake on the way out.

Copeland's, *547 West 145th Street between Broadway and Amsterdam (212-234-2356). Sunday–Friday 1 P.M.–11 P.M.; Saturday 4:30 P.M.–1 A.M.*

Copeland's is formal reservations dining with fresh flowers on the tables and harp music on Sundays. Harlem's high-finance, real estate, and media

African-Americans break bread here. The menu is mixed from soul to creole to sixteen-ounce New York–cut steaks. The corn fritters are crunchy and the Southern oxtails are a delicious specialty if you don't mind a lot of bones. There's a Copeland's cafeteria next door, but Copeland's experience is more than food.

Good Listening

From the blues shout to the jazz saxophone wail, Harlem is African-American music. It started with Scott Joplin rags and Baptist gospel. Harlem rent parties became the scene of piano battles and horn competitions. James P. Johnson perfected the New York ''stride'' piano style and Duke Ellington created a jazz band sound with symphony range. Harlem's Cotton Club was king in the twenties. The African-American arranger, Fletcher Henderson, taught Benny Goodman how to swing.

When jazz became too tight and predictable, Charlie Christian and Charlie Parker created a new jazz idiom. Minton's was the place for after-hours jams and be-bop. While Harlem went through bop and the birth of the cool, rhythm-and-blues stole the thunder. The music of the Clovers and Joe Turner was transformed into Bill Haley and Elvis rock'n'roll and a not-so-mad genius named Ornette was taking jazz beyond tomorrow. Eventually Harlem put it altogether and it spelled fusion and Miles Davis added a synthesizer.

Harlem is still the place for musical innovation. The players have the room to soar.

Ebony Lounge, *1496 Fifth Avenue between 119th and 120th Streets (212-289-9372). Monday–Saturday 3 P.M.–4 A.M.*

The jazz is more than background. The sets are not on a timeclock, and there is the sense of a spontaneous jam. Sometimes a name sits in, but the unknowns can be just as good.

The Lickety Split, *2361 Adam Clayton Powell, Jr., Boulevard near 138th Street (212-283-9093). Monday–Saturday 10 A.M.–4 A.M.*

The Lickety Split is happy jazz. The blues on the sunny side matches the good vibes and good talk. It's a place to laugh and drink good bourbon.

Billy's, *2246 Adam Clayton Powell, Jr., Boulevard near 132nd Street (212-283-8285). Monday–Saturday 9 P.M.–4 A.M.*

The jam sessions at Billy's take place on Tuesday and Thursday nights. Weekends are soul food with soul jazz, but in summer the music policy is loose and things shut down.

Showman's Lounge, *2321 Frederick Douglass Boulevard at 126th Street (212-864-8941). Daily noon–4 A.M.*

Lobster night and the weekend raffle take center stage and sometimes the music seems like an afterthought.

Black Drama and Dance

In an era when blacks were restricted from attending theater downtown—before 1945 only three Broadway theaters sold seats to blacks—the Harlem stage flourished. Blacks regularly attended the Crescent, the Lafayette, the Lincoln, and the Alhambra. They saw original dramas and musicals and black variations on Broadway hits. There were dancers on the Harlem stage as well as in the Cotton Club floor show. White producers like Florenz Ziegfeld purchased highlights of Harlem shows for their own productions.

Though blacks no longer have any problem attending the legitimate theater or a ballet, African-Americans have kept the performing arts in Harlem. It is a training ground for aspiring dancers, singers, and actors, and gives scope to black themes and identity.

Apollo Theater, *253 West 125th Street (212-749-5838).*

The legendary Apollo theater at 253 West 125th Street between Seventh and Eighth Avenues started out as a "whites only" burlesque theater in 1913. By 1934, in the competent hands of Leo Brecher and Frank Schiffman, it was presenting first-rate five-shows-a-day black revues. The Apollo audiences were noted for their critical eye and unbridled enthusiasm, and the stellar attractions were a Who's Who of black talent from the era of Bessie to Gladys Knight and the Pips. There was the comedy of Moms Mabley, an exuberant pre-Las Vegas Sammy Davis, Jr., and Little Richard with his mile-high hairdo.

In the 1970s the high salaries of stars and flagging box office forced management to switch to movies. In 1980 it was converted by new owners into a cable TV studio. The Apollo is making a comeback in the 1990s with a stage show policy and even amateur nights.

Dance Theater of Harlem, *466 West 152nd Street (212-690-2880).*

Arthur Mitchell brought ballet to Harlem sixteen years ago, and since then his Dance Theater has become one of the world's cultural treasures. Exacting Balanchine ballet standards are maintained, but there is a fresh approach to ballet classics that takes advantage of Harlem's artistic resources. The Dance Theater of Harlem is also a school. Prima ballerinas in training perform at a monthly open house.

National Black Theater, *2033 Fifth Avenue near 125th Street (212-926-1049).*

National Black Theater is creating a new black aesthetic. The drama is from the black perspective and about the black experience. The accomplished actress and writer, Barbara Ann Teer is the theater's creative force.

Black Place Marks

Harlem High Life

Most neighborhoods don't have any historic districts, but the wide-open spaces of Harlem have twenty-five, with three nationally known standouts: Hamilton Heights, Jumel Terrace, and Audubon Terrace. But they are part of a city history that often excluded black people. Harlem has districts where real black history was made; districts that are associated with leaders, celebrities, and milestones.

Sugar Hill

Directions: IRT-Seventh Avenue 1 to 157th Street.

These apartments on the bluff overlooking the Hudson were built for Harlem's white super-rich, with elevators, maid's rooms, and walk-in pantries. In one of the city's characteristic quick changes, it became the sweetest black neighborhood in Manhattan when black real estate brokers turned the tables on white developers. The Hill may not have an official designation, but this neighborhood, between St. Nicholas and Edgecomb Avenues from around 143rd Street to 155th Street, historically housed Harlem's rich and famous. Duke Ellington, Count Basie, Chief Justice Thurgood Marshall, and Sugar Ray Robinson all lived here.

Strivers' Row

Directions: IRT-Seventh Avenue 1 to 137th Street.

In the vicinity of Seventh and Eighth Avenues between West 138th Street and West 139th Street, Harlem goes high-hat. The King Model row houses were designed in 1891 by the city's leading architect, Stanford White, in neo-Italian Renaissance and neo-Georgian styles. These showplaces were custom-made for the city's tea-and-cucumber-sandwich set. It was an Equitable Life Insurance Company sure-thing investment.

In 1919, after being lily-white for two decades, it became the preserve of the black elite and earned the name of "Strivers' Row." W. C. Handy, Eubie Blake, and bandleader Noble Sissle belonged to the celebrity crowd along the Row. All the Strivers went to the Abyssinian Baptist Church on Sunday after partying on Lenox Avenue Saturday night.

Harlem Bright Lights—125th Street

Directions: IND A to 125th Street/Frederick Douglass Avenue, or IRT-Seventh Avenue 2 or 3 to 125th Street/Lenox Avenue.

Harlem's main drag hasn't changed; in the 1890s it was the Hammerstein Opera and in the 1990s it's the Apollo Theater. The street is the Harlem beat pounding like the A train coming uptown. It's the corner black nationalist handing out the latest ideology and the corner black capitalist playing "Let's Make a Deal." A man in Harlem cast-offs pushes a supermarket cart toward the park and a Spike Lee lookalike draped in Armani pushes the gas on his BMW. Tall, lithe women pass the Franco store gate mural of tall lithe African-American women. Aware black shoppers hunker down at Market and Mart 125 to bargain over Yoruba beads or a counterfeit Gucci bag.

—The Towers of 125th Street—

The Harlem State Office Building, *163 West 125th Street.*

Completed in 1973, the State Office Building is the state's recognition of Harlem political clout. The vast plaza opens up the street and provides a place for basking in the Harlem sunshine. The building is Harlem's highest and the design is a variation on Phillip Johnson modern. It adds gloss to Harlem traditional and the offices offer needed employment. Too bad it bumped the Lewis Michaux National Memorial African Bookstore, one of the community's intellectual lifelines.

Theresa Towers, *2090 Adam Clayton Powell, Jr., Boulevard at 125th Street.*

The elegant Hotel Theresa has been transformed into the Theresa Towers. Though some of the 1910 touches were removed in the 1971 renovation, it still lends high style to 125th Street. There are also the memories of a more opulent Harlem when celebrities like Fats Waller called it home. In its refined old age, Fidel Castro and Nikita Khruschev embraced on a Hotel Theresa balcony.

Harlem Culture

—Museums—

The Studio Museum in Harlem, *144 West 125th Street between Lenox Avenue and Adam Clayton Powell, Jr., Boulevard (212-865-2420). Wednesday–Friday 10 A.M.–5 P.M.; Saturday–Sunday 1 P.M.–6 P.M. Admission charge.*

The Studio Museum is a showcase for black artists. Gifted black painters, photographers, and sculptors exhibit. Shows are mounted with black cultural and historical themes. The museum is open space and modern with baby spots to highlight the art.

Black Fashion Museum, *157 West 126th Street (212-666-1320). Monday–Friday noon–8 P.M. By appointment. Contribution.*

Black fashion designers like Patrick Kelly have made it in high fashion and ready-to-wear, and the Black Fashion Museum is all about their fashion heritage. There are pictures and fashion illustrations and actual samples, from Yoruba headdresses to the runways of Paris.

Aunt Len's Doll and Toy Museum, *6 Hamilton Terrace between 141st Street and 142nd Street (212-926-4172). Tuesday–Sunday by appointment. Admission charge.*

There is an actual Aunt Len—Lenon Holder Hoyte, over eighty years young—who presides over this kingdom of ten thousand dolls. There are life-size Victorian relics and Tom Thumb miniatures, rag dolls, and dolls that cry, wet, and talk. The dolls are a United Nations of nationalities and colors.

Adam Clayton Powell, Jr., Gallery, *163 West 125th Street (No telephone.) Monday–Friday noon–3 P.M.*

On the second floor of the State Office Building a space has been set aside for exhibiting the art work of the community. The Studio Museum coordinates the shows. Whether it's sculpture or collage or a neo-realist painting, the black experience is part of the aesthetic.

Benin Gallery, *240 West 139th Street (212-926-8025). By appointment.*

In the vicinity of Strivers' Row, aspiring black artists exhibit, and artifacts of Africa are on display. There are art workshops and audiovisual programs dealing with the black artistic experience.

The Grinnell Gallery, *800 Riverside Drive at 158th Street (212-927-7941). Six shows a year open to the public. Call for times and by appointment.*

The Grinnell is a multimedia adventure into being black. It is a platform for African-Americans and Caribbeans. Poets and players perform and artists and photographers exhibit.

The Schomburg Center for Research in Black Culture, *515 Lenox Avenue at 135th Street (212-862-4000). Monday–Wednesday noon–8 P.M.; Thursday–Saturday 10 A.M.–6 P.M.*

Arthur Schomburg believed in black culture and black history, and wanted to preserve that legacy. His collection first became public in a branch of the New York Public Library. Today it is housed in a modern brick building and a full-time staff of sixty keeps it expanding. It has over three million separate items, including manuscripts of black greats like W. E. B. Du Bois and Langston Hughes and a hundred thousand books about the black experience. The Schomburg is a total media center with paintings, photographs, film, and video.

Harlem Houses of Worship

St. Phillip's Protestant Episcopal Church, *204 West 134th Street (212-862-4940).*

St. Phillip's is the most exclusive and the most sedate church in Harlem. The original congregation was founded in 1809 at Five Points and followed the black population to Mulberry Street and later to the Tenderloin. The church itself sold off its Tenderloin holdings to become one of the largest black property holders in Harlem. It is reputed to be the wealthiest congregation in Harlem.

Abyssinian Baptist Church, *132 West 138th Street (212-286-2626).*

When Strivers' Row was high-accomplishment Harlem, the Abyssinian Baptist Church on Sunday was a social as well as a spiritual obligation. The church had a magnificent pulpit in the round and it boasted the city's most spellbinding cleric, Adam Clayton Powell, Sr. His equally charismatic son would succeed him and also become Harlem's representative to Congress.

The church now possesses a memorial to Adam Clayton Powell, Jr., with mementos of a life spent defending the cause of human rights. The Reverend Samuel Proctor continues the church's committed preaching tradition. The incomparable church choir is the joyful noise unto the Lord every Sunday at 11:30 A.M.

Canaan Baptist Church, *132 West 116th Street (212-866-0301).*

This Baptist celebration is a gospel levitation. The singing and shouting and preaching are ecstatic; the participation is personal and moving. The church is not just sound and fury, it takes charity and social activism seriously.

St. Martin's Episcopal Church, *230 Lenox Avenue near 122nd Street (212-534-4531).*

St. Martin's is where Harlem's West Indians have been praying since 1928. The services are West Indian staid and proper; the sanctuary is Romanesque. The church has a forty-bell carillon that fills Harlem with music.

Masjid Malcolm Shabbazzn, *102 West 116th Street (212-662-2200).*

Malcolm X made his reputation preaching here when he was a follower of Elijah Muhammad and, despite his falling-out with the Nation of Islam, it still bears his name. It's four stories high and topped by a star and crescent. The mosque complex includes a food store and restaurant with many products from the Muslims' own farms.

Festivals

African-American Day Parade

All Harlem turns out for the African-American Day Parade on the first Sunday in September. It is one New York parade where the spectators still outnumber the marchers. The line of march is along Adam Clayton Powell, Jr., Boulevard and the reviewing stand is located on the plaza of the Adam Clayton Powell, Jr., Office Building at the corner of 125th Street and the Boulevard. The mood is a kind of good-natured militancy, marching to an African beat.

The Grand Marshal of the parade is more likely to be wearing a dashiki than a cutaway. This is one event where even the politicians unbend. The marching bands are precision, but the music is wailing Basie saxophones and the steps are Michael Jackson. The bands generally pass on John Philip Sousa for Quincey Jones arrangements. There are drums of Africa played by dignified men in long colorful robes and conga drums played by Dominicans in straw hats. New York's black cops of the Guardian Society walk with a military step, while some kids from the PAL do an Ali shuffle. The floats are cultural artifacts of the Yoruba and Timbuktu and the black broadcasters on KISS or WLIB. The flower of black womanhood gaily wave to the crowd from a float in the colors of black liberation.

Harlem Week

Harlem likes to do things in a big way and Harlem Week is actually a two-week event. It is a celebration of Harlem's existence and a reflection on its past and future. All of Harlem's cultural resources get into the act. There are special exhibits of Harlem memorabilia at the Schomburg and a retrospective of great black artists at the Studio Museum. There are symposiums and Harlem symphonies and Harlem's dance theaters keep everyone on their toes. This August bouquet to Harlem is sponsored by the Uptown Chamber of Commerce.

Martin Luther King, Jr., Day Parade

The Martin Luther King, Jr., Day parade is on the third Sunday in May, the original Armed Forces Day. The choice of the day may have something to do with the sponsoring organization, the 369th Veterans Association. The 369th—otherwise known as the Harlem Hellfighters—was no ordinary fighting unit. Pershing, the commander of American forces in World War I, went out of his way to commend Harlem's black heroes. In World War II, the 369th saw some of the bloodiest combat in the European Theater. They remained patriots to a cause and died fighting for a country where they were second-class citizens in segregated units.

Dr. King was the most important leader of the movement that finally brought black people in the U.S. legal equality. He was the pacifist champion of these African-American fighting men. It is fitting that the 369th leads the commemorative parade.

The line of march follows Fifth Avenue from 44th Street to 86th Street. It is not exactly solemn, but it is more low-key than other black parades. There are lots of high school and youth organization bands with energetic musicians and acrobatic baton twirlers. There are unions representing hospital workers and social workers conscientiously trying to keep up with the line of march. The military veterans are spit-polish smart, arms swinging to sharp cadences. The veterans of the alphabet corps (such as SNCC and CORE) of the civil rights wars are relaxed, middle-aged informality, cheerfully acknowledging the clapping and cheers. Leaders of the 1960s boycotts and protests make their eulogies and try to recapture the March on Washington hopefulness.

West Indians

History

The West Indians of the British Caribbean endured more brutal conditions under slavery than blacks in the American South. It was cheaper to replace slaves than to treat them humanely. But these slaves who did not have the benefits of plantation paternalism and were forced to raise their own food and support their own families did not lose their native self-sufficiency.

West Indians were emancipated earlier than American blacks with a transitional period to prepare them for a life of freedom. Their material situations didn't change; they still were dependent on the white plantation owners who controlled the cash-crop economy. Black West Indians learned early that emigration was a one of the few alternatives to serfdom.

In the early part of the nineteenth century, West Indians began arriving in New York in significant numbers. Many had their introduction to American mores and economic possibilities working on the construction of the Panama Canal. They brought to the city ambition, thrift, and a willingness to make the maximum effort.

They became Harlem's leading entrepreneurs. These mainly urban West Indians with a British education had a real advantage over rural African-Americans. By 1901 they already controlled 20 percent of Harlem's businesses.

West Indians were also cultural innovators in the Harlem Renaissance. James Weldon Johnson was a stunning stylist of the Harlem ideal, and Langston Hughes was the poet of the Harlem everyman. Claude McKay boldly aspired to a juster America.

There was friction between the West Indian "interloper" and New York's African-Americans. West Indians were sometimes scornful of Southern blacks and Southern blacks in turn resented the highhandedness of West Indians. The Southerners were confused by the West Indian social conservativism and radical politics and found their British manners affected.

West Indians in the twenties started the trek out of Harlem via the expanding IRT Line to Brooklyn. They were drawn to the solid one- and two-family houses that had for decades housed elite professionals and members of the financial community in Bedford and Stuyvesant.

Whether from Jamaica, Trinidad, Barbados, the Bahamas, St. Kitts, or Domenica, this aspiring middle class was intent on "buying house." Many owned businesses, proving the old adage that "as soon as a West Indian gets ten cents above a beggar he buys a business." West Indians who worked in construction or were even small contractors were especially primed for home ownership.

Through their own independent credit unions and informal rotating credit associations, they were able to finance the handsome houses of East Stuyvesant and West Bedford. Between 1930 and 1940 the black, mainly West Indian, proportion of newly united Bedford-Stuyvesant rose from a little more than a tenth to a third.

Whites refused to serve blacks in Bedford restaurants and there were even some attempts to keep them out of the Bed-Stuy real estate market. Whether by unconscious neglect or concerted policy, city services declined in this area over time affecting the homes that West Indians cherished and maintained with such care.

But West Indians did not halt their Brooklyn exodus. They expanded farther out along the tree-lined boulevard of Eastern Parkway into Crown Heights and Flatbush. They seeded their new enclave with West Indian businesses and island and hometown associations and soccer and cricket clubs.

In the 1950s the McCarran-Walter Act closed the doors on West Indian emigration. More than a decade later, the Hart-Celler Act of 1965 changed the quota system, stimulating West Indian emigration and reuniting West Indian families. Between 1965 and 1980, eighty-five thousand Jamaicans, representing the largest group of islanders, settled in the city.

The austerity policies of some West Indian governments, island unemployment, and political violence increased the flow of West Indians to New York in the 1970s and 1980s. They came from all strata of West Indian society, but were equally bent on success.

Most of these new arrivals from Jamaica and Grenada and Trinidad and Barbados head for the sprawling West India in Brooklyn. They are domestic houseworkers on contract and nurses and other professionals who will step right into jobs. Others start as low-level clericals, security guards, laborers, and domestics, but a high percentage go on to higher education and real white-collar employment. They keep up the West Indian home-owning tradition.

West Indian Brooklyn

Directions: IRT-Seventh Avenue 3, or IRT-Lexington Avenue 4 to Utica Avenue.

Introduction

The center of West Indian Brooklyn runs along Eastern Parkway between the Grand Army Plaza and Utica Avenue, following the line of march of the West Indian Day parade. It is a thoroughfare of Victorian grandeur, venerable brick mansions, and high-towered churches. On the south side of the parkway there is the best housing, mostly brick and stucco finished with high stoops and wide porches. The houses are well maintained and the sidewalks are swept clean.

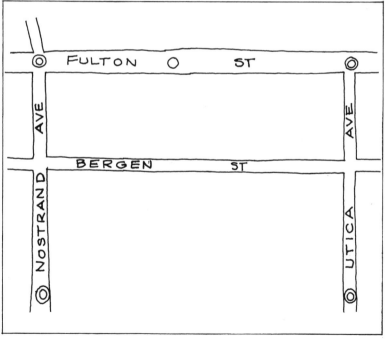

West Indian Crown Heights

West Indian commerce flourishes on Nostrand Avenue and Utica Avenue. The restaurants and bakeries are West Indian enterprises; the discount shops, groceries, and fishmongers are shared among Caribbean, Korean, and Arab merchants. On weekends these streets move to a reggae beat, as West Indian throngs take their time window-shopping along the avenue.

There are bearded Rastas in brightly colored caps and severe churchgoing women in old-fashioned turbans. Young and old, revolutionary and conservative gaily greet one another. The West Indians, man and woman, are tall and stand ramrod-straight. Though they have a weakness for the colors of the tropics, they carry themselves with a Quaker black dignity.

Island Eating

The cuisine of the West Indies borrows from the British colonizers, African slaves, and Indian indentured labor. While it has many ingredients in common with the Hispanic Caribbean, such as breadfruit, yams, plantains, dry cod, and the ever-popular pigeon peas or *goongo,* the black and British islands prefer hot chili pepper to the sweet, and make food additionally spicy with allspice, thyme, curry powder, nutmeg, and ginger. Coconut milk and other coconut products are also a regular staple in West Indian cooking.

Pigeon peas and rice is to the West Indies what beans and rice are to Mexico; when not eaten alone, it can accompany almost anything. The combination of coconut milk and hot scotch bonnet peppers in the preparation give it both richness and bite. West Indian meat patties with ground beef set off by Jamaican thyme and hot pepper is ubiquitous to the West Indies. A bland version is even sold with hot dogs on the sidewalks of New York. Callaloo is a West Indian green that gives its name to a memorable stew that runs the gamut from pork to crab meat and okra to grated coconut. Roti is a West Indian standby with an East Indian influence; Asian flat bread is wrapped around the vegetable or meat stew in a piquant takeoff of the Cornish pasty.

The West Indian eating place is usually somewhere on the continuum between restaurant and takeout. West Indians are people in a hurry even when they have nowhere to go, and they have taken to the New York practice of eating on the run. But after even a brief wait in line to make their order—which is usually not brief—it turns out that the main dishes from curried goat to calaloo are too heaping to fast-food consume. West Indian service does not stoop to conquer. The proprietor's singsong is peppered with wry humor.

Dewar's, *807 Nostrand Avenue (718-773-8403). Daily 8:30 A.M.–8 P.M.*

The Hollis family provides the warmth and the welcome at Dewar's. There are flowers in odd corners and a wall of pictures documenting the family's world travels. There is also warmth in their West Indian cooking, usually verging on the fiery. Curried goat is a taste easily acquired at Dewar's, the gaminess of the goat neutralized by the hot chilis. Breakfast West Indian at Dewar's with akee and saltfish. Akee is a tropical fruit that is transformed by frying with the fish into an omelet.

Gloria's In and Out, *991 Nostrand Avenue (718-778-4852). Tuesday–Saturday 11* A.M.*–10* P.M.

Don't mind the bars on the window or the counter enclosed by glass like a teller's window—they do let you out of Gloria's In and Out. It's mostly a lineup for takeout, but stop and set a spell at one of the picnic tables with a bowl of cow-heel soup with just a hint of scallion, thyme, and pepper. Drink a Jamaican ginger beer that has the tang of fresh ginger and watch the world go by.

Our People's Restaurant, *1052 Nostrand Avenue (718-756-5900). Sunday–Thursday noon–9:30* P.M.*; Friday noon–6:30* P.M.

The restaurant is a counter and a couple of booths small. It is intimate enough for people to talk like it's a living room. The owner is the resident philosopher with strong opinions about the nature of the world and West Indian cooking in particular. Don't let him steer you to his latest invention, the vegetarian gluten steak. The curried goat requires many glasses of chilled sorrel (a dry sweet and pepper drink from a tropical flower) to cool it down, but it's worth the exertions.

Singh's Hot Shop, *365 Utica Avenue (no telephone). Daily 7:30* A.M.*–8* P.M.

Singh's Hot Shop is the traditional Trinadadian roti that they hawk from carts on the streets of Port of Spain. The chicken, meat, and fish roti is hot as an Indian vindaloo and not for the faint-hearted.

"Bulla" Cake and Spice

West Indian baking crosses the divide between meat and sweet. The West Indians have taken something of India and something of England and the foods of the Caribbean to create their unique style of baking. They start with an English fruitcake and add rum and improvise with Indian breads and spices in their rotis and patties. Bland English-style breads are distinguished by coconut and cassava. Ordinary gingerbread is transformed into a subtly sweet and moist *bulla* cake. Don't be fooled by names—a spice bun is a ginger and spice cake, and a bread pudding is a flat cake flavored with rum.

Ronnie's Bakery, *892 Nostrand Avenue (718-756-4435). Monday–Saturday 9 A.M.–8:30 P.M.*

The West Indian rum fruitcake is strong enough to cause a hangover, the currant buns are rich with molasses, and the Jamaican patties are very peppery. This Ronnie is a Veronica who learned her trade from mother. She says her baking has a real island taste because she uses island-type flour.

Allan's Quality Bakery, *1109 Nostrand Avenue (718-774-7892). Monday–Friday 7:30 A.M.–9 P.M.; Saturday 7:30 A.M.–8 P.M.; Sunday 7:30 A.M.–6 P.M.*

Like the name says, Allan's uses quality ingredients and sells only freshly baked breads, tarts, and patties. The coconut bread is a unique compromise between cake and bread. The meat patties are authentic island orange with melt-in-the-mouth pastry, and the filling could burn the tongue. The apple turnovers are a pass, too bland and heavy.

Barbados Bakery, *229 Utica Avenue (718-493-5218). Monday–Friday 9 A.M.–8 P.M.; Saturday 8 A.M.–10 P.M.; Sunday 9 A.M.–3 P.M.*

The display case is full of unusual Bajian specialties like Bajian cheesecake with coconut milk and Barbados cornpone and the carrot cake called carrot pudding. The Bajian community from the whole metropolitan area comes here for their favorite sweets.

Gig Young, *366 Utica Avenue (212-773-9174). Daily 7 A.M.–11 P.M.*

The layer cakes in the window are mostly for display. The spice buns and the *bulla* cake are what sell like bread. Still, pride of place goes to hot Jamaican patties that could remove paint.

West Indian Rags

Calypso, the original West Indian folk music, started out in Trinidad. It's loose and lively and no holding back. The singers like Mighty Sparrow are free spirits ready to rip into politics and personalities. When calypso is played on a variety of oil drums, pots, and biscuit tins, the medium is the steel band message. The bands started in Trinidad in a spontaneous V-E Day celebration. Jamaica took reggae out of Harry Belafonte country and made it an urban Kingston idiom. The beat's insistent and the attitude's radical. Bob Marley was the reggae master, part prophet and poet and hip studio musician.

Straker's Caribbean Record World, *242 Utica Avenue (718-756-0340). Monday–Saturday 10 A.M.–7 P.M.*

Straker's is for Caribbean cult record buyers. It has the impossible-to-find from Grenada and St. Vincent and the early releases of Bob Marley and Jimmy Cliff. It is a place where people hang out to talk about Caribbean music.

Park Heights Records, *317 Utica Avenue (718-773-2891). Monday–Saturday 10 A.M.–10 P.M.; Sunday 10 A.M.–7 P.M.*

The reggae goes round and round and it stops right here, along with calypso and ska and steel bands that blast out of the outdoor speaker. Park Heights diversifies with Jamaica T-shirts, Rasta hats, and island carvings.

Rastafarian Rags

The Rastafarian religion is Jamaica's millennial faith. Ethiopia is the New Jerusalem and Emperor Selassie is the Messiah. He is the Christ, the Lion of Judah. Ganja is the wine and wafer of the faithful. Dreadlocks are the West Indian side curls. They believe in one creator, one aim, and one destiny.

At the corner of Utica Avenue and St. John's Place, the local Rastafarians gather around an informal church called Abyssinian Clothes. The African robes and dashikis and the Rastafarian leather and knit caps for covering dreadlocks are the colors of the rainbow with Rastafarian symbols. There is nothing more imaginative or better made in the craft shops of SoHo.

Island Builders

The blacks of Brooklyn are builders. The house strong and solid is the image of themselves and their community. They refuse to give in to urban decay. West Indians have taken the tradition of ''buying house'' a step further, rebuilding and restoring house.

The Bedford-Stuyvesant Restoration Center, *1360 Fulton Street.*

The Bedford-Stuyvesant Restoration took derelict warehouses and factories and turned them into a black enterprise zone. The Kennedy family supplied some of the inspiration and seed money but black Brooklyn did the building and planning. There's a spanking-clean complex of stores and offices, and even a theater named for ''Lady Day'' (Billy Holiday).

Weeksville Society, *1698 Bergen Street (718-434-7695).*

Weeksville is Bedford-Stuyvesant's answer to Williamsburg. It is a restoration of the old Hunterfly Houses, where free New York blacks lived before the Civil War. Weeksville is named for James Weeks, a proud independent black man who originally farmed this land. The Weeksville Restoration was sponsored by the city's Department of Housing Preservation and Development, but it was built by a new generation of self-sufficient blacks.

West Indian Carnival

Carnival is a centuries-old tradition in the Caribbean. The New York version that started in Harlem and moved to Brooklyn in 1960 (with most of Manhattan's West Indian inhabitants) evokes the energy and insistent rhythms of the islands with a flashy big-city quality. This New York–style extravaganza runs for five days and the preparations for next year's dazzling carnival costumes and elaborate carnival routines begin the moment it is over.

In workshops throughout the city, designers create costumes. It is only silver foil and aluminum tubing, painted cardboard and cane, but it somehow captures the spirit of myth and legend, with outer space creatures, and fairy-tale kings and queens. Meanwhile the dances are choreographed and the dancers go through their paces till the timing is instinctive. It is more than a celebration or putting on a show. For participants like designer Morris Stewart, it is the supreme form of self-expression.

The parade is the climax of this festival with carnival groups strutting their stuff to island reggae, calypso, and steel bands. There are also four days of special events featuring West Indian music, culture, and the carnival traditions and competitions. The West Indian-American Carnival is a vast reunion of all the city's hundreds of thousands of West Indian peoples. It is a time for Bamians, Jamaicans, and Trinidadians to get together to dance to the music and eat home-style hot cod cakes and curried goat, sold and prepared by the community's best cooks. It is one big West Indian block party.

Haitians

History

They are the boat people of the Western Hemisphere—risking it all in a leaky twenty-five-foot craft to escape oppression and want—twenty or thirty people to a boat, sharing hunger and thirst under the blazing sun for the seven hundred miles to Miami. In Haiti they committed the crime of questioning the violence of the Tonton Macoute or merely having something that someone in power desired. Like the Vietnamese, for them survival meant escape.

Haitians have been coming to New York since the 1790s, when French colonists and Creoles from San Domingue (the original name of Haiti) fled the slave rebellion. James Audubon, the naturalist, was among their number. Creoles in colorful West Indian prints were a familiar sight on the streets of New York in the first decade of the nineteenth century.

Haitian businessmen and professionals came to New York in the early years of the twentieth century to escape the country's political upheavals. Many of the city's five hundred Haitians were supporters of Marcus Garvey's Back to Africa campaign.

Following the American occupation of Haiti in 1934, a number of Haitians followed the American marines back to the States and settled in New York. At the same time, Haitians in the Columbia University student-exchange programs decided to remain in the city. After World War II, Haitians came to New York as live-in servants.

The mass migration of Haitians began with the election of Francois (Papa Doc) Duvalier in 1958. This supposedly simple country doctor and man of the people spawned a reign of terror in the process of picking clean his country's treasury.

The first to leave were the wealthy fair-skinned elite, who were against Papa Doc while he still represented himself as a black populist reformer. Trained and well educated, they could fit right into New York while they hatched a succession of unsuccessful coups and invasions. They were followed in the 1960s by a black middle class that couldn't live with the violence and economic insecurity of what one critic called the Duvalier ''kleptocracy.''

The first documented case of poor refugees fleeing Duvalier's brutality on the high seas occurred in 1963, but the wholesale flight of the boat people didn't start until the 1970s. Though they landed on the coast of Florida, most continued their journeys to New York.

At the beginning this outpouring of people was spontaneous, friends and relatives pooling their resources for a future in the States. By 1980 Haitian fast-buck artists with ties to the regime of Jean-Claude Duvalier (''Baby Doc'') were promoting these dangerous boat trips along with promises of employment in America. The kickbacks were supposed to go all the way to the presidential palace.

While the first emigrants of the Duvalier reign were managerial types, technicians, and professionals, the most recent arrivals are unskilled and semiskilled: laborers, factory workers, and domestics. Some have been forced to accept jobs of last resort because of their indefinite immigrant status.

Haitian immigrants in contemporary New York follow many of the same patterns as earlier immigrants from Italy and Eastern Europe. They band together in the same areas of the city with people from the same village or quarter. Despite the availability of city welfare, Haitians help one another through fraternities, associations, and credit groups. Group solidarity is also maintained through the Haitian newspaper *Haiti-Observateur*.

Though the Duvalier regime was finally deposed, conditions in Haiti have not measurably improved, and most Haitian New Yorkers, even among the elite, see their stay as permanent.

Bois Verna

Introduction

This Haitian colony, which is scattered in the West 80s and 90s between the Hudson River and Columbus Avenue, is named after Bois Verna, a crowded quarter in Haiti's capital, Port-au-Prince. The men and women of Bois Verna originally lived in the area's SRO hotels until they could find larger accommodations in the outlying boroughs. Since the Upper West Side started to gentrify and the hotels have made way for condominiums, the Haitian population has decreased. But on warm nights groups of Haitians huddle on the side streets and on Amsterdam Avenue, speaking their melodious patois. They have a reserve that is regularly broken by unforced laughter. Little Haiti in Manhattan keeps getting smaller, its people spreading out through Brooklyn, Queens, and the Bronx.

Creole Cooking

Creole cooking combines the French, African, and West Indian. The meat is primarily goat and pork and the starch comes from plantains, breadfruit, and all the root vegetables of the Caribbean. Coconut milk and cassava are the thickeners and *piment oiseau* is the spicy hot sauce. The *cabri* and the *lambi* are goat and conch in a peppery sauce and the *griot* is the spicy fried pork. *Poisson* is French for fish, but it is Haitian for a pan-fried snapper with tomato and spice. The Haitians make their own version of chicken fricassee, and instead of French duck, there is guinea hen with sour orange sauce.

Le Soleil, *877 Tenth Avenue between 56th and 57th Streets (212-581-6059). Monday–Saturday noon–11 P.M.; Sunday noon–9 P.M.*

In the center of Le Soleil, Madam sits at a counter taking the takeout orders and handing out copies of three Haitian newspapers. She smiles easily, as if she were presiding over a party rather than a frantically busy restaurant that only sounds like a party. The oxtail stew with a big bowl of brown beans and rice is best. The steak is tough and the goat is stringy.

Haitian Letters and "Livres"

Haitian Manhattan is intellectually active, with three newspapers and a host of magazines and Haitian-language radio. Haitians are proud of their culture and history, descended from the only blacks in the new hemisphere who rebelled and claimed their own freedom. They want to preserve their Haitian traditions and French heritage and remain culturally separate from British West Indians and other African-Americans.

Haitian Corner, *495 Amsterdam Avenue near 83rd Street.*

In place of cafés, Haitian intellectuals have their earnest conversations standing up in the Haitian Corner. The papers and books are from Haiti and Haitian-American Miami or New York. The recordings and cassettes are also local or imported. In between there are the visual arts, Haitian carving and painting. The store is already a second-generation business.

Haitian Primitives

Haitian painting began to be recognized in 1944, when De Witt Peters, an American artist, opened Le Centre d'Art in Haiti's capital, Port-au-Prince. Three years later, Haitian art was the talk of the Paris ateliers when the UNESCO show introduced Haitian artists to the art world. Later Selden Rodman, an art collector and a Rockefeller, brought Haitian murals to America. By 1949 Haitian paintings were as popular in America as the primitives of Grandma Moses.

The colors of Haitian painting—red, green, orange, and blue—are psychedelic bright. The subjects are simple rural daily life, a bus ride, or a bazaar. Haitian nature is rain-forest luxuriant. The technique ranges from childlike figures with no perspective to a high-fidelity surrealism. There are now Haitian masters like voodoo priest Hector Hyppolite and Enguerrand Gourgue, who is in the permanent collection of the Museum of Modern Art.

Haiti D'Art Inc., *145 East 92nd Street (212-427-9283). By appointment.*

Haitian art on the East Side is all about established names and the high end of the market. The paintings here set the standard for Haitian primitives.

Mehu Gallery, *21 West 100th Street (212-222-3334). Tuesday–Friday 11 A.M.–3 P.M., 5 P.M.–7:30 P.M.; Saturday, Sunday noon–6 P.M.*

Mehu shows the new Haitian masters and does retrospectives of the old ones. It also sells a wide selection of Haitian art books including Selden Rodman's tour de force, *Where Art Is Joy, Haitian Art.*

La Saline

Directions: IRT-Lexington Avenue 4 to Sutter Avenue/Rutland Road.

Introduction

Haitians looked for the good life in Brooklyn. They worked their way from Bed-Stuy roosts to sturdy brick houses in Crown Heights and have expanded on the south side of Eastern Parkway to Flatbush. Haitians have banded together with friends and relatives from Port-au-Prince and rural towns like Hinche and Jacmel. Their Brooklyn universe, which they call Le Saline after a district in Port-au-Prince, is their separate country.

The buoyant black faces of Haitian primitives speak in their molasses patois. This is their world and they express and carry themselves with loose-limbed freedom. They have endured a lot together in a country of Tonton Macoute and a New York of crime and racial politics. There is a closeness and a sense of intimacy in the ordinary Haitian relations of daily life on the streets of Brooklyn.

La Saline Tastes

The Haitian restaurants in Brooklyn are unsophisticated and family. It's all plastic placemats and familiar faces. But these Haitian eateries have Brooklyn security and the cash box and the cashier are behind a plexiglass wall. Still, nothing cramps the friendly Haitian style and the tasty home cooking and baking.

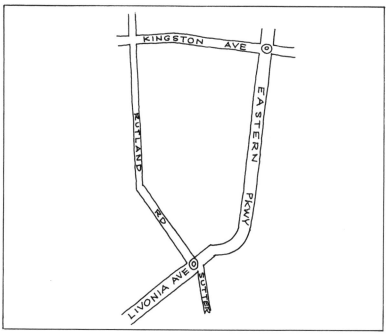

La Saline

Chez Price, *383 Kingston Avenue (718-756-9653). Daily 9 A.M.– midevening.*

Chez Price happily coexists on this Hasidic High Street. The place is cozy in sunny Haitian colors. The chicken stew is a tasty pepperpot with plantain and Irish potato. The *poisson* is their special event.

Rose Restaurant, *1046 Rutland Road (718-774-1635). Daily 9 A.M.–midnight.*

Rose's has a sense of space with last year's Christmas ornaments for decoration. At lunch it's single men at separate tables; dinner is a full house with animated families. The ragout is a big bowl of soup filled with every Caribbean root vegetable and knobs of bone with more fat than meat. It is enough for four and peppery without being hot. The *lambi* (conch curry) is one dish where the hot peppers complement the natural taste.

Bicentennial Bakery and Restaurant, *1037 Rutland Road (718-773-9772). Daily 8 A.M.–9 P.M.*

The Haitian biscuits are plain to a fault but the Haitian patties filled with fish can compete with the Jamaican.

St. Marc Boulangerie, *1065 Rutland Road (unlisted number). Daily 7:30 A.M.–9 P.M.*

Mornings on Rutland Road there is the incense of coconut bread and coconut cupcakes coming from the Boulangerie. While the cakes are a match for the heavenly aromas, the St. Marc with its one glassed-in window resembles a check-cashing office.

Haitian Sounds

Haitian music is a mixed bag. There are sentimental Creole versions of American pop and hot brass takeoffs of Dominican merengue and dance chants powered by a voodoo drum. Shak-shah is Haitian New York style, soul with a Creole accent.

St. Marc Records, *1020 Rutland Road (718-773-9507). Daily 10 A.M.–7 P.M.*

St. Marc has all the Haitian dance music, including boleros, that have disappeared from everywhere else. There is the latest Haitian-American music and drums of Africa folk music. St. Marc's is bare-looking when it's empty, but at its best it's filled with people enjoying Haitian sounds and occasionally buying a record or a ticket to a local concert.

Manoir Restaurant Banquet, *1744 Nostrand Avenue (718-282-8936). Call for information on special events.*

If it's not booked for a wedding, the mainspring of Haitian music in Brooklyn is the Manoir. There are stars directly from Haiti like the Super Stars Music Machine and Haitian-American groups like Skah Shah. Anything can happen at a Haitian concert. The audiences can't stand still.

Haitian Rites

Haitian Voodoo is what remains of African animism. It is a multilevel religion with its own symbols and rituals. Voodoo has *hungan* (priests) and *mambu* (priestesses) and the place of worship is the *humfort*. There is a pole in the center of the sanctuary, rising up like a steeple. Drums charge the ritual of whirling bodies and Voodoo trances. The *loa* (the gods) possess the body and the soul of the *mambu*.

St. Jacques Botanica, *1502 Nostrand Avenue (718-469-0769). Monday–Saturday 11 A.M.–6 P.M.*

St. Jacques has charms and primitive symbols and ceramic statues and plaster statues of black saints. There are herbal cures and miraculous cures.

The Hispanics

Introduction

Hispanic New Yorkers have a rich Hispanic culture. There are Latin American museums, schools, dance companies, theaters, newspapers, magazines, and radio and television stations. New York Hispanic covers a lot of territory, from Spanish diplomats to Dominican bootblacks. Even before the 1960s, when the Hart-Celler Act spurred Latin American emigration, there were seventeen Hispanic nationalities in New York, and they have multiplied with economic stagnation and political upheavals. The Latin New York of the 1990s represents racial and cultural diversity. The light-skinned European Argentinian and the Ecuadorian mestizo and the Afro-Caribbean of Puerto Rico or the Dominican Republic all share a Hispanic identity. They are New York's second city.

Puerto Ricans

History

Puerto Ricans may be known as the "airplane immigrants," but they were in New York as early as 1838, forming their own associations. They were merchants and planters in the sugar and coffee trade. They were temporary New Yorkers in town to do business and educate their children.

Some Puerto Ricans were political and plotted in New York against Spain. They spent their time writing manifestos and trying to organize skilled Puerto Rican workers. Dr. José Julio Henna, a society doctor, was the spokesman for the *independistas* and twice testified on Puerto Rican affairs before the U.S. Senate and House.

By the time the Spaniards got around to giving Puerto Rico autonomy the Americans were shopping around for their own territories. In a war trumped up by the Hearst papers, the U.S. remembered the *Maine* and made the hemisphere safe under the Monroe Doctrine. In 1900 Puerto Rico was placed under an American military government.

Puerto Rico was a poor country with a plantation economy. American food companies controlled the islanders' destiny. As the prices of coffee and sugar declined, Puerto Rican labor lost their jobs. Many *jibaros* (peasants) moved to the cities or hired out as contract labor on other Caribbean islands.

Small-scale local industry could not compete with American imports and Puerto Rican companies went out of business. Even the country's efficient cigar-making industry was forced to close down. The Puerto Rican unemployment problem was so desperate many were ready to leave for the mainland.

While the Puerto Rican economy was depressed New York was tooling up for World War I. Puerto Ricans found plenty of work in the city with the war blocking European emigration. They had the additional advantage of the Jones Act of 1917, which gave Puerto Ricans the right to travel freely and settle in the U.S. Their position was further solidified in 1920 by legislation that restricted European emigration.

Puerto Ricans were a mainstay of New York's light industry and service industries. As Jews and Italians left lower-level garment industry jobs, Puerto Ricans took their places. They also dominated the hotel and restaurant service sector. On the island Puerto Ricans were recruited by New York City plants that produced everything from pencils to biscuits.

Spanish-speaking doctors, lawyers, and pharmacists offered their services to the newcomers, easing the transition from plantation to big city. The Hispanic professionals provided leadership and advice. Spanish-language newspapers like *La Prensa* carried the news from home and made Puerto Ricans aware of local issues. New York's Puerto Rican entrepreneurs accounted for over 350 businesses in 1920.

Puerto Rican barrios began to honeycomb Brooklyn and Manhattan; there were Puerto Rican cigar-makers in Chelsea and the Lower East Side and San Juan stevedores on the Red Hook waterfront. In the 1920s Puerto Ricans moved into the Greenpoint section of Brooklyn to work in the hemp factories and sugar refineries.

In no time neighborhoods had a Puerto Rican flavor with *bodegas* offering papaya and *chaya* (a root vegetable) and *botanicas* selling amulets and statues. Puerto Rican restaurants cooked down-home *comidas criollas* (creole food), *mofongo* (mashed root vegetables), and *gandules verdes* (pigeon peas) with Caribbean root vegetables. The barbershops and boardinghouses had a warm relaxed *Boriqueno* feeling.

The majority of New York Puerto Ricans settled in El Barrio itself: East Harlem between 97th Street and 125th Street, an island in Manhattan bound by black Harlem in the north and west and Italian and Jewish Harlem in the east. It was the center of Puerto Rican cultural and community life. When Puerto Ricans thought about coming to New York, they dreamed about El Barrio.

There was no way of dealing with the economic depression that interrupted the progress of the thriving Puerto Rican community in 1930. The competition for even menial jobs became fierce. It was hard to find work—even washing dishes—and many a regretful Puerto Rican drifted back to the island. Just when things started to get better in the New York job market, World War II put a temporary hold on further Puerto Rican migration to the city.

Peace and the collapse of the sugar economy opened the floodgates of Puerto Rican migration. The airplane provided the Puerto Ricans with cheap and efficient transportation. A new life was eight hours and seventy-five dollars away. By the 1950s one out of every six islanders was leaving and the majority were coming to New York. Six hundred thousand made the trip in one decade.

These latest Puerto Rican New Yorkers were even less prepared for the city than their predecessors, the so-called *perfumadas* (the sweet-smelling ones) who were now starting to enjoy the fruits of the American dream. Most had no work experience and only one in ten had graduated from high school. They were at a disadvantage in an era when unskilled jobs were rapidly disappearing.

While the Puerto Rican mass migration to New York continued, the island was going through its own economic recovery. When Luis Muñoz Marín, leader of the Popular Democratic Party, became the first popularly elected governor of the Puerto Rican commonwealth, attention shifted from the statehood-independence controversy to the issue of economic development.

The benefits of tax incentives and cheap surplus labor combined with the appeal of a government Marshall Plan called Operation Bootstrap began to attract American industry and investment to Puerto Rico. Three hundred new factories meant the country went from creating six hundred new jobs to forty-eight thousand new jobs in a year; but it didn't stop the migration of thousands of Puerto Ricans.

Soon Puerto Ricans overflowed the borders of the Manhattan and Brooklyn barrios into the Bornx. They crossed the Harlem River to compete with other minorities for scarce housing space in Hunt's Point and Mott Haven. By 1950, sixty thousand Puerto Ricans were creating their own neighborhoods in a Bronx vacated by Jews, Irish, and Italians.

The time had come for Puerto Ricans to fight their own political battles. In 1953 Felipe Torres, a protegé of the regular Democratic organization, was elected to the State Assembly. When he became a family court judge in 1961, his son Frank ran against entrenched Irish Democratic power for his seat and won the Fourth District by fifty-two votes.

Puerto Ricans had their biggest political base in the Bronx and in the protest era of the 1960s they found their leader in a self-made man from Caguas. Herman Badillo was an orphan who earned a CPA while setting pins in a bowling alley and put himself through law school washing dishes. After a stint as the city's first Puerto Rican commissioner, Badillo became the first Puerto Rican borough president in 1965 and went on to capture the first Puerto Rican congressional seat in 1970. The latest Puerto Rican notables include schools chancellor Joseph Fernandez, who turned around the Dade County school system, and Bronx Congressman José Serrano, who is carrying on the Badillo tradition.

El Barrio
Direction: IRT-Lexington Avenue 6 to 116th Street.

Introduction

East Harlem was always poor Harlem. It was squatter and shack Harlem. It didn't have the estates and mansions of early West Harlem. The best it ever did was the Roosevelt farm at the turn of the nineteenth century, but that soon had to make way for the Harlem railroad.

Irish and German immigrants lived along the train tracks. They did odd jobs and raised a goat or two. They lived in rural squalor in a neighborhood called Goatville. Nineteenth-century East Harlem even had its feared youth gangs.

The Irish left the cold-water tenements to the Italians and Jews in the 1890s. It wasn't brownstone Harlem, but it was a step up from Mulberry Street and the Lower East Side. Both communities thrived with churches and synagogues and associations. They went from pushcarts to prosperous stores.

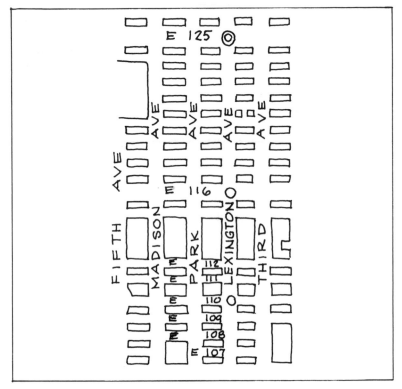

El Barrio

After World War I, Puerto Ricans entered East Harlem's ethnic picture. They moved into Jewish East Harlem between 110th and 117th Streets east of Madison Avenue. There were fifty Puerto Rican families there in 1916.

Eventually Puerto Rican New Yorkers concentrated around the open-air market along Park Avenue. The Jewish merchants in the market provided them with Caribbean foods and the housing was cheap. Rapid expansion of Spanish Harlem attracted Puerto Rican professionals.

Spanish Harlem was also developing culturally. Pura Belpre, the Puerto Rican librarian at the Seward Park branch, started the first program promoting Spanish writers and the Spanish language. She worked hard to bring Puerto Rican cultural values to the children of the community.

There were political circles around magazines like *Grafico* and literary circles around local Puerto Rican theaters. There was enough of an audience for Puerto Rican music for East Harlem to have its own Puerto Rican record store. Later in the 1940s and 1950s there were barrio theaters that showed only Spanish-language movies.

In 1926 East Harlem rioted. White ethnics attacked Puerto Ricans without provocation. It was one of the hottest summers on record, when complaints about Puerto Rican business competition and remarks about color lead to violence. Fists were thrown and bottles were thrown and there were minor injuries. Puerto Rican leaders calmed down Puerto Rican tempers and a Puerto Rican power broker from Brooklyn mediated between the communities.

Puerto Ricans were a political power waiting to happen. La Guardia, East Harlem's Italian congressman, realized that though the numbers of registered voters were small, the Puerto Ricans could play an important part in elections. He actively campaigned for their votes between 1922 and 1933.

Puerto Ricans found a champion in La Guardia's successor, congressman Vito Marcantonio. He helped his new constituents deal with the problems of housing and unemployment. His office guided Puerto Rican newcomers through the rules and regulations of the city bureaucracy.

In the 1950s El Barrio was inudated with Puerto Rican migrants making the cheap eight-hour flight from Puerto Rico. The Puerto Ricans of the 1950s were mainly unskilled and uneducated. They crowded together in crumbling tenements for their chance at the good life.

But they found a Puerto Rican glamour on 116th Street. It was Puerto Rican city lights with the raw vitality of immigrant hope. It was San Juan restaurants and casinos with immigrant energy and desire. *Jibaros* from the farms stared at the street scene with a feeling of wonder.

Despite the problems it was an El Barrio golden age with Puerto Ricans like José Ferrer and Rita Moreno on the Broadway stage and José Torres becoming middleweight champion. In 1957 Leonard Bernstein's Broadway musical *West Side Story* made Puerto Ricans part of the New York musical idiom.

Spanish Harlem, El Barrio, the city's classic "island in the city," stretches north from 97th Street to Mount Morris Park and 120th Street and from Fifth Avenue to the East River. The spine of this sprawling Puerto Rican neighborhood is still 116th Street.

It's the commercial center where people come to shop or enjoy Latino food or just hang out, listening to the salsa big bands from the record-shop speakers. It's surrounded by blocks of tenements ranging, from burnt-out to refurbished and high- and low-rise projects. El Barrio has lost some of the gloss from the old days, but it's still Puerto Rico's New York capital.

Comidas Criollas

The food of Puerto Rico is *criolla,* creole, combining the influences of the indigenous Taino Indians, the African slaves, and the Spanish conquerors.

The taste is robust without being excessively spicy or hot. *Adobo,* a seasoning for meat and poultry consisting of pepper, garlic, oregano, oil, and lime juice, and *sofrito,* an all-purpose flavoring of salt pork, ham, oregano, onion, peppers, coriander, and garlic, set the tone. The most common herbs are fresh *culantro* (coriander) and oregano. Lime rind and juice and fresh ginger give the food a characteristically Caribbean flavor as immediate as the sun and the sea. The color of the preparations comes from the *achiote* seed, which is mixed with lard or oil, the *naranja* (orange) of the island sun. *Plátanos* (green bananas) are a common side dish: fried, roasted, boiled, and baked like the American spud. Root vegetables and tubers such as breadfruit, yams, pumpkin, and beans called *gandules,* or pigeon peas, dominate the Puerto Rican table.

Popular dishes include *guisados* (stews), *rellenos* (stuffed meat and vegetables), and *frituras* (fritters). *Lechonarias* serve the national dish, *lechón asado* (barbecued pig), but seafood from *pulpo* (octopus) to *bacalao* (dried cod) has an equally large following. For snacking, there are *cuccifritos,* variations on the pork-rind theme.

On and off 116th Street there are restaurants and snack shops to take the edge off hearty Puerto Rican appetites. Whether in a corner lunch counter with a blaring radio or a white-tablecloth restaurant with pink lights and autographed pictures of celebrities, don't expect subtlety. The food is direct and unabashedly substantial and the service is straightforward, with none of the bowing waiter rituals.

Ponce De Leon, *171 East 116th Street (212-348-5580). Sunday–Thursday 7 A.M.–11 P.M.; Friday, Saturday 7 A.M.–1 A.M.*

Ponce De Leon has the pictures of the boss with the politicians and pretensions. Too bad the stained glass and exposed brick is only plastic. The restaurant is better with *criolla* than Spanish dishes like the *paella,* which is dried-out rice and rubbery shellfish. The *chuletas* (chops) are prepared with a classic *adobo* bringing out the natural taste of the meat with a Caribbean freshness.

Jimmy's Lechoneria, *1875 Lexington Avenue between 116th and 117th Streets (212-369-9613). Tuesday–Sunday 6 A.M.–11 P.M.*

Suckling pig turned slowly on a spit is a Puerto Rican passion. Jimmy's does the best it can, but it's just not the same indoors. The *mofongo* (seasoned, mashed root vegetables) is more like it.

Del Pueblo, *2118 Third Avenue at 116th Street (212-348-9164).*
Monday–Saturday 7 A.M.–10 P.M.

It's only a luncheonette, but it has the true spirit of El Barrio. People bounce
in like something's about to happen. The familiar faces nod and the salsa
never stops. The guys behind the counter sing along to the music and do rim
shots with the silverware. The *carne guisado* (stewed meat) is tingling with
coriander and garlic and too much to finish.

Puerto Rican Panaderia

The Puerto Rican *panaderia* is much more than a bakery. It begins with *pan*
de agua (water-base bread) and sweet rolls, and ends with a Cuban hero
packed with ham, roast pork, cheese, and pickles pressed on a hot grill. The
layer cakes are mile-high in shocking pink and blue with an icing bride and
groom and Batman or Mickey for the kids. There are Puerto Rican patties
(*pastelillos*) stuffed with guava, custard cream, and ground meat, and cakes
soaked with Puerto Rican rum. The coffee comes rich and black or with
steamed milk *con leche* and a buttered stump of bread. The barrio *panaderia*
is not on the scale of the typical Puerto Rican barn—it's smaller and not so
social.

Valencia Bakery, *1869 Lexington Avenue between 115th and*
116th Streets (212-991-6400). Monday–Saturday 9 A.M.–6 P.M.;
Sunday 9 A.M.–4 P.M.

This is the place to prepare for a party. Besides cakes shaped like a football
field or a baseball diamond, there are *toda ocasion cumpleaños,* a whole line
of party favors for birthdays. Saturdays and Sundays, parents and children
pace before the cake displays, making their choices.

La Nueva Bakery, *2129 Third Avenue between 116th and 117th*
Streets (212-876-2990). Monday–Saturday 7 A.M.–9 P.M.; Sunday
9 A.M.–9 P.M.

La Nueva has the best *pan caliente* (fresh warm bread) in the barrio and the
best Cuban sandwiches and everybody knows it. Come in the morning for a
café con leche and a *pan dulce* (sweet roll) that beats a Continental breakfast.

Capri Bakery, *186 East 116th Street (212-410-1876). Daily 7 A.M.–midnight.*

Capri looks like a Times Square snack shop. Pass on the Cuban sandwiches, but take a chance on the *pastelillos* with guava jelly and a black coffee. It's a good place to check out the 116th Street action.

116th Street Snacks

On the streets of the barrio, people are always eating and in-between bites they are talking. The Puerto Ricans are round-the-clock eaters and talkers; they have a variety of snack food to match their appetites. There are *cuccifritos* (giant pork rinds) that are salty and hard, and *alcapurias* (fried mashed plantains with pork), *papas rellenas* (fried mashed potato with pork and chick peas), and *bacalaitos* (croquettes of dried salt cod) that are heavy—and not to put too good a point on it, greasy. The *pastillo,* which is grated yucca with chopped pork, capers, and olives in a folded plantain leaf, can be memorable.

Puerto Rican junk food should be washed down with a *batido,* a tropical fruit shake with tastes like papaya and guava and orange. (New York Puerto Ricans have started adding milk for more body.)

The best Puerto Rican finger food is usually served in the smallest hole in the wall with the loudest conversation and eardrum-piercing salsa.

Lexington Restaurant, *1869 Lexington Avenue at 116th Street (212-534-4732). Monday–Saturday 5:30 A.M.–7 P.M.*

It has the look of a Times Square luncheonette, but the taste of a reed food stand on Luquillo Beach. The fried treats are made with a surprisingly light hand.

La Marquetta

La Marquetta, *Park Avenue between 110th and 116th Streets.*

East Harlem was once filled with pushcart markets on a down-to-earth Park Avenue. It was a multiethnic street scene, catering to the neighborhood's established Jews, Italians, and Irish, and the emerging Puerto Ricans. After Mayor La Guardia took the pushcarts off the East Harlem avenues, the vendors were relocated to stalls in a market under the Park Avenue railroad viaduct between 110th and 116th Streets. The market took on the character of the neighborhood's new ethnic majority—the Puerto Ricans—and came to be called La Marquetta.

La Marquetta is presupermarket Puerto Rico. Every seller has a specialty: produce, meat, fish, herbs, or folk medicines. The colorful Caribbean yuccas and batatas, eels and octopus are piled high in profusion. A whole suckling pig is hanging. Cleavers crack bone and fish-knives filet. A papaya is poked and sniffed. The sellers shout and the customers shout and the weighing looks like sleight of hand. The price is scrawled on the bag and paid.

The original 450 stalls have declined and some of the arcades have closed. La Marquetta has gone from a prosperous cooperative to a struggling, city-sponsored market. Early in the morning early in the week it's practically empty, but Saturdays are a replay of old El Barrio bustle, in the days when it was the only market for Latin New York.

Botanica Magic

In Puerto Rico the Church was associated with the Spanish white hierarchy. The clergy was alien and the Church was distrusted. Many Puerto Ricans practiced the religion of their African and Indian ancestors, a worship where spirits inhabit everything animate and fate is a potion or charm. *Santeria,* with its drums and chants, made the trip to Manhattan and the shamans opened up *botanicas.*

Botanicas prescribe the herbs and roots of traditional Puerto Rican folk medicine. They also sell wonder-working images, candles, amulets, and miraculous aerosols. The shops are a strange combination of vials and plants, statues of saints and African totems. Some of the supernatural paraphernalia looks as though it was lifted from a second-hand store.

Otto Chicas Rendon, *60 East 116th Street (212-289-0378). Monday–Saturday 9:30 A.M.–5:30 P.M.*

This is the oldest botanica in the city and is still going strong with two other branches. Roland, the inheritor of this botanica empire, applies modern management principles to the what-dreams-are-made-of elixirs and magic powders.

El Congo, *1789 Lexington Avenue between 110th Street and 111th Streets (212-860-3921). Monday–Saturday 9 A.M.–5:45 P.M.*

This botanica is serious *santeria* with books in Spanish and English explaining this mystical religion and its Yoruba roots. There are bamboo fetishes and miracle beads and dried herbs and leaves. The store is creative disarray, with a Puerto Rican rain forest motif.

Paco's Botanica, *1864 Lexington Avenue at 115th Street (212-427-0820). Monday–Saturday 8 A.M.–6 P.M.*

The music played in Paco's is sentimental serenades for the housewives who come in for an instant miracle . The setup is immaculate with miracle candles, wonder-working necklaces, and religious prints all in their places. The religious statues that take up most of the shop are shrink-wrapped in plastic.

Manhattan Boriqua

Boriqua or *Boricua* is the name of Puerto Rico's indigenous people. It is also the term Puerto Ricans use to refer to their own indigenous culture. They are proud of their culture, which, like American culture, partakes of Old and New World traditions and the European and the African experience. It is a culture that is always searching for its own identity.

—Museums—

El Museo Del Barrio, *1230 Fifth Avenue between 104th and 105th Streets (212-831-7272). Wednesday–Sunday 11 A.M.–5 P.M. Admission charge.*

El Museo is a museum with a human face. The guards actually speak and if someone left a hammer next to a crated painting, big deal. The art covers all the Puerto Rican bases from abstraction to nineteenth-century naturalism to folk art. Recent exhibitions included the primitive wooden *santos* and modern feminist painters. The gallery has workshops in Puerto Rican culture that involve the community.

Taller Boriqua, *1 East 104th Street (212-831-4333). Tuesday–Sunday 1 P.M.–6 P.M.*

Artists-in-residence put the artistic process in perspective. The artist and his work are side by side; the artist and his Puerto Rican heritage are one. The Taller Boriqua has a community outreach with film and video and a graphics show.

—Theater—

Teatro Moderno Puertorriqueño, *250 East 116th Street (212-289-2633).*

The Teatro Moderno Puertorriqueño is reality theater. It deals head-on with being poor and Puerto Rican in New York. The plays, which are the thing, are usually original or a new barrio slant to something familiar. The productions can be loose and experimental.

—Saucy Salsa—

Puerto Rico's original music was *bamba,* the beat of the bamba drum, fua sticks, and maraca. The bamba dancer duplicated the beat of the drum and the drummer duplicated dancer in a rhythmic can you top this. The music found words in the city and a harmonica and guitar were added, and it became *plena.* In the mountains near Bayamon, Spanish musical conventions were transformed into an *jibaro* serenade with guitar and bongo backing. Cuban *Son* came on the scene with its big brass sound driving the African dance of rhumba and mambo. It all came together in New York as the Puerto Rican sound met black America jazz. Salsa became the up-tempo Latin jazz of the barrio.

East Harlem Music School, *405 East 120th Street (212-876-0136).*

The East Harlem Music School teaches young players the whole Latin music vocabulary from bamba to salsa. There are classes in congas and bongos and marimbas and conventional brass and piano. Aspiring after-school musicians learn to respect themselves as they master the music. The school bands sound very professional and some students turn professional. The recitals are dancing in the aisles.

La Marketa Records, *100 116th Street between Lexington and Park Avenues. No telephone. Daily 9 A.M.–10 P.M.*

La Marketa is discount salsa records, compact discs, and cassettes.

The Day of the Puertorriqueño

The Puerto Rican parade is on the first Sunday in June. It is a day of cultural pride that spans the eighteen hundred miles that separate Puerto Rico and New York. Puerto Rican politicians and celebrities and ordinary people from the island in the sun and the island in the city march together up Fifth Avenue from 44th Street to 86th Street.

The Puerto Rican Parade has one of the largest turnouts on the city's parade roster. It's a family affair with kids sitting on their father's shoulders so they can see the floats and the marchers. Puerto Ricans are proud of their homeland and Puerto Rican flag-waving has not gone out of fashion. Puerto Rican red, white, and blue flags are everywhere along the line of march.

In the lead is the Grand Marshal, a celebrity actor like Raul Julia, or the leader of a Puerto Rican organization. The crowd, which is always in a state of near hysteria, goes wild for its dignitaries and matinee idols. Even the local politicos who follow get applause and whistles. But the real cheering is reserved for the political delegations from Puerto Rico and the mayors of localities like Bayamon and Ponce.

There are floats of Columbus's ships and the Morro Castle in San Juan and a local Puerto Rican radio station. Puerto Rican policemen and firemen and social workers show their colors and smile broadly to the crowd as a high school band from the Bronx does a medley of salsa hits. Salsa celebrities from Celia Cruz to Johnny Colon do their acts on tropical-colored floats and the word passes through the crowd and people stand on tiptoe for a better look. Finally it comes, spread out between twenty-five men and women, a giant Puerto Rican flag; all the flags among the spectators wave in unison.

Dominicans

History

The first Dominicans landed in New York at the end of the eighteenth century. They were whites and mulattos fleeing a slave insurrection from what is today the capital, Santo Domingo. The American Congress donated fifteen thousand dollars for relief.

In the nineteenth century the Dominican Republic was conquered and reconquered by Haiti and Spain. America took its turn in 1916 and ruled the Dominican Republic for eight years in conjunction with Standard Brands and American Fruit Company. When the American marines left in 1924 their Dominican dependents joined them in the States. Some Dominicans drifted into the Spanish-speaking neighborhoods of New York City.

Dominican emigration to New York was abruptly halted when military strongman Trujillo took over in 1930. The only Dominicans who now traveled to New York were polo-playing playboys like Rubirosa or intellectual exiles like Professor Galindez.

Dominicans only started coming to New York in any significant numbers when Trujillo was assassinated in 1961 and exit visas were no longer the privilege of the few. Though rising population and economic expectations spurred emigration, others were responding to the country's political instability that led to another American occupation in 1965.

The first-wave Dominicans who came in response to the Hart-Celler Act were mainly people who qualified for occupational immigration quotas. They were high-level professionals—doctors, engineers, and accountants—

and skilled labor—tailors and machinists. They moved into neighborhoods like Washington Heights that had Spanish-speaking Cubans with similar backgrounds and apartments with extra-large rooms.

Dominicans who settled in New York brought over other family members and gradually they began to form their own colonies on the Lower East Side and in Washington Heights and Corona, Queens. But most Dominicans were without technical skills or education and were barred from emigration to New York.

The next waves of Dominicans had more determination and will than qualifications, though they were above the Dominican average when it came to education and income. In New York, they worked as superintendents or did manual work in factories and often held down two jobs at once; they were intent on saving money to open a business or invest in land on their island.

These Dominican pioneers had a solid sense of family and a strong Catholic heritage. Their pride was personal and national. Often they left behind villages populated by the aged and very young. They would not send for their sons and daughters until they were really established.

For poor Dominicans, coming to New York is an obsession. Tourist visas are more valuable than gold. There is a steady traffic of small vessels plying the harbors of Florida and Puerto Rico who will assist these American dreamers for a price. Sometimes these extralegal emigration routes end in tragedy. On September 5, 1980, twenty-two Dominicans illegally headed for the ''promised land'' drowned in the ballast tanks of a Panamanian cargo ship while hiding from port police.

The Dominicans who have made it to New York have come of age. In Washington Heights in Manhattan they have their own Broadway, on Broadway from 155th Street to Dyckman Street. This Dominican scene is too self-confident and bright-lights big-city to be a ghetto. Dominican New York swings to a merengue beat more lightheartedly than any other *colonia* in the city.

Washington Heights

Directions: IND A or IRT-Seventh Avenue 1 to 168th Street/Broadway.

Introduction

The Dutch called it Harlem Heights, the highest elevation in the Harlem wilderness. When the Heights became the private property of English Colonel Roger Morris it was called Mount Morris. George Washington retreated to the Morris mansion after the defeat of Long Island. It became for a time his headquarters and the Heights was forever associated with his name.

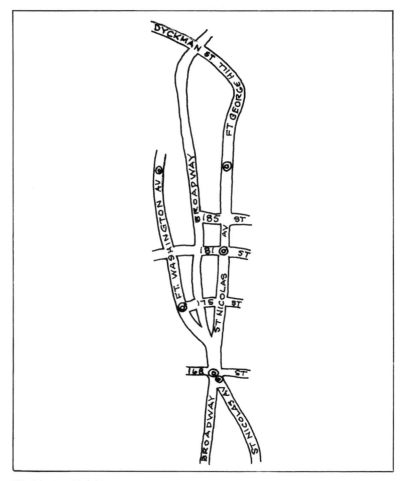

Washington Heights

The Heights remained estate territory for more than a century. It was the home of the naturalist Audubon and the publisher of the *Herald Tribune,* James Gordon Bennett. Chicago millionaire K. G. Billings had his racing stable in the rolling country of what would become Fort Tryon Park.

The IRT subway made the Heights accessible to working-class and middle-class New Yorkers in 1906. For a time, the Irish held the high ground and German-Jewish families moved into the valley of Broadway. In 1931 the neighborhood around 179th and 180th Streets was bulldozed for the George Washington Bridge linking New Jersey and New York.

German-Jewish refugees settled in the Heights before and after World War II, and Greek refugees came to the neighborhood to escape the Greek Civil War. In the 1950s the first Hispanics came on the scene from Cuba. They were fleeing a dictator named Batista and they were soon joined in the 1960s by Cubans fleeing Fidel Castro.

In the 1960s the Dominicans began coming to Washington Heights after the Trujillo government's travel and emigration restrictions were lifted. The early days were difficult: they had to find work and create a functioning Dominican community. In time they became the backbone of the garment district downtown and built their own Dominican business district in Washington Heights. Today they are the area's dominant ethnic.

Dominican Comidas Criollas

Dominican eating, from a friendly lunch counter to a formal sit-down, is pure *alegria* (joy). It is both the pleasure of the table and the pleasure of the company. Dominican eating is a team sport. Everyone urges everyone else on as they demolish everything from beans and rice to beefsteak. And Dominicans don't mind picking up the check; hospitality and generosity are traditional values.

Dominican cuisine is Hispanic-Caribbean, with the pork and beef rubbed with *adobo* and everything flavored with *sofrito*. It is rich *guisados* (stews) with peppers and olives and *mondongo* (tripe soup) and *mariscos* (shellfish) with dry rice or wet soupy rice. It has its own version of Puerto Rican *mofungo,* except the mashed plantains are mixed with scallions and it is eaten with cheese, sausage, or ham for breakfast. It is also African-Caribbean, with a dash of coconut milk and coconut oil.

Restaurant Caridad, *4311 Broadway at 184th Street (212-928-4645). Daily 6:00 A.M.–when the last customer leaves.*

The restaurant is spacious and splendid with a row of hanging plants dividing the dining room from the counter. It shows its Dominican colors with a map of the Dominican Republic on the counter's placemats. The dining area is strictly linen tablecloth. *Mariscos* Dominican style is the thing here. Six waitresses are kept busy ladling big bowls of *calamares* (squid) and *camarones asopao* (shrimp with soupy rice). There are mountains of rice and *habichuelas* (beans).

Mambi, *558 West 181st Street (212-568-5969). 1446 St. Nicholas Avenue (212-928-2760). 1446 Broadway at 179th Street (212-928-9796). Daily 24 hours.*

Mambi is a triple Dominican threat with three restaurants. The best is the new Broadway location. It's eating to a merengue beat with excellent meat selections. The day's specials are marked up on a blackboard. Look for the *costilla de cerdo con berenjena,* the pork rib with eggplant, which is Caribbean with a difference. You know it's authentic Dominican because it has *mangu* (boiled mashed plantains with oil and garlic) with cheese, sausage, and ham for breakfast.

La Nueva Cabana Restaurant, *1302 St. Nicholas Avenue at 175th Street (unlisted telephone). Daily 24 hours.*

In the back, *mamita* is slaving over a hot stove while her two daughters are serving up piles of food to stay or go. The restaurant is a no-frills twenty-four *horas del dia* operation. It's the food that gets all the superlatives. Leave the greasy *pollo frito* alone (it's supposedly the specialty of the house) and opt for the daily menu. There are great Dominican *guisados* (stews) with olives and peppers.

Dominican Merengue

The merengue—the dance and the music—is the essence of earthy Dominican. In northern Cibao, where most Dominican New Yorkers originate, the merengue was Spanish tinged with more European instrumentation and in the south it was African with hollow-log-drums rhythm. The merengue hollow log drum and maraca were part of the country's religious mysteries, saints' festivals, and religious brotherhoods. In the 1930s the split-personality merengues came together and the saxophone replaced the tribal drum. It went big band in the 1940s and adopted salsa in the 1960s. The merengue has its own festival every year in the Dominican Republic, when it is celebrated in all its glory and Dominicans from around the world join a pilgrimage to honor their music.

El Baturro, *1490 St. Nicholas Avenue at 185th Street (212-740-6135). Daily 11 A.M.–4 A.M.*

Dominicans say that the merengue is not the same in American dance halls but El Baturro tries to duplicate the true Dominican merengue experience. They don't do it self-consciously, it's simply that the groups and most of the dancers are just being themselves. It's a real show with a lot of couples doing a Dominican Ginger and Fred.

Dominican Record Shop, *3444 Broadway at 140th Street (212-926-9490). Daily 10 A.M.–10 P.M.*

The Dominican Record Shop is more than a place to buy merengue records. It keeps up with the whole Dominican Republic music scene and imports the Dominican top forty. It's also a community bulletin board that tells which groups are playing in which places.

The Parade with the Merengue Beat

The Dominican Day Parade is merengue bands and merengue dancers on floats. There are a few groups marching and folklorico ballets in ruffled skirts doing twirls and turns, but they are the exception. Dominican Day rolls up the Avenue of Americas from 44th Street to Columbus Circle on the Sunday closest to August 16. It is the day the Dominicans regained their freedom and the dictator Trujillo lost his to a hunting party of twelve.

Most of the floats that move along the line of march to the sounding brass and pounding congas are advertisements for beer companies, radio stations, canned beans, and the "real thing." No one notices or cares; everyone is lost in the music and the perpetual merengue motion. Even the button salesmen are dancing.

The Dominican beauty queens wave as if they really mean it and the Dominican community leaders have patriarchal Eisenhower smiles. The politicians, Dominican and American, look as though they are having too good a time to care. Along the line of march, Dominicans from the island politic among the spectators, many of whom have the right to vote in Dominican elections.

Cubans

History

Cuban politican refugees have been coming to New York since the middle of the nineteenth century. Cubans were the largest Latin group in the city before Puerto Rico became an American protectorate. They were intellectuals committed to the American ideals of freedom and a Latin American ideal of culture.

In nineteenth century New York, Cubans established a Spanish-language daily and thirty-four different magazines. The great Cuban novelist, Cirilo Villaverde, edited a newspaper in New York and José Martí, the George Washington of Cuba, founded two magazines in the city before his death in 1895.

Most of the Cubans who came to New York were white and well educated. Many were trained professionals who were quickly absorbed into the life of the city. Their children simply disappeared into mainstream American life.

Between 1867 and 1878 another strata of Cuban immigrants came to New York. These were skilled workers who were making a political statement by boycotting the Spanish-controlled tobacco industry. In New York they found freedom and better wages making American cigars.

Cuban cigar-rollers brought to New York an institution they shared with Puerto Rican workers—the factory reader. These highly literate workers paid a trained specialist to read plays, novels, and poetry to them while they worked. Some of these factory readers joined the Cuban theater company in New York.

When Cuba gained independence in 1898, Cuban emigration to New York slowed, though it did not stop. In the 1950s, during the dictatorship of Fulgencio Batista, Cuban political exiles returned to New York. By 1959 there were fifteen thousand Cubans on the Upper West Side.

In 1960, when it became clear that Castro would remake Cuba into the Soviet East, Cubans left in the thousands. The first Cubans to come to New York in the 1960s were society Cubans and Cubans from the military and business. They were white and well connected, but between 1960 and 1962, before flights from Cuba were stopped, there was a second wave of lower-middle-class and blue-collar Cubans.

While well-heeled Cubans could live lavishly outside of a barrio in New York, lower-level Cubans, who settled on New York's Upper West Side and in Queens, sought the support of their fellow countrymen. In Washington Heights and Jackson Heights they established small enclaves. Between 1965 and 1972 the Cuban airlift was renewed and thousands more came to the city.

In 1979 the Mariel boat lift brought more Cubans to the New York metropolitan area. The majority of these were true political refugees who went to the large Little Havana in New Jersey (Union City, West New York, and Weehawken) rather than to New York City. There are still small pockets of Cubans in the city, but their presence is mainly commercial.

It is the Cubans who run Channel 41, New York's Hispanic TV station, the Spanish-language press, and many of the Spanish-language radio stations. Cubans head Hispanic advertising agencies and Hispanic food companies. They are the entrepreneurs of the Hispanic community.

Cuban Taste

Cuban restaurants are not bound by the borders of a neighborhood; they are scattered throughout the city. There are country-club Cuban restaurants in the theater district and Cuban luncheonettes on the Upper West Side. The restaurants, high and low, share a pride in their food, which they consider Latino haute cuisine and the closest to the original Spanish. And they will prove it to you by having *gazpacho,* the cold Spanish soup, at the top of the menu.

Actually Cuban cuisine has much more in common with other Caribbean cuisines than with Spanish. It marinates meats in an *adobo* paste of garlic, salt, pepper, and lime juice or vinegar. Cuban food is more aromatic than spicy, and root vegetables like yucca and chayote and plantains (green bananas) are preferred to Spanish peppers. The Cubans make cornmeal tamales and a thick Caribbean soup/stew *ajiaco* with pork, oxtail, or tripe and all the tubers in the subtropical garden. *Ropa vieja,* a stew of shredded beef, is poor man's Cuba but very popular in America. Cuban fast food is a Cuban sandwich of roast pork, ham, cheese, and pickle and *chicharonnes de pollo,* fried chicken with a hint of coriander.

Eating out is a tradition of these middle-class immigrants. Cuban men in Havana socialized and did business in restaurants and cafés and on Sundays took the whole family out for a walk and dinner. Restaurants are still a big part of the male Cuban world, though Cuban women are no longer necessarily regarded as intruders.

Victor's Café 54, *236 West 52nd Street (212-586-7714). Sunday–Thursday noon–midnight; Friday, Saturday noon–1 A.M.*

When Victor's opened this big glossy restaurant on 52nd Street, leaving behind its more Bohemian Upper West Side location, New York's restaurant snobs scoffed as if this Victor were selling out and going tourist commercial. Actually this is the resaurant of choice for Cubans in the *colonia* in New Jersey; it is that special restaurant where Cuban families celebrate. Victor's Café 54 is Cuba before Castro with a string orchestra playing *danzon* music. Don't think about the corn tamales or *ropa vieja;* it is a place for lobster in *salsa verde* (a sauce of parsley and herbs).

Sabor, *20 Cornelia Street (212-243-9579). Daily 6 P.M.–11 P.M.*

Sabor is New York Cuban before Castro. The restaurant has ceiling fans and folkloric baskets on the walls and tries to look Cuban exotic, as if there never had been a Cuban airlift or Mariel. It's Cuban rum cocktails with little umbrellas and a watery *gazpacho* and a *ropa vieja* that tastes like rope.

Floridita, *3451 Broadway at 141st Street (212-281-1500). Daily 6 P.M.–1 A.M.*

The Floridita is attractive, glassed-in luxury on the Upper West Side, the flagship restaurant of the Floridita Cuban restaurant group. It is a place to relax and listen to Cuban *Son* on the state-of-the-art sound system and eat Cuban simple. It is black beans and rice and fried plantain Cuban. It is a place to order Cuban pot roast or stewed *bacalao* (salt cod).

The Other Cubans

Introduction

During World War I there were a hundred thousand Chinese living in Cuba, mostly working on the sugar plantations. But immigration restrictions reduced the numbers until there were only twenty-five thousand in 1960. These Chinese were thoroughly Cuban and in many ways had adapted to Cuban culture.

When Castro started to put socialism into practice, the Chinese merchants and businesspeople joined the airlift in 1960. Though they represented only a tiny percentage of the Cuban population, they made up 2 percent of the first series of airlifts from 1960 to 1962.

Five thousand Cuban Chinese settled in New York. They were spread out from Washington Heights in Manhattan to Jackson Heights in Queens to downtown Brooklyn. The Cuban Chinese in New York are trilingual, speaking Spanish, Chinese, and English with equal fluency. While they have kept their Chinese surnames, they have adopted Spanish first names.

The younger Cuban Chinese identify more with their Hispanic background and many intermarry with Cubans as they did before they left Cuba. But there is also an older Cuban Chinese generation who view themselves as being more Chinese and identify with their Buddhist heritage.

Oriente Oriental

Many Cuban Chinese went into the restaurant business when they came to the city, offering a menu that gave equal time to the Cuban and the Cantonese. The restaurants were a fad in the 1960s and became part of the landscape in the 1970s. In the 1980s they have fared best in Hispanic neighborhoods like the Upper West Side and the Bronx Concourse. In gentrifying areas like Chelsea, they have practically disappeared.

Asia de Cuba, *190 Eighth Avenue between 19th and 20th Streets (212-243-9322). Daily 11:30 A.M.–midnight.*

Asia de Cuba wasn't the first Cuban Chinese restaurant in New York, but it was the one to introduce Cuban Chinese to trendy eaters in the 1960s. The restaurant started out small and simple and cheap and wound up taking reservations. It still does special things with sweet and sour pork, and it's fun to end a Chinese meal with a Cuban coconut cream cheese dessert.

La Victoria China Restaurant, *2532 Broadway at 95th Street (212-865-1810). Daily 11:30 A.M.–11:30 P.M.*

The restaurant has been attracting young people on the West Side for the past thirty years. It is one Cuban Chinese that gets as big a play for the Cuban food as the Oriental. The *chicharron de pollo* is a Hispanic version of Chicken McNuggets with the spice of coriander and garlic.

═══════ Latin Jackson Heights ═══════

Directions: IRT-Flushing line 7 from 42nd Street to 82nd Street.

History

Jackson Heights, a slow starter at the beginning of the twentieth century, was known as the "cornfield of Queens." In 1906 the Queensboro Corporation designated a hundred blocks of Jackson Heights farmland for development. The corporation had the intention of attracting high-income Manhattanites.

The forward-looking project combined architectural styles from English Tudor to neo-Spanish. The large apartment houses had landscaped court-yards and the individual apartments had fireplaces and cathedral ceilings. The Jackson Heights houses were some of the city's first cooperatives.

In 1917 Jackson Heights was no longer a backwater, but connected to Manhattan by the IRT elevated line along Roosevelt Avenue. Five years later it became the first area in Queens to be serviced by Manhattan's Fifth Avenue bus line.

The Queensboro Corporation cashed in on the real estate boom of the 1920s and started to sell off its Jackson Heights acres. Development was no longer tightly controlled and planned parks and open spaces were shelved. In the 1930s it managed to remain a model middle-class garden community with golf courses and tennis courts.

Major changes came to Jackson Heights when the tiny North Beach Airport was converted into a major transcontinental terminal and renamed

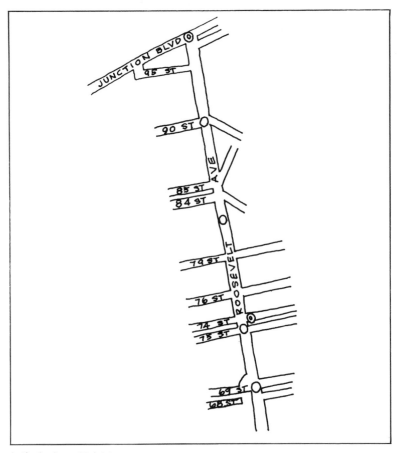

Latin Jackson Heights

La Guardia in 1947. By the time the airport grew to 650 acres, Jackson Heights gardens were concrete.

The neighborhood was solidly Irish and Italian ethnic in the 1940s and 1950s; it was working-class and second-generation with middle-class aspirations. As the neighborhood started to lose its glow and bodyshops replaced groceries, the ethnics relocated to the Long Island suburbs.

Argentinians were the first to claim Jackson Heights for the Latins in the 1960s. They were refugees of runaway inflation and unstable government. When Cuban exiles came to New York by the thousands escaping Castro collectivism, Jackson Heights was a comfortable Latin option.

Though there were older Irish and Italian holdovers, the neighborhood was shifting to young-family Hispanic. When the affluent Argentinians dispersed to Forest Hills and Rego Park, Colombians were the next new Latins on the block and the Peruvians and Ecuadorians were waiting in the wings.

Roosevelt Avenue and Junction Boulevard are the real New York Avenues of the Americas. One Latin American nation succeeds another: there is an Argentinian deli, a Colombian nightclub, a Cuban luncheonette, and a Peruvian takeout. The newsstands carry papers from every nation in South America. The parochial schools are administered by the Spanish Apostolate.

Colombians

Introduction

Colombians are among the latest Latin Americans on the New York scene. They came in the hundreds to New York at the end of World War I. They were solid middle-class accountants, technicians, nurses, and pharmacists on the lookout for economic opportunity. Over the years, Colombians staked out a community in Jackson Heights, an area offering good middle-income housing and easy access to the Manhattan job market.

The numbers of Colombians coming to New York multiplied in the era of "La Violencia." From 1945 to 1955 Colombia was a killing field—guerrilla bands ran rampant, and government troops were out of control. The peasants took refuge in the town and when the overcrowding and the unemployment became impossible, they emigrated to the Venezuelan oil boom and ultimately to New York.

The exodus was amazing—3 or 4 percent of the population was leaving annually. The trend continued into the 1970s with Colombian unemployment sky-high and the cost of air flights to New York relatively low. Many of the emigrants left unwillingly as a matter of economic necessity, and some who came to New York were undocumented.

Though Colombians put down roots in the city, they kept their attachment to their homeland. The newsstands of Jackson Heights carry five Colombian dailies. Many Colombians would like to think they are only temporary New Yorkers. The monotonous factory and warehouse jobs that they perform are viewed simply as a means to make a new life in Colombia. Unlike other recent immigrants, they are reluctant to become naturalized citizens.

The next generation of Colombians are learning about their heritage in Spanish parochial schools. They speak Spanish with a Colombian accent, which is considered the best in Latin America, and read Colombian books and listen to Colombian music. Colombians are still not ready to assimilate.

New York Colombians have even won the right to vote here in their own national elections. The campaigns are hard-fought on the streets of Jackson Heights. In 1975 the president of Colombia, Lopez Michelsen, made a special trip to the United States to speak to his countrymen assembled at the

Americana Hotel in Manhattan. He was acknowledging his debt to these absentee voters.

There are estimates that there are up to three hundred thousand Colombians in Jackson Heights. They are currently the largest Hispanic group there and sections of the Heights bear a resemblance to Colombian Cali or Medellin. Colombians own the majority of Jackson Heights businesses.

There are signs on Roosevelt Avenue advertising Colombian *speciales* in Spanish and Colombians eat *speciales* in Colombian restaurants while watching videos of Colombian variety shows. Every year the whole Colombian community turns out for soccer Colombian style when their local "Medellin" teams play. Two correspondents for Colombian newspapers cover the happenings in the Jackson Heights colony.

The Colombian neighborhood, which centers around 82nd Street and Roosevelt Avenue, is called "Chapinero" in honor of a middle-class Bogota suburb. The Colombians are gregarious, out-of-the-house people. The restaurants, bars, and even the travel agencies along the *avenida* are informal social clubs. The gestures and rhythms are slightly slower and more reserved than earlier Hispanic arrivals, but the gusto, the pure pleasure in living, and enjoying, is evident.

Montañero and More

Colombian cooking is hearty eating, part South American and part Spanish Conquistador. The *Arepes* (cornmeal tortillas) and *hallacas* (tamales) steamed in plantain leaves are pure Indian enhanced by Spanish fillings like *Chorizo* (pork sausage) flavored by garlic, onion, and culantro. Spanish meal-in-a-dish soups are fleshed out with indigenous root vegetables: yucca, yams, and plantain in a dish called *Sancocho*. Big Colombian appetites on Roosevelt Avenue opt for the *Montañero,* a mountain of food combining ground chuck, fried pork, and avocado, all topped by a fried egg.

Los Arrieros, *76-02 Roosevelt Avenue (718-898-3359). Daily noon–1 A.M.*

Colombian friendliness shines along with the simple dishes served in Las Arrieros. The simple empanadas are always good with coffee for just a snack.

Chibcha Restaurant, *79-05 Roosevelt Avenue (718-429-9033). Wednesday–Sunday 6 P.M.–4 A.M.*

The Chibcha is a popular watering hole for the Colombian open-shirt-and-gold-chain set. They come for the Cali bands and the top-choice *bistec* (beefsteak).

La Pequena Colombia, *85-08 Roosevelt Avenue (718-478-6528). Daily 9 P.M.–midnight.*

The workday over, groups of young men, sharp-eyed and Colombian, unwind around the table. They ahve to catch their breath but it's not from fatigue, it's La Pequena Colombia's *aji pique*. It's a hot sauce that really sizzles on a flaky Colombian cornmeal empanada.

Cali Viejo, *84-24 Roosevelt Avenue (718-898-9812).*

Cali Viejo II, *73-10 Roosevelt Avenue (718-424-9812). Daily 11 A.M.–10 P.M.*

Cali Viejo I and II are gourmet Colombian in casual surroundings. The dishes themselves are far from delicate but the preparation is flawless. Even if it's just an *arepe* (cornmeal tortilla) wrapped around a *chorizo* (spicy sausage), it's perfection. The tamales and empanadas draw food sophisticates from Manhattan.

The Others

Colombians dominate Jackson Heights, but there is a sampler of other Hispanic nationalities who are growing in size or have already left the neighborhood. Their restaurants and shops dot Roosevelt Avenue.

La Cabana Argentina, *95-51 Roosevelt Avenue (718-429-4388). Daily 3:30 P.M.–11 P.M.*

La Cabana is a typical Argentinian restaurant with the grilling as the floor show. The secret of the mixed grill is the marinade and quality *churasco* (flank steak) and spicy *chorizo*. The chicken and meat empanadas are flaky, melt-in-the-mouth pastry.

El Sitio Restaurant, *68-28 Roosevelt Avenue (718-424-2369). Monday–Thursday, Sunday 10 A.M.–1 A.M.; Friday 10 A.M.–3 A.M.; Saturday 10 A.M.–4 A.M.*

The new owner is from Spain and it is evident in the savory *arroz con pollo* (chicken and rice) and the Spanish-style tortillas, a moist omelet with a mashed-potato taste. But it still continues its Cuban tradition with dishes like *ropa vieja* (stewed shredded beef).

La Nusta, *90-01 Roosevelt Avenue (718-429-8401). Wednesday–Sunday noon–9 P.M.*

La Nusta has a way with seafood. Their shrimp dishes are delicious, with the spicy touches of coriander and pepper that are characteristic of Peruvian food.

Brazilians

Introduction

Since the 1960s New York Brazilian is multinational big business or poor undocumented alien. The extremes of Brazilian society are reflected in the city's Brazilian emigrants. There are the business school graduates and conquistador descendants from Rio de Janeiro and Brasília and the peasants from Belo Horizonte.

When the Brazilian economy went austerity with a multibillion-dollar debt, the poor undocumented Brazilians began to outnumber the affluent. The Regine types are staying home while the men and women of Mineiros are working—in the city's restaurants, on construction projects, and in shoe repair shops shining shoes.

Though the Brazilians are limited in numbers, they have a large and influential musical population that keeps New York current with Brazilian jazz and samba and the latest dance craze like the Lambada. Some of Brazil's top stars, like the jazz singer Flora Purim and the group Airto, are practically permanent Manhattanites.

The more mundane elements of the Brazilian population are widely scattered through the five boroughs. Though they don't have a significant presence, things Brazilian have caught the city's fancy. It is something very basic and very open that strikes the right chord. Brazil is all about desire and the senses and a spirit that is part pagan and pure play. It is life lived as a carnival to the insistent rhythm of the samba even if tomorrow's an early breakfast and a business meeting at the Plaza.

On 46th Street (and a sliver of 45th) between Fifth and Seventh Avenues, the Brazilians have staked several claims to restaurants and retail stores. It is the closest they come to a neighborhood.

Feijoada Plus

Brazilian cooking is a combination of Portuguese, Aftican, and Amazon Indian. The Portuguese brought over the salt cod and took the local shellfish and steeped it in sauces of wine, tomato, and garlic. The Indians and Africans added the subtropical beans, fruits, and vegetables. The *caldo verde* is Brazil's most popular soup. The chicken stock is green with kale and collard greens and thick with potatoes and sausage.

The national dish is *feijoada* with various meats, including beef tongue, dried beef, *chorizo* (sausage), pig's trotters, and slab bacon cooked with black beans and mixed with rice and garnished with manioc and orange slices. In the northern region of Bahia there are African flavors of hot peppers and coconut milk with seafood. In cosmopolitan Rio de Janeiro, beef and pork are seasoned with onions, garlic, tomato, and coriander.

Most of the area's restaurants have been around a while and have proved themselves to their native clientele. One has to wonder whether they have become complacent or the regulars less demanding. The food's not bad, just not inspired. But whether the food is magnificent or mediocre, Brazilian diners are animated to the point of being hyperactive. They like life frenetic and the restaurants can get high-decibel.

Brazilian Coffee Restaurant, *45 West 46th Street (212-768-2766). Sunday–Friday noon–10 P.M.; Saturday noon–11 P.M.*

The Brazilian Coffee Restaurant has the most authentic *feijoada* in the city with enough pig's ears and pig's tails to delight the *feijoada* aficionado. Too bad it's only a Wednesday and Saturday special.

Cabana Carioca, *123 West 45th Street (212-581-8088). Daily noon–11 P.M.*

Cabana Carioca is a one-flight-up restaurant with gaudy Brazilian painting and loud Brazilian diners. It's tropical sunshine and a joyful noise and though the tables are a little close together, it's easy to get used to. The *camarao frito* is delicious and light even with the shrimp deep fried in white wine and garlic sauce. The *bacalhau a braz* is what rich peasant food is made of, with salt cod, black olives, onions, eggs, and potatoes.

Via Brazil, *34 East 46th Street (212-997-1158). Daily 11 A.M.– midnight.*

Via Brazil is Brazilian mahogany trim and water colors on white walls and samba in the background. The restaurant serves a very special African-Brazilian *maquecas,* fish stew with tomatoes and coconut milk. The salt cod *maqueca* is better than the more expensive lobster and shrimp.

Brazilian Shopping

The resident Brazilian population comes to 46th Street to do its shopping—get the Rio newspapers, buy manioc to sprinkle over *feijoada,* and get the latest Baden-Powell guitar album. The stores are plain but the people are interesting.

Coisa Nossa, *57 West 46th Street (212-719-4770). Monday–Saturday 9 A.M.–7 P.M.*

Brazilians come here for papers and magazines and conversation. There's also a good selection of Brazilian music and videos.

Latin American Products, *142 West 46th Street (212-302-4323). Monday–Saturday 9 A.M.–7 P.M.; Sunday 10 A.M.–3 P.M., but often until 6 P.M.*

The name is not exactly inspired, but it does sell Latin American products with the emphasis on the Brazilian. This is the place to get all the fixings for a *feijoada.*

Carnival on 46th Street

New York Brazilians celebrate their Independence Day on the first Saturday in September. The city closes 46th Street to traffic and the samba takes over from nine in the morning to nine at night. The Brazilians like to party and they do it full throttle. Man, woman, and child are possessed by the drum and possessed by the samba. Though the amateur dancers steal the show, there are professional singers and musicians performing Brazilian jazz and bossa nova on a stage at the Avenue of the Americas corner.

It's difficult to move through the dancers and the press of people to the stalls and stands lining 46th Street. But what's a little inconvenience in a carnival? The neighborhood's Brazilian restaurants have taken to the streets, serving heaping portions of *feijoada.* There are also Brazilian carvings and brightly colored papier-mâché figures for sale, along with the T-shirts and buttons that inevitably appear at any ethnic event. They close with the American and Brazilian national anthems.

Little Spain in Chelsea

Directions: IND Sixth Avenue D or F or Eighth Avenue A or E to 14th Street.

History

In 1750, Captain Thomas Clarke was a merchant seaman who earned enough on the high seas to occupy an estate that covered the present area from 14th Street to 24th Street and Eighth Avenue to the Hudson River. He named it Chelsea in honor of the Soldier's Hospital in London.

His grandson, Clement Moore, who spent his time preparing Greek lexicons and writing verse like the "Night Before Christmas," closely supervised Chelsea's residential development. Every house had a ten-foot setback, and stables and alleys were strictly forbidden.

The Hudson River Railroad shattered Chelsea's suburban calm and soon the neighborhood was glue factories and slaughterhouses. In 1871 the Ninth Avenue El completed the destruction of society Chelsea and Irish immigrants with Tammany connections took over.

Before the turn of the century, Spanish seaman from the poor northern province of Galicia settled in New York near the Hudson River waterfront from 14th Street to 23rd Street. In a more carefree age they traveled back and forth between Spain and New York, raising families and operating businesses on shore leave. Though the colony was small in numbers, it had the closeness of a Spanish village and the people formed many organizations, from workingmen's clubs to merchants' associations.

New York's Spanish population had an active cultural life. The millionaire philanthropist, Archer M. Huntington, founded the Hispanic Society in 1904, providing Spanish New Yorkers with a first-rate Spanish museum and library. Huntington brought over great figures in Spanish culture, such as critic Ramon Mendez Pidal and scholar Federico de Onis.

In the 1920s Spanish political refugees came to New York in increasing numbers. They were democrats and anarchists and socialists who couldn't live under the military dictatorship of Primo Rivera. The new Spanish emigrants had their own theater and magazine; guitarist Segovia gave concerts and poet Frederico García Lorca gave readings.

The Spanish Civil War brought more Spanish refugees to New York and the Spaniards for a brief time were the dominant Hispanic group in the city. Fourteenth Street was their "Great White Way," with twelve Spanish restaurants and numerous Spanish food stores and bookstores. Flamenco guitars and dancers were a nightly event, and Casa Moneo was the city's Spanish supermarket and all-purpose bazaar. Latins from both hemispheres browsed its aisles.

New York Bohemians in the 1960s tried to turn Chelsea into another Greenwich Village, and Little Spain started to look passé. Meanwhile, the younger Spanish and Galician generation weren't interested in local color and left for suburban comfort and safety. The rising real estate costs of the gentrifying 1980s completed the change from Little Spain to trendy Chelsea.

Chelsea's Spanish era is over, but a 14th Street remnant remains.

Galician Cooking

Manhattan cuisines come and go, one year it's barbecue spareribs and the next it's nouvelle cuisine, and overnight it changes from chow mein to pasta. While the food fads play musical chairs, Galician/Spanish cooking has held its own on 14th Street, The food is uncomplicated garlic and oil and *salsa verde* (a piquant sauce with basil and greens), Spanish seafood and *paella* (saffron rice with shellfish or chicken and *chorizo*). It is too much back to basics for eaters to ever get jaded. Lately food snobs from the Upper East Side have been coming down here, "slumming" for budget lobster.

Spain Restaurant, *113 West 13th Street (212-929-9580). Monday–Saturday noon–1 A.M.; Sunday 3 P.M.–1 A.M.*

The restaurant is old-days' Galician. The only thing not casual about the Spain is the red awning. The waiters are absentminded but friendly. The shrimp and the langosta (crayfish) in the *salsa verde* are the light at the end of this tunnel.

Meson Toledo Restaurant, *318 West 23rd Street (212-691-0529). Daily noon–midnight.*

The Meson Toledo is giant two-and-quarter-pound lobster at lobster tail prices. Somehow seafood that is a struggle to eat makes people more congenial, and the Meson Toledo is at its best in a big group. A pound-and-a-quarter lobster in tomato, garlic, or green sauce is one of life's small Spanish pleasures.

Nueva España

The Spain of the post-Franco economic boom has its headquarters in the high-rent districts of Manhattan. It's a Spain of chic stores and highbrow culture. Manhattan Latins go the opera to see Placido Domingo and attend a private showing of Velazquez. It's part of a new Spain that includes a Socialist prime minister King Juan Carlos.

The Spaniards are masters of fine finished leathers in shoes and bags and small accessories. They have won the low-end of the market away from the Italians and are now working on the upper.

J. S. Suarez, *26 West 54th Street (212-315-5614-5). Monday 10 A.M.–5 P.M.; Tuesday–Saturday 10 A.M.–6 P.M.*

The shop goes back to the 1960s when Suarez father and son had their first place in the Empire State Building—"a lifetime ago." Noted for copies of designer bags—Hermes and Gucci, among others—they also design their own very elegant models. High fashion for the ladies who lunch.

Farrutx, *456A West Broadway (212-473-4349). Monday–Saturday 11 A.M.–7 P.M.; Sunday noon–6 P.M.*

The name may be unpronounceable, but the Spanish shoes for men and women are high-priced couture for New York trendsetters. Sybilla is their avant-garde designer who approaches shoes like an abstract sculpture. The thousand-square-foot retail space is part of the flash and fun image.

Loewe, *711 Madison Ave. (212-308-7700). Monday–Saturday 10 A.M.–6 P.M.; Sunday 10 A.M.–5:30 P.M.*

Loewe is the leading leather shop on Madrid's "Gran Via", its Fifth Avenue. On New York's Madison, it's winning a wealthy following for its beautiful leather bags, accessories, and clothes. The salesgirls are all Spanish-speaking, and fine Castilian is spoken by its Spanish clientele. It's a worthy if expensive competitor for Italian leather goods.

Place Marks

Spanish culture spans the ages from El Greco to Picasso, from a Gothic church to Gaudi church. Despite a culture that sometimes seems too traditional, Spaniards are great innovators. Cervantes created the novel and Dali invented surrealism. New York has its own outposts of Spanish culture.

Spanish Institute, *684 Park Avenue at 68th Street (212-628-0420). Daily 11 A.M.–6 P.M. Call for times of special events.*

The Spanish Institute is housed in a neo-Federalist wonder designed by Stanford White's architectural firm. The elegant building draws the visitor inside to see elegantly mounted exhibits of Spanish painters and sculptors.

There are lectures in an upstairs drawing room concerning serious developments in Spanish arts and Spanish history. The elegant library has the feel of a fashionable club. It is a private nonprofit organization that offers educational fellowships and prizes.

Casa de España, *308 East 39th Street (212-689-4232).*

The Spanish government sponsors this cultural *casa* in a Spanish country-style stucco building. Inside, the rooms have heavy Spanish furnishings and Spanish wrought iron on the windows. It's just the right setting for exhibits of Spanish art and films and videos. The Casa attracts the Spanish Consulate crowd and the cab driver from Galicia or Asturias and New York Spanophiles.

Fiesta de Santiago Apostole

For four days at the end of July Little Spain celebrates the festival of Spain's patron saint, St. James the Apostle. It is a nostalgic return to a Spanish past, with a procession carrying the shrine of St. James and an open-air mass. There are booths with Spanish souvenirs—mostly about bulls and Seville—and food stands with *tapas* (Spanish snacks—bits of Spanish omelet and chorizo).

The Church of Our Lady of Guadalupe, which was the first New York church to be part of the Spanish Apostolate, is the setting for the grand fiesta. The stands and the stalls and the games of chance and the portable stage with entertainment are outside the church door on 229 West 14th Street between Seventh and Eighth Avenues. While the church has Spanish masses and Spaniards in the congregation, it is actually dedicated to the patron saint of Mexico.

The fiesta is sponsored by the Little Spain Merchants' Association, which does nice things for the neighborhood like plant trees. Señor Joe Castro is the president of the organization and the neighborhood's unofficial historian.

══════ Hispanic Manhattan ══════

Introduction

In recent years New York had been the objective of an all-Hispanic landing. It's become as a consequence a New York Organization of American States with small groups and individuals from South and Central America and the Spanish Caribbean. They haven't the numbers as yet to create an impression or profile. They are too ill-defined to have stamped their identity on the city. But they have added a new string to the New York guitar with a Latin taste or store or even an item in a shop. Some of these ethnics in time will have their own parade or institute and others, maybe the majority, will be assimilated into the New York melting pot.

Hispanic Imports

Hispanic imports are mostly handicrafts and folkloric costumes. There are toys and masks and carvings and baskets. There are sweaters and blouses and ponchos. The stores are usually labors of love for the owners, who have visited the countries and met the people.

Clothes

Putumayo, *857 Lexington Avenue at 64th Street (212-734-3111). Monday–Saturday 11 A.M.–7 P.M.; Sunday noon–5 P.M. 339 Columbus Avenue (212-595-3441). 147 Spring Street (212-966-4458). Both Monday–Saturday 11 A.M.–8 P.M.; Sunday noon–6 P.M.*

Putumayo is folk Mexican ceramic candlesticks in bright colors and a Guatemalan coat of many colors. It is South American gift items and South American casual clothes, machine- and hand-made.

Pan American Phoenix, *153 East 53rd Street (212-355-0590). Monday–Friday 10:30 A.M.–6:30 P.M.; Saturday 10 A.M.–6 P.M.*

This long-time resident of the Citycorp Center has a selection of Mexican and Latin American clothes and accessories as well as hand-worked figures, ceramics, and silver jewelry. This crowded store on the main floor can easily be missed, but not to be missed are the beautiful cotton pleated wedding dresses.

Back from Guatemala, *306 East 6th Street (212-260-7010). Monday–Thursday noon–11 P.M.; Friday, Saturday noon–midnight; Sunday 2 P.M.–10 P.M.*

Back from Guatemala is crafts and clothes from thirty-five countries, including large parts of Latin America. The handmade wall hangings and puppets are among the more unusual items. Everything from the Andes to the Rio Grande is chosen with care and affection.

Hispanic Books

Hispanic books and letters are the world's leaders. While other literatures are standing still, the Hispanics are creating new styles and experimenting. The Hispanic Renaissance includes a Marquez, Fuentes, and a Vargas-Llosa in one generation.

Libreria Hispanica, *610 Fifth Avenue between 49th and 50th Streets (212-581-8810). Monday–Saturday 10 A.M.–6:15 P.M. 115 Fifth Avenue at 19th Street (212-673-7400). Monday–Saturday 10 A.M.–6 P.M.*

The selection of Hispanic books, newspapers, and magazines is outstanding. The clerks know their stuff, whether it's bestsellers or high art.

Place Marks

Hispanic Society of America Museum, *Audubon Terrace, Broadway and 155th Street (212-690-0743). Tuesday–Saturday 10 A.M.– 4:30 P.M.; Sunday 1 A.M.–4 P.M. Free.*

The Hispanic Society is a testament to Archer M. Huntington and his passion for Hispanic culture. The museum is pure Spanish magnificence with terra cotta floors and two-story skylights and Valencian tapestries. Its impressive collection of Spanish paintings includes Goya, El Greco, and Velazquez and it also has fine examples of Latin American art. The Hispanic Society has a library dedicated to Hispanic culture with a hundred thousand manuscripts and books.

Americas Society, *680 Park Avenue at 67th Street (212-249-8950). Tuesday–Sunday noon–6 P.M. Contribution.*

The main gallery exhibits the whole range of Latin American art from pre-Columbian to contemporary. Peruvian weaving is side by side with Brazilian photographs. In Latin America, folk arts and fine arts coexist with ease.

Repertorio Español, *138 East 27th Street (212-889-2850).*

Repertorio Español is the theater of Spain and the theater of Latin America with adaptations of foreign theatrical works into Spanish. The company bridges the centuries between Calderon and Lorca and also does contemporary musical comedies. The city's Latin American wordsmiths contribute plays dealing with current issues.

Hispanic-American Day

Hispanic-American Day falls on the Sunday closest to Columbus Day, with the Hispanics getting equal time with the Italians, who have their parade on Monday.

The Hispanic parade attracts a Hispanic cross section from slight, almond-eyed Hondurans to round-faced, copper-skinned Mexicans to lean, eagle-eyed Argentinians. The new Hispanics come in families with thermoses and sandwiches to stand for hours until their country strides up the Avenue. At that moment any shyness disappears and their eyes gaze with recognition and pride as they shout greetings and encouragement in Spanish.

Even with such a diversity of groups and affiliations, the organizers have kept the parade uniquely nonpolitical. The only political statements are nonspoken, like the uniformed anti-Castro Cubans marching with Cuban flags.

The parade is a full-scale organization of American states. They march up Fifth Avenue from 44th Street to 79th Street in national dress and dance down the Avenue to their national music. The costumes are theatrical and wildly colorful: Bolivians in turned-up-brim hats and striped blankets kick up their heels with bells on their boots; Peruvians in devil masks and clown pants shake their arms like witch doctors; Cubans wearing Stetson hats and chaps gallop by on horses. The parade is organized in alphabetical order, beginning with Argentina and ending with Uruguay. It is the longest parade of the year.

The Asians

Introduction

The Asians are New York City's new immigrant achievers. The city's Chinese, Vietnamese, Korean, and Indian newcomers are filling the ranks of the professions and creating successful businesses. These Asians are high-profile New Yorkers, treating patients in city hospitals and serving customers in retail businesses and restaurants. The family-oriented Asians are passing the torch to the next generation, who are winning places in the city's prestigious high schools. In two decades they have made the leap from crowded city streets to the suburbs.

Chinese

History

In the early part of the eighteeth century, the Chinese Emperor forbade emigration under penalty of death. Later, in the early part of the nineteenth century, the imperial government lifted its restrictions in the era of the Chinese "open door" policy, enabling the poor rural populations of south China to cross the Pacific to California in time for the Gold Rush.

Caught between rural poverty and an expanding population and pressed by the high taxes of an arbitrary imperial government, the southern Chinese were forced to emigrate. They didn't intend to settle in the American West or a northeastern Chinatown; they just wanted to support their families and have enough left over to buy land in their ancestral village.

At the time the Chinese were building the western section of the transcontinental railroad and working the mines of the Far West, Chinese were a novelty in New York. The Chinese sailor who jumped ship or the Chinese acrobat on the New York stage were objects of wide-eyed wonder. Crowds collected around a Chinese junk that landed in New York harbor. P. T. Barnum literally put Chinese on display in the carnival sideshow he called the American Museum.

Public opinion on the West Coast abruptly changed in the 1870s. The Chinese, who had been viewed as model workers and model citizens, were now the "Yellow Menace." Demagogues East and West called for the abrogation of the Burlingame Act of 1868, which gave Chinese the right to work and live in America.

Anti-Chinese sentiment in the West led to restrictive local legislation. Chinese were forced out of jobs and off the land. They were physically attacked and their homes and businesses were burned. Finally, the federal government responded by passing the Chinese Exclusion Act of 1882, which barred the entrace of Chinese laborers.

Chinese went east in search of work (frequently limited to laundries) and the solace of a closed Chinese community. In New York, a "China Town" grew up in the garrets and cellars of Lower Manhattan. The neighborhood was self-sufficient, people worked in their own restaurants, curio shops, laundries, and garment workshops. They consciously refused to compete with the white population of the city. They were suspicious of Anglo-Saxon justice; they made their own agreements and settled their own disputes.

In 1890 New York's three thousand Chinese existed outside the usual channels of city government and society. They were isolated by their language, an alien culture, and discrimination. The federal government's restrictive immigration and naturalization policies created a mainly male community where families could never be reunited.

It was an uneventful existence with many single men crowded into small rooms. The literate read histories and novels and threw the I Ching. Others gambled at *f'an t'an, mah jong,* or *bok-a-bou* in back rooms hidden behind restaurants and stores. But mostly they talked over endless cups of tea about homes and villages they would never see again. The money they sent overseas kept their families alive and paved the streets and built many schools in Kwangtung and Fukien.

The bachelor society of Chinatown depended on a network of organizations to provide the lost world of family and place for these "birds of passage'' who could no longer fly home. Family associations, district associations, and the secret societies were the main sources of community.

Family associations like the Lees and Wangs helped the elderly and the unemployed and provided credit. District associations were also involved in community welfare, working with people from a particular geographical area of China. They also were the key organizers of traditional Chinese observances like the Moon Festival and Chinese New Year.

The secret societies in China offered some recourse to the all-encompassing state and a position in the world for the dispossessed. In New York the Tongs had an unsavory reputation for criminal activity, but they did supply the isolated people of Chinatown with traditional distractions like gambling, which were legal in their own country. In 1933 they signed a truce in the consul general's office, putting an end to the periodic clashes over territorial control.

While Chinese laborers were forbidden to enter the United States, merchants were not barred by the Chinese Exclusion Act, and many ordinary Chinese presented themselves as merchants to the immigration authorities in order to enter the country. Chinese also came into the country falsely as children who were conceived during an overseas visit.

Despite stories spread by the tabloid press about Chinese hatchetmen and white slavery, the Chinese community was generally safe and stable by the 1920s. The Chinese Consolidated Benevolent Association (CCBA) in the city brought together many disparate elements in the community and created unity in a hostile world. The Confucian concept of harmony reigned.

Even Tongs that competed for Chinatown spoils now donned the mantle of respectable merchant associations, the On Leung and Hip Sing, and sat on the board of the CCBA together.

The whole complex CCBA organization was reorganized in 1940 to meet the challenges of a wartime situation. The officials of the CCBA represented commercial, family, and governmental Chinese interests. They were mostly from Toishan, one of ninety-eight Kwangtung districts, but they maintained a fair distribution of power by alternating the chairmanship with other groups.

In this same era, other types of organizations were formed to deal directly with the Occidental world. The Chinese-American Citizens Alliance took legal action against discriminatory legislation, while the Chinese Laundry Association fought whisper campaigns against Chinese businesses. The National Chinese Welfare Council lobbied against the deportation of Chinese aliens.

Although in 1880 only 3 percent of Chinese were east of the Rockies, by 1940 it was up to 40 percent, and the second largest concentration of Chinese were in New York. There was also a new element in New York's Chinatown, a class of Chinese professionals, engineers, and scientists, who were stranded in the country by the surprise Japanese invasion of 1937.

They became the foundation for a new Chinese middle class. These high-achieving Chinese first became a statistic in 1940, when it was reported that Chinese had the highest proportion of high school graduates in the city to go on to college.

Once China and America were allied in World War II, attitudes toward the Chinese changed and bigotry subsided. In 1943 discriminatory laws were lifted and Chinese G.I. brides were eligible to become naturalized. After the war, the eight thousand Chinese who had worn the uniform of a country that didn't recognize their right to be citizens were granted permanent citizenship.

The Chinese were no longer regarded by the government as innately alien to American values and were allowed modest immigration quotas. The Chinese who came to New York on these quotas were mainly middle-class and professional and many had close ties to the Nationalist Chinese on Taiwan. While this elite entered New York legally, thousands of undocumented Chinese were smuggled into the city to work in restaurant kitchens and garment sweatshops.

The Hart-Celler Act of 1965 abolished the old national origins quotas and Chinese immigrants for the first time in eighty-five years were put on a par with other groups entering the country. Chinese from all levels of society, rich and poor, skilled and unskilled, flocked to New York.

The new immigrants differed from their Chinatown forebears; they were urban Chinese from Hong Kong and Taiwan who may have originally come from northern China and Shanghai. The newcomers came with families, wives, and children, and from the beginning were committed to the United States. They were Westernized and prepared to follow the American dream.

These Chinese were no longer willing to live passively outside the mainstream. They became involved in the "War on Poverty" and worked with the Chinatown Planning Council to get funds for employment, housing, legal aid, and education programs. They protested against the war in Viet Nam and even staged their own Mao-style cultural revolution to protest the community's conservative leadership.

In 1974 Chinatown activists had their greatest victory. They organized protests against a city building project in their own neighborhood that had not one Chinese employee. They closed down the Confucius Plaza construction site until the unions promised to hire forty Asian-Americans.

Young Chinese immigrants from Hong Kong, who could not cope with the New York education system and confronted unemployment and dead-end jobs, joined gangs like the Ghost Shadows and Flying Dragons. They became involved in the latest protection rackets, and Chinese gang violence was again on the front pages of New York's tabloids.

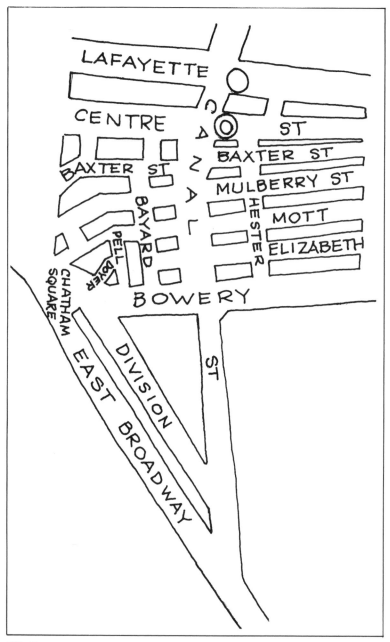

Chinatown

Despite the publicity, the gangs were primarily an extension of the old Tongs and membership was never large. The community has learned to stand up to this threat, which doesn't seem half as dangerous as the current trend to gentrification. The real story of Chinese youth in the community is about merit scholarships and the awards for excellence in science and math. It is the high number of Chinese students who win slots every year in New York's elite schools like the Bronx High School of Science.

The 1980 census estimated the Chinese population in New York to be just over 150,000. This included 80,000 Chinese in Chinatown and communities spread out through downtown Brooklyn and Sunset Park, and the Queen's neighborhoods of Jackson Heights, Flushing, and Elmhurst.

The Chinese who are moving to the suburbs, like earlier ethnics, are upwardly mobile. They are architects following in the footsteps of I. M. Pei and financial experts emulating Dr. Gerald Tsai. They are accountants for the IRS and lawyers for the district attorney's office. They run family-owned garment factories in Manhattan and some even own Chinese restaurants.

Chinatown

Directions: IRT-Lexington Avenue 6 to Canal Street.

Introduction

When the area that became Chinatown was still British, it was known as the Plow and Harrow district in honor of a seventeenth-century tavern. In American New York it was a neighborhood of contrasts, with Federalist row houses occupied by wealthy merchants and sea captains and hovels filled with the poorest Irish immigrants. By 1858 it had its first Chinese resident, a Kwangtung merchant named Wo Kee, who made his home at 8 Mott Street.

Poor Chinese lived in the cellars and attic rooms of the damp and decaying houses on Baxter and Park (now Moscu Street) Streets. In 1870 there were twenty-nine Chinese living in the area bounded by Canal, Baxter, Worth, Park, and Bowery, which would eventually be called Chinatown. In this early era the Chinese sold cigars and papers on the streets and some even married Irish immigrants from the neighborhood. Twenty years later, there were three thousand Chinese in this densely populated enclave.

The Chinese were ''sojourners,'' isolated from a world that would not accept them. The majority were rural people from Toishan, one of ninety-eight districts in Kwangtung. They were restricted to working in laundries or restaurants or to domestic employment. The only thing that they sold outside of Chinatown were tickets to the Chinatown lottery.

In the popular press Chinatown was opium dens and white slavery. Since the ratio of Chinese men to Chinese women was on the order of two thousand to one, the absence of vice would have been surprising. The gambling and other extracurricular activities were controlled by the Tongs, who had one of their bloodiest battles at the "bend" in Doyers Street, which was dubbed the "bloody angle."

The Chinese Consolidated Benevolent Association had its headquarters on Mott Street. It was the law in Chinatown till quite recently. While it was hardly a model of legality, it was the only protection the Chinese had against a hostile outside community. It also provided the credit essential for developing Chinese institutions and businesses.

China's Prince T'sai Chen visited Chinatown in 1902 and made an impassioned speech to his people. He encouraged them to learn to speak English and practice American customs and move out of their segregated community. Despite the Prince's words, New York's Chinatown remained relatively stable.

Though there were screaming headlines about bloody Tong battles with guns and knives in 1912 Chinatown, that did not deter adventurous tourists from visiting. They nervously navigated Chinatown streets and, like present-day tourists, peered into Buddhist temples and shops selling exotic Chinese clothes and curios. They went to American-style Chinese restaurants serving chop suey, a dish of odds and ends invented in Chicago in the 1980s.

Chinatown's community of bachelors had a reputation for being passive, but Chinatown had its own civil rights organizations that were not afraid to protest. The Chinese Civil Rights League fought the extension of Chinese exclusion in the Geary Act. Later the Chinese-American Citizens Alliance campaigned in 1915 to eliminate all anti-Chinese restrictions.

In the 1930s, with war breaking out on the Chinese mainland, Chinatown made peace, with an invisible line down Mott Street dividing Tong territories. Chinatown's establishment, the CCBA, supported the Chinese Nationalists, and its local unit, the Chih Tang, was more active than Chinatown's Democratic Party. There were local Nationalist newspapers, like the *Chinese Republic* and the *Nationalist Vanguard,* and Nationalists sat on the board of the CCBA.

The increase in Chinatown's population after World War II revitalized an aging Chinese community. Gift shops and restaurants and markets multiplied. Garment factories became key contractors for New York's garment center. The women employed in these factories joined the International Ladies Garment Workers Union and the Chinese, for the first time, were part of the city's labor movement. Some of the factory owners were recent Hong Kong immigrants who started with nothing and became millionaires.

In the 1960s Chinese youths, who had been characterized as well behaved and industrious, became part of the anti-Vietnam protests. Chinatown organizations used the techniques of student protesters to fight racial discrimination in hiring and forced the construction unions to hire Chinese workers for Chinatown's Confucius Plaza project. Chinatown activism continued into the 1980s, when the community was galvanized to block the building of a correction facility.

Chinatown has grown from a community of four thousand in the 1930s to a community of eighty thousand in the 1980s. The Chinatown of shabby tourism has given way to a Chinatown of banks and shopping malls and local industry; it is prospering, with three hundred restaurants and four hundred factories; it is also booming culturally with Chinese theater companies and art galleries; and it now publishes many Chinese books and magazines and twelve Chinese newspapers.

The community has organized groups to help new immigrants from Hong Kong and Taiwan adapt. They have worked with the city through groups like the Chinatown Planning Association to provide English-language programs and vocational training for new immigrants. They have established centers to try and solve the social problems that have led to the Chinese youth gang warfare.

In recent years Chinese big business from Hong Kong has also emigrated to Chinatown. They are moving their money out of the English colony and investing in New York's Chinese colony. They have brought Hong Kong sophistication to Chinese restaurants and shops, which are now larger and glossier. While they have expanded Chinatown's horizons to include international finance, they have been buying up the neighborhood. Chinatown's real estate prices have skyrocketed and the old Chinatown image has changed.

The borders of old Chinatown have broken down and the Chinese, in a spirit of manifest destiny, have enlarged their territory. Aging Jewish and Italian ethnic enclaves and stagnating businesses have been superceded by Chinese enterprise. The Chinese are on the move: traversing Canal Street and crossing into Little Italy; breaching the Bowery and occupying the Jewish Lower East Side from East Broadway to Allen Street. Chinese retail businesses, trading companies, banks, restaurants, movie theaters, and Buddhist temples mark their progress.

The Chinatown feeling is confident; the Chinese on the streets have dropped the diffidence. They are more New York and more hurried. The new Chinese have helped the old to open up. New York slang and matter-of-fact New York mannerisms are just as common as the musical rise and fall of Cantonese. Young Chinese men and women have taken on American irreverence and dress in the latest fad styles. Chinatown is assimilating as it expands.

The Chinese Banquet

Confucius said that "Chinese food is the start of Chinese culture." More than mere nourishment, it's the scrupulous arrangement of texture, color, and flavor and the musical counterpoint of courses. It is the painstaking millennial development of the perfectly balanced taste. Chinese chefs are philosophers.

Chinese food is prepared in twenty-two ways, from stir-frying to boiling. There are braised ducks in pieces and whole fried bass. The meat and fowl and fish and vegetables for wok cooking are chopped, diced, and slivered in advance. The vegetables are very different from the Occidental table, with bean sprouts, bamboo shoots, Chinese squash, winter melons, and winter beans taking pride of place. The natural flavors are enhanced by soy, oyster, and plum sauces and accented by fermented black beans, aniseed, and coriander. Ingredients like shark fins, sea slugs, offal, tree fungi, and snake add to the variety of tastes.

Chinatown is populated with eighty thousand people and sometimes it seems to have as many restaurants. (By the latest count there are 367.) Chinese restaurants were always an important part of New York Chinese life, a link to the homeland and a link between people. The Chinese, like other immigrant groups, also found what passed for American cooking alien and unappetizing. In a time of employment restrictions, the Chinese restaurant also represented one route for economic survival.

Today Chinatown's restaurants range from the cramped and drab to multilevel Las Vegas glitz. A bowdlerized Cantonese concocted for the tourists has been superceded by authentic regional cuisines. Szechuan cooking was the first new arrival, its fiery flavors residing in red chilis. Later, there was the salty taste of the sea from Shanghai and Beijing barbecue. The mountain people called the Haaka contributed their hearty peasant fare, with meats and fowl baked in salt. Now the Hong Kong Chinese have come with their authentic Cantonese.

The price range of Chinatown restaurants is very wide. It depends on ambience, the reputation of the cuisine, and the possession of a liquor license. But even the high end is modest by Manhattan's expense-account standard.

Lately with the rise in Chinatown real estate values and the infusion of Hong Kong money, Chinese restaurants and the best Chinese chefs have been playing musical chairs. Even restaurant landmarks like the popular Say Eng Luk are not sacred.

The Chinatown restaurants start early and close late. Hours are freeform and don't conform to Occidental ideas of breakfast, lunch, and dinner. Chinatown restaurants are nonstop, up to midnight and beyond.

Peking Duck House, *22 Mott Street (212-962-8208).*

The Peking duck, crisp skin, pancake, and company is naturally the choice at the Peking Duck House. The hoisin sauce is Chinese nectar. The duck does not come cheap.

Hunan House, *45 Mott Street (212-962-0010).*

Hunan House is the landmark restaurant of hot cuisines—it was one of the first to move into the Cantonese territory of Mott Street. Concessions are made to American tastes regarding the red pepper. Hunan House does things with snails and black bean sauce that would suprise the French.

Mandarin Court, *61 Mott Street (212-608-3838).*

The Mandarin Court is that rarity, an all-around Chinatown restaurant. It is sleek black on mauve modern and the people are uptown and Hong Kong money. It has excellent *dim sum* and fine Hong Kong Cantonese cooking.

Hong Fat, *63 Mott Street (212-962-9588).*

Hong Fat in its day was long lines and long waits in the wee hours of the morning, when you could count on having strangers join you at your table. The service has the good-guy-abrasive quality usually associated with old-fashioned Jewish delis. The duck or pork *chow fun* (wide stir-fried noodles) and the roast pork are the high points of a Hong Fat pig-out.

House of Vegetarian, *68 Mott Street (212-226-6522).*

Vegetarian cooking at the House of Vegetarian is something of a gimmick, with vegetarian versions of pork and oyster that are hard to differentiate from the real thing. The spring rolls are superior to most of the meat-filled variety.

Yun Luck Rice Shoppe, *17 Doyers Street (212-571-1375).*

Yun Luck Rice has the *New York Times* seal of approval and the dinners to prove it, but it wouldn't win a beauty contest. It has real *chow mein* with pan-fried noodles and superb sea bass.

Four, Five, Six, *2 Bowery at Doyers Street (212-964-5853).*

The Four, Five, Six is another Chinese restaurant that is bad-rapped for its appeal to Occidental diners, as if that alone makes its Shanghai cuisine less authentic. The Shanghai cook-your-own hot pot, where you drop everything from squid to lamb in a steaming broth, is a fun food experience.

Mandarin Inn Pell Restaurant, *34 Pell Street (212-267-2092).*

Mandarin Inn Pell is a relief from the Chinatown frenzy. It's a relaxing place, not too big and impersonal nor small and cramped. It has a pleasant dining area with gold and red tile and a Chinese mural of wild horses. It holds its own in the Szechuan and Hunan sweepstakes.

Rice Stops

At the lower end of the Chinese restaurant market there are rice shops featuring very basic meat-and-vegetable mixtures served over heaping portions of rice. The vegetables may be mostly Chinese cabbage and the cuts of meat or fowl aren't exactly choice, but the food is more tasty than the local coffee shop at half the price. In the front of most of the rice shops, roast duck, chicken, pork, and spare ribs hang all in a row. It's hard to figure out, but at the rice shops all the Chinese eat with forks and all the Occidentals work the chopsticks.

Tai Tung Rice Shop, *244 Canal Street (212-431-9632).*

There are two counters near the entrance, one with a stainless-steel coffee urn and *dim sum* and the other with the slabs of roast pork and hanging roast ducks and chicken. Take a table in the back and refuse all the tourist exotica in favor of a simple Chinese beef stew on rice.

Sun Say Gay Restaurant, *220 Canal Street (212-964-7256).*

The basic no-frills rice shop with some specials. The Chinese fish cake with pickled vegetables is a taste worth acquiring. The Vietnamese sesame ball is a good change of pace.

Chao Sing Restaurant, *77 Mulberry Street (212-233-8988).*

Chao Sing is less frenetic than the rice shops on Canal and the customer doesn't feel obliged to race through the meal. Simple is better with dishes like pepper steak on rice and spare ribs with spicy black bean sauce on rice.

Oodles of Chinese Noodles

Chinatown's noodle shops are a source of good inexpensive meals. Noodles and *won tons* are served in a broth that has subtlety and body. Greens, scallions, spices, and enough meat to add savor complete this traditional one-dish Hong Kong or Vietnamese Chinese luncheon. The service is very quick and customers don't linger. Even the crowd noise cannot compete with the sound of the customers slurping up the soup.

Chao Fu Lau Restaurant, *89–91 Bayard Street (212-732-5122). Closes at 10:30 P.M.*

The broth is sweet as sugar with a choice of some of the most interesting combinations in Chinatown. Try curry chicken flat noodle and the mushroom with duck egg noodle.

Won Ton Garden, *52-56 Mott Street (212-966-4886).*

The Won Ton Garden caters to the tourists having their first fling at noodle-soup dining. The fish balls are their specialty.

Bo Ky Restaurant, *80 Bayard Street (212-406-2292).*

Bo Ky is eating on the run in a Chinese soup kitchen. The bowls are chipped and the service is just about civil, but the jumbo shrimp flat noodle and shredded chicken flat noodle will make you forget everything.

Some Dim Sum

Chinatown's better restaurants specialize in elaborate, belt-loosening banquets. They must be arranged in advance except during the Chinese New Year when a set banquet menu is offered to the public prix-fixe.

The order of a traditional Chinese banquet can be confusing for Westerners. Soup ends rather than begins the meal and sweets like sugared apple slices comes before the two final meat courses. The banquet usually leads off with four cold appetizers, including salted shrimp and sliced kidneys, and has at least eight main courses with some kind of steamed fish and a whole duck. Tiny cups of rice wine keeps everyone convivial.

During the afternoon many restaurants serve a kind of banquet in miniature called *dim sum*. Waiters or waitresses pass among the diners, wheeling carts filled with appetizer-size portions of Chinese delicacies. There are steamed dumplings or baked buns filled with pork or shrimp or bean paste, noodles stuffed with meat and fish, chicken feet and other things too numerous to mention. If you still have an appetite after several rounds of *dim sum*, follow the Chinese example and have a main course.

Hee Seung Fung Teahouse, *46 Bowery between Canal and Chatham Square (212-374-1319). Dim sum 7:30 A.M.–5 P.M. daily.*

Success has only half spoiled HSF. The ladies pushing the carts usually put out plenty of the steamed *har kow* (shrimp dumpling) and *shiu mai* (pork dumpling), but what about some of the more arcane dishes like pork taro dumpling or the sticky rice *dim sum*?

Silver Palace, *50 Bowery at Canal Street (212-964-1204). Dim sum 8 A.M.–3:30 P.M. daily.*

The Silver Palace is Chinese swank with lush red decor and golden dragons and a great view of the bridge to Brooklyn. Connoisseurs of *dim sum* say it's too commercial, but the beef balls, pan-fried pork dumplings, and even the humble spring roll are excellent. Don't forget to leave a tip or a waiter (not the young woman energetically pushing the *dim sum* cart) will follow you half-way down the stairs.

The Nice Restaurant, *35 East Broadway (212-406-9510). Dim sum 8 A.M.–5 P.M. daily.*

It's a wonder how this huge high-volume multilevel restaurant retains its high quality. The mixed meat dumpling and the chicken rice roll stand out.

Chinese Baking

Chinese baking—like most things Chinese—always seem to come hot straight out of the oven. Chinese baking is buns, balls and tarts baked and fried. It's made with bean paste, sticky rice, and yeast cake. The fillings don't take sweetness to extremes, whether it's coconut or egg custard or yellow bean. There are pastries with meat centers and cookies that are sculpted to look like fish or birds.

Lung Fong Chinese Bakery, *41 Mott Street (212-233-7447) Daily 8 A.M.–9:30 P.M.*

Lung Fong has an excellent assortment of pastries and cookies, all clearly marked for the non-Chinese customers. The cream sponge and the lotus seed pastry are sweet without being cloying; the big Buddha and fish cookies both look and taste good.

Maria's *148 Lafayette Street. Monday–Saturday 7:30 A.M. –7:30 P.M.; Sunday 8 A.M.–7 P.M.*

Maria's bakery may be a multimillion dollar Hong Kong chain, but its buns and pastries can't compete with Chinatown's Mom and Pop operations. Their restaurant next door is in between Chinese and American and doesn't satisfy a taste for either.

Mee Sum Mee, *48 Mott Street (212-233-8155). Daily 7 A.M. –8:30 P.M.*

Mee Sum Mee is the busiest bakery on Mott Street. He gets most of the Chinese trade and would get the tourists too, if they were willing to wait in line.

Teahouses and Tea Ceremonies

Tea is the favorite beverage in Chinatown. It is aromatic and light or dark as coffee and in its own way as rich. There are teas for relaxing and teas that supply energy. Chinese teas are graded in quality and prepared in blends. Tea tasters discriminate the fine shades of difference.

In old China, tea drinking was a stylized ritual and there was a special tea ceremony that is still performed today. Tung Lu, the Chinese philosopher of the Tang Dynasty, devised his own logic of tea drinking and precisely described how it should be consumed. Chinatown is more offhanded in its treatment of tea and unceremoniously chugalugs it from chipped coffee cups and water glasses; but it still steeps the leaves in boiling water and hasn't taken the fatal leap to tea bags.

Chinese teahouses take the place of cafés. The teahouse is sipping tea and speaking to friends and unwinding from a long day. The teahouse is the midmorning or midafternoon break to recharge and go back to business. The tea accompaniment is Chinese pastry and buns and *dim sum,* and in the better places, they are prepared on the premises. Chinese teahouses are casual and all hours.

Ten Ren Tea and Ginseng Company, *176 Canal Street (212-925-9822). Daily 10 A.M.–8 P.M.*

The Ten Ren Tea Company is Taiwan modern with large technicolor photos of waterfalls and gardens. It has thirty different teas, from fermented Green Tung Tin to fermented black. They all come in bags or fancy gift boxes in 120 grades. Tea sets in clay or celandon porcelain are also on sale. The back area is reserved for tea ceremonies and a videotape sales pitch about teas.

Mayflower Tea Parlor, *76 Mott Street (212-421-6216). Daily noon–11:45 P.M.*

The Mayflower Tea Parlor is a Chinese café, older Chinese sitting over tea and *dim sum* or a pastry and batting the breeze. The *dim sum* are fresh from the kitchen and go very quickly. Sit at the counter and make your picks as they come out. The pork dumpling and the shrimp ball and the steamed bun are perfect with chrysanthemum tea.

Baguio Tea Parlor, *131 Lafayette Street (212-966-7622). Daily 7 A.M. –9:30 P.M.*

The Baguio is a large tea parlor with the care and quality of a small one. They have a huge selection of *dim sum* and pastry that are first-rate and low-priced. The baked pork bun, which is a throwaway in most Chinese bakeries, is wonderfully sweet and savory.

Chinatown Marketing

Chinatown markets are controlled chaos, the battle of the buyers and sellers, Chinese-style. Inside and out, everyone wants to be next. Constantly the clerks restock and stack the shelves, and truckers arrive from the central market with new produce. The noise of cleavers chopping and ice spread out on a jerry-built stall and boxes being broken open combine with shouts of prices and shouts of frustration and the never-ending engine of crowd hum. The problem is not enough room along steep Canal Street or along the aisles of a Chinese frozen-food department.

Dairy Farm Food Product, *132G Lafayette Street (212-966-2020). Daily 8:30 A.M.–8:30 P.M.*

Dairy Farm is one Chinese supermarket where the clerks are not too busy to smile. The market has shelves of teas including a special "jasmine slimming tea" and a deep freeze with frozen *moo shu* shells (pancakes to wrap *moo shu* pork) and frozen lotus seed buns. The store's Chinese apothecary has shark's fins and deer's tail extract.

Canal Food Corp., *224 Canal Street (212-966-2524). Daily 9 A.M. –8 P.M.*

This busy outdoor fish market stops pedestrian traffic with its red snapper, tile fish, and fluke on ice. The fish are fresh and men in rubber boots and rubber aprons keeps replenishing the supply. Inside it's all meat, including *lop chong,* a slightly sweet dried Chinese sausage.

Lye Yan Inc., *226A Canal (212-966-0237). Daily 7 A.M. –11:30 P.M.*

Lye Yan is shopping bedlam but it does have the best and most reasonably priced selection of Chinese vegetables. The only answer you'll get from the harried clerks is the price.

Kam Kuo Food Inc., *7 Mott Street (212-349-3097). Daily 9 A.M.–9 P.M.*

Off frenetic Canal Street, Kam Kuo feels less crowded than some of the other supermarket-size Chinese markets. It has all the staples from noodles to bean curd and also some surprises including fresh ginko nuts, black sesame oil from Taiwan, melon juice from Tienjin, and Szechuan spice mix from the Szechuan.

Canton Noodle Manufacturing, *101 Mott Street (212-226-3276). Monday–Saturday 8:30 A.M.–5 P.M.*

Canton Noodle is an adventure. Enter a factory and come out with everything necessary to make *won ton* or spring rolls from scratch. It has all the fresh noodles in the Chinese kitchen.

Wing Fat Company, *33-35 Mott Street (212-962-0433). Daily 9 A.M.–8 P.M.*

This is old Chinatown without the supermarket fixtures. There are snails and clams in the baskets and dried fish suspended from the ceiling. Some of the produce is in boxes and some of it is in bags. Maybe this will change after the next sixty years.

Chinese Curios and Antiques

Chinatown gift shops run the gamut from souvenirs to genuine antiques. Some look like everything just came off the assembly line and others resemble small museums. They are havens for browsers. The merchandise includes carved ivory and jade, lacquered Chinese screens, framed calligraphy, fine porcelain, and ceramic figures. The better shops seem to be run by venerable Chinese gentlemen with ear-to-ear smiles. They are very knowledgeable about which dynasty produced which objets d'art.

Wardward China and Porcelain Inc., *130 Lafayette Street (212-219-0240). Daily 10 A.M.–7 P.M.*

Wardward is fine china and porcelain, tea sets and bowls, and delicate figurines. The stock is endless but it rarely descends to the cute or kitsch.

Din Lay Co., *5 Mott Street (212-227-0945). Daily 10 A.M.–11 P.M.*

Din Lay is creative chaos—a profusion of carved ivories, lacquered plates, Chinese scrolls, and painted fans. The Tang horses are not originals but wonderful all the same.

Don Enterprises, *36 Mott Street (212-267-5765). Daily 10 A.M.–10 P.M.*

Don is a curiosity in itself. It is a tiny store that carries the most monumental urns. Each one could fit two of the owner, Mr. Don Cho.

Tai Heng Lee Company, *60A Mott Street (212-925-2233). Daily 10 A.M.–10 P.M.*

Tai Heng Lee is the class of Chinatown. It has fine antique furniture and porcelains and tasteful copies. Does anyone actually sit on the chairs or have dinner at the tables? It has a wide variety of pictorial panels, cloisonne vases, lacquered screens, and statues of lions and grinning Buddhas. Take your time wandering through and discover your own treasures.

Hong Kong City, *40A Mott Street (212-962-7981). Daily 10 A.M.–9 P.M.*

The kid minding the store is glum because he's not home watching the World Series, but that doesn't affect his enthusiasm as he hustles the fans, tea cup sets, and ceramics of Confucian scholars. It's a friendly souvenir shop.

Hong Kong Gold

Before the Hong Kong Chinese came, Canal Street was the place where young couples came to get discounts on wedding rings or parents bought their child an inexpensive I.D. bracelet. The jewelers on Canal Street were the last remnant of the old Jewish diamond district. Today's Chinatown Canal Street is paved with gold, the kind that is sold in the form of chain necklaces, bracelets, and medallions. The stores have names like Treasure Island Jewelry. It is mostly fourteen carat and heavy and extreme. The pendants include three-inch disks with dollar signs and huge heads of the pharaoh with a ruby eye. There are gold necklaces that easily could be worn as belts and bracelets that could be worn as necklaces. The clerks are demure Oriental women and the clientele nouveau riche street. The stores are more a curosity than for buying. Recently jewelry has become so big in Chinatown that two exchanges have opened. The Canal Street exchange is one of Chinatown's flashiest buildings, a high-rise red pagoda.

Canal Street Jewelry Exchange, *255 Canal Street (212-966-2020). Daily 9:30 A.M.–7 P.M.*

Chinatown's Cultural Umbrella

Chinese-American Arts Council, *456 Broadway (212-431-9740).*

The Chinese-American Arts Council was founded in 1975 to expand and implement cultural programs that had been initiated by Chinatown's Chinese-American Planning Council. It started as the administrative arm of the Chinatown Summer Outdoor Festival and went on to sponsor Chinese art exhibits, concerts, plays, operas, and dance companies. It presents this Chinese art to the community for little or no payment. The Chinese-American Arts Council publishes a bimonthly newsletter and books of cultural interest to Chinese New Yorkers.

Place Marks

—Chinatown Originals—

While the new neighborhood takes shape, the original preserves its past and builds for the future. Chinatown has weathered the tourist traffic and kept its authenticity. It is a functioning ethnic community as well as convention bureau sights. The Chinatown experience gets off to a flying start as you exit the subway at Canal Street and Center Street.

Golden Pacific National Bank, *corner Canal and Center Streets.*

The Golden Pacific National Bank was constructed in 1983 in the manner of Forbidden City, Beijing. The facade is startling—bright red, gold, blue, and green with pagoda roofs and Oriental galleries. Outside it is as good gaudy fun as the inside jewelry exchange it now houses.

The Chinese Merchants' Association, *85 Mott Street.*

The headquarters are on the southwest corner of the intersection of Canal and Mott Streets. The building is a wild combination of Chinese baroque and Western functional dating from the first real estate boom in the 1950s. It houses the On Leong Tong, which in these sophisticated times takes the trappings of a business group.

The Eastern States Buddhist Temple, *64B Mott Street.*

The atmosphere is subdued, the golden Buddha transfixed, and aromatic incense rises in the air. Chinese housewives sit in chairs arranged around the wall as the candle flames waver. Behind the alter you can glimpse more golden Buddhas in different poses.

Chinese Consolidated Benevolent Association and the Chinese Community Center, *62 Mott Street.*

Next door to the temple are the offices of the unofficial government of Chinatown. The aged informally drop in like it's a clubhouse, while younger people take advantage of its employment services. Meanwhile, Chinatown's mandarins, representing the families and regions of another place and another time, make the tradeoffs and set policy. The building also houses the Chinese School, which helps perpetuate the Chinese language and culture and has an enrollment of three thousand.

The Church of the Transfiguration, *25 Mott Street.*

The church was consecrated as an Episcopal church in 1801, but today it has masses in Chinese for the local community. The church is pure Georgian with a spire as an afterthought. On Saturday, amid the tourist crush, Chinese wedding parties try to pose for pictures.

8 Mott Street.

This is the address of the original premises of New York's first Chinese merchant, Wo Kee.

13 Pell Street.

The Hip Sing Tong has its headquarters behind a door marked number 13. It is just steps away from the bend in Doyers Street called the "Bloody Angle," where the Hip Sings and the On Leungs fought for control of the lucrative opium trade and gambling and prostitution rackets in the not-so-gay 1890s.

—The New Face—

Where Mott Street ends in Chatham Square, the new face of Chinatown begins. It is the closest Chinatown comes to a panorama of tall buildings. The cityscape centers on a green and black marble Confucius, thoroughly American but proud of its Chinese ancestry. The open space of the square comes as a relief after the closed narrow confinement of old Chinatown. It was once terminal decay with its street abutting the Bowery, but now the smart money from Hong Kong is investing here.

The Kim Lau Memorial, situated on a traffic island in the square, is dedicated to the Chinese dead of two world wars, combining a triumphant arch with a Chinese pagoda. Southwest of the square a modern office building rises, providing Chinese professional services, from tax attorneys to traditional acupuncturists.

Across the square on Division Street is Confucius Plaza, a public housing development built for the community. Though not notable for its institutional architecture, it is a landmark to Chinese activism. The Confucius Plaza protest marks the first time the Chinese community mobilized to seek satisfaction from an unresponsive city government. They used techniques of civil disobedience to secure jobs for Orientals on the Plaza project.

Another controversy followed concerning the not-quite-monumental statue of Confucius to be erected near the development. The CCBA wanted it, while local Maoists thought the philosopher-king of bureaucrats should be shelved. Today Confucius looks down benignly on Division Street as the tourists snap pictures.

Chinese Culture

Calligraphy is the oldest Chinese visual art. This highly disciplined execution of the Chinese character transcends meaning. Originally it was a matter of carving in wood or stone. After the invention of paper in the first century, it was inky brush strokes on paper or silk.

Chinese classical painting had its roots in calligraphy. It uses the calligrapher's brush and inkstone. In the spirit of classic calligraphy, the representations are simple, idealized, and poetic. The artist is deft and quick; nothing in the painting can be worked over or changed. The moment is captured. The Chinese moderns who studied in Paris built on these traditions.

Chinese art, traditional and modern, is part of the Chinatown Renaissance. The arts of classical painting and calligraphy are promoted alongside abstract sculpture and minimalist water colors.

Gallery 456, *456 Broadway (212-431-9740). Monday–Friday noon–5 P.M.; Saturday 1 P.M.–5 P.M.*

Gallery 456 is located in SoHo gallery country and wants to introduce new Chinese artists to a wider artistic community. It changes its exhibits every month and shows traditional as well as modern Chinese artists.

Oriental Gallery, *83 Bowery (212-226-8461). Daily 10 A.M.–8 P.M.*

The Oriental Gallery is a place where young Chinese artists can exhibit their work and learn and grow in the process. The emphasis is on painting and sculpture in this Chinatown training ground.

—Chinese Performing Arts—

The traveling storyteller and the folk traditions of Chinese festivals and religious ritual brought forth Chinese dance, drama, and song. All the forms developed individually in different regions of China and they came together in China's all-encompassing opera.

Chinese opera, or *Ch'ing Hsi,* is the Chinese national art form. It combines traditional music and song, old-fashioned melodrama and mime. The costumes, masks, and makeup are elaborate, and the gestures and movements are highly stylized. Though the sets are bare bones, the graceful, almost balletic, actors provide a grand spectacle.

The plots of the typical Chinese opera include wild coincidences and outrageous changes of fortune. Somtimes the romance verges on American soap opera. The cast of characters is bound to include rulers, scholars, warriors, and even a god or two. Costume color is an indication of character, with red for loyalty and black for integrity.

Chinese operas are updated in the Chinese action movies that play Chinatown. The heros and villians are pure stereotypes and good always triumphs over evil. The fight scenes in the Hong Kong Kung Fu epics may not be very realistic but they provide real operatic spectacle.

Though modern American Chinese theater has used the techniques of Chinese opera as a stylistic device, Chinese playwrights in New York work mostly through European dramatic forms even when they experiment. But their plays are concerned with the Chinese experience in the West, the injustices and the accomplishments of the past, and the problems of identity in the present.

Pan-Asian Repertory Theater, *74A East 4th Street (212-565-5655).*

The Pan-Asian Repertory Theater is directed by Tisa Chang and is associated with La Mama Experimental Theater Club and shares their facilities. For more than a decade it has encouraged Asian actors and writers in the pursuit of theatrical excellence. It introduced John Lone, the star of the film *The Last Emperor,* and launched the popular play, *Eat a Bowl of Tea,* which was turned into a film.

Four Seas Players, *Transfiguration Church, 29 Mott Street (212-962-5157).*

This is grass-roots theater at its best, with productions in English, Mandarin, and Cantonese. The members of this community theater go back to the Chinese classics for their sources and sometimes bring them up to date.

Chinese Dance Company of New York, *50 East Broadway (212-966-4747).*

These performers chase away the evil spirits in the ceremonial Lion and Dragon dances. The harvest dances gracefully mark the passage of the seasons.

Asian-American Dance Theater, *26 Bowery (212-233-2154).*

The theater is two flights up to Chinese flights of fancy. There are traditional dances like the sword dance with traditional music and modern dances based on the folk forms or the dances of Chinese opera.

Rosemary Theater *133 Canal Street (212-431-1185).*

The Rosemary is the place for Chinese-language flicks from Kung-Fu epics to adaptations of Chinese opera. Whatever the genre, dialogue takes second place to action and the audience is pure spectacle.

Martial Arts

China's martial art, Kung Fu, means "heroic excellence." It's a discipline and an art form and a personal quest. In Chinatown martial arts are not a hobby, they are a way of life. There are different Kung Fu techniques with different philosophies, from the delicate dance of *tai chee chuen,* to the sudden attack of Eagle's Claw, but they all demand total dedication.

Tony Chu Kung Fu School, *27-29 Division Street (212-340-8858).*

Tai Chee Chuen Association, *211 Canal Street (212-226-9912).*

Yase, *263 Canal Street (212-219-1659).*

Yase claims to have everything in martial arts paraphernalia. The clerks know their stuff and there are also books for the uninitiated. The store handles mail order.

Festivals

—New Year—

Whether the new lunar year is the year of the ox, the snake, or the rabbit, Chinatown is bound to have its biggest blowout celebration. Chinese men and women crowd the markets, outdoor and indoor, stocking up on holiday foods for the traditional feast. Golden oranges and fat fish are good luck for the New Year, while lotus seeds ensure fertility for the coming moon year.

Everywhere in stands and stores, symbolic New Year's birds and pagodas are suspended from red streamers, and there are bells to ring in the New Year. *Sui Xien* roots are sold in earthenware bowls, holiday symbols of growth that will sprout into delicate yellow flowers.

In the gift shops of Mott Street, the Chinese buy New Year's cards and batches of red envelopes, *bao,* for gift money for the children and a prosperous New Year. Old men walk with small children to the Buddhist shrine; it is also a time for prayer and reflection.

The giant drums are beaten and the lion goes into its dance at the stroke of midnight. It's a frenetic dance with one man fiercely tilting the papier-mâché lion's head while a second swings the lion's tail. The third dancer, head bobbing and body bouncing, baits the lion like a toreador without a cape. Total pandemonium reigns along the twists and turns of Mott, Pell, and Bayard Streets. Local Chinese and visiting tourists press forward for the best view as fusillades of firecrackers go off in the night.

—Lantern Festivals—

The fifteenth day after the Chinese New Year, the mood becomes more solemn. The Lantern Festival marks the end of the wild celebration. The lanterns that are carried in processions by the children of Chinatown represent the torches that people once carried to attract the wandering spirits set loose at the time of the full moon. The dragon dances in the street with its head and scaly body held aloft by poles. Gongs ring out and firecrackers are thrown in its path.

It's a carnival holiday celebrated with puppet shows and Chinese opera. Children eat the round *yuan hsaio* (sticky rice cake), symbolic of the new moon and perpetual rebirth.

—Moon Festival—

The Moon Festival occurs in the autumn on the fifteenth day of the eighth lunar month. The moon is supposed to be at its brightest on this day and the god of the earth is thanked for the harvest. In this Chinese thanksgiving, young girls ask Yueh Lao, the man in the moon, for a vision of their future husband and burn incense in the temple. Moon cakes are the traditional food with black bean, lotus seed, egg yolk, and red bean.

—Chinatown Cultural Festival—

During the back-to-the-roots cultural explosion of the 1960s the Chinese-American Planning Council organized a series of Chinese cultural exhibitions in Columbus Park. In 1970 the exhibitions were broadened to include musical performances and drama with the support of the New York Council on the Arts and the China Institute.

In 1971 these efforts led to the staging of the first Summer Chinatown Cultural Festival. It is now an annual multimedia event from mid-July to mid-September. The Chinese-American Arts Council is the community bulletin board for all the plays, concerts, exhibits, and dance recitals in and out of Chinatown.

Indo-Chinatown

Introduction

In April of 1975 America began its wholesale evacuation of South Vietnam. Many Vietnamese joined the airlift or followed months later, using their own resources. By May there were 130,000 Vietnamese refugees in America with 60,000 in relocation camps outside of the country.

The Vietnamese who came to America were mostly middle-class, urban, and Catholic. Many were originally from North Vietnam and had fled an earlier Communist victory. They settled primarily in the warmer climes of California and Texas but some with New York sponsors settled in the city.

By 1979 there was a new Vietnamese mass migration. Life in Vietnam had become so unbearable that Vietnamese crowded leaky boats to make the long and dangerous voyage to freedom. A large number of these boat people were ethnic Chinese who were in a vulnerable position after the 1979 Chinese invasion of Vietnam.

Though the Vietnamese New York population is small, they are highly visible in Chinatown. It is not just the handful of Vietnamese shops and restaurants. Vietnamese has become a third language in Chinatown. In the markets and stores the signs are increasingly trilingual, and there are products like *nuoc mam,* geared to the Vietnamese.

The majority of New York's Vietnamese are of Chinese extraction and their relationship with ethnic Vietnamese is not always cordial. In Vietnam the Chinese were resented as an old hereditary foe and a wealthy minority. But both groups share a nostalgia for a time and place that is increasingly bringing them together in New York. Vietnamese of all backgrounds are scattered through Chinatown and Flushing and the Bronx.

Vietnamese Nouvelle Cuisine

Vietnamese cooking is sometimes called the nouvelle cuisine of the Orient. It is light and subtle and sprightly seasoned with the freshness of mint and

coriander. The Vietnamese table is international, combining the sophistication of the French and the technique of the Chinese. It borrows the curry,
cocoa, and tamarind from India and lemon grass and hot chilis from Thailand. Vietnam's own unique contribution is *nuoc mam,* the essence of
fermented anchovies, which is salty and slightly fishy and does service as an
all-purpose condiment.

Vietnam's national dish is the spring roll, *cha gio,* which has a thin
rice-paper wrapper and a filling that combines diced mushrooms, pork,
shrimp, crab, and noodles. It is wrapped in fresh lettuce leaves and plunged
into *nuoc mam.* The *ga xao xa* chicken with lemon grass is a typical
Vietnamese entree. It is chicken at its most succulent with just a hint of
pepper and citrus.

The Vietnamese are soup fanatics and even eat it for breakfast. The
Vietnamese breakfast of champions is *pho bo* with thick beef broth poured
over rice noodles, raw beef, scallions, coriander, and *nuoc mam.* The eel
with tamarind and pineapple is the soup for the evening and very hot.

Saigon Restaurant, *60 Mulberry Street (212-227-8825). Sunday–*
Thursday 11:30 A.M.–10:30 P.M.; Friday–Saturday 11:30 A.M.–11
P.M.

Saigon is a family-run restaurant with Mom at the cash register and her two
daughters patiently explaining the ins and outs of Vietnamese cooking to a
mainly Occidental crowd. The food is very good, especially the lemon grass
chicken and the Vietnamese pork and shirmp crepe.

New Vietnam, *11 Doyers Street (212-693-0725). Daily 9 A.M.–1*
A.M.

The New Vietnam is a friendly downstairs restaurant where the waiters have
a sense of humor. The Vietnamese curries and sweet and sour eel soup are
hot stuff.

Shopping Vietnamese

Hoa Thanh, *217 Canal Street, 121 Canal Street (212-966-5225).*
Daily 10 A.M.–1 A.M.

Hoa Thanh on Sundays is a Saigon reunion. While people buy their chilis
and lemon grass and hunt for banana leaves, they discover old friends from
another time and place. Vietnamese music plays in the background.

Southeast Asia Food Trading Company, *68A Mott Street (212-431-5012). Daily 7 A.M.–11 P.M.*

Southeast Asia has choice Vietnamese products among its all-Asian assortment. The *nuoc mam* is the authentic article from Phuc Quoc, an island on the south coast of Vietnam.

Chinese Culture Uptown

The Astors and the Rockefellers and other members of the Four Hundred were connoisseurs and collectors of Chinese art. They endowed institutions to support their enthusiasms and the dealers in Chinese antiquities came uptown.

China Institute, *125 East 65th Street (212-744-8181). Monday–Saturday 9 A.M.–5 P.M.; Saturday 11 A.M.–5 P.M.*

The Chinese Institute is a dignified brick town house containing the city's best exhibits of Chinese art. Guest curators mount regular exhibits of the old and the esoteric. It also has lectures and courses touching on many aspects of Chinese culture. On special occasions like the Chinese New Year, it offers authentic Chinese entertainments and banquets with discussions of Chinese culture.

The Metropolitan Museum of Art, *Fifth Avenue between 80th and 84th Street (212-535-7710). Tuesday–Thursday, Sunday 9:30 A.M.–5:15 P.M.; Friday,Saturday 9:30 A.M.–8:45 P.M. Contribution, except Friday and Saturday evenings.*

The Metropolitan has pieces covering the whole chronology of Chinese art. The holdings include primitive pottery and jade from the Neolithic and remarkable bronzes from the eleventh century B.C. There is the famed "Female Dancer" of the Han Dynasty and a notable Buddha from Mongolia dated A.D. 524. The Douglas Dillon Gallery has a roundup of fine Chinese painting, and the Astor Court is a re-creation of a Ming scholar's Suzhou Garden. The second floor is the site of these Chinese treasures.

J. T. Tai, *18 East 67th Street (212-288-5253). By appointment only.*

J. T. Tai deals in the very precious. His customers are the elite of New York collectors. If you are looking for high-caliber Ming ceramics or Shang bronzes, J. T. Tai has it or will find it.

Barry Chan, *948 Madison Avenue (212-288-0798). Tuesday–Friday 10 A.M.–6 P.M.; Saturday 10 A.M.–5 P.M.*

Barry Chan specializes in eighteenth- and nineteenth-century extravagant Chinese furniture. It also carries an assortment of elegant wall decorations, porcelain, and cloisonne vases and bowls.

Koreans

History

The Koreans are a typical New York phenomenon, the overnight immigrant success story. One day they are selling wigs on street corners and driving taxicabs, and the next they own retail businesses in every neighborhood in the city and are moving into real estate and shopping centers.

The city's original Koreans were academics and Christian converts who settled in the Columbia University area. In 1920 there were seventy Koreans in the city and thirty of them formed their own Christian church on 633 West 115th Street, attracting students and political refugees.

At the conclusion of the Korean War, Korean war brides flocked to the city with their G.I. husbands. They did not attempt to join the established Korean community or start their own, though they did maintain contact with other war brides. They felt liberated by the freedom America offered women and they took the assimilationist route.

In the era of the Cold War, the United States encouraged Korean students to attend American universities, and Korean physicians were offered American internships. Some were even able to stay in the country after their schooling and training and chose to live in the city. Korean pharmacists came directly to New York to practice, since they could be licensed by passing a single exam.

The 1965 Hart-Celler Immigration Act, with its preferences for skilled occupations and professions, opened up the city to an influx of educated Koreans. Korean doctors and nurses became a highly visible component of New York's private and municipal health system. There were more Korean doctors in New York than in rural Korea. Korean accountants, chemists, engineers, and technicians signed on with American corporations.

While the medical professionals thrived, it gradually dawned on the other Korean professionals that advancement was slow or nonexistent. Ambitious New York Koreans took their green cards and futures in their own hands. Relying on capital amassed before emigrating or the earnings of two jobs or a lump sum from an informal Korean credit association, a *gye,* they opened small businesses.

These aspiring Korean entrepreneurs were also helped by business classes that were held by their consulate. In the early stages the Korean consul acted as a liaison between Korean-American businessmen and Korean wholesalers. Later, when the profit margins became too small, Korean New Yorkers started their own wholesale businesses and became their own suppliers.

Some Koreans started their business lives peddling made-in-Korea wigs, handbags, and sweatsuits in black and Puerto Rican areas deserted by Jewish and Italian retailers. They purchased the items with a line of credit from an overseas Korean company, and peddled them on the street.

In time they were able to open their first fruit and vegetable stores and discount clothing and bag stores in transitional neighborhoods. Whether the Koreans were welcomed or resented, crime and racial tension were part of the cost of doing business. Many Koreans soon outgrew marginal neighborhoods and made it to the fleshpots of Manhattan's Upper East Side; others have replaced them, and their businesses still thrive in the high-crime areas of the outer boroughs.

Koreans concentrated on fruit and vegetable selling because it was labor intensive and didn't require a large outlay to start. In the early days, five thousand dollars was the start-up cost. Their profit margin came from working around the clock and employing only members of their family. They also weren't hampered by any shortcomings in English. These Korean businesses caught on with innovations like salad bars.

They formed their own organization, the Korean Produce Retailers Association, for mutual assistance and to deal with problems in the produce business. Soon, determined Koreans were hiring the latest immigrants from South and Central America and moving on to other businesses, like liquor stores and cleaning shops, that required higher capitalization.

The success of Koreans also inspired resentments. There was friction in minority neighborhoods and even demonstrations and boycotts. Local groups in Harlem demanded that Koreans hire black employees. There was a whisper campaign that associated Korean business success with the Unification Church and the high-living Reverend Sung Yung Moon. Koreans were even the objects of racial attacks.

In 1977 the Koreans at the Hunt's Point produce market had enough of the racial slurs and the shabby offhanded treatment. Reacting to a racist incident at the market, the low-profile Korean community went uncharacteristically public and picketed. In short order, they made their point and collected three thousand dollars from the wholesalers for the KPRA and a public apology.

New York's Korean community is growing. In 1980 it numbered twenty-two thousand; a decade later it had climbed above a hundred thousand. The community, which is scattered throughout the city, has kept its cohesion through organizations and associations.

Korean groups form around different businesses, like the community's thousand dry cleaners of three hundred fifty fishmongers. In the tradition of old ethnic fraternities and social clubs, they provide the members with health insurance and other benefits. There are also Korean "prosperity associations," where Korean Horatio Algers pool ideas about business and sponsor community programs. Local Korean Protestant churches are also sources of group solidarity.

The new Koreans are mainly middle-class and urban from South Korea's capital, Seoul, and Pusan. They have brought their cosmopolitan culture to the city. The latest Korean bestsellers, magazines, videos, and cassettes are readily available. Cable television shows recent Korean programs. There are two New York Korean dailies and four imported South Korean newspapers. Even the *gisengs* (modern bar/restaurants with hostesses) have made their appearance in New York.

Empire State's Korea Town

Introduction

New York's wealthy classes retreated to Fifth Avenue and the 30s to escape the immigrant advance in the nineteenth century. There were mansions and luxury hotels. The first Waldorf was built at 34th Street and Fifth Avenue for the then-amazing figure of thirteen million dollars to attract the swells who ate off silver plates. By the time the area was mainly big department stores in 1929, the Waldorf was superceded by the biggest building in the world, the Empire State Building.

Manhattan's Korea Town is in the shadow of Manhattan's number-one tourist attraction, the Empire State Building, but it doesn't attract anything like the crowds of the Chinese enclave downtown. For the most part, the twenty Korean restaurants and bars between Fifth and Broadway on 32nd and 33rd Streets are all Korean faces. The Koreans aren't looking for the tourist trade; they cater to the Korean merchants in the neighborhood.

Korea Town proper is a purely commercial strip on Broadway between 23rd Street and 31st Street. While there are other ethnics in the area, it is the center for Korean wholesalers in the city, and Korean retailers buy here regularly. The buyers and sellers deal in electronics, inexpensive clothing, handbags and luggage, cosmetics, and jewelry. There are 350 Korean wholesalers, importers, and corporations, as well as branches of the important Korean banks and the offices of three Korean newspapers.

24-Hour Kimchi and Barbecue

Korean cooking is the full-bodied of Asia. The Koreans made the haute cuisine of the Chinese and the Japanese approachable and human. The food is barbecued steak and short ribs and rich soups with dumplings. The Koreans take meat eating so seriously that they eat it raw in their own versions of steak tartar and liver tartar. They also like their fish raw in Japanese sushi. The Korean national dish is *kimchi,* pickled cabbage laced with hot peppers. It keeps everyone warm during the long Korean winter.

The Korean restaurants in Manhattan are mostly all-night nonstop affairs. The Koreans are a people who never sleep and these round-the-clock workers need twenty-four hour restaurants. The restaurants come out of the same mold, whether they are two-floor football fields or four tables and a sushi bar. The tables and chairs are light wood and simple and the rooms are Oriental screens and rice-paper paneling. In the better restaurants, there are ceiling beams and photographic blowups of Pusan or the New York skyline.

Kang Suh Restaurant, *1250 Broadway (212-564-6845).*

Kang Suh is banquet-hall sized and rambling with three men manning the sushi bar downstairs and six waitresses in white in the upstairs dining room. In the middle of the night it is constant motion, with Korean greengrocers popping in before or after the Hunt's Point market. It is barbecue and sushi all night long.

Kom Tang Soot Bul House, *32 West 32nd Street (212-947-8482).*

Kom Tang is open twenty-four hours a day, 365 days a year. They open their back room for private parties and do a lot of business with Korean and Japanese business travelers. They are masters of Korean tripe.

Empire Restaurant, *28 West 33rd Street (212-563-3695).*

The staff are obliging even in the wee hours of the morning. They are specialists in steak and barbecued short ribs (*kalbi*).

The Korean Protestant Ethic

The Koreans are the city's only Protestant Orientals. A majority are Protestant Christians who take the Protestant ethic seriously. They are success-oriented believers in self-sacrifice. In every Korean neighborhood, commercial or residential, there are Protestant gift shops that look like Hallmark Card stores. Korean churches often dominate the social lives of New York's Koreans and are a source of important business contacts.

Koryo Books, *35 West 32nd Street (212-564-1844). Monday–Saturday 10 A.M.–9 P.M.*

The store carries framed quotations from the Bible and a complete selection of religious books. There are also cassettes of Korean and classical music and Korean greeting cards. The selection of books about Korea in English is excellent.

Galilee Books, *22 West 32nd Street (212-686-6680). Monday–Saturday 8:30 A.M.–7 P.M.*

It is the size of a small department store. It combines cosmetics with its shelves of religious books and framed religious mottos (all in Korean). On its mezzanine it has a travel agency. The clerks follow the customers around, either out of courtesy or suspicion.

Korean Roots

Korea has its own tradition of natural medicine, with folk doctors prescribing herbs and roots. Its miracle drug is the ginseng root—not exactly a cure but a source of energy and virility.

Korea Ginseng Trade Center, *65 East 59th Street (212-935-6789). Monday–Friday 10 A.M.–7 P.M.; Saturday 10 A.M.–6 P.M.*

Moon Young Moon was the Korean to introduce ginseng to Manhattan, and his Upper East Side customers still swear by it. He has branched out to the yin and yang of Chinese barefoot doctors and has Dr. Yao Yang from Beijing on hand to prescribe the right Chinese extracts.

Korean Brush Strokes

Korea has its own tradition of high arts and folk arts. There is Korean calligraphy and naturalistic painting. The celadon and porcelain work bears comparison with the best Chinese. Korean furniture and inlaid chests and lacquer work have attracted New York collectors.

Korean Art & Antiques Inc., *963 Madison Avenue between 75th and 76th Streets (212-249-0400). Monday–Saturday 10 A.M.–6 P.M.*

The Korean Art & Antiques treats any stray visitor like a guest. They specialize in antique Korean furniture, but the store also has fine ceramic pieces and lovely wall hangings.

Korea Gallery, *The Consulate General of the Republic of Korea, 460 Park Avenue (212-759-9550). Monday–Friday 10 A.M.–5 P.M.; Saturday noon–6 P.M.*

The exhibition openings are important events for the Korean diplomatic and resident community. The showings seem to alternate between traditional and modern works.

News of Korea

Korean newspapers are everywhere. They are sold in supermarkets and religious gift shops and are available in twenty-four-hour restaurants. The local Korean press is active in the community and has offices in Korean neighborhoods and on the streets of Manhattan.

Korea News, *48 West 88th Street (212-695-5444).*

Korea News is Korean New York's daily grapevine. It handles the latest news from Korea and the local news from Korean neighborhoods. Unlike other ethnic papers, it doesn't soft-pedal its homeland's problems and is willing to deal with local controversies, like Korean youth gangs.

Korean Day Parade

The Korean Day Parade is timed to coincide with the Korean Moon Festival, which is the Korean holiday of thanksgiving. It takes place annually on the third Saturday in October. The parade makes its way from the Avenue of Americas and 44th Street down Broadway to 23rd Street.

Korean Day is part marching bands and part Korean folkloric groups, the drums and brass contrasting with singing strings—the drill team following Korean country maids in flowing silks. Young men in martial arts uniforms bounce down the Avenue to the hammering beat of an Oriental drum.

There are the flags of South Korea and official Korean delegations leading the way for American-Korean Associations. The greengrocers march and the dry cleaners march and the fishmongers march. The Korean churches and Buddhist temples float down the Avenue on floats along with TV stations and beauty queens.

Japanese

Introduction

The Japanese in Manhattan and upscale Riverdale are multinational corporation New Yorkers. They are here on assignment for one of the hundreds of Japanese companies headquartered in the city. They are New Yorkers for only a short duration and not about to go native, and that gives their local cultural institutions added vitality.

New Yorkers are also intrigued and attracted by Japanese culture. There is a vogue in things Japanese, from fashions to cosmetics to Wall Street takeovers. Japanese black on black is the look and Japanese hi-tech is the content. The city has taken to Japanese religion and meditation and made a religion out of sushi.

The Japanese themselves are now part of the landscape as they move conservatively suited in groups through Manhattan's boardrooms and financial centers. The Japanese, though numbering in the tens of thousands, are not that high profile; they entertain themselves in Japanese bars and restaurants and edify themselves in Japanese museums. They have their own organizations and even their own hotel.

Sushi Bars and Tatami Rooms

Japanese cuisine is simple and severe, like Japanese design or the lines of a Japanese flower arrangement. The fish delicacy is raw *sashimi* or with vinegared rice, sushi. The Japanese catch includes tuna, yellow tail, and fluke set off with shaved ginger and radish. The Japanese also lightly batter-fry shrimp with vegetables in a tempura. When it comes to meat, it is a straight forward barbecue teriyaki, on or off skewers, and *sukiyaki* thinly sliced with vegetables and cellophane noodles cooked at the table. Noodles, the wheat kind, are a Japanese obsession.

Japanese restaurants in the early days, before they discovered that New Yorkers didn't necessarily know the difference, had across-the-board quality, very small portions, and very limited menus. The sushi was an afterthought. Today only the restaurants that are expensive or have a regular Japanese clientele walk the extra mile.

The Japanese in Japanese restaurants are out for a good time. The dinner is their entertainment with scotch and saki. Japanese haven't had a Puritan revival, so they are able to drink, smoke, and laugh with impunity until the hostess diplomatically tells them it is time to close. In some restaurants the

Japanese can do this in the privacy of a *tatami* room, eating Japanese style, shoes off, on mats.

Genroku Sushi, *365 Fifth Avenue between 34th and 33rd Streets (212-947-7940). Monday–Friday 11 A.M.–8 P.M.; Saturday 11 A.M.–7:30 P.M.*

Genroku Sushi is gimmick-Japanese with everybody sitting around a ''modern times'' conveyor belt, watching the Japanese appetizers go around like airport luggage. The sushi, *hajiki* (seaweed salad), and *shumai* (steamed dumplings) probably taste better than the plastic models of the appetizers in the window.

Mitsukoshi, *461 Park Avenue at 57th Street (212-935-6444). Monday–Saturday noon–2 P.M., 6 P.M.–10 P.M.*

Mitsukoshi is high-flyer expense account dining below the Park Avenue premises of New York's most elegant Japanese boutique. Japanese agree it has the freshest, firmest, and shapeliest sushi in the city. The surgeon/chefs at the sushi bar are artists. Reserve a *tatami* room in advance.

Hatsuhana, *17 East 48th Street (212-333-3345). Monday–Friday 11:30 A.M.–9:30 P.M.*

Hatsuhana is upstairs/downstairs with a sushi bar on each level. The sushi is excellent, from the dark tuna to the orange roe. But sushi is just the beginning of the Japanese good tastes in small packages. There are fried tiny crabs and fried chicken bits, morsels of boiled beef, and slices of broiled duck.

Dosanko, *217 East 59th Street (212-752-8088). Monday–Friday 11 A.M.–9:30 P.M.; Saturday noon–5 P.M.*

Dosanko is luncheonette Japan with noodles in broth and stir-fried. The noodle soup is the big seller, which Japanese diners demolish in jig-time, lifting up the bowl to get the last drop. This is the flagship of a chain of five.

Hakubai, *66 Park Avenue at 37th Street (212-686-3770). Daily 7:30 A.M.–9:30 A.M.; noon–2:30 P.M.; 5:30 P.M.–10 P.M.*

Hakubai is eating in Japan or at least that portion of Japan that is New York's Japanese Hotel Kitano. The food from *miso* (clear soup) to *sukiyaki* is exceptional. There are *tatami* rooms and also tea ceremonies for Japanese and American visiting firemen. It is expensive but a one-of-a-kind experience.

Culture Clubs

The Japanese are not all business. In Japan, arts are avocations for the men in the boardrooms and the men on the assembly lines. Things the West takes for granted, like kite making and flower arrangements, are art and matters of exacting technique. The Japanese also have their own art forms like Kabuki, a kind of Japanese ballet where dance becomes total theater. Japanese following the Japanese tradition pursue these arts collectively.

Japan Society, *333 East 47th Street (212-832-1155). Monday–Saturday 11 A.M.–5 P.M.*

The stated purpose of the Japan Society is to provide Americans with information about Japanese arts, literature, and culture. It presents traditional Japanese music and dance and past and current Japanese films. There is a gallery where there are exhibits, from Japanese scroll painting to contemporary abstractions. There is a library and demonstrations of crafts like paper cutting. New York's Japanese community takes full advantage of its attractive Japanese-style facilities.

Nippon Club, *145 West 57th Street (212-581-2223).*

The Nippon Club promotes Japanese-American friendship while it promotes Japanese arts. It has a wide variety of lectures and exhibits in Japanese and English. There are concerts and dance recitals and classes in the art of flower arrangement, the Japanese thirteen-string *koto,* the tea ceremony, and brush painting.

Buddhism and Zen

In some Buddhist sects, religion is long mystical explanations and abstract reasoning. There are complex rites and rituals with sutras and mandalas. Zen Buddhism is a way to awareness, a meditation and a paradox. The Zen Koan is an unanswerable question and a self-contradictory statement that the Zen master places before the initiate. Both ways are embraced by the Japanese and New Yorkers looking for meaning.

Japanese Buddhist Temple, *332 Riverside Drive at 106th Street (212-678-9214).*

This is traditional Japanese Buddhism with chanting and gongs and kneeling. On the Saturday nearest to June 15, Japanese Buddhists celebrate the *obon,* in commemoration of the selfless act of a disciple of Buddha from the sixth century. The daughters of the temple dance in modest kimonos with mincing steps.

All the Zen institutions offer training and "meditation time" for a fee.

The First Zen Institute of America, *113 East 30th Street (212-684-9487).*

New York Zen Center, *440 West End Avenue near 81st Street (212-724-4172).*

Zen Studies Center, *223 East 67th Street (212-861-3333).*

Japanese Books and Galleries

For the Japanese the art of the word and the visual arts are not that far apart. Chinese calligraphy was an integral part of literary forms like *Haiku* (poems) and it was the precursor of the *sumi-e* brush and ink painting. In New York, Japanese bookstores sell prints and curios, and galleries show Japanese wood-block prints.

Zen Oriental Book Store, *521 Fifth Avenue between 43rd and 44th Streets (212-697-0840). Monday–Saturday 10 A.M.–7 P.M.*

The bookstore draws the Japanese crowds, but there is a lot of room for non-Japanese browsing. Besides the Japanese books, cards, and magazines, there are books in English about Japanese literature and art, including the martial and Zen. There are also dolls, ceramics, Japanese fans, lacquer boxes, and calligraphy.

Ronin Gallery, *605 Madison Avenue between 57th and 58th Streets (212-688-0188). Monday–Saturday 10 A.M.–6 P.M.*

The Ronin is a landmark gallery that shows antique jade jewelry with seventeenth-century wood-block prints and even an example of the bamboo basketmaker's art or the swordmaker's skill.

Japan Gallery, *1210 Lexington Avenue between 82nd and 83rd Streets (212-288-2241). Hours vary, call in advance.*

The Japan Gallery is chrysanthemum Japan with delicate water colors and fine examples of *sumi-e* brush and ink blossoms and bamboo reeds.

Bonsai and Other Japanese Gardens

The bonsai trees are exquisite Japanese miniatures of cherry, pomegranate, buttonwood, plum, and jasmine. They are formed by painstaking pruning and pinching. The bonsai have to be mother-henned like delicate children. They cannot be placed in direct sunlight or be exposed to extremes of temperature, and must be root-pruned and repotted every few years. In Japan and Japanese New York, there are bonsai masters who look upon bonsai as a mystical mission.

Bonsai Dynasty, *851 Sixth Avenue near 30th Street (212-947-6953). Monday–Saturday 7:30 A.M.–6 P.M.*

Bonsai Dynasty has all the tools, plants, and books to become a bonsai master. They have rare nursery stocks for the bonsai gardener.

Bonsai Garden, *135 West 28th Street (212-947-6953). Monday–Saturday 7:30 A.M.–5:30 P.M.*

The Bonsai Garden is a tranquil museum of every variety of dwarf tree. The staff are interested and friendly and will explain the ins and outs of things like drainage and fertilizing.

The Japanese garden is a state of mind—calm and meditative. It is gravel and rocks or a hill and a pond or water falls set off by shrubs. It is the perspective of the observer and the shrine in the distance from a summerhouse. The Japanese garden is a vast park or the corner of a courtyard or a room. It is a place for contemplation.

Brooklyn Botanic Gardens, *1000 Washington Avenue (718-622-4433). November–March, Tuesday–Friday 8 A.M.–4:30 P.M.; Saturday–Monday 10 A.M.–6 P.M.; April–October Tuesday–Friday 8 A.M.–6 P.M.; Saturday–Monday 10 A.M.–6 P.M.*

The Japanese Garden is by the Japanese master, Takeo Shiota. There is a pavilion and a pond, and within the pond the gateway to a shrine. The hill opposite is five small falls splashing over the shrubs. The Ryoanji Garden is raked gravel cut off by a wall, a temple wall. It is a place for meditation.

The Asia Society, *725 Park Avenue at 70th Street (212-288-6400).*
Tuesday, Wednesday, Friday, Saturday 10 A.M.–5 P.M.; Thursday
10 A.M.–8:30 P.M.; Sunday noon–5 P.M.

The Japanese garden is framed by a trellis and surrounded by red granite. It
is a moment of silence in the center of the city. The exhibits of Asian art have
a timeless beauty.

The Japan Society Gallery, *333 East 47th Street (212-832-1155).*
Monday–Saturday 11 A.M.–5 P.M.

The Japanese garden is an interior garden with a skylight softening the hard
edges and adding depth to the rock and spaces.

Indians

History

The first East Indians entered New York in the early part of the twentieth
century, between 1904 and 1914. They were a very small group comprised
of political refugees, educators, and artists. They were joined by Punjabi
agricultural laborers from California who were looking for work in the city
after the failure of the harvest.

In 1917, court rulings barred immigrants from Asiatic countries. The only
East Indians who were able to enter the city were from the West Indies; and
once these Indians gained resident status they had difficulty getting naturalized. The courts were arbitrary, classifying some Indians as white and
eligible for naturalizaition, and others as nonwhite and ineligible.

A ruling by the Naturalization and Immigration Authority regarding
classification in 1926 resulted in the revocation of the citizenship of forty-six
Indians. Prafulla C. Mukerjii, a New York Bengali, demanded his day in
court and even protested to the U.S. Senate. He testified before Congress for
a bill to reinstate all forty-six but it was killed in committee. He finally was
able to regain his own citizenship on a legal technicality.

Mr. Mukerjii, who was one of New York's leading Indian citizens and the
president of the prestigious Tagore Foundation, was not satisfied with the
ruling on the case and the response of the government. He was determined
to win equal rights for the Indians and formed the Hindu Citizenship
committee to fight the injustice.

New York's Indian community celebrated in 1946 when the law was rescinded and Indians could become citizens and enter the country on a limited quota. There was a slight setback in 1952, when the McCarran-Walter Act with its rigid immigration ceiling based quotas on racial characteristics rather than country of origin, and Western Hemisphere Indians and Indians from the Indian subcontinent were included in the same small quota.

The Hart-Celler Immigration Act, which went into effect in 1968, finally dispensed with the racial and country of origin quotas. Visas were awarded on the basis of familial relationship or scarce occupational skills, and Indians were now able to enter New York in substantial numbers.

These Indian newcomers were English-speaking, highly educated, and familiar with Western-style American customs. The new immigrants were skilled professionals and mainly male: engineers, scientists, and doctors. While the Indian doctors readily found positions in New York's health system, Indian engineers who were trained abroad did not always have the requirements desired by New York firms.

The Indians who had problems being placed started their own businesses or took jobs selling insurance or real estate to their own upscale community. As Indian New Yorkers became more settled, they left the bachelor apartments they usually shared with other Indians and began bringing over their families, who received special preference under the Hart-Celler Act.

The Indian immigrants who settled in New York were diverse. They represented the countries of India and Pakistan and, later, Bangladesh. They were Hindus, Muslims, Sikhs, Christians, Jains, and Parsis. Others identified strongly with their native Indian states and native languages and viewed themselves and one another as "Northerners" and "Southerners."

They had different habits and customs. There were meat-eaters, fish-eaters, and strict vegetarians who would not touch milk or eggs. While caste was less important than in the past, it also played a part in differentiating Indian New Yorkers. There were fair-skinned Aryan Indians and the darker Dravidians.

New York's Indians formed their own societies and fraternal groups. They had over forty-four associations and organizations. The purpose of these groups, from the northern Cultural Association of Bengal to the southern Kerala Samaj of New York, was primarily social.

In 1971 New York's Indians incorporated the Association of Indians in America, AIA, to confront issues that affected the whole Indian community and to deal directly with American society. AIA formed a tier of professional organizations to defend Indian doctors and engineers who were sometimes characterized as poorly trained and culturally maladjusted. AIA organized an "honor banquet" recognizing the accomplishments of Indians and Indian-Americans to improve the image of the community.

In the 1990s AIA has been joined in its efforts to defend Indian interests by the Federation of Indian Associations. The new group also represents Indian commerce and issues an annual community directory. The new Indian merchants have a higher profile than the generation of professionals.

New York's Indians have bought up many of the newsstands and candy stores and stationery stores that sell the city's newspapers. They have even purchased the Union News, which controls many of New York's most important magazine and newspaper franchises. By the nature of their newspaper connection they have become a neighbor to most New Yorkers and no longer an exotic.

Little India in Mid-Manhattan

Introduction

The first Indian New Yorkers congregated uptown around Columbia University; though many lived together in dormitory-type arrangements, they did not have the numbers to form a neighborhood. They did their shopping on Lexington Avenue, where an Armenian named Kalyustan supplied them with Indian spices and grains. When it came time for the Indians to open their own shops and restaurants in the city, they located them in the same area between Park and Lexington Avenues, 30th and 27th Streets.

A few families even occupied apartments above the shops, but the area never became more than an Indian commercial strip. New York's affluent Indians headed for the suburban borough of Queens: Flushing, Rego Park, Elmhurst, and Forest Hills. They could afford to live among New York's successful second-and third-generation ethnics and didn't need the security of their own separate neighborhood. The only full-fledged Indian enclave developed in Flushing with later waves of immigrants and a deepening sense of Indian identity and consciousness.

Eating and Drinking

Indian cuisine is not all hot curries and sweet chutneys. Although the combination of spices in curry may be its core, Indian cooking has as many variations as the regional checkerboard of the Indian subcontinent. In the north, wheat is king and breads are the staple of the table, while in the south, rice is the staff of life. Southerners tend to be vegetarians while Bengalis are fish fanatics. The northern Bengalis also break the north-south divide by preferring rice. The Indian shortening *ghee* lends body to their cooking, especially the vegetarian dishes.

Indian flat breads are more than the staff of life. There are light puffs of deep-fried *poori* and a baked leavened bread stuffed with potato (*aloo paratha*) and *papadam* (a circular spicy crisp that is the king of crackers). There are clay oven kebabs and chicken tandoori. The curries are hot and spicy and reach the peak of heat in the *vindaloo*. *Raita* (yogurt and cucumber) and chutney (sweet pickle) and *dal* (yellow lentils) are the relishes neutralizing the chilis. The Bengalis make *biryanis,* a flavored rice made with nuts and saffron.

Madras Palace, *104 Lexington Avenue between 27th and 28th Streets (212-532-3314). Monday–Saturday 11:30 A.M.–3 P.M.; 5:30 P.M.–10 P.M.*

The food is Madras vegetarian and the atmosphere is subdued if not the hot and spicy in the cooking. The *chola batura* (a bread baked with chick peas) and the *bonda* (dumplings filled with vegetables) are a good way to start the meal. Madras is the only Indian restaurant in the city certified strictly kosher by a rabbi.

Maurya, *129 East 27th Street (212-689-7925). Daily noon–3 P.M., 5 P.M.–11 P.M.*

Maurya is traditional tandoori clay pot cooking in a sleek cosmopolitan setting. More than chicken, the tandoori surprises include *shahi paneer* (cheese with herbs) and fish *tikka* (fish marinated with spices and herbs). The inexpensive luncheon buffet is all-you-can-eat.

Shaheen Sweets, *99 Lexington Avenue at 27th Street (212-683-2139). Monday–Saturday 11 A.M.–10:30 P.M.; Sunday 11 A.M.–9:30 P.M.*

Shaheen is fast-food Indian, steam-table style, with the richest Indian sweets. The atmosphere is casual—cafeteria-style eating and Indians relaxing, being themselves. The curry makes no allowances for American tastes but there's a water tap conveniently in the back. While a full line of sweets is available at a counter in front, the *kheer,* rice pudding with rose water and pistachios, is a dessert suited for Occidental tastes.

Annapurna Restaurant, *108 Lexington Avenue between 27th and 28th Streets (212-679-1284). Daily 11:30 A.M.–3 P.M.; 5 P.M.–10 P.M.*

Annapurna is Kerala southern cuisine, with a Miami mural of sheltering palms and shuffling waiters. The Indian Emperor Shahjahani had his sauces flavored with almond paste, which go well with Annapurna's lamb. The southern style *dhosa* (crepes filled with vegetables) are very good dipped in coconut chutney.

Shopping on the Avenue

The Lexington Avenue Indian Bazaar is best seen on weekends when Indians arrive en masse to stock up on short-grain Indian rice and yellow lentils, shop for saris, or bargain for an appliance. It's a real family outing, with Dad searching for a parking space, while the wife and kids start their circuit of the stores, sometimes with an autocratic mother-in-law in tow. The kids keep their restlessness in check, while the grownups look at the saris one after another, third-degree a merchant over a sewing machine, or pick through the fresh produce. They know at the end of the day they will be rewarded with an ultrarich sweet or even a curry chow-out.

Indian food shops have the sweet spicy aroma of the East and plastic envelopes of spices from coriander to cumin line the shelves along with sticks of incense. There are burlap bags of Basmatti rice, short-grain brown, and long-grain white, large enough to feed an army, and an exotic assortment of dried beans and grains including three varieties of lentils (*malka masoor*). The produce counter looks alien to the American eye with its ginger roots, giant kaunda squashes, hot chilis, and Chinese radishes.

The stores stock a wide variety of prepared and canned Indian foods and Indian and English cleaning products with an overwhelming odor of disinfectant. Though the clientele is mostly Indian and Pakistani, there are also West Indians who cook with Indian ''heat'' and amateur chefs from Murray Hill. At the counter in front, by the tapes of Indian music and magazines, the Indian proprietor chatters with cronies, never missing a beat on the register as he rings up sales.

Kalustyan's, *123 Lexington Avenue between 27th and 28th Streets (212-685-3451). Monday–Saturday 10 A.M.–7:30 P.M.; Sunday 11 A.M.–6 P.M.*

Kalustyan's is a holdover from the old Armenian neighborhood, but deserves a mention since it was the first to import Indian food and spices into the city. Despite the competition from Indian retailers, it holds on to its trade with exceptional products like its own spice mix for *garam masala*. It also has a full line of Middle Eastern foods and exotic coffees and teas.

Spice and Sweet Mahal, *135 Lexington Avenue at 29th Street (212-683-0900). Monday–Saturday 10 A.M.–8 P.M.; Sunday 11 A.M.–7 P.M.*

Neater and less sprawling than the other markets, it somehow contains everything in its smaller spaces. It is Eastern exotic with sweets dipped in rose water and the perfume of spices. The people behind the counters are all business.

Annapurna Grocery, *126 East 28th Street (212-889-7540). Monday–Saturday 10 A.M.–7:30 P.M.; Sunday 11 A.M.–6 P.M.*

Annapurna has posters in front advertising Indian concerts and religious festivals. It is the right place to find out what's happening culturally in the Indian community. The store is long and narrow and crowded with people cruising the shelves for spice, rice, and grains in all their Indian varieties.

India Spice World, *126 Lexington Avenue between 28th and 29th Streets (212-686-2727). Daily 10 A.M.–7:30 P.M.*

India Spice World is neatly arranged with a long wall of shelves like a library of Indian foods. The prices are clearly marked, which is a problem in some stores. India has a large following from the West Indies and Guyana, where they cook with Indian spices.

Sari Silks

Though most Indian men have opted for Western-style dress, Indian women still favor the sari and wear it with considerable flair. The sari is six yards of cloth that makes an elegant cultural statement. The draping of the sari is second nature to Indian women—with one expert motion the fabric is wound around the body and flung over a shoulder. The traditional sari fabric reflects regional designs and colors, but nowadays bright Benares embroidered silks have been replaced by inexpensive Japanese and Hong Kong synthetics. A tight blouse called a *choli* and a half-slip are worn under the sari.

Women from the north and central part of India wear pastel saris; southern women prefer dark colors with gold-brocaded edges. Generally the upper part of the sari, the *palau,* is worn over the left shoulder, but Gujarati women drape it over the right shoulder. In Madras the sari is comprised of nine yards of material. Punjabi women entirely forsake the sari, favoring a tunic called the *kurta* worn over tight trousers, set off by a diaphanous scarf over the shoulders. Rajasthani women replace the sari with long print skirts decorated like Indian figurines with mirrors and a form-fitting short-sleeved jacket.

Sapna Sari Palace, *116 East 29th Street (212-689-6182). Monday–Saturday 10 A.M.–7 P.M.; Sunday 1 A.M.–6 P.M.*

The Indian women survey the sari collections with scorn mixed with irony; the saleswoman stands diplomatically aside. The customers try one and another on and the bargaining begins. Trimmings, bangles, cologne, and blouses are also on sale.

Sapna hasn't decided whether it's in the sari or electronics business. Half the store is cassette players and electric shavers; the other half is saris and suitings.

Little India in the East Village

In the days of the hippie East Village, enterprising Indians were selling the counterculture Indian blouses and love beads along with the Eastern philosophy. Indian restaurants followed with meals even a hippie could afford. The fad for Indian clothes subsided in the 1970s but the Indian restaurants that satisfied Bohemian appetites remained and prospered. This Indian restaurant row covers the south side of 6th Street between First and Second Avenues with tributaries on both avenues.

East Village Indian Restaurant Bargains

Sonali Restaurant, *326 East 6th Street (212-505-7517). Daily noon–1 A.M.*

Come dinner time, Sonali resembles the rush-hour IRT. People are lined up at the door, squeezed between the narrow lanes of tables. The rush-hour mood extends to the service, though to be fair, the staff are ever cheerful and obliging. But the food is worth the bother, from the lighter than air *paratha* to the richly satisfying lamb masala. The Indian dinners, the vegetable and meat *thalis,* are a real bargain with soup, *nan* (Indian bread), a main dish, and dessert for the price of a single entree uptown.

Prince of India, *342 East 6th Street (212-228-0388). Daily noon–midnight.*

The decoration awkwardly contrasts natural hanging plants and plastic roses. The food also has a split personality, with curries neutralized for Western tastes and shrimp tandooris that could charm a maharajah.

Ganges Restaurant, *342 East 6th Street (212-228-3767). Daily noon–midnight.*

The chicken in this restaurant is marinated in a magical mixture of herbs and spices; the white meat transcends tender and juicy. Regulars in this no-nonsense restaurant swear by the chicken *tikka mostom,* with its delicately sweet cream and almond sauce.

Mitali, *334 East 6th Street (212-533-5208). Daily noon–midnight.*

Mitali is spacious seating and obliging service. They don't try to hustle you out the door when they really get busy. Come with a big group and eat family-style with plenty of *pakora* (cheese and vegetable fritters) and *samosa* (deep-fried pastry filled with vegetable or meat) appetizers and a variety of curries.

Gaylord's Indian Restaurants, *87 First Avenue between 5th and 6th Streets (212-529-7990). Daily noon–midnight.*

Gaylord's has returned to feed the limousine set, but it's quite a distance from their former midtown location. The curries are mild and the sweets are strong. The palm reader that used to entertain the customers between courses is gone.

Indian Newspapers to Ragas

Indians may no longer live in Manhattan, but it's the cultural headquarters for the whole community. The concerts, the community festivals, and the newspapers all emanate from Manhattan. Manhattan has the prestige and the power and the Indians have their front-line offices here.

Indian Consulate General, *3 East 64th Street (212-879-7800). Monday–Friday 9:30 A.M.–5 P.M.*

Though the New York Indian community is not geographically united, institutions like the Indian consulate keep it close knit. The consulate provides local Indians with a library, including editions of home newpapers, and acts as a clearing house for information about Indian cultural happenings from films to festivals. The consulate also maintains contact with the wide range of Indian ethnic organizations. The consulate has its own cultural artifacts, with a many-armed Shiva in the lobby and a bust of Ghandi in the library.

India Abroad Publications, *43 West 24th Street (212-929-1727).*

At the counter of every Indian grocery there are stacks of *India Abroad*. The paper is a clearing house for information about Indian exhibits, community activities, and concerts with Indian musicians. The paper is more of a community bulletin board; the news is more social than serious.

The World Music Institute, *10 West 27th Street.*

World Music is the only producer of Indian concerts in New York and is involved in ten concerts a year. Town Hall and Lincoln Center are the type of sites, with performers like the Beatles' favorite sitar player, Ravi Shankar.

Festivals
India Day Parade

The India Day Parade celebrates Indian Independence, an August 21st Indian national holiday. The parade is organized and sponsored by the Federation of Indian Associations. The marchers are members of Indian organizations representing all the regions of India and all its language groups. The feeling is more solemn than Fourth of July.

In its first years it went along Lexington Avenue, passing Little India, but today the parade is a Madison Avenue march from 34th Street to 21st Street. Indian dignitaries in limousines and open cars lead the line of march, followed by the leaders of the Indian Federation.

The parade is Indian dance troops in gold lamé and American marching bands in high-collar uniforms and caps and Indian raga players in white. There are floats representing the moment India won its freedom, with gentlemen in cutaway coats, and floats with Indian beauties in evening gowns, throwing flowers. The crowd in small but enthusiastic, waving flags with Brahman dignity. Later the marchers and the spectators join together for Independence celebrations in Lexington Avenue restaurants.

India Festival

The Federation of Indian Associations takes over the Central Park Mall in the last week of May or the first week of June to celebrate the India Festival. It is an affirmation of the Indian identity, transcending religion and geography. There are the haunting rhythms of the sarod and sitar and dancers in extravagant costumes. Indian crafts are on display and voluptuous Indian women put on a sari fashion show. Home-cooked Indian food—breads, curries, rice pulao, and kebabs—are served out by members of participating organizations. There are smiles all around and not just from the politicians, as long-lost friends and relatives exchange greetings and children play on the grass. The festival originated in 1974 with the support of Indian community leaders from around the country.

Divali

In November, all Hindus observe Divali, the Indian New Year and the festival of lights. The celebrants light lamps to guide the departed souls back to earth. It is the Indian thanksgiving, though no one is eating turkey. There are processions with resemblances to the Macy parade with floats that are massive painted shrines with a whole range of Hindu dieties and the beating of drums and the trill of Indian woodwinds. In the spirit of other New York holidays, the Indian merchants hold sales. The Indian Consulate has the information about time and locations of Indian processions.

═══════════ Asia in Flushing ═══════════

Introduction

The Dutch dubbed it Vlissingen in 1643 after a Dutch town, but it was settled by English dissenters. Governor Stuyvesant tried to block their Quaker meetings and they issued a written remonstrance that struck a blow for the colony's religious freedom.

The English anglicized Vlissingen to Flushing. It was the garden spot of colonial Queens, with the nation's first large-scale nursery. While George Washington admired William Prince's botanic gardens, he was less enthusiastic about Flushing's citizens, who were diehard Loyalists.

In the middle of the nineteenth century, Flushing was a popular resort for wealthy Manhattanites. It was elegant summerhouse country along the Flushing River. In 1910 Flushing, which had been incorporated into New York, took its first tentative steps toward development and by the opening of the 1939 World's Fair in Flushing Meadow, it had two hundred small apartment houses.

The theme of the World's Fair in 1939 and the later Flushing Fair in 1964 was the world of the future. The future for Flushing turned out to be Asian

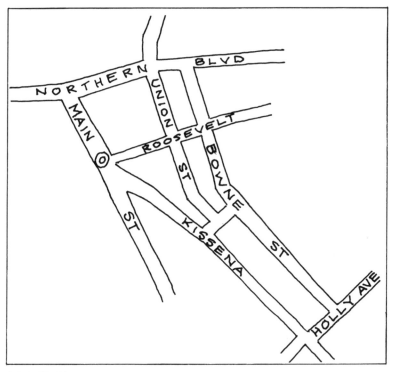

Asia in Flushing

international: Chinese, Koreans, and Indians have added the energy of the East to historic Flushing.

In the years before the Asians came, Flushing was losing steam. Main Street couldn't compete with the suburban malls, and the housing was showing its age. Landmarks from the colonial times and the Gilded Age were allowed to decay.

The new immigrants turned Main Street around and picked up the pulse of the city. They opened new businesses and started families. The older residents, who remember a greener, more rural Flushing, couldn't help but approve.

Asian Flushing is women in saris wheeling baby carriages and Chinese kids with arms full of books heading to the public library and tired Koreans getting off the subway at sunrise returning from stores in Harlem or the Bronx. It is the markets with exotic squashes and the restaurants with twenty-four hour service. It is a Hindu temple and a Taiwan cultural center.

Chinese Flushing

Introduction

The Chinese are the largest Asian group in Flushing. They are upward mobile Chinese and thoroughly middle-class. They look at Flushing as a stepping stone to the more-affluent suburbs. Many of these Chinese are later arrivals from Hong Kong and Taiwan who never experienced anti-Chinese discrimination and are comfortable with Chinese customs and American culture. Chinese Flushing is confident and on the make, but still values family and duty above everything.

Chinese Eating

The restaurants in Chinese Flushing are mostly on Main Street and on 40th Avenue and on Prince Street behind St. George's Episcopal Church. It's a smaller version of Manhattan's Chinatown, and many of the restaurants had their original branches on Mott and Division Streets. They are new and glossy in restaurant red and gold with lions and dragons and Chinese vases by the cash registers. The clientele, which is mostly Chinese keeps the standards high.

Stony Wok Restaurant, *137-40 Northern Boulevard (718-445-8535). Daily 11:30 A.M.–3 A.M.*

The Stony Wok is Taiwanese cooking and Taiwanese hospitality. The hot pot is the national dish prepared at a built-in stove at the table. It takes no time to get the hang of it—dipping meat and shellfish and Chinese vegetables into the bubbling broth till it's cooked to taste.

The Happy Dumpling, *135-29 40th Road (718-445-2163/4). Monday–Thursday 11 A.M.–10 P.M.; Friday–Sunday 11 A.M.–10:30 P.M.*

The Happy Dumpling has a hostess who makes that extra effort. The food is well prepared and graciously served. The dumplings, fried and boiled, and the noodle dishes are the house specialties.

Yao Han, *135-21 40th Road (718-359-2828). Daily 11 A.M.–9 P.M.*

Yao Han's owners are Chinese from Saigon and specialists in Chinese and Vietnamese noodle dishes. The Vietnamese beef noodle soup, made with eye of round, flank steak, and brisket is a meat-eater's delight.

Little Peking, *125-23 40th Road (718-886-2011). Sunday–Thursday 11:30 A.M.–10 P.M.; Friday, Saturday 11:30 A.M.–10:30 P.M.*

Little Peking is why Manhattan food lovers take the subway to Flushing. It is a source for such Peking delicacies as the piquant cabbage and pork buns and the sweet yogurt dessert. Little Peking's special *wor shu* pancake features Chinese polenta in place of rice.

Yuet Tung Restaurant, *136-11 38th Avenue (718-461-1859). Daily 11 A.M.–2 A.M.*

Yuet Tung is a large formal dining room with expensive plates and exquisite antiques. The food turns out to be Hakka, a Chinese equivalent of country soul cooking with pork belly gravy and salted chicken.

Chinese Shopping

The Chinese shops in Flushing attract Chinese from all over the metropolitan area who want to avoid the Chinatown crowd scene. For the Chinese of Flushing the shops of Main Street and 40th Road and Roosevelt Avenue are their neighborhood stores and there is a communal feeling here that doesn't quite break through in anonymous Manhattan.

Kam Sen, *41-79 Main Street (718-939-2560). Monday–Saturday 9 A.M.–8:30 P.M.; Sunday 9:30 A.M.–8 P.M.*

There is chinese muzak in the background as Chinese shoppers push their carts down the aisles. At the door there are roots and herbs to cure what ails you and Gillette razor blades. There are miles of aisles of soy sauce and noodles (dry, rice, sheet, and instant). The rice is in twenty-five-pound bags and the vegetables run to bok choy and bean sprouts.

Shun An Tong, *132-24 Roosevelt Avenue (718-445-9358). Daily 9 A.M.–8 P.M.*

Shun An Tong is Chinese traditional medicine keeping the healthful balance of yin and yang through the proper roots, extracts, and herbs. Some of these elixirs can cure anything from fallen arches to the common cold. The ginseng here is from Northern China and more potent because of its age. There are ginseng teas and ginseng cosmetics and ordinary health supplements like wheat germ.

Flushing Seafood, *135-17 Roosevelt Avenue (718-353-8585).
Daily 9 A.M.–7:30 P.M.*

The fish is so fresh it jumps out of the tank and into the skilled hands of the
fishmongers for fast, on-the-spot filet. Besides the pick of shellfish, they
have Chinese delicacies like sea slugs and sea cucumbers.

Rochelle Bakery, *135-19 Flushing Road (718-353-6100). Monday–Saturday 7 A.M.–8 P.M.; Sunday 7 A.M.–7 P.M.*

The bakery has light sweet Chinese cakes and buns that are filled with lots
of good things, from cream custard to yellow bean. The bakery has some
tables where elderly Chinese while away the afternoons over tea and cakes
and shoppers have a quick snack.

The Chinese Corner

The Middle-class Chinese of Flushing are as organized as the "sojourners"
of Chinatown. The close-knit Chinese community provides social and
cultural outlets for the Chinese population.

The Taiwan Center, *137-44 Northern Boulevard (718-445-7007).*

The Taiwan Center was the first community center for the Chinese in North
America. It has a small library with books dealing with Taiwan and regularly
receives current Taiwanese newspapers and magazines. The center sponsors
the performances of musicians and dancers from Taiwan and provides
information regarding immigration questions. Recently it has become the
focus of demonstrations concerning the Taiwan government.

The Flushing Chinatown Planning Council, *41-25 Kissena Boulevard (718-358-8981).*

This social service originated in Chinatown but it has branched out to any
area where there is a significant Chinese population. It has implemented day
care and medical care programs and has helped Chinese in Flushing obtain
housing and employment. It has supported Chinese arts in the community
and sponsored performances of Chinese musical, dramatic, and dance
groups.

Korean Flushing

Introduction

Koreans may do business in Manhattan, but they live in more-suburban Queens. Flushing is a favorite Korean residential area. Hardworking Korean families occupy cozy brick houses and high-rise apartments in the vicinity of Union Street and 37th Avenue. It is only second in population to Los Angeles's Koreatown. There are a variety of businesses catering to the special needs of the Korean community on Union Street and Flushing's multiethnic Main Street. The first Korean establishments were the restaurants.

Neighborhood Restaurants

Cosy House, *36-26A, Union Street (718-762-0167). Monday–Friday noon–1 A.M.; Sunday noon–midnight.*

Don't look for the name, it's nowhere to be found (in English) outside this closet-size restaurant. The restaurant may be plastic tablecloths and mismatched silver, but it is thoroughly Korean. It will take a while for the surprised Korean waitress to find the English menu. The Korean dumplings in broth and the Korean barbecue beef are good choices for people who don't like their food red hot.

Ko Hyang Restaurant, *42-96 Main Street (718-463-3837). Daily 11 A.M.–3 A.M.*

Ko Hyang is the place to relax for Korean greengrocers after an eighteen-hour day of hosing and pruning and sorting fruits and vegetables. The lights are dimmed and the dark wood room and leatherette booths spell comfort. It's late but a cold beer and *koo-chul-pan* Korean pancakes filled with shredded beef and black mushrooms help to unwind.

South River, *45-05 Main Street (718-762-7214). Daily 24 hours.*

South River is the restaurant in the Korean community to see and be seen. The parking lot is the image of the crowd—bumper-to-bumper Mercedes and BMWs. The host is brash and fast-talking in English or Korean. The Japanese sushi is limp and the monkfish is hot and the decor is Japanese rock-garden modern.

Greengrocers to the City

The Koreans gained high visibility in New York City when they became the local fruit and vegetable store and New Yorkers deserted the supermarkets for Korean high quality. New Yorkers were also impressed by the care Koreans took in preparing and displaying their produce. They also liked the fact that they always stayed open. The high prices came later, along with the salad bars and the Chinese buffets. In Flushing they have the greengrocers' greengrocer.

Green Farm, *42-01 Main Street (718-961-6179). Daily 24 hours.*

Green Farm has Korean delicacies like singo pear, which is used to make their raw liver specialty. It also has the cheapest if not the best produce in Flushing.

The Korean Produce Retailers Association

The Korean Produce Association has its headquarters in Flushing, where a large portion of the membership live. While it deals with laws and regulations that affect the industry, it provides the membership with insurance, legal services, and training seminars.

Koreans have their own supermarkets in Flushing, which also carry products for the Chinese and the Japanese communities. They are streamlined affairs, no different from an American chain supermarket except for the products lining the shelves.

Han Ah Reum Market, *29-02 Union Street (718-445-5656). Daily 9:30 A.M.–9:30 P.M.*

The market in the heart of the Korean residential district is an interesting Korean cross-section. Smartly dressed young women from a nail salon sort through the prepared *kimchi* and the greengrocer with five o'clock shadow and a permanent yawn stocks up on fish sauce.

Sam Bok, *42-21 Main Street (718-359-7345). Monday–Saturday 10:30 A.M.–8:30 P.M.; Sunday 10 A.M.–7 P.M.*

Sam Bok has all the Korean brands in canned and frozen foods. There are taro roots for Korean soup and frozen Korean dumplings. The seafood counter specializes in Korean seafood salads like squid in pepper sauce.

Korean Curiosities

The Korean handicrafts are embroidery and cabinet making, and they have a tradition of lacquer work and inlaid boxes. Korean crafts decorate the living rooms of Union Street.

G. Youn and Company, *36-14 Union Street (718-359-1187).*
Monday–Saturday 9:30 A.M.–8 P.M.

G. Youn is Korean gifts: gaudy ceramics and mother-of-pearl boxes that practically glow in the dark. The furniture is also heavy on the decoration and even the slippers are embroidered with iridescent colors.

Indian Flushing

Introduction

During the week Indian Flushing is women and children; it is as if the men went off to war, though only their business hours are long. The Indians in Flushing have kept the extended family and in the Indian groceries and sari shops on Main Street between Franklin and Holly Streets there are usually three generations with age wielding authority. The scene in Flushing is less sophisticated than Manhattan; these are the later arrivals who don't necessarily speak English. People seem to express themselves more freely in the battle between proprietors and shoppers, though the women have a modesty and shyness that hasn't been worn down by New York directness. The professional long-time resident Indians are already in Long Island and the New Jersey suburbs.

Neighborhood Shopping

Indian shops in Flushing are all in a row and nondescript; their only decoration is the Indian script on the signs advertising specials. The prices are lower than in Manhattan and people buy in larger quantities, but the stock is identical. The area in front of the stores is paved with asphalt and Indian families are always milling around, women are wheeling baby carriages, and men working on their cars. After school the children rush in for *julabi* pretzels (a rich sweet made with chick pea flour) and *ras gola* (cream cheese balls in syrup). On weekends the crowds can block the street. There is a sense of real community in the activity around the stores, as though it is the center of the Indian village.

Indian Bazaar, *42-67 Main Street (718-358-5252). Daily 10 A.M.–8:30 P.M.*

The Indian Bazaar is an Indian market plus a very large selection of music and videos. The owners are Muslim and have announcements and fliers for events involving the Muslim community.

Dana Bazaar, *42-69 Main Street (718-853-2818). Daily 10 A.M.–8:30 P.M.*

Dana Bazaar subtitles itself the "House of Shamiana Sweets" and even if people do their big shopping somewhere else, they come in for *ras malai* (cheese soaked with cream) and almond fudge.

Japan Sari House, *42-73 Main Street (718-886-0457). Daily 10 A.M.–8:15 P.M.*

The fabrics come from Japan and the rest of the Orient; some, at least on the hangers, don't look very appropriate. This is the K-Mart of saris.

The Temple of Flushing

The Hindu Temple is a place of prayer and offerings (*puja*) where the priest (*pundit*), a high caste Brahmin, leads the praises to the Indian pantheon.

Hindu Temple of North America, *45-57 Bowne Street between Holly and 45th Avenues (718-539-1587).*

Flushing's Hindu Temple of North America is the real thing; its gray pagoda tower is ornamented with Indian gods and its solid walls are the work of a hundred skilled craftsman from the southern state of Andra Pradesh. In 1976 this twenty-ton granite structure was reassembled by twenty-five of these workmen.

Statues of the god Shiva, the six faces of Shanmuga, and the goddess of wealth, Lakshmi, have places of honor, but Ganesh the elephant god is at the center. Ganesh is wisdom, he solves problems; but he is also the god of gluttons.

On weekends and Hindu holidays the rituals are more elaborate, with the congregation sitting cross-legged, chanting, and the *pundit* in his white dhoti regaling the gods with milk and rose petals and tropical fruits while perfumed incense fills the sanctuary.

In September the Hindus of the south celebrate Ganapathy when Ganesh rises from the underworld. On this day women adorn Ganesh with flowers and spread before him a banquet of coconuts, bananas, oranges, and avocados. The floor of the altar is covered with flower petals. Worshipers bow to the image while throwing handfuls of rice and periodically put their fingers on a flame carried on a silver tray and touch their foreheads.

After a vegetarian feast, the worshipers drive to the Flushing Meadow Lake and put a replica of Ganesh in the water to return to the land of the dead.

TRAVEL AND CULTURE BOOKS

"World at Its Best" Travel Series
Britain, France, Germany,
Hawaii, Holland, Italy, Spain,
Switzerland, London, New York, Paris

International Herald Tribune
Guides to Business Travel in Asia and
Europe
New York on $1,000 a Day (Before Lunch)
Mystery Reader's Walking Guides:
London, England
Everything Japanese
Japan Today!
Japan at Night
Japan Made Easy
Discovering Cultural Japan
Bon Voyage!
Business Capitals of the World
Hiking and Walking Guide to Europe
Where to Watch Birds in Britain and
Europe
Living in Latin America
Frequent Flyer's Award Book
Guide to Ethnic London
Guide to Ethnic New York
European Atlas for Travelers
Health Guide for International Travelers
Travel Guide to British/American English
Chinese Etiquette and Ethics in Business
Korean Etiquette and Ethics in Business
Japanese Etiquette and Ethics in Business
How to Do Business with the Japanese
Japanese Cultural Encounters

Passport's Regional Guides of France
Auvergne, Provence, Loire Valley,
Dordogne, Languedoc, Brittany, South
West France

Passport's Regional Guides of Indonesia
New Guinea
Bali
Spice Islands

Passport's Travel Paks
Britain, France, Italy, Germany, Spain

Passport's China and Asia Guides
All China; Beijing; Fujian; Guilin,
Canton & Guangdong; Hangzhou &
Zhejiang; Hong Kong; Nanjing &
Jiangsu; Shanghai; The Silk Road; Tibet;
Xi'an; The Yangzi River; Yunnan; Egypt;
New Zealand; Australia; Japan; Korea;
Thailand; Malaysia; Singapore

Passport's India Guides
Bombay and Goa; Dehli, Agra and
Jaipur; Burma; Pakistan; Kathmandu
Valley

Southwest China off the Beaten Track

On Your Own Series
Brazil, Israel

"Everything Under the Sun" Series
Spain, Barcelona, Toledo, Seville,
Marbella, Cordoba, Granada, Madrid,
Salamanca, Palma de Majorca

Passport's Travel Paks
Britain, France, Italy, Germany, Spain

Exploring Rural Europe Series
England & Wales, France, Greece,
Ireland, Italy, Spain, Austria, Germany,
Scotland

"Just Enough" Phrase Books
Just Enough Dutch
Just Enough French
Just Enough German
Just Enough Greek
Just Enough Italian
Just Enough Japanese
Just Enough Portuguese
Just Enough Scandinavian
Just Enough Serbo-Croat
Just Enough Spanish
Multilingual Phrasebook
Let's Drive Europe Phrasebook

Passport Maps
Europe; Britain; France; Italy; Germany;
Holland, Belgium & Luxembourg;
Scandinavia; Spain & Portugal;
Switzerland, Austria & the Alps

 PASSPORT BOOKS
a division of *NTC Publishing Group*
4255 West Touhy Avenue
Lincolnwood, Illinois 60646-1975